REFORMING THE DOCTRINE OF GOD

REFORMING THE DOCTRINE OF GOD

F. LeRon Shults

WILLIAM B. EERDMANS PUBLISHING COMPANY
GRAND RAPIDS, MICHIGAN / CAMBRIDGE, U.K.

Wm. B. Eerdmans Publishing Co.
255 Jefferson Ave. S.E., Grand Rapids, Michigan 49503 /
P.O. Box 163, Cambridge CB3 9PU U.K.

Printed in the United States of America

10 09 08 07 06 05   7 6 5 4 3 2 1

Library of Congress Cataloging-in-Publication Data

Shults, F. LeRon.
Reforming the doctrine of God / F. LeRon Shults.
p.   cm.
Includes bibliographical references.
ISBN-10: 0-8028-2988-0 / ISBN-13: 978-0-8028-2988-7 (pbk.: alk. paper)
1. God.   I. Title.

BT103.S45   2005
231 — dc22

2005053937

www.eerdmans.com

To Ray S. Anderson

Contents

• PART II •

TRAJECTORIES IN THE DOCTRINE OF GOD

Contents

Abbreviations

ANF	Ante-Nicene Fathers
CC	Calvin's *Commentaries*
CD	Karl Barth, *Church Dogmatics*
CSR	*Christian Scholar's Review*
DTEL	Schmid, *The Doctrinal Theology of the Evangelical Lutheran Church*
Elenc.	Turretin, *Institutes of Elenctic Theology*
GOTR	*Greek Orthodox Theological Review*
Inst.	John Calvin, *Institutes of the Christian Religion*
LW	Luther, *Luther's Works*
NIDNTT	*New International Dictionary of New Testament Theology*
NPNF	Nicene and Post-Nicene Fathers, Series 1 and 2
NRSV	New Revised Standard Version
PG	*Patrologia Graeca*
PL	*Patrologia Latina*
PRRD	Muller, *Post-Reformation Reformed Dogmatics,* 4 vols.
PWD	*Philosophical Writings of Descartes*
RD	Heppe, *Reformed Dogmatics*
SCG	Thomas Aquinas, *Summa Contra Gentiles*
SumTh	Thomas Aquinas, *Summa Theologica*
SVF	*Stoicorum veterum fragmenta*
TI	Rahner, *Theological Investigations*

· 1 ·

INTRODUCTION

E very presentation of the Christian doctrine of God should aim to conserve the intuitions of the living biblical tradition by liberating them for illuminative and transformative dialogue within a particular cultural context. How can we articulate the gospel of the biblical God within our own contemporary setting? For an increasing number of people both inside and outside the Christian community the proclamation of the existence of a timeless immaterial substance, whose absolute subjectivity is the predetermining first cause of all things, does not seem like good news. The early modern categories that guide these ways of articulating the doctrine of God have been challenged by developments in biblical scholarship, historical research into the theological tradition, late modern philosophical reflection, and discoveries in the natural and social sciences.

Alongside these concerns three trajectories in the doctrine of God emerged in the twentieth century: the retrieval of divine Infinity, the revival of trinitarian doctrine, and the renewal of eschatological ontology.[1] The conceptual space opened up by these trajectories provides us with an

---

1. I outlined these trajectories in "Sharing in the Divine Nature: Transformation, *Koinonia* and the Doctrine of God," in *On Being Christian . . . and Human,* ed. T. Speidell (Eugene, Ore.: Wipf & Stock, 2002), 87-127, and explored their soteriological and ecclesiological implications in chapter 2 of *The Faces of Forgiveness: Searching for Wholeness and Salvation,* with Steven J. Sandage (Grand Rapids: Baker Academic, 2003). Part II of the current book will spell them out in greater detail.

opportunity to present the Christian understanding and experience of divine knowing, acting, and being as the *gospel* in our contemporary culture.

This book is an exploration of this conceptual space, but it is important for us to begin by recognizing that this academic exercise should not — and in fact cannot — be divorced from the practical and liturgical space of Christian life. As the sixteenth-century Reformers saw so clearly, the calcification of particular formulations of doctrine can cripple the praxis and worship of the Christian community. *All* dimensions of the church — its theological formulations as well as its ministry and doxology — are *semper reformata et reformanda,* called to reformation by the grace of God.

Martin Luther protested against the "Babylonian captivity" of the medieval church, but in the twenty-first century we are threatened with a different kind of bondage. Much of our theological language is imprisoned by particular philosophical and scientific categories that constrain our proclamation of the good news about the biblical God. It is love for the gospel that leads us to take up the task of reforming theology, to protest whenever and wherever it is being fettered. However, the desire to love God with all of our minds (Matt. 22:37) is also accompanied by a trembling fascination with the absolutely uncontrollable presence of divine grace.

§1.1. The Delightful Terror of Theology

The intensification of fear and desire that accompanies the task of reforming theology ought not to surprise us. If the "fear of the Lord" is the beginning of knowledge and wisdom (Prov. 1:7; 9:10), we should acknowledge and embrace the existentially delightful terror of theology. In the first chapter of his 1559 *Institutes of the Christian Religion* John Calvin emphasized the existential "dread and wonder" that surround and permeate theological inquiry. He also insisted that "without knowledge of self there is no knowledge of God" and "without knowledge of God there is no knowledge of self." Indeed, these are so intertwined that "which one precedes and brings forth the other is not easy to discern" (*Inst.,* I.1.1). In *Reforming Theological Anthropology* I focused on the anthropological side of this dialectic and outlined a reconstructive presentation of *human* knowing, acting, and being in relation to God and neighbor, organized around the traditional loci of human nature, sin, and the image of God. In this book I attend primarily to the theological side. *Reforming the Doctrine of God* outlines a presentation of *divine* knowing, acting, and being, but the existential tension of the dialectic is maintained. Does God *know* us? How can God *act* for us? Will God *be* there for us? The gospel is that the biblical God is the origin, condition, and goal of our longing for a true, good, and beautiful life.

Many Christians resist the biblical call to *fear* God because it seems to contradict the call to *love* God. How can we love that which we fear? If we define fear as our response to a perceived inability to control an existentially relevant object, then we can begin to see that fear and love are not mutually exclusive. Even in the experience of human love, we find a dialectical relation between fascination and fear. A true lover does not desire to control the beloved, but rejoices in the freedom of the beloved to respond to love. The beloved is the beloved precisely as a delightfully uncontrollable existentially relevant object. If controlled, the beloved ceases to be the object of *love*. In this sense, "fear" is an essential element of love. Part of the ecstasy of human intimacy is the trembling that occurs in the presence of the unmanipulable beloved. True love does not eradicate the element of fear, but takes it up into itself, transforming it into delight in the other. Human love of God includes the element of fear, but it is infinitely transformed in the joy of worship.[2]

It is our fear or love of other things that keeps us from reforming theology. We fear cognitive dissonance (or love the safety of psychological inertia) and so we resist the reconstruction of cherished formulations of doctrine. We love the affirmation of those with ecclesial power (or fear their political retribution) and so we are tempted to maintain the theological status quo. On the one hand, some are tempted to respond *de*-constructively to the challenges of contemporary culture, leaving behind the intuitions of the biblical tradition in order to engage in the postmodern play with the "other." The danger here is the dissolution of Christian faith. At the other extreme, some are tempted to respond *paleo*-constructively, resisting engagement with culture in order to stay behind with the "same" fossilized formulations of Christian intuitions that have been unearthed from modern (or premodern) discourse. The danger here is the petrification of Christian faith.

---

2. For a more detailed treatment of the role of fear and love in theology, cf. my *Reforming Theological Anthropology: After the Philosophical Turn to Relationality* (Grand Rapids: Eerdmans, 2003), chap. 3. The significance of this "trembling delight" will be incorporated into the presentation of the doctrine of God in Part III.

The *re*-constructive response must navigate a way between these two temptations.[3] Reforming theology is the ongoing task of presenting the internal coherence and explanatory power of the Christian understanding of God in each new context. The reconstructive theological presentation that follows is guided by four interwoven desiderata: a faithful interpretation of the biblical witness, a critical appropriation of the theological tradition, a conceptual resolution of relevant philosophical issues, and a plausible elucidation of contemporary human experience. Reforming theology is both dangerous and difficult, but it is also delightful — insofar as it serves the gospel of God.

The phrase "reforming theology" indicates both the dynamic *reconstruction* of theology and the *reformative* dynamics of theology. Because the conceptual space of theology is wrapped up within the practical and liturgical space of our lives, the struggle to articulate the doctrine of God will also *reform us*. Reflecting critically on the way we talk and think about God can facilitate the renewal of our minds (Rom. 12:2). Theology is not simply a set of propositions "out there" that we can decide whether or not to engage. What we think and how we think are not so easily separated. It is important for us to thematize not only the beliefs onto which we hold but also how we "hold on" to our beliefs. The reconstruction of concepts within our consciousness is an important part of the process, but radical transformation occurs only as the way in which our consciousness orders concepts is itself reformed.[4] God's gracious reformation of our fear and desire can be mediated through philosophical reflection on the categories that structure our theological formulations.

The reciprocity between religious desire for God and philosophical categories will be a recurrent theme throughout this book. Some readers may wonder whether the "god of the philosophers" has anything to do with "the God of the Bible." In 1654 Blaise Pascal had an intense religious experience that led him to pen the following note: "FIRE. God of Abraham, God of Isaac, God of Jacob, not of the philosophers and scholars. . . . God of Jesus Christ . . . let me never be separated from him." It is important to ask *which* philosophers Pascal had in mind here. The philosophical

---

3. Cf. my *The Postfoundationalist Task of Theology* (Grand Rapids: Eerdmans, 1999), xiii, and my *Reforming Theological Anthropology,* 7-8.

4. For a discussion of some of the psychological dynamics involved in theological inquiry, cf. *Reforming Theological Anthropology,* chap. 2.

categories that dominated much of seventeenth-century theological scholarship had led to a description of the divine nature as a rational causative substance. It was difficult indeed to link this description to the God of the Bible. We can understand why Pascal felt he had to choose. However, if late modern philosophical discourse is no longer constrained by these categories we may find new opportunities for articulating our passion for the "God of Jesus Christ" in contemporary culture.

§1.2. The Philosophical Turn to Relationality

In contemporary philosophy the category of "relation" plays a more significant role than it did for most ancient Greek and early modern philosophers. The pre-Socratics were interested in defining the basic elements of "being," and the notion of "substance" was the dominant hermeneutical and metaphysical category for Plato, Aristotle, and most of the Stoics. Because I have traced this philosophical "turn" in some detail in *Reforming Theological Anthropology,* and the following chapters offer several concrete examples of the impact of this categorical shift, a brief introductory overview will suffice for our purposes here.[5] Although the story is most easily told in chronological order, the following narrative is not meant to imply a simple line of ascent away from substance and toward relationality. As we will see, an emphasis on relationality may be found in many thinkers throughout the history of philosophy and theology, especially Christian authors whose imaginations were captured by the inherently relational ideas of the Trinity, the Incarnation, and Pentecost. Our purpose here is simply to point out some of the important moments in the philosophical history of these categories.

Aristotle's book on *Categories* has been particularly influential in Western philosophy. He argued that "things that are said" simply (not in combination with other things) fall into ten categories: "each signifies either substance or quantity or qualification or a relative or where or when or being-in-a-position or having or doing or being-affected" (1^b25).[6] Not

---

5. *Reforming Theological Anthropology,* chap. 1. Cf. my "The Philosophical Turn to Relationality" in *Redemptive Transformation in Practical Theology,* ed. Dana Wright and Robert Kuentzel (Grand Rapids: Eerdmans, 2004), from which the following overview borrows heavily.

6. Quotations and references are from *The Complete Works of Aristotle,* ed. Jonathan Barnes, 2 vols. (Princeton: Princeton University Press, 1984).

only is the term *substance* first on Aristotle's list, it also has a material priority over the other categories because it is a necessary component of every predication. In other words, making an affirmation (or negation) requires combining a substance, such as "the man," with a predicate that fits into one of the other categories, such as "running" (doing). Aristotle's theory of predication and his theory of substance are intimately connected; the structure of language re-presents the structure of being. He clearly gives the category of substance *(ousia)* priority over the category of relation, which describes the "toward something" *(pros ti)* of a thing. What we might call a thing's "towardness" does not really get at its "whatness" for Aristotle. In the *Metaphysics* he explains that "the great and the small, and the like, must be relative to something; but the relative is *least of all things a real thing or substance,* and is posterior to quality and quantity; and the relatives are accidents of quantity" (1088ᵃ21-25).[7] Aristotle's hard distinction between "substances" and "accidents" (including relations) implies that the latter are not essential to what a thing *is.*

Both the Platonic and the Stoic lists of categories were less dismissive of relationality. The five "kinds" in Plato's *Sophist* are "that which is," "rest," "change," "the same," and "the different" (254ᵈ-255ᵉ). Although "being" is still first, Plato also insists that "the different" (which is the basis of relationality) "pervades" all of the kinds, which "share" in the type of the different insofar as they are in relation to the others, which they are not. The Stoics proposed four basic categories: "substance," "quality," "disposed in a certain way" and "disposed in a certain way in relation to something else" *(pros ti pōs echonta).* Their "dispositional" emphasis in metaphysics has been recovered in several streams of late modern philosophy, but the Stoic list still begins with substance, which is privileged over the other categories. In the third century A.D., the Neoplatonist Plotinus rejected the Stoic list in favor of Plato's. In his exposition of the five "kinds," Plotinus goes out of his way to stress that the term "Relation" is "remote from Being." He asks: "But how could 'relation', which is like a sideshoot, be among the first [general]? For the state of being related is of one thing to another and not of a thing to itself" (*Enneads,* VI.2.16).[8]

In the early Middle Ages we find a mixture of Neoplatonic and Aristo-

---

7. Emphasis added. Cf. *Posterior Analytics* (83ᵃ15-24).

8. Plotinus, *Ennead VI .1-5,* trans. A. H. Armstrong, Loeb Classical Library (Cambridge: Harvard, 1988), 157.

telian influences in the theological appropriation of the categories of substance and accidents. Porphyry, who was a pupil of Plotinus, had accepted the ten Aristotelian categories in his *Isagogue,* but asked very Plotinian questions about them. Do genera (e.g., "brown," "horse") exist only in the human understanding or also outside of it? Are they corporeal or incorporeal? Do they have existence apart from sensible things? When the Christian theologian Boethius translated the *Isagogue* into Latin in the sixth century, he also offered his own answers to these kinds of questions. This set the stage for the medieval debate over the nature of "universals," in which most of the interlocutors shared a metaphysical assumption: to be "real" is to be a "substance." As we will see in Part I, theories of knowing (and language) developed hand in hand with theories of being and (to a lesser extent) theories of acting.

While many early modern philosophers (e.g., Descartes and Spinoza) continued to rely heavily on the category of substance, others began to question its dominance and even its coherence. In *An Essay Concerning Human Understanding* (1689), Locke argued that the ideas of substance and accidents are not of much use in philosophy, because we do not know what "Substance" is, and we have only an obscure and confused idea of what it does, namely "supports Accidents" (II.13.19). He also observes that "the *Ideas* which relative Words stand for, are often clearer, and more distinct, than those Substances to which they belong" (II.25.8). David Hume spelled out the logic of this critique in his *Enquiry Concerning Human Understanding* (1748). If Locke's "substance" (or substratum) is merely a "something we know not what" then we cannot predicate anything of it, or know anything about it. Hume argued that anything we do say about "substances" is merely habit or convention. Immanuel Kant, who credited Hume for waking him from his "dogmatic slumbers," offered his own Table of Categories in *Critique of Pure Reason* (1787). Explicitly referring to his dissatisfaction with Aristotle's approach, Kant made "substance and accident" a sub-category of the broader category "Of Relation."

Relationality was emphasized even more strongly by several nineteenth-century philosophers. In his *Science of Logic* (1812-1819), G. W. F. Hegel agreed with Kant's privileging of the category of "relation," but challenged the basic separation between the categories of substance and accident. For Hegel, the "whole" (or totality) is not determined by "being" (or essence) but by the dialectical unity of substantiality and accidentality in the reflective movement of the *"absolute relation,"* which is the highest category in the objective logic. Charles Sanders Peirce developed his own "New List" of categories in 1867. Initially he proposed five categories: a major division between substance and being, with the latter having the sub-categories of quality, relation, and representation. In his later work, these sub-categories, which he came to call Firstness, Secondness, and Thirdness (the three "classes of relations"), became more dominant.[9] Peirce's "synechism" — the doctrine that everything is continuous — also illustrates his fascination with relationality.

The importance of relationality is also evident in the "phenomenology" of Edmund Husserl and his followers. Here the focus is less on developing a list of categories and more on understanding the types of relations (or distinctions) that appear in consciousness through "categorial intentionality." We can see the influence of the renewed interest in relationality at work in the writings of twentieth-century philosophers like Heidegger and Sartre, who both struggled with making sense of the relations inherent in being, although they interpreted these differently insofar as they attended more closely to the human experiences of time and nothingness, respectively. In *Process and Reality* Alfred North Whitehead set out his own eight "categories of existence": Actual Entities (actual occasions), Prehensions, Nexus, Subjective Forms, Eternal Objects, Propositions, Multiplicities, and Contrasts. He explicitly rejects the Aristotelian idea of "individual substances, each with its private world of qualities and sensations," and criticizes what he calls the "substance-quality" doctrine of actuality. Unlike Descartes (and others), for whom a physical body has the attribute of extension, for Whitehead physical "occasions" have the primary *relationship* of extensive connection to all things.

Throughout the following chapters we will explore additional examples of this philosophical turn to relationality. We will see how these philosophical reflections are connected to developments in the natural and social sciences, which have increasingly thematized the importance of relationality for interpreting the world (e.g., "relativity" and "systems" theory). Our theological response to this "turn," however, should not be guided primarily by these developments, but by our interpretation of the

---

9. Cf. Peirce, "On a New List of Categories," in *The Essential Peirce, Volume 1*, ed. Nathan Houser and Christian Kloesel (Bloomington: Indiana University Press, 1992), and the Harvard Lectures on Pragmatism in *The Essential Peirce, Volume 2*, ed. the Peirce Edition Project (Bloomington: Indiana University Press, 1998).

biblical tradition. As we will see in Part II, several streams of the tradition throughout the history of the church have utilized inherently relational categories to articulate the doctrine of God. This means that, with reference to Christian theology, we should more properly speak of a *re*-turn to relationality. This book aims to participate both in the recovery of these resources and in the ongoing task of refiguring theological categories for the sake of the gospel.

§1.3. Refiguring Theological Categories

Categories figure largely in theological discourse. Our interpreted experience of God configures our experience of interpretation, and vice versa. As we focus on figuring out answers to particular questions, we sometimes fail to recognize the underlying categories that have shaped their formulation. In Part I we will outline three of the basic categories that shaped significant streams of early modern theology: the idea of God as an immaterial substance, single subject, and first cause. Although these concepts were tightly interwoven and mutually implicated within a general understanding of God as a rational causative substance, for the sake of analysis we will distinguish the three strands within this theological cord. These categories became entrenched in many Protestant doctrinal formulations as theologians engaged the prevailing early modern ways of thinking about matter, person, and force — all of which were shaped by substance metaphysics.

These categories also structured the formulation of many of the questions about God's foreknowledge, predestination, and timelessness. Does God's mind contain some or all future contingents? Does God's will control some or all creaturely events? Does God exist inside time or outside of time? As we will see, arguments over these issues have led into a theological cul-de-sac. The shared premises in these debates lead both sides to conclusions that are logically and existentially problematic. Unfortunately, this contributes to the sense among Christian laypersons (and non-Christians) that theology is either self-contradictory or irrelevant (or both). If we back up and challenge the assumptions that have led to these logical antinomies and existential absurdities, we may be able to find another avenue for articulating a Christian understanding of divine knowing, acting, and being in late modern culture. Part I explores developments in philosophy, science, and biblical scholarship that have contributed to the (re)turn to relationality and raised questions about the helpfulness of some aspects of the early modern road map for contemporary theology. In Part II we ask for directions from the biblical tradition and explore some of the paths forged by leading twentieth-century theologians who have recovered and refigured traditional emphases on the ideas of Infinity, Trinity, and Futurity.[10]

The struggle to release theology from the strictures of the categories of substance dualism, autonomous subjectivity, and past-oriented causality has been driven in large part by a sense that these concepts no longer provide an adequate conceptual matrix for articulating belief in the biblical God. The Hebrew Bible and the New Testament show little interest in an abstract divine "substance," pointing instead to the experience of a dynamic presence that confronts, addresses, and calls humanity into covenant relation. Attempts to depict God as one of the types of being in the world were condemned as idolatry. The intimate unity of Jesus' relation to the Father through the Spirit led the early church to creedal and liturgical expressions saturated with references to three divine persons. Those who depicted God simply as *a* person (a single subject) were immediately suspect of collapsing into Arian subordinationism, Sabellian modalism, or some other christologically or pneumatologically deficient heresy. The apostles were not interested in proving the necessary existence of a first cause of the world, but in directing their readers' attention to a presence that called them into a proleptic experience of sharing in the eternal reign of divine peace. It was this radical metaphysical hope in an already arriving eschatological kingdom that marked off Christians from their fatalistic religious neighbors.

It is important to emphasize that the problem is not the Protestant Scholastics, who have unfortunately been demonized or canonized at the ends of the liberal-conservative spectrum.[11] The problem is our unwilling-

10. Capitalization of these terms is a way of signifying that they are being used to indicate a particular way of speaking about God, which will be outlined in §5.5, §6.5, and §7.5.

11. Several of the stereotypes that have plagued the historiography of the sixteenth to eighteenth centuries are being overcome as the literature on the period of Protestant Orthodoxy has grown exponentially in the last few years. The most significant and comprehensive contribution to date is Richard Muller's four-volume *Post-Reformation Reformed Dogmatics* (Grand Rapids: Baker Academic, 2003). Cf. Willem J. van Asselt and Eef Dekker, *Reformation and Scholasticism: An Ecumenical Enterprise* (Grand Rapids: Baker Academic, 2001); Carl R. Trueman and R. Scott Clark, eds., *Protestant Scholasticism: Essays in Reassessment* (Carlisle: Paternoster Press, 1999).

ness to follow their example by engaging in rigorous dialogue with the philosophical and scientific categories that shape our own context. What were the intuitions that early modern theologians were trying to uphold as they spoke of God as an immaterial substance, single subject, and first cause? The biblical God is not reducible to nor determined by the categories of the material world, and so if our only options were that God is either a material or an immaterial substance, we would embrace the latter. The biblical God is not less than personal but intensely personal, and so if we felt forced to choose between describing God as impersonal or as a single (personal) subject, we would select the latter. The biblical God is not dependent on creatures for power or being, and so if we were caught in a dilemma between depicting God either as an immanent part of a cause-effect nexus or as a transcendent first cause, we would gladly impale ourselves on the latter horn of this dilemma. In each case the Protestant Scholastics attempted to maintain deep Christian intuitions about the relation of God to the world within the constraints of the categories of early modern cosmology, which forced these choices.

The main function of Part I will be to argue that we are no longer compelled to formulate the questions in the doctrine of God in terms of these either-or dichotomies. For the sake of parsimony I will sometimes refer generally to "early modern theological projects" and to "late modern theological trajectories." This is not meant to imply that all theologians during a particular historical period formulated doctrine in the same way. Broadly speaking, an early modern "theological project" refers to a way of doing theology, to a "research program"[12] that is largely guided by specific ways of construing God as rational causative substance. The categories behind these formulations had already begun to harden in the work of some medieval theologians, and they continue to guide the organization of themes in some contemporary theological presentations. We will also observe significant differences among those who contributed to the late modern "trajectories" in Part II. The differentiation between "early" and "late" modern is not intended to draw a line between two time periods, nor to suggest that later theology means better theology. As we will see, the

12. For an introduction to the concepts of a "research program" or "research tradition" in the philosophy of science, cf. Imre Lakatos, *The Methodology of Scientific Research Programmes* (Cambridge: Cambridge University Press, 1978); and Larry Laudan, *Progress and Its Problems: Towards a Theory of Scientific Growth* (Berkeley: University of California Press, 1977).

momentum that propels the "late modern" trajectories was already operative at the origins of the Christian tradition.

Theologians of every generation have been faced with the task of engaging the plausibility structures of their own culture as they sought to articulate the gospel. As patristic, medieval, and early modern theologians wrestled with the anthropological, cosmological, and theological implications of Neoplatonism, Aristotelianism, and materialism, their concern was to present the Christian understanding and experience of the biblical God in a way that captured the imagination of their contemporaries — a reconstructive task that is passed on to us. Resistance to reforming the doctrine of God may be particularly strong in some streams of "evangelical" theology, in which orthodoxy is defined in terms of the crystallization and repristination of a particular historically embedded seventeenth-century synthesis.[13]

I will suggest that the best way to conserve the gospel *(euangelion)* is to liberate it from categories that hinder its presentation for illuminative and transformative dialogue in our contemporary context. Understanding the significance of philosophical and scientific debates over particular categories can help us gain the critical distance required for the task of reconstruction. It may also help us acknowledge our own inescapable participation with(in) contemporary symbol systems, which is equally important for reforming the doctrine of God today. Rather than trying to immunize theology from philosophy and science — which is impossible at any rate — we can thematize the messy reciprocity between our ideas about God and everything else, humbly entering into the delightful terror of reforming theology.

13. Cf. Daniel Alvarez, "On the Possibility of an Evangelical Theology," *Theology Today* 55, no. 2 (July 1998): 175-94 at 185.

· PART I ·

CHALLENGES IN THE DOCTRINE OF GOD

· 2 ·

GOD AS IMMATERIAL SUBSTANCE?

W e begin by exploring a category whose waxing and waning influence in philosophy, science, and theology clearly illustrates the (re)turn to relationality that we traced briefly in §1.2. Early modern Protestant theologians often described the divine nature as an "utterly incorporeal essence," a "thinking independent substance," wholly uncontaminated by "materiality."[1] This terminology had been inherited from the earlier tradition. For example, in his seventh-century attempt to summarize the consensus of the orthodox faith, John of Damascus maintained that it "must be assumed that the Deity is incorporeal." However, he immediately went on to insist that this is not a "definition" of the divine essence but an indication of what God is not: God does not belong to "the class of existing things" but is "above all existing things, nay even above existence itself."[2] Most of the Protestant Scholastics agreed that God is not defined as one type of substance over against creaturely substances, but the Renaissance appropria-

---

1. For representative quotes, cf. Richard Muller, *Post-Reformation Reformed Dogmatics*, 4 vols. (Grand Rapids: Baker Academic, 2003), 3:271-77, 298ff. (hereafter *PRRD*); Heinrich Heppe, *Reformed Dogmatics: Set Out and Illustrated from the Sources*, rev. and ed. E. Bizer, trans. G. T. Thomson (London: Allen & Unwin, 1950), 52ff. (hereafter *RD*); Heinrich Schmid, *The Doctrinal Theology of the Evangelical Lutheran Church*, 3rd ed., ed. and trans. C. A. Hay and H. E. Jacobs (Minneapolis: Augsburg, 1961), 115ff. (hereafter *DTEL*); Robert D. Preus, *The Theology of Post-Reformation Lutheranism*, 2 vols. (London: Concordia, 1972), 2:64-79.

2. *De Fide Orthodoxa*, I.4; NPNF2, 9:3.

tion of ancient classical philosophy and the rise of modern science contributed to a cultural milieu in which the meaning and relevance of the idea of an "immaterial substance" became increasingly complicated. The function of this idea in theological discourse was deeply affected by semantic shifts in the meaning of the category of "matter" itself.

In order to understand the significance of this category in the seventeenth century, we must recognize that three general views of matter and its relation to divinity were competing, each of which may be traced back to ancient Greek philosophy. Plato had divided "all that is" *(to on)* into two types of being — intelligible things and visible things (*Republic*, 509[d]). The realm of invisible Forms (or ideas) is eternal and immutable, whereas the material realm is characterized by coming-to-be and ceasing-to-be (525[b]).[3] How could such radically different realms interact? Plato's solution was to propose a "participation" of corporeal substance with immutable substance, which was made possible by the mediating efforts of the creative Demiurge, who mixed together the two types of being (*Timaeus*, 35[a]). For Plotinus, whose philosophy contributed to a movement that later came to be called Neoplatonism, matter is simply privation. It is that which has only a "certain measure of existence," which opposes authentic (rational) existents (*Enneads*, II.4.16). Matter is primal, absolute evil — Evil itself — and has no share in the Good (I.8.4-5). In his cosmology, the first principle is the One, which is the absolute Good without limit, beyond being, and even beyond Form as the supreme source of all Forms (VI.7.17; VI.8.9).

Aristotle noted the ambiguity of Plato's dualistic cosmology, laconically observing that precisely what participation is, or how it works, was "left an open question" by his teacher (*Metaphysics*, 987[b]).[4] Rather than dividing matter *(hylē)* and form *(morphē)* into separate realms, he argued that these always appear together in particular substances as hylomorphic composites.[5] Change occurs through the composition, de-composition,

---

3. Cf. *Sophist*, 248[a]; *Philebus*, 54[a]; *Timaeus*, 29[c]. Quotations are from *Plato: Complete Works*, ed. John M. Cooper (Cambridge: Hackett, 1997). For a discussion of the various ways in which ancient Greek philosophers used the term "being" *(ousia)*, and the impact on early Christian theology, see Christopher Stead, *Divine Substance* (Oxford: Clarendon, 1977).

4. Quotations are from *The Complete Works of Aristotle*, ed. Jonathan Barnes, 2 vols. (Princeton: Princeton University Press, 1984).

5. Aristotle defines matter as the "primary substratum of each thing, from which it comes to be, and which persists in the result, not accidentally" (*Physics*, 192[a]32). He uses the term "substance" in different ways, sometimes referring to matter (or potentiality), some-

and re-composition of the potential (material) and actual (formal) constituents of things (*On Generation and Corruption*, 327^{a}30-328^{b}25). Only the divine substance is exempt from this process of compositional change. As essential actuality, or pure form, God is absolutely "simple" and without potentiality — thought thinking itself (*Metaphysics*, 1072^{a}19-1073^{a}13). What these philosophers held in common was a view of the divine as that reality in the world that is as far as possible from matter, but somehow at the same time functions as its ultimate formative principle.

In addition to Platonism and Aristotelianism, another option in ancient Greece and Rome was materialism, a view that was manifested in distinctive ways among the Atomists, Epicureans, and Stoics. In contrast to the (Neo)platonists and the Aristotelians, these schools denied the existence of a separate type of substance that was immaterial. Leucippus and Democritus argued that nothing exists except the "void" and an infinite number of indestructible, indivisible material "atoms." All change can be explained in terms of the collision of atoms, which forms new compounds and dissolves old ones. Epicurus adopted this atomism, but argued further that, because God is imperishable and does not experience affect in relation to this ongoing composition and dissolution, we have no reason to fear divine intervention in this mechanical process. Epictetus, and most of the Stoic philosophers who followed him, were also materialists. According to Galen, they commonly defined a body as that which is extended in three dimensions with resistance.[6] Even the divine, active principle of the cosmos, variously called *pneuma* or creative fire, is material and finite.[7] Although they conceived of the world in more organic terms, the Stoics were notoriously fatalistic; God is the all-pervading, rational principle that governs all things.

The explanatory power of early modern scientific theories had more in common with these mechanistic and atomistic views of matter than with the Neoplatonic and Aristotelian models upon which medieval natural philosophy had been built. In response to these developments, sixteenth- and seventeenth-century theologians struggled either to deny

---

times to form (or actuality), and sometimes to that which is compounded of both (e.g., *On the Soul*, 412^{a}1-11). In his *Categories*, he differentiates between "primary" substances (particular things or subjects) and "secondary" substances (genera or attributes).

6. "*ousian sōmatikēn trichē diastatēn meta antitupias.*" *Stoicorum veterum fragmenta*, ed. H. von Arnim, 3 vols. (Leipzig: Teubner, 1903-1905), 2.381 (hereafter *SVF*).

7. *SVF*, 2.528, 2.614.

the validity of one (or more) of these ancient philosophical schools, or to demonstrate their potential coherence with the Christian understanding of God and the world. In some cases, this involved careful engagement with the philosophical sources, as in Leonard Lessius's correlation of Christian theology to Stoic determinism,[8] or Gassendi's adoption of Epicurean atomism.[9] In other cases, we find a simplistic appeal to the "literal" interpretation of Scripture, which led conservative Protestant authors like John Biddle to insist that God has a body.[10]

§2.1. Cartesian Anxiety

The physical and theological proposals of René Descartes (1596-1650) were shaped by these debates over the nature of matter in relation to divinity. He is best known for his epistemic anxiety (the search for indubitable foundations for knowledge), which was driven in part by the success of mathematical method in science — itself buoyed by a new appreciation of Greek mathematicians such as Pythagorus and Archimedes. However, Descartes's epistemological worries were inextricably linked to his *metaphysical* anxiety about the relation between God and the material world.

Descartes found himself pulled apart intellectually by competing philosophical schools. As a Roman Catholic, he was well aware of the church's appreciation of Thomas Aquinas' synthesis of Aristotelian philosophy and Christian thought, which had been embraced at the Council of Trent. However, like the Cambridge Platonists, he also found inspiration in Augustine's cosmology and anthropology, which had more in common with Neoplatonic dualism. By the seventeenth century Christian theology had come to rely heavily on the ideas of divine immutability and simplicity. These Neoplatonic and Aristotelian categories often overlapped and reinforced each other within particular theological projects.[11] However,

---

8. Cf. Michael J. Buckley, S.J., *At the Origins of Modern Atheism* (New Haven: Yale University Press, 1987), 42-55.

9. Cf. William B. Ashworth, Jr., "Christianity and the Mechanistic Universe," in *When Science and Christianity Meet,* ed. David C. Lindberg and Ronald L. Numbers (Chicago: University of Chicago Press, 2003), 61-84.

10. Cf. Philip Dixon, *Nice and Hot Disputes: The Doctrine of the Trinity in the Seventeenth Century* (London: Continuum, 2003), chap. 2.

11. Augustine also utilizes the concepts of simplicity and composition theory (e.g., *De*

the medieval picture of the world, in which all things are imbued with living principles, formed by their varying degrees of participation in being, and in which the basic elements of fire, air, water, and earth each had their "natural" place, held together by the movements of the celestial spheres, was rapidly collapsing.[12] Descartes's own *Principles of Philosophy* (1644) was in fact a major contribution to its demise.

Like Augustine and Thomas before him, Descartes wanted his understanding of God to cohere with his understanding of creation. Two intrinsically related regulative concepts guided his philosophical and theological project: substance dualism and the dictum *cogito ergo sum*.[13] Descartes connected these to his idea of God in both the *Principles* and the *Meditations on First Philosophy* (1641), although not in the same order of presentation. The key points in the argument may be summarized as follows. The foundation of knowledge must be beyond doubt, or we can never achieve certainty. Although we can doubt our sensations and most of our thoughts, we cannot doubt that we are doubting and so thinking: *je pense, donc je suis*. This clear idea of Descartes's own existence as a thinking thing is prior to and distinct from any certainty about his knowledge of corporeal things. This immediately implies another idea, which is equally certain — a clear distinction between two types of substances: "thinking" things and "extended" things.

The other ideas in his mind represent a variety of different things; this raises the question of the cause of these ideas. Descartes accepts the Neoplatonic correlation between degrees of being and causative power. He applies this to ideas: "the greater the amount of objective perfection they contain within themselves, the more perfect their cause must be" (*Princi-*

Civitate Dei; XI.10, *De Trinitate*, V), and Thomas also makes use of the categories of immutability and participation (e.g., *SumTh*, I.9; *SCG*, I.40.3, II.15.5). These philosophical categories did not dictate what they could say about God, but they did often condition their expressions of the relation of the Creator to creation.

12. Cf. N. Max Wildiers, *The Theologian and His Universe: Theology and Cosmology from the Middle Ages to the Present* (New York: Seabury, 1982), chaps. 1-3; Edward Grant, *The Foundations of Modern Science in the Middle Ages: Their Religious, Institutional, and Intellectual Contexts* (Cambridge: Cambridge University Press, 1996), chap. 4.

13. In *Rules for the Direction of the Mind* (12) Descartes argues that the following propositions are necessarily conjoined: "I am, therefore God exists" and "I understand, therefore I have a mind distinct from my body" (*The Philosophical Writings of Descartes*, 3 vols., trans. John Cottingham et al. [Cambridge: Cambridge University Press, 1985-1991], 1:46 [hereafter *PWD*]). They are two moments in the same intuition.

ples, I.17). Among the ideas in his mind is that of a supremely perfect being who necessarily exists. In the *Meditations* (III), he says that by the word "God" he understands "a substance that is infinite, independent, supremely intelligent, supremely powerful, and which created both myself and everything else (if anything else there be) that exists."[14] As an imperfect doubter, he cannot be the cause of this idea of a perfect being. Its cause must have objective perfection at least equivalent to the idea, which includes necessary existence; therefore, a perfect being necessarily exists. This idea of God is utterly clear and distinct, having the same level of certainty as mathematical truths (*Meditations*, V). A *perfect* being would be wholly Good and so not a deceiver,[15] therefore Descartes can be certain that every other clear and distinct idea is true. This becomes the foundation of all scientific knowledge and method.

We will return to an assessment of this "ontological proof" in chapter 10, but our interest here is in the underlying theological basis of Cartesian natural philosophy. The idea of "infinity" itself, which is at the core of his understanding of divine substance, threatens the stability of Descartes's foundationalism. On the one hand, he believed that we *must* think of God as a clear and distinct idea, for the idea of an infinitely perfect being authorizes the certainty of human knowledge. If he did not have this idea indubitably secured, he could never be quite certain about anything else. On the other hand, we *cannot* think of God in this way because, as Descartes himself realized, the very idea of "infinity" itself would be destroyed. In his Replies to Objections, published together with the French edition of the *Meditations*, Descartes acknowledged that "God cannot be taken in by the human mind, and I admit this, along with all theologians. . . . God cannot be distinctly known by those who look from a distance as it were, and try to make their minds encompass his entirety all at once." He was aware that "the idea of the infinite, if it is to be a true idea, cannot be grasped at all, since the impossibility of being grasped is contained in the formal definition of the infinite."[16] In other words, the very idea of the in-finite itself requires that it not be de-finable in clear and distinct terms.

Another tension in Descartes's theology is between a mathematical

14. *PWD*, 2:31.

15. Here, too, Descartes seems to be presupposing a Platonic view of the divine as inherently good and so not deceitful (*Republic*, 379b-382e).

16. *PWD*, 2:81, 253. He approvingly quotes Thomas Aquinas's observation that knowledge of God is within us "in a somewhat confused manner."

and a metaphysical use of the term "infinity." In the former case, infinity is understood as the indefinite extension of a series, such as the natural numbers. Descartes sometimes describes God in ways that use the idea of extension: "everyone has the form or idea of understanding; and by indefinitely *extending* [emphasis added] this he can form the idea of God's understanding. And a similar procedure applies to the other attributes of God."[17] The metaphysical use of the term "infinity," however, more commonly refers to that which is absolute, perfect, or all-embracing. In a letter to Henry More, Descartes noted the great difference between the "indefinite" vastness of bodily extension and the infinite vastness of the divine substance — "I do not say 'divine extension', because strictly speaking, there is none."[18]

Descartes longed to emulate the certainty of mathematical method in all other forms of knowledge. His rationalist approach in theology may very well have been motivated in part by his desire to provide a method that could ameliorate the explicit hostility between religious factions that contributed to the Thirty Years' War. However, he was aware that the majority of the Christian tradition had always insisted that divine infinity cannot be grasped by human reason. How, then, was he to explain rationally how an infinite, unextended divine substance could have a causative relation to the world of extended matter? This problem parallels the mind/body puzzle in Cartesian anthropology. To explain the interaction between immaterial Creator and material creation, Descartes is pulled toward a participative ontology, in which "being" is a genus common to both. For Descartes, the unextended human soul becomes aware of God not through examining the extended world of matter, but by contemplating the perfect being in which it participates.[19]

Anxiety about the relation of matter to an infinite God continued to shape the philosophers who responded to Descartes throughout the early modern period. As the author of the third set of Objections to Descartes's *Meditations,* Thomas Hobbes challenged both the idea that reality (being) admits of more or less and the possibility of conceiving of an infinite substance. He articulated these concerns in more detail in his *Leviathan* (1651), suggesting that we must think of God as having a body in some sense

---

17. *PWD*, 2;130-32.
18. Letter to Henry More, 5 Feb. 1649 (*PWD*, 3:364).
19. Cf. *Discourse on the Method*, IV (*PWD*, 1:128).

(I.3.12; III.34.5). If Hobbes resolved the anxiety in favor of materialism, George Berkeley represents the opposite extreme, claiming in his 1710 *Principles of Human Knowledge* that all that exists is incorporeal substance (I.7-9).

Spinoza tried to resolve the problem by conflating material and immaterial substance. All that exists is Absolute Substance *(Deus sive Natura)*. In his *Ethics,* which was published soon after his death in 1677, he insisted that "thinking substance and extended substance are one and the same substance." Because no substance can be (or be conceived) apart from God, "extended substance is one of God's infinite attributes."[20] Leibniz described Spinoza's metaphysics as an "exaggerated Cartesianism," and saw these two as the leaders of a revived Stoicism that threatened Christian theology. His own approach, which postulates a divinely preestablished harmony of monads, is defended in part II of his *Theodicy* (1713) in constant dialogue with contemporary interpretations of Atomism, Epicureanism, and Stoicism, which illustrates the extent to which these ancient schools continued to impact theological reflection on the relation between God and the world.

§2.2. Infinity in Early Modern Theological Projects

The Protestant Scholastic systems of theology were forged in this philosophical upheaval and scientific revolution. They fought against materialism with the tools they had inherited — a mixture of the Neoplatonic and Aristotelian categories of divine immutability and simplicity. For example, at the beginning of his presentation of the doctrine of God in 1626, Johannes Wollebius speaks of the "immutable life" of God and defines divine simplicity: "he is not compounded of parts . . . of potentiality and act" (I.1).[21] Francis Turretin maintained the simplicity of God against the Socinians later in the century (1679) by arguing that divine perfection rules out mutability: God is "a most pure act having no passive admixture and

20. Baruch Spinoza, *Ethics,* trans. Samuel Shirley (Cambridge: Hackett, 1992), 67, 40. He defines God as an "absolutely infinite being" because finitude involves negation (I. Def. 6, explication), while "to be infinite is the unqualified affirmation of the existence of some nature" (I.8, Scholium 1).

21. *Compendium Theologiae Christianae,* trans. and ed. John W. Beardslee III, in *Reformed Dogmatics* (New York: Oxford University Press, 1965), 39.

therefore rejecting all composition."[22] Rejecting the renovated Stoic and Epicurean ways of conceptualizing the relation between materiality and divinity, these theologians were guided by the Aristotelian dictum that "whatever comes to be is always complex" (*Physics*, 190^{b}12), as well as the Neoplatonic intuition that the absolutely perfect One is untouched by change (Plotinus, *Enneads*, V.4).

Most early modern theologians, along with the majority of the Christian tradition, were careful to avoid the Greek tendency to speak of God as one part of the world, defined as the formative principle over against a material or passive principle. They accepted the doctrine of *creatio ex nihilo*, insisting that God was not dependent on forms to shape preexisting matter, but created both form and matter out of nothing.[23] Like Augustine and Thomas, they saw the main function of the doctrines of simplicity and immutability as underlining the Christian intuition that human thought cannot grasp or define divinity as it does material things. It became increasingly difficult to uphold this intuition as rationalism and materialism began to permeate Western philosophy and science. Theologians were tempted to immunize faith from reason (by emphasizing biblical revelation as the only source of theological knowledge) and to isolate God from the world (by privileging transcendence over divine immanence).

The way in which semantic shifts in the concepts of matter, form, substance, and infinity impacted the doctrine of God may be illustrated by observing the early modern theological distinctions between the divine essence and the divine attributes, and among the attributes themselves. As we noted in chapter 1, the substance-attribute distinction itself derives from Aristotle's *Categories*, where he explains how to define a particular substance. The definition of a thing (identifying its genus and differentiae) marks off its essence, but we may also attribute various accidental qualities to the thing (such as its relations to other things). How are we to define God? On the one hand, a strict doctrine of simplicity would imply no dis-

22. Francis Turretin, *Institutes of Elenctic Theology,* trans. George Musgrave Giger, 3 vols. (Phillipsburg, N.J.: P&R Publishing, 1992), 1:191 (hereafter *Elenc.*). Originally published 1679-1685. For additional examples of Reformed treatments, cf. *RD*, 63-64; *PRRD*, 3:227-324. For Lutheran examples, cf. *DTEL*, §§15-18.

23. For example, cf. Tertullian, *Against Hermogenes* (ANF, 3:481, 486); Basil of Caesarea, *Hexameron*, Homily II, NPNF2, 8:58-65. Cf. Gerhard May, *Creatio ex nihilo: The Doctrine of 'Creation out of Nothing' in Early Christian Thought,* trans. A. S. Worrall (Edinburgh: T&T Clark, 1994).

tinction between the divine essence and attributes. All of God's attributes would have to be essential attributes, and in fact identical to the divine essence and to each other. On the other hand, Scripture and religious experience lead us to attribute qualities like "mercy" to God. If such qualities are essential attributes of God, however, then they must be eternal, which suggests that the relation to an object of mercy must also be eternal. To avoid this conclusion, several classifications of divine attributes were developed: e.g., between absolute and relative, internal and external, incommunicable and communicable attributes. Because such distinctions could not be "real," the Protestant Scholastics borrowed and adapted categories from medieval debates, describing them as conceptual, modal, formal, or nominal distinctions.

However, this did not wholly alleviate Cartesian anxiety. On the assumptions of substance metaphysics, any divine attributes that were "really" communicated to creatures or dependent on God's relation to creatures would threaten divine simplicity and immutability. But if the divine essence is not related to mutable, dependent creatures, how can we claim that God is "really" present in the religious experience of divine mercy? Too much stress on the relative attributes could imply pantheism, but too much emphasis on the absolute attributes could lead to deism.

It became increasingly common in the seventeenth century to speak of the attribute of the infinity of God not only with reference to the divine essence, but explicitly in terms of divine *immensity* in relation to space and of divine *eternity* in relation to time.[24] God is not circumscribed by the limits of space and time, but is present to all spaces and times. Turretin urged us not to think of God's presence as extended like bodies, but as "containing the whole world . . . just as eternity holds in its embrace all time and coexists with it indivisibly."[25] He emphasized that God's repletive presence is everywhere, "even in the most filthy places," but the divine majesty does not come into physical contact with material things. For the most

---

24. In his 1685 *Theologia Didactico-Polemica*, Quenstedt makes this explicit: the infinity of God is the absolute interminability of the divine essence, which in relation to time is called eternity and in relation to space is called immensity (1:288). In his 1624 *Syntagma Theologiae Christianae,* Polanus explicitly says that the infinity of God is both eternity and immensity (Synopsis libri II). Cf. *DTEL,* 119, and *RD,* 61-66. Arminius also applied infinity to time and space, deriving eternity and immensity; cf. Richard Muller, *God, Creation, and Providence in the Thought of Jacob Arminius* (Grand Rapids: Baker, 1991), 135-36.

25. *Elenc.,* I:200.

part, theologians during this period were careful to insist that divine infinity should not be conceived in mathematical but in metaphysical terms.[26] However, tying divine infinity to the negation of the limits of time and space intensified the problem of God's interaction with an extended temporal and corporeal world.

The struggle to articulate the relation between an immaterial God and a material world during the early modern period is reflected in the debates over the relation between divine and creaturely substances in Jesus Christ and in the Eucharist. How can an immutable, immaterial substance become united with a finite, material substance? Is the finite capable of bearing or containing the infinite *(finitum capax infiniti)*? The coherence of faith in the incarnation and in the real presence in the Lord's Supper was at stake in the debates between the Lutherans and the Reformed over this question. Does the divine Word communicate all or only some of its attributes (or properties, *idiomata*) to the human nature of Christ? The Lutherans tended to argue that all of the attributes were shared, else it would not be a true union, while the Reformed usually maintained that some of the attributes of the divine Logos are simply incommunicable and so outside of the union *(extra Calvinisticum)*. A similar metaphysic colored the debates over what happens during the prayer at the communion table. Is the substance of the bread and wine changed into the body and blood of Christ, while their accidental attributes (e.g., taste, texture) remain the same? The particular structure of these early modern Christological and sacramental debates was shaped by the deeper metaphysical shifts in the concept of matter, which made it difficult to conceive of the relation between material and immaterial substances.

The categories that led to Cartesian anxiety continue to shape some streams of the Christian tradition. The nineteenth-century American theologian Charles Hodge used Turretin's *Institutes* as the framework for constructing his own theology, as he attempted to defend the rationality of early modern theological formulations of the doctrine of God. Hodge insisted that we have a "perfectly *clear and distinct idea* of the infinity of God" and that "we know God in *the same sense* in which we know our-

---

26. Edward Leigh insists on this in *A Treatise of Divinity* (1646-1651): God "is infinite not according to the Etymon of the world, which respects an end only; for he is both without beginning and end; and although the word be negative, yet we intend by it a positive attribute and perfection." Quoted and translated in *PRRD*, 3:332.

selves and things out of ourselves."[27] This view of theological predication is metaphysically laden, and may easily be taken to imply that God is a type of substance in the world, marked off by human language. Taken to its extreme, such a model would depict divine infinity in terms of the extension of human attributes.

The temptation to rely upon univocal and quantitative predication in the doctrine of God has not always been sufficiently resisted among American theologians who find themselves in the current of this early modern theological stream. For example, Millard Erickson suggests that "whenever God has revealed himself, he has selected elements that are *univocal* in his universe and ours." Moreover, "God is powerful as humans are powerful, but *much more* so. . . . God has humans' knowledge *amplified* to an infinite *extent.* . . . Although what we know of him is *the same* as his knowledge of himself, the *degree* of our knowledge is *much less.*"[28] This approach presupposes a basic dualism between God and the world, between two "universes" that can be spanned by language, although one is "much" larger.

If Cartesian rationalist dualism or Spinozist mystical monism were the only options, theology would be forced to choose between them. However, the early modern epistemological, cosmological, and linguistic assumptions that uphold this dichotomy have all been challenged in late modern philosophy and science.

§2.3. Alterity in Late Modern Philosophy

As we saw in chapter 1, Plato listed five general "kinds" — that which is, rest, change, the same, and the different (*Sophist*, 254^d-255^e). The success of mathematical analyses of motion *(rest* and *change)* and the linguistic shift toward univocity *(the same)* in early modernity contributed to the rationalist impulse to exert a conceptual reign over *that which is,* including God. During this period, *the different* was often seen as problematic — that which must be manipulated or overcome by the same, whether scientifically, politically, or conceptually.

In much of late modern philosophy, however, attending to the novelty

27. Charles Hodge, *Systematic Theology,* 3 vols. (Grand Rapids: Eerdmans, 1981), 1:359, 365. Emphasis added.

28. *Christian Theology,* 2nd ed. (Grand Rapids: Baker, 1998), 205-6. Emphasis added.

of that which is otherwise (*aliter*) has become as important as understanding the repetition of that which is similar (*identidem*). In some cases, the category of "the other" (*alter*) is even construed as anterior to "the same" (*idem*). This indicates a preference for Plato over Aristotle, for whom difference — relation to the other — was "accidental." The category of being was usually privileged in Plato as well, but he also emphasized the significance of the different: it "pervades" all of the other kinds, which share in the different insofar as they are in relation to each other and to the different. This emphasis was taken up and strengthened by several twentieth-century philosophers. For example, Heidegger's critique of early modern onto-theology led him to begin not with the sameness of thinking and being, but with the oblivion of the "*difference* between Being and beings," which gives rise to thought.[29]

This fascination with alterity and "the other" has radically impacted late modern philosophical (and theological) discourse on "infinity." Emmanuel Levinas insisted that language does not grasp the infinite, for language is itself the relation between the other and the same made possible by the anteriority of the infinite, which constitutes conversation (and ethics) as the presence of the absolutely Other. This Other is "prior to every initiative, to all imperialism of the same." Its alterity is not simply a limit of the same "for in limiting the same the other would not be rigorously other: by virtue of the common frontier the other, within the system, would yet be the same."[30] This is why the truly "infinite" cannot be de-fined by its negation or extension of the finite. As Levinas puts it elsewhere, "the *in* of infinity is not a *not* like any other. . . . The difference between the infinite and the finite is a non-indifference of the infinite to the finite."[31] Calvin Schrag has argued that we should link alterity and transcendence, but not simply in a way that takes God to be the "different," for this is still one of the "kinds" of being. He suggests we take the Platonic hint that the Good is "beyond being" to indicate an alterity of infinite love that can only be received as absolute Gift, which is irreducible to the economy of finite being.[32]

29. Martin Heidegger, *Identity and Difference,* trans. Joan Stambaugh (Chicago: University of Chicago Press, 2002), 50.

30. *Totality and Infinity,* trans. A. Lingis (Pittsburgh: Duquesne University Press, 1961), 39.

31. Levinas, "God and Philosophy," in *Basic Philosophical Writings,* ed. Adriaan T. Peperz et al. (Bloomington: Indiana University Press, 1996), 129-48 at 138.

32. Calvin Schrag, *God as Otherwise than Being: Toward a Semantics of the Gift* (Evanston, Ill.: Northwestern University Press, 2002).

How did this shift occur? We have already alluded to the tension between two general ways of discussing the concept of infinity in the history of philosophy and theology. The common *mathematical* use of the term refers to a series that may be limitlessly extended or divided, while its *metaphysical* use more often indicates that which is absolute, perfect, or all-encompassing.[33] In order to understand the late modern interest in the latter, it is important to recognize how deeply entrenched the former became in early modern philosophy.[34] Descartes tried to hold together infinity and perfection in his idea of God, but as the seventeenth century progressed the term increasingly came to refer only to a mathematical ideal. In his 1689 *Essay Concerning Human Understanding*, John Locke treated the idea of infinity (as he did all other ideas) by exploring how it arises in the mind through sensation and is developed through reflection. The finite and the infinite are looked upon by the mind as *"Modes of Quantity,"* and apply to number, space, and duration. He argued that we cannot have a positive clear idea of infinity, for whatever idea of supposedly infinite length is in the mind may again be imaginatively doubled. For the mind to have a positive idea of the infinite, it would have to place a boundary around that which has no bounds — so the mind cannot have such an idea.[35]

Kant's attempt in the late eighteenth century to mediate between rationalism and empiricism had ramifications on his treatment of the idea of infinity. In the *Critique of Pure Reason* (1787), he treated the idea of "extensive" magnitude as a "mathematical" principle, connected to the axioms of intuition, which deal with space and time. However, "intensive" magnitude is the key to the "analogies of experience," which are the "dynamical" principles of pure understanding (B200-B218). Extension has to do with the homogenous (and quantitative), but intension applies to the heterogenous

---

33. Cf. A. W. Moore, *The Infinite*, 2nd ed. (London: Routledge, 2001); J. Seppänen, "Infinity — An Outline of Conceptions in Mythology, Cosmology and Natural Philosophy," in *Finite Versus Infinite: Contributions to an Eternal Dilemma*, ed. C. S. Calude and G. Paun (London: Springer-Verlag, 2000), 257-83; Jill Le Blanc, "Infinity in Theology and Mathematics," *Religious Studies* 29 (1993): 51-62.

34. For an overview and analysis of the concept of the "positive" metaphysical infinite and "perfection" during this period, cf. Philip Clayton, *The Problem of God in Modern Thought* (Grand Rapids: Eerdmans, 2000).

35. Locke acknowledged that "the great GOD, of whom and from whom are all things, is incomprehensibly infinite," but our narrow thoughts apply this idea to "his Duration and Ubiquity," which theologians call eternity and immensity (*Essay*, II.17, 210).

(and qualitative). This distinction fuels his attempt to resolve the first antinomy of pure reason, i.e., the question of the limits or infinity of the world in regard to time and space. In the *Critique of Judgment* (1790) Kant dealt with the sublime — that which is absolutely great, without comparison (beyond quantity), that which has to do with the quality of the beautiful, the aesthetic. Pure reason cannot have an idea of the mathematical infinite in space and time, but aesthetic judgment can "think" of nature as an exhibition of the unconditioned, the absolute magnitude (§§25-29).

Hegel reacted against the way in which the mathematical (quantitative) infinite had dominated early modern science, banning "spirit" from the material world. He argued that the quantitative and the qualitative are inherently related and sublate themselves in each other, positing their immediate unity.[36] Hegel argued for a vision of the metaphysical infinite as a self-related Absolute that could include finitude without being limited by it. He was ruthless in his critique of what he called the "spurious" infinite, i.e., any idea of the infinite that is determined by its polarity to the finite. A contradiction occurs in the positing of such a polarity "as a direct result of the circumstance that the finite remains as a determinate being opposed to the infinite, so that there are *two* determinatenesses; *there are* two worlds, one infinite and one finite, and in their relationship the infinite is only the *limit* of the finite and is thus only a determinate infinite, an *infinite which is itself finite*."[37]

For this reason, Hegel refused to oppose spirit and matter as mutually limiting (de-fining). The "true" infinite embraces both itself and finitude; it is a process that raises its difference from itself into the affirmation of itself, and through this mediation is becoming itself. Hegel applies "true infinity" to God explicitly in his *Lectures on the Philosophy of Religion*. Absolute Spirit must encompass finitude within itself, for "if it did not have it [finitude] within itself, and thus if it confronted finitude from the other side, then its infinitude would be a spurious infinitude. . . . If God has the finite only over against himself, then he himself is finite and limited."[38]

The philosophical emphasis on alterity has often taken a deconstructive form. Jacques Derrida emphasized the negativity of differánce, the deferral of the consummation of meaning, and the opening of absence

36. *Hegel's Science of Logic,* trans. A. V. Miller (Amherst, N.Y.: Humanity Books, 1999), 372; cf. 79.

37. Ibid., 139-40 (emphases in original).

38. *Lectures on the Philosophy of Religion,* trans. P. C. Hodgson et al., 3 vols. (Berkeley: University of California Press, 1998), 3:263-64.

in all attempts at signification, which he took to be irreducible traces of the different.[39] However, even in deconstructive forms of the (re)turn to alterity, we can hear echoes of the apophatic intuition of the Christian tradition,[40] which has always insisted that God is beyond human language and creaturely being. The link between the contemporary metaphysical interest in "difference" and resources in the Christian tradition that have resisted the reduction of the divine Other to idolatrous signification has been explored by several Christian philosophers and theologians.[41] Such explorations are part of a broader theological concern to stress what Kierkegaard called the "infinite qualitative distinction" between God and the world, to attend to the Infinite and Unknown as the "frontier that is continually arrived at . . . the absolutely different."[42]

The recovery of this traditional emphasis on intensive, qualitative infinity will be explored in chapter 5 and integrated into our attempt to reconstruct the doctrine of God in part III. Our interest here, however, is noting that, although these philosophical developments challenge the early modern theological tilt toward univocity and the reliance on the idea of extension in the doctrine of divine attributes, they also provide an opportunity to retrieve resources from the biblical tradition that have emphasized the infinite qualitative distinction between Creator and creature.

§2.4. Mathematics and Linguistics in Contemporary Science

The anxiety that pervaded early modern reflection on the relation between God and the world was shaped in part by the idealization of mathematical methods, which led to a search for apodictic foundations (or axioms) as the

---

39. Cf. his *Of Grammatology,* trans. G. C. Spivak (London: Johns Hopkins University Press, 1998), and *Writing and Difference,* trans. Alan Bass (Chicago: University of Chicago Press, 1978).

40. This is especially evident in Derrida's 1986 "Comment ne pas parler: dénégations." For discussion, see Graham Ward, *Barth, Derrida and the Language of Theology* (Cambridge: Cambridge University Press, 1995), 252ff.

41. For example, cf. Merold Westphal, *Overcoming Onto-theology* (New York: Fordham University Press, 2001); Oliver Davies, *A Theology of Compassion: Metaphysics of Difference and the Renewal of Tradition* (Grand Rapids: Eerdmans, 2003).

42. *Philosophical Fragments,* trans. Howard V. and Edna H. Hong (Princeton: Princeton University Press, 1985), 44.

basis for all scientific knowledge. In late modernity, however, developments in metamathematical discourse itself have led to a rejection of this foundationalist method. For centuries the postulates of Euclid, which were taken to be self-evident and necessary, formed the basis for geometry and mathematics. His fifth postulate, which refers to parallel lines that are indefinitely extended, created a problem that was often ignored by mathematicians. The human mind cannot actually follow these lines indefinitely to discover if they are indeed infinite.

Some mathematicians tried to expunge this trace of infinity from the Euclidean model,[43] but the notion of ideal elements at infinity within this axiom was required for the analysis of complex mathematical relations, which led to the infinitesimal calculus. Gauss's distinction between the agreement of a mathematical system with the physical universe and its logical consistency opened the way for non-Euclidean systems such as Riemannian geometry, from which Einstein developed his theory of general relativity. The ideal infinity nestled in Euclid's fifth postulate and other geometries suggested that mathematics could not function without postulating the inaccessible.

Another blow to mathematical foundationalism came with the Gödelian Incompleteness Theorems (1931), which showed that any consistent formal system of mathematics will be incomplete, because some true statements in the system will be unprovable or undecidable from within this system. Self-referential statements (e.g., "this statement is unprovable") within any system require the formation of a higher system that can refer to the lower system as a whole. Gödel observed that this undecidability is reiterated in each new system and can be continued into the transfinite.[44]

The idea of infinity also has a central role in the story of Georg Cantor's development of set theory, during which he discovered that mathematics cannot secure itself with self-evident (or provable) foundations. Aristotle had rejected the idea of an "actual infinite" as incoherent, for a limitless series cannot be thought as a whole. Cantor challenged this assumption, which had guided mathematics for over two millennia. He de-

43. Cf. Eli Maor, *To Infinity and Beyond: A Cultural History of the Infinite* (Princeton: Princeton University Press, 1987), chap. 16.

44. Cf. Raymond M. Smullyan, *Gödel's Incompleteness Theorems* (Oxford: Oxford University Press, 1992); Gregory J. Chaitin, *The Unknowable* (London: Springer-Verlag, 1999); idem, *The Limits of Mathematics* (London: Springer-Verlag, 2002).

fined a set as a collection of things, or as a many that may be thought of as a one. Finite sets have equal cardinality if there is a one-to-one correspondence between the elements in each set. Cantor applied this idea to infinite sets. An infinite set is a set that may be put into one-to-one correspondence with a proper subset of itself. So the natural numbers $\{1, 2, 3, \ldots\}$ are an infinite set because they may be placed in a one-to-one correspondence with a proper subset of the natural numbers; for example, $\{10, 20, 30, \ldots\}$.

It seems appropriate to suppose that all infinite sets would have the same cardinality. However, Cantor demonstrated through a diagonalization argument that the set of real numbers (which also includes all the decimal numbers between the integers) may not be placed in a one-to-one correspondence with the set of natural numbers, which is one of its proper subsets. Elements of the infinite set of real numbers are always left over, which means this set has a higher cardinality than the set of natural numbers. He also showed that an infinite set (like a finite set) cannot be placed into one-to-one correspondence with the set of all of its subsets. The set of all subsets of an infinite set has greater cardinality than the set itself. In other words, surprisingly, some infinite sets are "larger" than others.

This comparison among transfinite sets led to the question of the cardinality of the "set of all sets." This raises a paradox. If the set of all the subsets of the "set of all sets" has greater cardinality than that set (which it must have, given the definition of an infinite set), then the "set of all sets" does not contain that set, in which case it is not the set of *all* sets. This of course may be reiterated for the new infinite set of all that set's subsets, *ad infinitum*. At this point, Cantor argued that we must postulate an Absolute Infinity, which is beyond the Transfinitum, else we could not make sense of the functions of set theory that make arithmetical analyses possible. The idea of Absolute Infinity is explicitly theological for Cantor *(Infinitum aeternum increatum)* and transcends mathematical formulation.

Set theory obviously does not "prove" the existence of an infinite God. However, it did lead to developments in the twentieth century (such as the failure of Hilbert's program), which confirmed that mathematical rationality is intrinsically limited. Demonstrating the consistency of mathematical functions within any set always depends on the postulation of a set with higher cardinality. The indefinite postulation of inaccessible cardinals is inescapable and so mathematics has no self-contained foundation.[45]

45. For a discussion of "inaccessible cardinals" in contemporary metamathematics, cf.

These developments in metamathematics have led to a renewed interest in the relation between the intelligibility of mathematical structures and the idea of God.[46]

Early modern assumptions about language have also been challenged in the wake of the "linguistic turn." As we saw in chapter 1, Aristotle's theory of predication and his theory of substance were intimately connected; the structure of language represents the structure of being. Descartes accepted this substance-accident model, imagining that ideas in the mind represent (mirror) distinct objects in nature, which are their substantive cause. As Nancey Murphy explains, this led to early modern "referential-representative" theories of language, in which meaning resides in the "atoms" of particular words or propositions.[47] However, the linguistic turn in all of its various forms challenges this model by insisting that human knowledge cannot step out of its "subjective" embeddedness within language to confirm the adequation of its propositions to "objective" reality. We are inextricably embedded within "language games" (Wittgenstein), and we cannot escape the linguistic mediation of the horizons of our experience (Gadamer) and communicative praxis (Habermas).

Furthermore, research in the anthropological sciences indicates that language does not simply deal with ideas in the mind that may be foundationally secured independently of the knower's embodied context, for the emergence of language in children is mediated through their psychosocial relations.[48] If the capacity for language (symbol use) evolved

---

Solomon Feferman, "Does Mathematics Need New Axioms?" *American Mathematical Quarterly* (Feb. 1999): 99-111.

46. For discussion of Cantor's set theory and its relation to theology, cf. Ignacio Jané, "The Role of the Absolute Infinite in Cantor's Conception of Set," *Erkenntnis* 42 (1995): 375-402; Adam Drozdek, "Beyond Infinity: Augustine and Cantor," *Laval théologique et philosophique* 51, no. 1 (1995): 127-40; Joseph W. Dauben, "Georg Cantor and Pope Leo XIII: Mathematics, Theology and the Infinite," *Journal of the History of Ideas* 38, no. 1 (1977): 85-108; Robert J. Russell, "The God Who Infinitely Transcends Infinity," in *How Large Is God? The Voices of Scientists and Theologians,* ed. J. M. Templeton (Philadelphia: Templeton Press, 1997), 137-65.

47. Nancey Murphy, *Anglo-American Postmodernity* (Boulder, Colo.: Westview, 1997). Cf. Richard Rorty, *Philosophy and the Mirror of Nature* (Princeton: Princeton University Press, 1979).

48. Cf. Leslie Milroy and Matthew Gordon, *Sociolinguistics: Method and Interpretation,* 2nd ed. (Oxford: Blackwell, 2003); Michael Garman, *Psycholinguistics* (Cambridge: Cambridge University Press, 1990).

along with the brain in early hominids,[49] this suggests that the distinctive function of human language is to manipulate finite symbols for the sake of communicating the relation between them. We ought not to be surprised when this tool does not work on true infinity, which is beyond finite differentiation. Such shifts in the understanding of the function of language may open a way out of the scholastic debates over the theological use of "analogy," which always contains an element of univocity as well as equivocity.

These developments in linguistics and mathematics are part of a broader movement that rejects the foundationalist rationality of early modern philosophy and science.[50] Elsewhere I have challenged the assumption that these developments force us to choose between the Scylla of foundationalist dogmatism and the Charybdis of non-foundationalist relativism.[51] While foundationalism emphasizes experience as the basis of belief, the unity of truth, reason in the individual, and the universality of explanation, non-foundationalism stresses the way in which webs of belief condition experience, the plurality of knowledge, the rationality of the community, and the particularity of understanding.

The "post-foundationalist" approach attempts to avoid the horns of this dilemma by accommodating the legitimate intuitions of each of these approaches without collapsing into the polarizing tendencies of either extreme. This middle way can be summarized in four couplets. Interpreted experience anchors all beliefs, and a network of beliefs informs the interpretation of experience (PF1). The objective unity of truth is a necessary condition for the intelligible search for knowledge, and the subjective mul-

---

49. Cf. Terrence W. Deacon, *The Symbolic Species: The Co-evolution of Language and the Brain* (New York: Norton, 1997), 336; William Noble and Iain Davidson, *Human Evolution, Language and Mind: A Psychological and Archaeological Inquiry* (Cambridge: Cambridge University Press, 1996); Andrew Carstairs-McCarthy, *The Origins of Complex Language: An Inquiry into the Evolutionary Beginnings of Sentences, Syllables and Truth* (Oxford: Oxford University Press, 1999); N. Rescher, *A Useful Inheritance: Evolutionary Aspects of the Theory of Knowledge* (Savage: Rowman and Littlefield, 1990); Steven Mithen, *The Prehistory of the Mind: The Cognitive Origins of Art, Religion and Science* (London: Thames and Hudson, 1996).

50. The post-foundationalist move in the philosophy of mathematics is illustrated in Thomas Tymoczko, *New Directions in the Philosophy of Mathematics: An Anthology,* rev. ed. (Princeton: Princeton University Press, 1998). The linguistic turn in theology is illustrated in D. Z. Phillips, *Faith After Foundationalism* (Boulder, Colo.: Westview, 1995).

51. Cf. my *The Postfoundationalist Task of Theology* (Grand Rapids: Eerdmans, 1999), chap. 2, and J. Wentzel van Huyssteen, *The Shaping of Rationality* (Grand Rapids: Eerdmans, 1999).

tiplicity of knowledge indicates the fallibility of truth claims (PF2). Rational judgment is an activity of socially situated individuals, and the cultural community indeterminately mediates the criteria of rationality (PF3). Explanation aims for universal, trans-contextual understanding, and understanding derives from particular contextualized explanations (PF4).

As we have seen, the hubris of early modern foundationalist rationality crashed on the "reef of the infinite,"[52] but this does not mean we are condemned to drown in the sea of relativism. On the contrary, these developments provide us with an opportunity to recover a metaphysically intensive understanding of divine Infinity, to discover with Augustine that God is infinite in a different way *(infinitum aliter).*[53] Chapter 5 is dedicated to tracing the retrieval of these resources, but it is important at this stage to observe that the driving force behind this theological trajectory was not merely philosophical and scientific shifts in culture but a fresh awareness that early modern categories in the doctrine of God had obscured aspects of the biblical witness.

§2.5. Biblical Experiences of Infinity

The authors of Scripture did not rely on the categorical distinction between material and immaterial substance to express their experience of the biblical God. They did not spend their energy trying to hold together divine transcendence and immanence. Nor were they obsessed with the philosophical tensions between human freedom and divine foreknowledge, or between the existence of evil and divine predestination. Their experience of the redemptive activity of the biblical God was a being-encountered by a powerful presence that was wholly beyond their finite control. The absolute reality of this intensive presence bore down on them in a way that opened up the possibility of new life. The philosophical and scientific categories of early modernity created a conceptual matrix in which it became increasingly difficult to offer a coherent presentation of this experience. How can an immaterial, timeless substance be causally related to material, temporal substances? We can begin to respond to these

52. Cf. Karsten Harries, *Infinity and Perspective* (Cambridge, Mass.: The MIT Press, 2001), 282-99.
53. Cf. *Confessions* 1.7; 7.14.

challenges by showing that dependence on the category of immaterial substance is underdetermined by the biblical witness to an experience of God as an incomparable divine *presence.*

My interest here is not in deducing the doctrine of divine Infinity from propositional statements found in Scripture, but in demonstrating how the experience of an incomparably intensive presence underlies the development of the biblical understanding of God. Several passages in the Hebrew Bible express the idea that God's greatness cannot be defined in comparison to creaturely greatness. "All the nations are as nothing before him; they are accounted by him as less than nothing and emptiness. To whom then will you liken God, or what likeness compare with him?" (Isa. 40:17-18). In the New Testament, Paul declares that the sufferings that he has experienced in his ministry "are *not worth comparing* with the glory about to be revealed to us" (Rom. 8:18). What he calls "this slight momentary affliction" does not crush him because he is anticipating "an eternal weight of glory *beyond all measure*" (2 Cor. 4:17). The experience of this incommensurably redemptive presence transforms the way in which the people of God interpret the conditions of their finitude.

The doxological expressions of the biblical authors indicate that their experience of God's "greatness" is qualitatively different from creaturely greatness. "Great is the LORD, and greatly to be praised; his greatness is unsearchable" (Ps. 145:3). The "limit of the Almighty" cannot be found out because it is "higher than heaven" and "deeper than Sheol" (Job 11:7-8). However, this limitless presence is not simply beyond the extensive limits of the cosmos as Job's friends understand it. The Psalmist describes his experience of an intense presence that cannot be escaped because it holds us together: "Where can I go from your spirit? Or where can I flee from your presence? If I ascend to heaven, you are there; if I make my bed in Sheol, you are there. If I take the wings of the morning and settle at the farthest limits of the sea, even there your hand shall lead me, and your right hand shall hold me fast" (Ps. 139:7-10). As Solomon prays at the dedication of the temple, it seems strange to suggest that God will dwell on the earth since "even heaven and the highest heaven cannot contain you" (1 Kings 8:27). On the other hand, God is present to all things: "Do I not fill heaven and earth? says the LORD" (Jer. 23:23-24). The experience of being embraced by the intensive reality of YHWH was expressed not in terms of an immaterial substance but as an incomparable presence that both contained and filled all things.

God's presence does not "fill" in a way comparable to finite "fillings." The divine *plērōma* (fullness) does not extend through space and time the way finite creatures do; rather, it is the reality "in" which they have their spatio-temporal becoming. As Paul reminds the philosophers at Athens, God is the one *in whom* we "live and move and have our being" (Acts 17:28). His critical appropriation of Epicurean philosophy[54] in this passage illustrates the reconstructive task of theology; Paul refigures their categories in light of the experience of God in Christ through the Spirit. The presence of the Creator is not simply the presence of one thing among many things but the metaphysically infinite *plērōma* that conditions *all things.* As Paul explains in Romans 11:36, "For from him and through him and to him are all things. To him be the glory forever. Amen."[55]

The mediation of the fulfilling presence of God through the Spirit of Christ is more explicit elsewhere in the Pauline literature. The inner being of the members of the Christian community is strengthened through the Spirit and indwelled by Christ as they are grounded in love, so that they may "be *filled* with all the *fullness* of God" (Eph. 3:16-21). The "one God and Father of all" is "above all and through all and in all" (Eph. 4:6). The resurrected Christ shares in the divine reign and ascended so that "he might fill all things" (4:10). The Father of glory is at work in Christ in the upbuilding of "his body, the *fullness* of him who *fills all in all*" (Eph. 1:17-23). This Christian experience of the divine *plērōma* suggests a truly infinite presence that is not simply defined over against that which it fills.

Three ideas in particular emphasize this experience of divine Infinity in Scripture: the name, the reign, and the face of God. We will return to these three concepts in the reconstructive chapters of part III, but it will be helpful to introduce them here since they point to the experience of an intensively infinite presence. The ancient Israelites refused to speak the name of YHWH because their religious experience told them that this One is not like other objects in the world of experience that can be "named," compre-

---

54. Cf. Marilyn McCord Adams, "Philosophy and the Bible: The Areopagus Speech," *Faith and Philosophy* 9, no. 2 (April 1992): 135-49.

55. This passage opens up a trinitarian way of conceptualizing God's presence to "all things." It is ironic that so much of the debate about "sovereignty vs. free will" focuses on Romans 9–11 but fails to account for this consummating verse, which then opens up Paul's discussion of the way the Christians in Rome should work out their freedom in the presence of this God. In Part III we will explore how the revival of Trinity (and Futurity) can help us move beyond the impasse.

hended, or grasped. The divine "name" does not name one finite thing among many, but is the reality through which all things are named (cf. Eph. 3:15). Similarly, the idea of absolute divine sovereignty emerged in response to this presence that cannot be controlled, but rules all things. The kingdoms of the nations are "as nothing" before God (Isa. 40:17). The divine reign cannot be judged by comparing it with other reigns; the peace of God's kingdom is not like the peace the world gives (John 14:27), which is dialectically defined by the temporary absence of war. Finally, the scriptural use of the metaphor of the face of God is also connected to the experience of the incomparable divine presence. When the biblical authors describe an ambiguous longing for the divine countenance (Num. 6:26) and the manifestation of divine glory in the face of Jesus Christ (2 Cor. 4:6), they are testifying to an experience of an inescapable promising presence that evokes creaturely desire.

Interpreting the biblical witness to the experience of God primarily in terms of substance and immateriality too easily leads to a conception of the divine as dialectically defined over against material substances. As Robert Sokolowski observes, "The reason the pagans could not conceive of anything like the incarnation is that their gods are part of the world, and the union of any two natures in the world is bound to be, in some way, unnatural, because of the otherness that lets one thing be itself only by not being the other. But the Christian God is not a part of the world and is not a 'kind' of being at all."[56] The divine presence is not one type of substance in the cosmos that is either "close" or "far" in contrast to other substances. The difficulty with the relation between two substances in the incarnate Christ also applies to the relational unity between the infinite Holy Spirit and the finite human spirit in the Christian understanding of regeneration. Under the strictures of the category of immaterial substance, basic Christian doctrines like creation, incarnation, and regeneration can seem confusing and contradictory. It was precisely the experience of being confronted by the incarnate Christ and being filled with the Holy Spirit that led early theologians to challenge the negative (and extensive) view of infinity in relation to the divine that dominated Greek philosophy (cf. chap. 5 below).

In some cases, however, it seems that the hermeneutical category of immaterial substance forced biblical interpretation through a dualist

---

56. *The God of Faith and Reason* (Washington, D.C.: Catholic University Press, 1995), 36.

metaphysical grid. St. Augustine, who often praised Plato's insight into divine things, explicitly acknowledged two types of "substance," changeable and unchangeable, and argued that God alone is the latter. This naturally led him to interpret biblical passages that indicate God does not change (e.g., Ps. 102:25-28; Mal. 3:6-7; Heb. 13:8; James 1:17) in terms of divine immutability (cf. *De Trinitate*, I.1.2; I.6.9; V.2.3; *De Civitate Dei*, XI.21). A similar hermeneutic was operative in the work of Origen, who argued that John 4:24 — "God is Spirit" — was an ontological assertion distinguishing incorporeal from corporeal reality. His conflation of the ideas of *pneuma* (spirit) and *nous* (mind) led him to conclude from this text that God is "undivided intellectual nature . . . all reason," and the most superior of all "intelligent, that is, incorporeal beings" (*De Principiis*, I.1.3-6).[57] As we will see later, this contributed to the problem of spurious infinity, since the idea of a mind seems to be dialectically defined in relation to objects of knowledge.

The important point here, however, is that the biblical understanding of the spiritual presence of the Creator in and to the world is not built on a harsh dualism between spirit and matter. The earliest traditions of Israel see the Spirit *(ruach)* as the life-breath, which is received from God and is the basis of all embodied creaturely life (Gen. 2:7; 7:22).[58] The Spirit (or breath) of God is initially what distinguishes the human creature from other animals in the second creation story (Gen. 2:7), but Ecclesiastes 3:21 indicates that the animals too have "spirit." The book of Job acknowledges a general dependence on the divine Spirit for life: "The spirit of God has made me, and the breath of the Almighty gives me life" (33:4; cf. Gen. 1:2; Isa. 44:3-4). However, particular experiences of the divine Spirit can also lead to an intensification of the relation to God (as in prophecy and worship). The *ruach* of YHWH is not a "substance" but the self-disclosing "presence" of God through which embodied creaturely life is given and called to renewal.

After we recover theological resources in part II that can help us artic-

57. Cf. ANF, 4:243.

58. For a discussion of the difference between the common Greek usage of *pneuma* and the Hebrew idea of *ruach* (which was carried over into the New Testament), see John Breck, *Spirit of Truth: The Origins of Johannine Pneumatology* (Crestwood, N.Y.: St. Vladimir's Press, 1991), especially chap. 5. Cf. George T. Montague, S.M., *The Holy Spirit: Growth of a Biblical Tradition* (New York: Paulist Press, 1976), chap. 1; Alasdair I. C. Heron, *The Holy Spirit* (Philadelphia: Westminster, 1983), 4-10.

ulate the qualitative presence of divine Infinity, we will turn in part III to a more detailed presentation of the way in which the authors of the New Testament invite readers to participate in the intensive life of God through the Spirit of Christ. But first we must complete our portrayal of the other early modern categories that have been challenged in contemporary discourse about the doctrine of God.

· 3 ·

GOD AS SINGLE SUBJECT?

If one accepts a philosophical substance dualism between thought and matter, the idea of God as an intelligent agent seems to follow naturally from divine immateriality. In this chapter we turn our attention to ways in which early modern theological projects were shaped by philosophical and psychological assumptions about the concept of "person." The covenantal themes of the Hebrew Bible testify to the religious experience of being confronted by a powerful personal presence. On the basis of the manifestation of the relational unity of the Father, Son, and the Spirit in the New Testament, the early church insisted that Christian faith required speaking of *three* divine persons. However, the notion of God as essentially a *single* subject slowly crept back into Christian theology. As we will see, the Protestant Scholastics spent considerable energy in disputation over the relation between the powers of the divine "intellect" and "will" in the single divine essence. The doctrines of simplicity and immutability complicated the discussion, for any distinctions between or within divine faculties could not be "real," nor could God "essentially" be related to the mutable creaturely experience of divine revelation. These concerns may be traced back to patristic and medieval sources, but defending the doctrine of the Trinity against the Socinians, Racovians, Anthropomorphites, and others in the seventeenth century, became increasingly difficult as early modern individualism colonized the category of person.

To understand the theological significance of this concept we need to back up and summarize the ancient and medieval faculty psychology that was inherited by early modern theologians.[1] Plato compared the structure of the human soul *(psyche)* and its faculties to a charioteer who tries to control two powerful horses, leading them upward toward heaven (*Phaedrus,* 246[a], 253[c]). Elsewhere he divided the soul into three parts — the rational, spirited, and appetitive aspects (*Republic,* 435[b]-444[a]). The good and just soul is one in which reason rules, and in some of the earlier dialogues Plato portrays the god Zeus as the ideal soul. In the *Timaeus,* he describes the Demiurge as guided by reason in the fashioning of the universe in the "image of the intelligible Living Thing" (30[b], 92[c]).

Just as Aristotle criticized Plato's way of distinguishing between form and matter, so too he developed a different model of the soul and its powers. The soul is not separate from the body, but its "form" — the actualizing power that enlivens it (*On the Soul,* 412[a]20). Aristotle describes various psychic powers, which he calls the nutritive, the sensory, the locomotive, and thinking (414[a]29). All living things are enlivened by the formative presence of one (or more) of these actualizing powers. However, only human beings have a "rational" soul, which ought to dominate the other powers in a virtuous human being. As we have seen, Aristotle's concept of the divine also privileges reason — God is thought thinking itself (*Metaphysics,* 1072[b]20).

These sources were influential for the first-century Jewish philosopher Philo of Alexandria, who interpreted the "image of God" in Genesis 1:27 in terms of the concept of *nous:* "For after the pattern of a single Mind, even the Mind of the Universe as an Archetype, the mind in each of those who successively came into being was moulded."[2] In each of these models, the faculty of reason is privileged in both the divine and the human being. The impact of this tendency, which we will call the *intellectualist* ideal, is evident in Boethius's influential definition of the person as "an individual substance of a rational nature,"[3] and his assertion that "understanding *alone* is the property of the divine."[4]

Another option in ancient Greece, however, was characterized by an

1. Cf. my *Reforming Theological Anthropology,* (Grand Rapids: Eerdmans, 2003), chap. 8.

2. Philo, *De Opificio Mundi,* 23.15 §69, in Philo, trans. F. H. Colson and G. H. Whittaker, Loeb Classical Library (London: Heinemann, 1929), 1:55.

3. *Persona est naturae rationalis individua substantia.* Boethius, *De persona et duabus naturis* 3 (PL 64: 1343).

4. *Consolation of Philosophy,* trans. Joel Relihan (Indianapolis: Hackett, 2001), 142. Emphasis added.

emphasis on assent or decision as equal (or even prior) to understanding in human experience. This stress on the volitional power of human beings contributed to the formation of a concept that would later become called the "will."[5] Let us call this the *voluntarist* ideal. Although Epicureanism also contributed to this minority report,[6] it is most easily illustrated in Stoicism. Simplicius reported that the Stoics commonly identified four basic genera: "substance," "quality," "disposed in a certain way," and "disposed in a certain way in relation to something else" *(pros ti pōs echōnta)*.[7] This dispositional metaphysics affects both theology and anthropology. The *pneuma* that permeates the cosmos is purposive and intentional — the active, divine principle that rules all things. Since divine and human rationality are not qualitatively different for the Stoics, they often depicted God as *a* person. Human beings are rational because they share in the purest form of the *pneuma*.

Rather than distinguishing faculties within the soul, the Stoics tended to speak of the individual as a whole. A person's rational *pneuma* is the leading principle *(hēgemonikon)* that determines all her actions. The Stoic theory of "assent" *(sunkatathesis)* refers to the "motion of the soul" in adult human beings whereby they judge a sense impression. Belief formation requires that the individual assent to the validity of the impression.[8] Epictetus introduced the concept of *proairesis* to indicate dispositional agency or choice, and argued that the individual is autonomous in the sense that her assent cannot be hindered (*Discourses*, I, 17.20-26).[9] The Stoics' emphasis on the ruling power of *pneuma* was intimately connected to their materialist ontology, and initially had less impact on the Christian tradition. Along with the early modern scientific retrieval of Stoic models of matter and motion, however, came a renewed interest in the autonomy

---

5. Cf. Charles H. Kahn, "Discovering the Will: From Aristotle to Augustine," in *The Question of "Eclecticism": Studies in Later Greek Philosophy*, ed. J. M. Dillon and A. A. Long (Berkeley: University of California Press, 1988), 234-59.

6. Cf. J. M. Rist, *Epicurus: An Introduction* (Cambridge: Cambridge University Press, 1972).

7. *SVF*, 2.369.

8. Cf. *SVF*, 2.836, 3.177. For the reports of Plutarch and Cicero on this issue, cf. Karlheinz Hülser, ed., *Die Fragmente zur Dialektik der Stoiker*, 4 vols. (Stuttgart: Frommann-Holzboog, 1987-1988), 1:363, 363A (hereafter FDS).

9. Epictetus, *The Discourses as Reported by Arrian*, trans. W. A. Goldfather, 2 vols. (Cambridge: Harvard University Press, 1925), 1:119.

of the individual, which complicated the role of the concept of person in the doctrine of God.

§3.1. Ockhamist Anxiety

Although William of Ockham wrote during the early fourteenth century, as founder of what came to be known as the *via moderna* he provides an entry point into understanding the anxiety that pervaded early modern theological discourse about God as a single subject with an intellect and will. Attending to the singular *individual* thing[10] was a regulative principle of Ockham's theology and philosophy. Any postulates that are not necessary for an explanation should be cut out, and he applied this razor to the belief in the existence of abstract universal natures, which was central to the (moderate) realism of the *via antiqua* represented by Thomas Aquinas. Ockham argued instead that general terms like "human" are merely names *(nomina)*. This opened up space for the concrete analysis that increasingly came to characterize early modern science. However, his severing of the close connection between human logic and universal causative substances, which had been the basis of the medieval proofs for the existence of God, contributed to the growing fissure between reason and faith.

Ockham was a Franciscan theologian, and his emphasis on the *volitional* power of the soul, in contrast to the intellectualist ideal prevalent in the Dominican theology of Thomas, may in part have been related to the distinctive spiritualities practiced by these orders. In light of the debates following the Condemnations of 1277, Ockham emphasized that the absolute power of God *(potentia absoluta)* is not constrained by God's *potentia ordinata*, the divine power revealed in the ordering of the actual world. He argued that not even the "ideas" in the divine intellect constrained the determining power of the divine will.[11]

These features of Ockham's thought resonated with the Atomist's attention to particulars and with the Stoic's emphasis on assent, and his philosophical efforts shaped the reception of these ancient models in early modernity. However, they also led to an intensification of several theologi-

---

10. Armand Maurer, *The Philosophy of William of Ockham* (Toronto: PIMS, 1999), 540.

11. For analysis, cf. Frederick Copleston, *A History of Philosophy*, 9 vols. (Garden City, N.Y.: Image Books, 1985), 3:95, 100ff.

cal problems. If God is an eternal, immutably good person whose omniscient intellect knows all future contingents and whose omnipotent will determines all creaturely events, how can we make sense of the human experience of freedom and the existence of evil?

This anxiety was shaped by the psychological models for God as *a* person that Ockham had inherited. Boethius's definition of a person as an "individual substance of a rational nature" had been influenced by Augustine, whose faculty psychology incorporated Neoplatonic and Stoic themes. Augustine argued that the human mind, the mind's knowing itself, and the mind's loving itself are three things (substances), but so mutually related that they are one essence — equally substantial with each other (*On the Trinity*, IX.3-5). He also described the relational unity of the faculties of memory, understanding, and will, which are one essentially but three relatively (X.11). The human soul is an image of the Trinity because (like God) it is one substance that knows and loves itself. Applying this faculty psychology to God leads Augustine to describe the Son as the wisdom or *intellect* of the Father, and the Spirit as issuing from the divine *will* (XV.16-19). This is the *locus classicus* for the psychological analogies for the Trinity that came to dominate so much of Western theology.

Thomas Aquinas's anthropology reflected the Aristotelian model of faculty psychology,[12] which he also applied to God as a person. Although the doctrine of simplicity requires that there can be no real distinction between God's substance, intellect, and will (*SumTh*, I.14; I.19), Thomas adopts and adapts Augustine's psychological analogies: the procession of the Word (Son) from God is explained in terms of the *intellect* (I.34.1), and the procession of Spirit from God is linked to the operation of the divine *will* (I.27.3). He argues that "person" signifies "what is most perfect in all nature — that is, a subsistent individual of a rational nature." Everything that is perfect must be attributed to God; therefore "this name *person* is fittingly applied to God" (I.29.3).

In addition to the material emphasis on God as a person with an intellect and will, Ockham also inherited the practice of formally separating discussions of God's essence from treatments of the three persons of the Trinity. The beginnings of this divorce may be traced to the hardening of a distinction between the nature of God *(theologia)* and the works

---

12. Thomas's psychology is a modified Aristotelianism, and he explicitly claims that (considered absolutely) the intellect is higher and nobler than the will (*SumTh*, I.82.3; cf. I.77.4).

of God in creation *(oikonomia)* developed among some patristic theologians.[13] In the "economy" of salvation, God is clearly revealed in the relations between the persons of the Father, Son, and Spirit. How is the divine "essence" (God in Godself) related to this economy? A harsh line drawn between *theologia* and *oikonomia* challenges the validity of divine revelation, but the blurring or erasure of the distinction raises the spectre of pantheism.

Thomas Aquinas's formal presentation of the doctrine of God in the first part of his *Summa Theologiae* treats divine unity, goodness, knowledge, power, and several other themes that examine the divine essence before arriving at a discussion of the trinitarian persons in Q. 27.[14] Even "How God Is Known by Us" (Q. 12) is not concerned with the economy of revelation but with the power of the human intellect. While the formal organization of themes is not determinative for the subject matter of theology, it surely conditions the interpretation of the relations between theological ideas. In fact, this formal separation contributed to the bifurcation between reason and faith; the unity of God could be proven by appeal to the Aristotelian logic of simplicity, but this problematized the real relations of the persons in the Trinity, which then must be accepted on faith.

Ockham's nominalism and voluntarism intensified the problems inherent in both the material psychological analogies for God and the formal separation of the divine essence from the doctrine of Trinity. His nominalism led him to a definition of person that even more strongly emphasized the subsistence of the individual substance *(suppositum)*, which is "incommunicable by identity, not suited to inhere in anything, and not sustained by anything." A person is a *suppositum* that is a complete intellectual nature — "that does not exist in another as in a subject, and it cannot form a substantial unity with something else as its part."[15] If this definition is applied to the *three* persons of God, tritheism appears inevitable. Ockham affirmed the doctrine of the Trinity as articulated by the early church, but he

---

13. In *De Principiis,* I.1.9, Origen says that he has now investigated the nature of God, although he had not yet treated the Trinity at all. For a history of the separation of *theologia* from *oikonomia* and its impact on the doctrine of Trinity, cf. Catherine Mowry LaCugna, *God for Us: The Trinity and Christian Life* (San Francisco: HarperCollins, 1991).

14. Until Thomas, most theological education in Europe involved commenting on the *Sentences* of Lombard, for whom the Unity and Trinity of God were treated together in Book I: *De Dei Unitate et Trinitate.*

15. *Reportatio* 3.1; quoted and trans. in Maurer, *Ockham,* 451-52.

emphasized more strongly than Augustine or Thomas that it could not be proven by human logic. This widened the divorce between reason and faith.[16]

The attempt to resolve his anxiety about the relation between predestination, God's foreknowledge, and future free contingents led Ockham to emphasize distinctions within the divine intellect — between *scientia necessaria* and *scientia libera*. God's knowledge of God's own substance and will, and all possible worlds, is "necessary" since these are all eternal objects. However, God's knowledge of the actual created world cannot be of the same type, since it is not eternal. Created objects are known by God's "free" knowledge. Ockham notes that "it is impossible to express clearly the way in which God knows future contingents. Nevertheless it must be held that He does so, but contingently."[17] These objects are not known necessarily because they are contingent — dependent on the absolute freedom of the divine will.

Ockham's understanding of divine knowledge is an idealization of his understanding of human intuitive cognition, expanded to all past, present, and future. God has intuitive cognition that is perfectly clear, knowing which propositions about the future are true and which are false. God's knowledge of these propositions derives from God's willing of them; nothing escapes divine knowing because every created thing is dependent on divine willing. The value of these distinctions was clouded by Ockham's acknowledgement of divine immutability, which would allow only a logical (not a chronological) priority of the will over the intellect, and of divine simplicity, which demanded that the divine intellect and will are essentially identical, negating any real distinction in the first place.

Ockham's proposed solution also intensified the problem of evil; if the divine will is all-powerful and not dependent even on divine ideas, why

16. "Thus Ockham helped to transform faith as much as reason: while the latter came increasingly to rest upon empirical observation and natural causation, the former was directed increasingly towards a positive theology, with its own independent truth. . . . Certainty lay in faith alone without the need of intermediaries. At one and the same time, a growing empiricism was giving rise to a growing fideism." Gordon A. Leff, *Medieval Thought* (Atlantic Highlands, N.J.: Humanities Press, 1980), 291.

17. Ockham, *Predestination, God's Foreknowledge and Future Contingents,* trans. Marilyn McCord Adams and Norman Kretzmann (Indianapolis: Hackett, 1983), 50; cf. 68. Although it is only "nominal," since God is absolutely simple, this distinction is the key to Ockham's attempted solution.

would God "volunteer" to create an actual world with so much suffering? By the mid-sixteenth century, the intellectualist ideal had made a comeback as part of the general revival of Thomism in Roman Catholic theology. In response to the voluntarist tendencies in some elements of the Reformed tradition, the Jesuit theologian Fonseca proposed the idea of *scientia media* in his 1556 *De praedestinatione, libero arbitrio et gratia contra Calvinum*. This third type of divine knowledge, which is allegedly "between" necessary and free knowledge, is God's knowledge of conditioned, consequent possibilities. These objects, which include free human choices, are independent of the divine will, an idea that smacked of Pelagianism to the voluntarists. The theologian most closely associated with this approach is Luis de Molina,[18] who emphasized that this divine middle knowledge stands *prior* to any free act of God's will. But such a solution still appears to be in conflict with the doctrines of simplicity and immutability. If the divine intellect and will are actually identical, and God timelessly wills which of these objects of middle knowledge to actualize in creation, the Molinist solution does not really work. Meanwhile, reflection on the generative power of the distinctive Christian understanding of God as three persons took a back seat to arguments about the faculties of a single divine subject.

§3.2. Trinity in Early Modern Theological Projects

The doctrine of the Trinity was defended by seventeenth-century Protestant Orthodoxy, but for the most part it was articulated *materially* with analogies that implied a single subject (as with Augustine), and separated *formally* from the treatment of the nature and attributes of the one God (as with Thomas). The reduction of the trinitarian relations to the psychological structures of the intellect and will of a single divine essence is often explicit. For example, in his 1611 *Systema Sacrosanctae Theologiae* Keckermann observes: "In an essence in which there is perfect knowledge bending back upon itself, an Image is begotten and a Spirit proceeds on the impulse of the will. And yet these things inhere in the one, most single essence of God."[19] In Turretin's treatment of the doctrine of God in the

---

18. Molina, *On Divine Foreknowledge (Part IV of the Concordia)*, trans. by Alfred J. Freddoso (Ithaca: Cornell University Press, 1988).

19. Quoted and translated in *RD*, 107.

Third Topic of his 1679 *Institutes of Elenctic Theology,* a discussion of the "Holy Trinity" comes only after twenty-two *Quaestiones* dealing with themes such as the unity, simplicity, knowledge, and will of God. The first point to be made about the Trinity is that it cannot be proven by reason but must be received by faith (*Elenc.,* I.3.23.1).[20] With notable exceptions like Peter van Mastricht and Jonathan Edwards, the formal privileging of Unity over Trinity continued to dominate Protestant theology throughout the eighteenth century. By 1831 Schleiermacher would relegate the Trinity to a brief concluding section of his presentation of *The Christian Faith,* where he argues that it is not an "immediate or even a necessary combination of utterances concerning the Christian self-consciousness," and the "main pivots" of church doctrine "are independent of the doctrine of the Trinity."[21]

Ockhamist anxiety over the relation between divine knowledge (and will) and creaturely freedom was at the heart of many of the seventeenth-century debates on the doctrine of God. The majority of Reformed theologians were voluntarists and were satisfied with the distinction between necessary and free knowledge or, as some preferred, between God's *scientia naturalis* and *scientia visionis.* Introducing his argument against the proposal that God has a third kind of knowledge that is not preceded by the divine will (or decree), Turretin curtly observes: "The Jesuits, Socinians and Remonstrants affirm this; the orthodox deny it" (*Elenc.,* I.3.13.8). In fact, the intellectualist ideal was a defining element of the theology of Arminius, who even went so far as to say that the divine will is considered the "second faculty" of the divine life because it "follows the divine intellect and is *produced from it.*"[22]

Arminius's acceptance of the idea of middle knowledge may have been motivated by his worry that the voluntarist option led to the conclusion that God sins, and is the only sinner.[23] Some of the Lutheran Scholastics

---

20. We can also hear Ockham in the background of Turretin's definition of the term "person" as an intellectual *suppositum* (*Elenc.,* I.23.7).

21. F. D. E. Schleiermacher, *The Christian Faith,* trans. H. R. MacKintosh and J. S. Stewart (Edinburgh: T&T Clark, 1989), 740-41.

22. *Disputationes Publicae,* IV.xlix. Quoted and trans. in Richard Muller, *God, Creation and Providence in the Thought of Jacob Arminius* (Grand Rapids: Baker, 1991), 145. Emphasis added.

23. Cf. "A Declaration of the Sentiments of Arminius," in *Works of James Arminius,* 3 vols. (Grand Rapids: Baker, 1983), I:630.

also were amenable to the idea of middle knowledge, although it was not as central to their doctrine of God.[24] The vast majority of Reformed Scholastics, however, rejected middle knowledge because they believed it made both God's will and intellect dependent on objects outside of God, threatening divine aseity, simplicity and immutability. The main point for our purposes in this brief overview of early modern theology is that all of these debates are guided by the idea of God as *a* person with faculties of a certain sort, creating problems for understanding the relations between the three persons of the Trinity, which are generally treated later in the presentation of the doctrine of God.

The theological significance of the concept of person is also evident in the trinitarian controversies that shook the Church of England in the seventeenth century. As nominalism took root in English philosophy, the term "person" became colored by the renewed interest in the autonomy of the individual. In contrast to Boethius, whose definition of person relied on Platonic and Aristotelian categories, Thomas Hobbes explicitly appealed to the Stoic philosopher Cicero. In chapter 16 of *Leviathan* (1651), Hobbes argues that a *person* "is the same that an *actor* is, both on the stage and in common conversation; and to *personate,* is to *act* or *represent* himself or another."[25] He argues that God too may be "personated," as when God speaks through Moses to the Israelites, but is later "personated" by the Son of man and by the Holy Ghost working in the apostles. In John Locke's *Essay Concerning Human Understanding* (1689), the term "person" stands for "a thinking Intelligent Being, that has reason and reflection and can consider it self as it self, the same thinking thing in different times and places; which it does only by that consciousness, which is inseparable from thinking, and as it seems to me essential to it."[26] The punctual consciousness of the individual is the basis for the identity of the self, and this we call a "person."

This idea of person applied to God naturally led to Unitarianism. Denying the Trinity was punishable by imprisonment or even death, and ecclesiastical and political sanctioning led even Isaac Newton to hide his anti-trinitarian views. Hobbes' view of the Trinity was condemned as a "Strange Wheemsie," and Locke was accused of being a "well-willer to the

---

24. E.g., Quenstedt, *RD*, 126-27. Cf. Muller, "Patterns in Arminius's Theology," 442 n. 43.

25. *Leviathan* (Oxford: Oxford University Press, 1996), 106. Emphasis in original. Cf. 108.

26. *Essay*, II.27.9, 335.

Racovian way,"[27] but by the eighteenth century Unitarianism came out of the closet both in England and in the North American colonies. Theological attention slowly shifted away from articulating the doctrine of the Trinity and the focus turned toward defending the idea of God as *a* person actively involved in the world (theism) against the deists and a-theists. The nominalist concept of person made modalism a more respectable option, for *ex hypothesi* the only other option was an impersonal God.

Ockhamist anxiety continues to plague some streams of American systematic theology. Charles Hodge spent more space on a critique of "mysticism" than on the doctrine of the Trinity, and for the most part followed Turretin's lead in explaining the distinctions between the divine intellect and will. The impact of this early modern project on contemporary systematic theology is evident in the work of Millard Erickson. In his presentation of the doctrine of God ("What God Is Like"), the chapter on the Trinity comes last — after the discussion of the divine attributes and God's relation to the world. Although Erickson emphasizes that the doctrine is incomprehensible to reason, he does offer some psychological analogies for the Trinity; for example, Erickson himself is a father, a professor and a husband, yet one person.[28]

Vestiges of the early modern concept of person also haunt many of the debates among contemporary Christian philosophers of religion. For example, Alvin Plantinga defines theistic belief as "the belief, first, that there exists *a* person of a certain sort — a being who acts, holds beliefs and has aims and purposes."[29] In his *Warranted Christian Belief,* he describes the "theistic" component of Christian belief as the assertion that "God is a *person:* that is, a being with intellect and will."[30] Although it is sometimes

27. Cf. Philip Dixon, *Nice and Hot Disputes: The Doctrine of the Trinity in the Seventeenth Century* (London: Continuum, 2003), chap. 5.

28. *Christian Theology,* (Grand Rapids: Baker, 1998), 366. This analogy would obviously imply modalism if taken seriously. Erickson concludes this chapter with the following sentiments about the Trinity: "Try to explain it, and you'll lose your mind; but try to deny it, and you'll lose your soul" (367).

29. Plantinga, "Reason and Belief in God," *Faith and Rationality* (Notre Dame: University of Notre Dame Press, 1983), 82. Emphasis added. In *The Coherence of Theism,* Richard Swinburne says that "by a 'God' [the theist] understands something like a 'person without a body (i.e., a spirit) who is eternal, free, able to do anything, knows everything, is perfectly good'" (2nd ed.; Oxford: Clarendon, 1993), 1; cf. *The Existence of God,* rev. ed. (Oxford: Clarendon Press, 1991), 102.

30. (Oxford: Oxford University Press, 2000), vii.

called "Reformed" epistemology, Plantinga's own solution to the problems of creaturely freedom and evil involves a mixture of an Arminian emphasis on human free-will and a reworked version of "Ockham's way out."[31] If the only way to defend divine "personality" was through a projection of faculty psychology onto God as a single subject, Ockham's might seem to be the only way out. Besides obscuring the centrality of the distinctively Christian understanding of God, however, this continued reliance on early modern categories also fails to engage late modern dynamic and relational concepts of person.

§3.3. Personality in Late Modern Philosophy

The philosophical turn to relationality had a major impact on the concept of person. The rise of Idealism and Romanticism was in large part a reaction to the alienation of personal experience from the mechanistic explanations of "reality" in modern science. Many philosophers increasingly took "personality" as a key hermeneutical, ethical and even metaphysical category. Schleiermacher used the term "Personalismus" in his 1799 *On Religion: Speeches to Its Cultured Despisers,*[32] but it did not become influential until the late nineteenth and early twentieth century when it was taken up in the development of personalist philosophy.[33] The category of an autonomous individual substance was no longer adequate for describing the phenomena of personal experience.

A significant step in the liberation of the concept of person from the category of substance was taken by Hegel in the early nineteenth century. In his *Phenomenology of Spirit* (1807), he described human knowing as participation in the Absolute Knowing of the Spirit, by which the Spirit becomes what it *is* in self-consciousness; substance is objectified and be-

31. Plantinga, "On Ockham's Way Out," in *The Concept of God,* ed. Thomas V. Morris (Oxford: Oxford University Press, 1987), 177. Cf. idem, *God and Other Minds* (Ithaca, N.Y.: Cornell University Press, 1990), chap. 6.

32. Trans. and ed. Richard Crouter (Cambridge: Cambridge University Press, 1996), 103.

33. In the influential North American philosophical school called "Boston Personalism," the concept of person was the basic metaphysical category. Cf. Paul Deats and Carol Robb, eds., *The Boston Personalist Tradition in Philosophy, Social Ethics and Theology* (Macon, Ga.: Mercer University Press, 1986).

comes Self in this process.[34] In his *Science of Logic* Hegel explicitly critiqued Spinoza for stopping with the notion of Absolute Substance, which left him with the problems of necessitarian pantheism. We should recognize the moment of truth in Spinoza but move beyond him: it is not Substance but "Subject" that is Absolute; as the self-comprehending pure Notion, the Spirit (as Subject) consummates Spinoza's concept of substance by sublating its necessity into the freedom of the Notion.[35] Whether Hegel avoided pantheism himself is questionable, but the point here is that his negation and elevation of substance into *subjectivity* as the higher category opened the way for a variety of "phenomenological" analyses of human consciousness that attended more closely to the relational processes of personality.

We may point for example to Kierkegaard's definition of the self in his 1849 *The Sickness unto Death* as "a relation that relates itself to itself or is the relation's relating itself to itself in the relation; the self is not the relation but is the relation's relating itself to itself."[36] The impact of this shift toward relational models of personality on twentieth-century anthropology is easy to illustrate. One of the most well known examples is Martin Buber, who emphasized the importance of the "between" in which one is addressed and faced by a Thou. "The primary word *I-Thou* establishes the world of relation." This relation is not simply something that is later added to the *I*. "In the beginning is relation . . . the *a priori* of relation," in which meeting and dialogue occur and the *Thou* is formed.[37] Although Buber's concept of the "between" has been criticized, his deeply existential prose had and continues to have a profound effect on the philosophical concept of person. In the work of Emmanuel Levinas, for example, the face of the

34. Hegel, *Phenomenology of Spirit,* trans. A. V. Miller (Oxford: Oxford University Press, 1977), 479-93.

35. *Hegel's Science of Logic* (Amherst, N.Y.: Humanity Books, 1999), 580-82. Traces of Neoplatonism and Augustinian psychological analogies are still present in Hegel, for whom a "trinitarian" explication of the Absolute Spirit was still the coming-to-self of a single subject. Cf. *Lectures on the Philosophy of Religion,* vol. III.

36. Kierkegaard, *The Sickness unto Death,* trans. Howard V. and Edna H. Hong (Princeton: Princeton University Press, 1980), 13.

37. *I and Thou,* trans. Ronald Gregor Smith, 2nd ed. (New York: Charles Scribner's Sons, 1958), 6, 27. For Buber, Spirit is not in the I, but between I and Thou. The Spirit, which makes human life real, cannot be controlled but only received as gift (ibid., 129-30). Cf. Buber, *The Knowledge of Man,* ed. and trans. Maurice Friedman (New York: Harper & Row, 1965).

other has priority in the establishment of subjectivity. The "primordial re-lation" of the face-to-face, in which the responsibility to and for the other constitutes subjectivity, is irreducible to "essence."[38] The category of per-son functions less as a statement about a kind of "being" (or substance) and more as a description of a way of becoming in relation.

The claim that personality is inherently relational poses an enormous challenge to modern "theism." One of the most significant attacks on the early modern concept of God as a single subject was the projection cri-tique of protest a-theism. It protested against the "theistic" idea of God as a single subject, a Master whose glory was defined by its absolute domin-ion over the subjects of creation. This protest found its voice most power-fully in Ludwig Feuerbach's 1841 *The Essence of Christianity*. He suggested that all of the attributes that traditional Christianity applies to God — in-cluding "consciousness" itself — are "projections" of human desires and wishes. He also argued that God and humanity are in opposition: therefore either God is free or humans are free. Either God has power or humanity has power. "The impoverishing of the real world and the enriching of God is one act. Only the poor man has a rich God. God springs out of the feel-ing of a want, what man is in need of . . . that is God."[39] Human persons are alienated from themselves when they project their desire for power onto an imaginary heavenly person; Feuerbach encouraged an affirmation of the infinity of humanity itself.

The "masters of suspicion" have built on this projection critique, bol-stering the protest of a-theism. For Marx, religion was the "opiate of the masses"; the phenomena can be explained (and cured) through the cate-gories (and actions) of economics. Nietzsche argued in the *Genealogy of Morals* that religion is a function of the resentment of the weak masses, and the madman in his *The Gay Science* proclaimed the new possibilities that arise once we recognize that God is dead. For Durkheim, religions are a reflection of the societies in which they emerge; a culture projects "per-sonality" onto forces it cannot control, often in ways that apotheosize its own values.[40] Freud observed the tendency of small children, like Durkheim's animistic societies, to "personalize" nature as a way of con-

38. Cf. Levinas, *Otherwise than Being or Beyond Essence,* trans. Alphonso Lingis (Pitts-burgh: Duquesne, 1998).

39. *Essence of Christianity,* trans. George Eliot (New York: Harper & Row, 1957), 73.

40. Durkheim, *The Elementary Forms of Religious Life,* trans. J. W. Swain (New York: The Free Press, 1915), 463-64.

trolling and making sense of the world. Religion is a "universal neurosis" that emerges out of the Oedipus complex, fear of the "father," projected as wish-fulfillment; it is based on an "illusion."[41]

The projection critique should not be dismissed simply as a puerile resistance to divine authority. The idea of a single divine subject was challenged on the basis of its philosophical incoherence. The a-theistic projection critique had its roots in the German philosophical discussion in the late eighteenth century *Atheismusstreit* surrounding Fichte. The latter had suggested that the concept of personality (or consciousness), which we discover within ourselves, presupposes finitude — a self conscious of itself over against other objects. How could this apply to an *infinite* Reality? Already in the late seventeenth century Spinoza had followed out the logic of attributing intellect and will to God, showing how this denied both simplicity and immutability. Because a divine and a human intellect (or will) can have no more in common than the name, he argued that continuing to use such terms in theology is equivocation.[42]

In fact, several ancient Greek philosophers had already raised the projection critique. In the third century A.D. Plotinus refused to attribute *nous* to the Good or the One, which is beyond Intellection (e.g., *Enneads*, I.7). This follows from the meaning of the terms "Absolute" (unconditioned) and "mind" (knower). The concept of a *nous* implies a basic distinction between the subject itself as knower *(nous)* and that which is known *(noēton)*. Further, if knowing occurs (which is presupposed in calling the subject a knower), this requires positing a principle of unification that makes knowledge *(noēsis)* possible. In other words, the existence of a *noēton* and a principle of *noēsis* are conditions for the existence of a *nous*. The idea of an unconditioned eternal single mind is contradictory, and would run afoul of the criterion of true infinity. The same problem is reiterated in any exemplarist solution that attempts to maintain the essential simplicity of the Absolute. However, the projection critique may be traced back even further. In the mid-sixth century B.C. Xenophanes attacked anthropomorphite language for the divine, noting that "the Ethiopians say their gods are snub-nosed and black, the Thracians that theirs have light

---

41. Freud, *The Future of an Illusion*, trans. James Strachey (London: Hogarth Press, 1968).

42. Divine and human intellect and will "could be no more alike than the celestial constellation of the Dog [Canus] and the dog that barks." *Ethics* (Cambridge: Hackett, 1992), 45.

blue eyes and red hair."[43] Although such critiques may threaten particular versions of "theism," they are not necessarily a threat to Christianity — is not the warning against idolatrous imaging of God in human form already central to the Hebrew Bible?

If the only options are either God as a single personal subject or the denial of a personal God, most Christians would feel compelled to embrace the former. The projection critique is obviously a challenge to "theism," but it is also an opportunity to reconsider the philosophical assumption that it shares with a-theism, that God is as *a* person of a certain sort. The marginalization of the doctrine of the Trinity coincided with the rise of modern a-theism. When mechanistic science seemed to squeeze personality out of a deterministic world, and the ideal of personhood became the autonomous individual, many early modern theologians responded not with resources from the dynamic relations of the trinitarian understanding of God, but with ancient Greek categories mediated through medieval psychology and cosmology.

Michael J. Buckley argues that in early modernity Christianity "transmuted itself into theism" in order to protect its "god" from the challenges of mechanistic science. When Christian theology surrendered to philosophy the fundamental task of describing the divine nature, it accepted the claim that the only evidence of a personal God is an impersonal nature. Buckley points out that "modern atheism took not only its meaning but its existence from the self-alienation of religion."[44] As we will see in Chapter 6, many leading twentieth-century theologians have attempted to move beyond the impasse between theism and a-theism, aiming to overcome this self-imposed estrangement from late modern culture by recovering the illuminative power of robustly relational trinitarian symbols.

§3.4. Feeling and Acting in Contemporary Science

The concept of a person as an "individual substance of a rational nature" with the powers of intellect and will has also been challenged by developments in contemporary psychology and other anthropological sciences. In *Reforming*

---

43. G. S. Kirk, J. E. Raven, M. Schofield, *The Presocratic Philosophers,* 2nd ed. (Cambridge: Cambridge University Press, 1987), 168.

44. *At the Origins of Modern Atheism* (New Haven: Yale University Press, 1987), 346-47, 359.

Theological Anthropology, I examined the way in which holistic and dynamic models of human personhood not only bring challenges to the Christian doctrine of humanity, but also provide an opportunity for articulating a theological anthropology that is consonant with contemporary biblical scholarship.[45] Turning to the doctrine of God, we can see how these developments add insult to the injury of the projection critique; we are not even projecting a plausible understanding of the *human* person onto God. The point of this brief review of contemporary scientific concepts of person is not to suggest that along with human rationality we also project human feelings and behavior onto God, but to illuminate the extent to which early modern anthropological assumptions have become deeply attached to the idea of God as a single subject — providing even further motivation to participate in the revival of trinitarian doctrine. The central categories that structure the Boethian definition of person have been challenged by developments in the sciences of neurobiology, psychology and other anthropological sciences.

First, personal existence is no longer defined only in terms of a *rational* nature, abstracted from embodied agency. The early modern philosophical retrieval of voluntarism with its emphasis on the power of persons to act underlined the limitations of the intellectualist ideal, but anthropological models that maintained substance dualism continued to privilege the powers of the soul over the powers of the body (appetites, passions, or emotions). The abstraction of rationality from embodiment has been increasingly criticized by feminist social scientists, who argue that human knowing and acting (as well as feeling) are mediated by the embodied relations of the knower.[46] Even the meaning of the term "intellect" has undergone significant alteration. To make sense of research that shows how intelligence is not reducible to ratiocination, Howard Gardner has theorized that every person has "multiple intelligences," which include spatial and bodily-kinesthetic intelligence. These cannot be understood apart from each other, but work together in the functioning of the whole person.[47]

---

45. In *Reforming Theologial Anthropology,* chap. 8. Cf. Fraser Watts, *Theology and Psychology* (Aldershot: Ashgate, 2002); N. H. Gregersen et al., eds., *The Human Person in Science and Theology* (Edinburgh: T&T Clark, 2000); Mary Stewart van Leeuwen, *The Person in Psychology: A Contemporary Christian Appraisal* (Grand Rapids: Eerdmans, 1985).

46. See, e.g., Mary Field Belenky et al., *Women's Ways of Knowing: The Development of Self, Voice and Mind* (New York: Basic Books, 1986).

47. H. Gardner, *Frames of Mind: The Theory of Multiple Intelligences* (New York: Basic Books, 1985).

Neuroscientist Antonio Damasio also demonstrates the connection between thinking and embodied brain. His work is particularly insightful for our purposes because he explicitly interprets his findings in light of the philosophical options provided by Descartes and Spinoza. After summarizing his studies of the brain and exploring their implications, Damasio concludes that Descartes's error comes down to this: "the suggestion that reasoning, moral judgment, and the suffering that comes from physical pain or emotional upheaval might exist separately from the body."[48] His other two major books have focused on the separation of thinking from "feeling." In *The Feeling of What Happens,* he demonstrates from his laboratory work that for better or for worse, biologically triggered emotions, the feelings associated with them, and consciousness of these feelings, are all integral to the process of reasoning and decision making.[49] In his more recent *Looking for Spinoza,*[50] Damasio searches more explicitly for a philosophical position to undergird his neurobiological findings about feelings, especially the expression of human joy and sorrow.

Second, human personality is no longer interpreted primarily in terms that focus on an *individual* substance. For most contemporary psychologists, the key to understanding the dynamics of "personality" is not the isolation of an autonomous individual ego nor the identification of a punctual consciousness. To be a human person is to be emerging and upheld within a dynamic context of social and cultural systems. Interpersonal relations are intrinsic to personal formation; even if a person is later isolated from society, the absence of these relations remains a formative presence. The recognition of the importance of sociability and society for the formation of persons developed over several centuries in the human sciences.[51]

The cultural and communal factors that shape personal formation have been addressed by virtually every school of social science in the 20th century, whether the emphasis is on the mediation of the self through the other in society (Mead), on the action frame of sociological reference (Parsons), the deep enmeshment of the I in the collective unconscious (Jung),

48. *Descartes' Error: Emotion, Reason, and the Human Brain* (New York: Avon, 1994), 250.

49. *The Feeling of What Happens: Body and Emotion in the Making of Consciousness* (New York: Harcourt and Brace, 1999), 41.

50. *Looking for Spinoza: Joy, Sorrow and the Feeling Brain* (New York: Harcourt, 2003).

51. Cf. Roger Smith, *The Human Sciences* (New York: Norton, 1997), chaps. 8 and 12.

or the ongoing adaptation of the self through assimilation and accommodation (Piaget). More recent research has confirmed that the emergence of intentionality in small children is dependent on their social interaction with other "intending" knowers.[52] However, understanding and appreciating the intrinsic significance of relationality within the formation of one's own personality apparently require a sufficiently complex order of consciousness that often does not emerge until early adulthood (if at all).[53] The turn to relationality in psychology has virtually banished the once dominant emphasis on the lone individual, the "man of reason," as the ideal for understanding the concept of person.

Finally, personality is no longer understood as the *substantiation* of an abstract nature, but as an ongoing dynamic process. Ockham had assumed that the substance of a person's mind is untouched by relational changes to objects of knowledge. In fact, this is the basis of his claim that God's knowledge of creatures does not threaten divine immutability. God can at one time know a proposition "and at another time not, and know one after He did not know it, and not know after He did know, and know a proposition that He did not know earlier, *without any change in Him* [emphasis added] as a result . . . because *our* intellect can [do this] without any change in it."[54] Contemporary social science has overthrown this medieval anthropological assumption — our intellect can *not* do this, for the process of knowing *does* change who we are, or better, who we are becoming. The whole point of developmental psychology is that the person has to be understood in the context of a process of becoming that takes time and space. The power of this insight can be therapeutic as well as explanatory, which partially explains the use of systems theory and the exponential growth of narrative approaches in contemporary therapy.

Personal human being is being-in-relation, and all of a person's feeling, thinking and acting substantively changes the structures of relationality within which she continues to find her being. I will argue in Part III that

52. Among the animals, the emergence of "intentions" is intense in humans in a way that is unique. Cf. Raymond W. Gibbs, Jr., "Intentions as Emergent Products of Social Interactions," in *Intentions and Intentionality: Foundations of Social Cognition,* ed. Bertram F. Malle, Louis J. Moses, and Dare A. Baldwin (Cambridge, Mass.: MIT Press, 2001), 105-22.

53. Cf. Robert Kegan, *The Evolving Self: Problem and Process in Human Development* (Cambridge: Harvard University Press, 1982); idem, *In Over Our Heads: The Mental Demands of Modern Life* (Cambridge: Harvard University Press, 1994).

54. Ockham, *Predestination,* 60.

our noetic, moral, and aesthetic desire are also inextricably interwoven in our experience of God. Emphasizing the importance of feeling and acting in human life can help us remember that we need to integrate our concerns about doxological and practical space within our reconstruction of conceptual space (cf. chapter 1). Thinking, acting and feeling are all operative in the irreducibly personal task of theology.

The model of God as a single subject, to which protest a-theism objected, presupposes a faculty psychology that was already collapsing in the seventeenth century. The demise of this view of person provides an opportunity for theology to explore other ways of articulating the personal presence of the biblical God. The concept of personality as dynamic being-in-relation is not at all hostile to the doctrine of the Trinity. In Chapter 6, we will trace this underlying theme in several theological treatments of the trinitarian relations, but our final task in this chapter is to indicate the extent to which late modern challenges to the idea of God as a single subject derive not simply from philosophy and science, but from biblical scholarship.

§3.5. Biblical Experiences of Trinity

Like "Infinity" the term "Trinity" does not appear in Scripture. One strategy for defending the Trinity has been to attempt to establish a foundation for proving the doctrine by showing that it is logically implied by biblical propositions. This approach usually begins by quoting passages that speak of God as one (e.g., Deut. 6:4, 5; Isa. 45:5; Mark 12:29; 1 Cor. 8:4; Gal. 3:20; Jas. 2:19). The next step is to adduce passages that state (or suggest) that the Father is God (John 8:41; Eph. 4:6), the Son is God (John 1:1, 18; Heb. 1:8) and the Spirit is God (Acts 5:3-4; 1 Cor. 3:16). Other passages are listed to demonstrate that they are distinct and personal (e.g. Mark 1:10-12; 2 Cor. 13:13; John 14:26; Eph. 4:30). The conclusion that follows: God is one and God is three. With slight variation, this is the approach of the early modern project that may be traced from Turretin through Hodge and to their contemporary followers.

This is problematic not only because of its reliance on foundationalist epistemology and rationality but also because it sets up the debate in logical terms that entail either incoherence or heresy. It suggests that the term "God" is a genus of which there are three particular instances, and calls them "persons." Insofar as a person is understood as an individual substance or autonomous subject, tritheism is implied. Insofar as the one God is understood as a single subject, modalism is implied. As we will see, the biblical tradition has significant resources for articulating the experience of the trinitarian God in ways that are not bound to these early modern categories. Our limited purpose in this section, however, is to demonstrate how the early Christian experience of being redeemed through participating in the relation of Christ to the Father through the Spirit led naturally to robust expressions of the inherently relational life of God in Scripture.

Many biblical scholars are hesitant to affirm that the doctrine of Trinity is laid out in (or even implied by) the New Testament. This is understandable since the question of substances and hypostases clearly does not dominate Scripture. We may be able to articulate the doctrine of the Trinity more adequately if we begin by emphasizing the explicitly trinitarian shape of the Christian experience of redemption. Paul spells out the relational structure of salvation: "If the Spirit of him [the Father] who raised Jesus from the dead dwells in you, he who raised Christ from the dead will give life to your mortal bodies also through his Spirit that dwells in you" (Rom. 8:11). The experience of redemption "through Christ" involves gaining "access in the one Spirit to the Father" (Eph. 2:18). These robust relations permeate the New Testament presentation of the Gospel and structure the practical and liturgical space of Christian life.

However, because these passages are often read through the lenses of particular categories of substance and person, we often unwittingly think like tritheists while reading the Bible but talk like modalists when asked to describe God's nature or attributes. Here we are dealing with a tension between two intuitions: God is the one absolute Creator of all and God is revealed in the personal relations of the Father, Son and Spirit. As we saw earlier in this chapter, the separation of these intuitions (*theologia* vs. *oikonomia,* divine essence vs. divine economy), which began among some patristic theologians and was reinforced in Western medieval scholasticism, became hardened in the early modern period. Acknowledging the philosophical (re)turn to relationality, however, can help us rediscover the central hermeneutical significance of the triune relations for understanding the biblical experience of salvation. The twentieth-century revival of trinitarian doctrine (cf. chapter 6) aimed to recover the intrinsically relational thought-forms of the biblical tradition.

The Johannine literature includes some of the most explicitly relational language about the trinitarian persons. The teachings and prayers during the Passover before Jesus' crucifixion (John 13–17) describe the intimate relational union of the Son and the Father and the way in which the disciples are called to share in this union in the Holy Spirit. In his first epistle John summarizes the command of the Father: "believe in the name of his Son Jesus Christ and love one another" — this cannot be separated from "abiding" in the Spirit (1 John 3:23-24). Eternal life involves knowing God and Jesus Christ, whom he has sent (John 17:3). However, Matthew 11:27 claims that "no one knows the Son except the Father, and no one knows the Father except the Son." Salvation is entry into this relational knowing and being known, which occurs through life in the Spirit since "no one comprehends what is truly God's except the Spirit" (1 Cor. 2:10-13).

Paul describes the experience of unity among the diverse community of believers as made possible by the relational unity of God: "Now there are varieties of gifts, but the same Spirit; and there are varieties of services, but the same Lord; and there are varieties of activities, but it is the same God who activates all of them in everyone" (1 Cor. 12:4-6). In the first chapter of Romans, Paul describes the Gospel of God (our Father) concerning Jesus Christ, who was "declared to be the Son of God with power according to the Spirit of holiness" (1:4). This triune dynamic is presupposed or explicitly expressed throughout the Pauline literature. For example, it is the Father who is called upon to grant the Ephesians strength in their inner being "through his Spirit," so that Christ may dwell in their hearts — so that they "may be filled with all the fullness of God" (Eph. 3:14-19).

In the reconstructive chapters of Part III, we will explore in more detail the biblical witness to the experience of the robust relations of the trinitarian God. This experience involves sharing in the way of Jesus Christ and intensification in the life of the Spirit in relation to the Father. The concepts of the divine name, reign and face of God will also help us spell out the doctrine of God in explicitly trinitarian terms. At this early stage, however, it is important to note briefly these key relational themes. First, new converts are to be baptized "in the name of the Father and of the Son and of the Holy Spirit" (Matt. 28:19). The divine name was holy for the ancient Israelites, and the linking of Jesus and the Spirit to it represents a radical development in the understanding of God. Second, the reign or kingdom of God is also explicitly trinitarian. The kingdom is the Father's (e.g., Matt. 26:29) yet it is made present already in the ministry of Jesus through the Spirit (cf. Matt. 12:28). The reign of God involves a reciprocal empowering of the Father and the Son through the Spirit (cf. Phil. 2:5-11 and 1 Cor. 15:20-21). Finally, the theme of the divine face (or presence) also takes trinitarian form in the New Testament. The glory of God is revealed in the *prosōpon* of Jesus Christ through the presence of the Spirit of freedom (2 Cor. 3:17–4:6). In order to avoid the abstraction of the doctrine of God from these relational experiences of the divine, we will incorporate the doctrine of Trinity (as well as Infinity and Futurity) into the heart of every aspect of our reconstructive presentation.

If the trinitarian shape of salvation was so clearly emphasized in the New Testament, how did the description of God as a single subject become so deeply entrenched in later Western theology? We have already observed some of the theological and philosophical factors that contributed to this model, but it is important to recognize that it also had putative warrant in the biblical text. After all, the Hebrew Bible does often emphasize that God is one, and this is carried over into the New Testament. It is precisely this tension that is often considered to be at the core of an irreducible contradiction within the Christian understanding of God. However, several observations may help to resolve this tension. Although the relational nature of God is manifested in the shared life of the Father, Son and Spirit in the New Testament, already in the Hebrew Bible we find intimations of a robustly relational understanding of God. Hearing the Word and receiving the Spirit were essential dynamics in the encounter with YHWH. The Spirit and the Word mediate not only the creative presence (e.g., Gen. 1:2; Ps. 33:6-9) but also the redemptive presence of God (e.g., Ps. 51:10; Isa. 55:10-11).

More importantly for Christian theology, however, is the fact that in the New Testament itself the term "God" is almost always applied to the "Father." We will return to the issue of gender in the naming of the biblical God in §8.2, but here our concern is with the connection in the minds of the biblical authors between the terms God and Father. This is true first of all on the lips of Jesus: "It is my Father who glorifies me, he of whom you [the Jews] say, 'He is our God'" (John 8:54). When he is addressed as "good teacher," Jesus insists that "no one is good but God alone" (Mark 10:18; Luke 18:19). Several of the Pauline epistles begin with a blessing of grace and peace "from God our Father and the Lord Jesus Christ" (e.g., Rom. 1:7; 1 Cor. 1:3; 2 Cor. 1:2; Gal. 1:3; Eph. 1:2).

Sometimes it is more explicit that the Father is the God *of* Jesus Christ (cf. Rom. 15:6; Col. 1:3; 1 Pet. 1:3). For example, the author of Ephesians prays that "the God of our Lord Jesus Christ, the Father of glory, may give you a spirit of wisdom" (Eph. 1:17). When Galatians 4:6 says that "God has sent the Spirit of his Son into our hearts," the term clearly applies to the Father. The name "Lord" is often applied to Jesus Christ (e.g., 1 Cor. 12:3) and to the Spirit (2 Cor. 3:17), but usually the "one God" refers to the Father (e.g., 1 Cor. 8:6). First Peter is written to those who have been chosen "by God the Father and sanctified by the Spirit to be obedient to Jesus Christ" (1:2). This does *not* mean that the incarnate Word and the indwelling Spirit are not "God," for Scripture indicates that they are (e.g., John 1:1; Acts 5:3-4). But it does mean that we must be clear when we use the term theologically that we do not distort the intention of the New Testament, which usually means "the Father of our Lord Jesus Christ" when it says "God."

The failure to recognize this biblical practice is at the root of the hardening of the idea of God as a "single subject." The New Testament does speak of God as a single subject, but almost always it has the Father in view. Take for example the idea of the "mind" of God. The apostle Paul concludes his discussion of God's salvific relation to the people of Israel in Romans 9–11 by marveling at the scope of the knowledge of God. "O the depth of the riches and wisdom and knowledge of God! How unsearchable are his judgments and how inscrutable his ways! 'For who has known the mind of the Lord? Or who has been his counselor?'" (11:33-34). Here Paul is referring to Isaiah 40:13, and it is clear that "the Lord" refers to the one God of Israel, who Paul now believes has shown mercy and grace through Jesus Christ in the Spirit. When 1 John 3:20 indicates that "God is greater than our hearts, and he knows everything," the term God is referring to the Father who calls us to believe in the Son and gives us the Spirit (3:23-24). It is natural that the New Testament authors usually reserved the name "God" to refer to the one true God of Israel; what is radical is that they also argued that divine knowledge can no longer be expressed merely in terms of a single subject. Rather, the knowledge of God is the mutual knowing and being known of the Father and Son (cf. Matt. 11:27), which cannot be separated from the deep searching of the Spirit (cf. 1 Cor. 2:10-13). Their encounter with Christ and their immersion in the Spirit led them to think of divine knowledge as essentially relational.

The same observation may be made about the New Testament usage of the idea of the "will" *(thelēma)* of God. Unless explicitly indicated otherwise, the divine will distinctly refers to the will of the Father. For example, Paul speaks of himself as "called to be an apostle of Christ Jesus by the will of God" (1 Cor. 1:1; cf. 2 Cor. 1:1; Eph. 1:1 Col. 1:1). It is the will of the Father that calls him to proclaim the Gospel of the Son. Paul urges the Thessalonians to "give thanks in all circumstances; for this is the will of God in Christ Jesus for you," reminding them not to "quench the Spirit" (1 Thess. 5:18). The divine will here is the will of the Father, which is materially connected to the redemptive operation of the Son and the Spirit in the church. In the mouth of Jesus, the "will" of God always refers to his heavenly Father whose Spirit rested upon him. In the light of the resurrection and the outpouring of the Spirit we may understand the divine *thelēma* as the dynamic redemptive power of trinitarian love, in which we (like Jesus) are invited to share through intensification in the life of the Spirit.[55] In Part III we will return to the antinomies of divine foreknowledge and predestination, which are based on the idea of God a single subject with an intellect and will. Our initial point here is that when the New Testament speaks of the knowledge and will of "God," it typically is referring to the Father whose creative and redemptive presence is mediated through the Son and the Spirit.

It is also important to remember one of the insights gained from our initial discussion of divine Infinity: all human language is limited in relation to God. Just as descriptions of the "arm" or "seat" of God are anthropomorphic, so too are descriptions of the divine "intellect" and "will." These concepts are not exempt from the limitations of human predication. This does not mean that this language is not truly revelatory but it does mean that the absolute presence that is being revealed cannot be grasped by these finite definitions. At any rate, the question is not whether our concepts grasp God, but whether our experience of being grasped by God is obscured by our concepts.

Late modern philosophy, science and biblical scholarship have all challenged particular conceptions of God as a single subject. In Part II, we will explore theological trajectories that may help us recover resources in the Christian tradition for engaging contemporary culture. But first we must tease out one final ingredient in the early modern concept of God as rational causative substance.

---

55. I outline a model of this intensification in the context of reforming Pneumatology in Part I of F. LeRon Shults and Steven J. Sandage, *Transforming Spirituality* (Grand Rapids: Baker Academic, forthcoming 2006).

· 4 ·

GOD AS FIRST CAUSE?

The question of the relation between divine and creaturely causality has been implicit in our brief review of the debates over the relation of a personal God to a material world. We turn now explicitly to an examination of the way in which shifts in the concept of *force* also shaped the early modern doctrine of God. Some of the Protestant Scholastics relied heavily on the idea of God as *causa prima:* the independent, simple, unchangeable divine will — which is identical to the divine essence — is the eternal, infinite, free, and effective first cause of all things.[1] Both Scripture and the early creeds emphasized the power of God Almighty, but the stress on *efficient* causation that became prevalent in early modern mechanistic science complicated the theological articulation of this Christian doctrine. The primacy of the Creator as the origin of all creaturely reality was emphasized throughout the patristic period and early Middle Ages. However,

1. For illustrative quotes from and analysis of the Reformed Scholastics, cf. Francis Turretin, *Institutes of Elenctic Theology [Elenc.],* trans. George Musgrave Giger, 3 vols. (Phillipsburg, N.J.: P&R Publishing, 1992), VI.1.9; Heinrich Heppe, *Reformed Dogmatics: Set Out and Illustrated from the Sources [RD],* rev. and ed. E. Bizer, trans. G. T. Thomson (London: Allen & Unwin, 1950), 81-92, 155-72; Richard Muller, *Post-Reformation Reformed Dogmatics [PRRD],* 4 vols. (Grand Rapids: Baker Academic, 2003), 3:365-475. For the Lutheran Scholastics, cf. Heinrich Schmid, *The Doctrinal Theology of the Evangelical Lutheran Church [DTEL],* 3rd ed. and trans. C. A. Hay and H. E. Jacobs (Minneapolis: Augsburg, 1961), §19, §21; Robert D. Preus, *The Theology of Post-Reformation Lutheranism,* 2 vols. (London: Concordia, 1972), 1:96-107, 208-21.

as mechanistic models of linear cause and effect came to the fore in early modern science, natural philosophers became increasingly focused on identifying the causal order in a series of determined events. This impacted the concept of time itself, which required fresh reflection on the relation of temporal experience to an immutable and eternal God. Philosophical and scientific views of the world as a great machine made it more difficult to articulate the Christian experience of being called into a life of freedom by the dynamic ever-promising presence of the trinitarian God.

Once again we may introduce this problem by pointing to the conflicting options that had been passed down from ancient and medieval philosophy and refigured in the early modern period. For Plato, motion is caused by the living presence of Soul in all things. The world is a "truly living thing, endowed with soul and intelligence" by the god who is described as the Maker or Craftsman (*Timaeus*, 30^c). In this sense Soul is the first cause of all phenomena, including the movement of the heavens (*Laws*, 899^c). Things that are (beings) are defined in terms of their capacity or power to move and be moved (*Sophist*, 247^e). The causal power of any substance and the perfection of its being are intrinsically related. The power of the intellectual Forms derives not from any external agency or willing on their part, but from their very being, which "causes" things that have less being to "imitate" them, to "participate" in their being. Plato's conception of the Good as the ultimate object of desire indicates a view of the divine as the absolute ideal toward which souls are drawn (cf. *Republic*, 505^e-509^b; *Symposium*, 189^d-197^e).

Plotinus argued that all things inherently desire the Good, and movement is caused by this longing to participate in it (*Enneads*, VI.8). The important point for our purposes here is the Neoplatonic insistence that the perfection of a thing's mode of existence is related to its power; substance and causation are coincident. The productive power of the One (or Good) is absolute since it is the perfect source of all being. This power overflows in the Intellect, in which order and structure are expressed. The power of the Intellect produces Soul, in which the intelligible order is further articulated. The material world of successive time and space is produced by the power of the Soul, which governs all its movement, as it reverts back contemplatively toward the One (cf. *Enneads*, III.2).

Aristotle's treatment of causation was more attentive to the changes in particular things in everyday experience. He aimed for a more precise answer to the question "why" a thing moves. In Book II of the *Physics*, Aristotle enumerates the four types of causation in every natural change: that out of which a thing comes to be and which persists, its form (archetype or essential definition), the primary source of its change or rest, and that for the sake of which it is done (194^b16-35). Answering "why" requires identifying each of these, which are commonly called the material, formal, efficient, and final causes of a thing. Aristotle deals with the same four causes in *Metaphysics* (1013^a24-1013^b3). In that context he gives the example of a statue, which may be helpful in distinguishing the four causes, all of which are present in the coming to be of a thing. The *material* cause is the bronze from which the statue is made, the *formal* cause is the pattern (or definition or essential structure) of the sculpture, the *efficient* cause is the sculptor, and the *final* cause is the goal (or "end") of the sculpting, which we might call aesthetic presentation. For Aristotle, God as the first unmoved mover is the ultimate "final" cause, that for which and towards which all things move (*Metaphysics*, 1072^a19-1072^b13). The existence of this unmoved mover is necessary in order to explain the movement of all things toward their natural "telos."

The Stoics tended to think of the whole cosmos as a living ensouled being, ruled by an active, divine principle. However, causality is explained with only two categories: the passive principle (matter) and the active principle of the cosmos. This latter principle is a conflation of Aristotle's other three "causes." Zeno of Citium, usually considered the founder of Stoicism, is reported to have spoken of this vital principle as "fire," the *stoicheion* of everything.[2] Unlike Plato, however, both the passive and active principles (or *archai*) are bodies *(sōmata)*. For the Stoics, all events come about by fate, directed by the seminal principles *(spermatikoi logoi)* that are woven together by the agency of the divine *pneumatikos tonos* — an all-pervading, cohesion-providing *pneuma*. In an attempt to soften this determinism, some Stoic philosophers such as Chrysippus (as reported by Cicero) developed distinctions between hidden and evident causal factors, between antecedent and assisting causes, and complete and principal causes.[3]

2. This report comes through Aristocles and Eusebius; cf. *SVF*, 1:98. See also the depiction of the Stoic view of movement and providence in Diogenes Laertius, *Lives of the Philosophers*, 2 vols., trans. R. D. Hicks (Cambridge: Harvard University Press, 1925), 2:236-63 (VII.132-60).

3. Cicero, *De fato*, 41-42. Cf. *M. Tulli Ciceronis scripta quae manserunt omnia*, Fasc. 46, *De divinatione, De fato, Timaeus*, ed. Remo Giomini (Leipzig: Teubner, 1975), 170.

The other major philosophical option for explaining force in Greek antiquity was Atomism. Epicurus argued that all movement can be accounted for by the collision of infinite impenetrable atoms (within the void). There is no need for the additional hypothesis of living or active forces. All that exists is material, including the animating force of the human soul. Most Epicureans also believed that God exists, but taught that it would be inappropriate to think of the divine nature as intervening in the ongoing motion of the material atoms.[4] The concept of movement (and force) in the cosmology of the ancient Atomists was explicitly mechanistic and anti-teleological. The understanding of force that came to epitomize early modern mechanistic science had more in common with Epicurean materialism and Stoic determinism than with the vitalist, organic, and teleological models of Plato and Aristotle.

§4.1. Newtonian Anxiety

The theological significance of these developments was not lost on Isaac Newton. His own formulation of the laws of motion in the *Principia Mathematica* (1687) contributed to the establishment of the metaphor of nature as "machine," but he struggled even within the pages of his magnum opus to secure a place for divine causality within the cosmos. Newton was attracted to aspects within each of the various philosophical schools that were battling in the seventeenth century. Like the Cambridge Platonists, he resisted the idea of a completely mechanistic and materialist view of nature. In the *Opticks* he insisted that the main business of natural philosophy is to "argue from phenomena without feigning hypotheses, and to deduce causes from effects, till we come to the very first cause, which certainly is not mechanical."[5] Newton's well-known fascination with alchemy and occult forces is evidence of the lure which the Neoplatonic idea of active principles in nature exerted on him. Like the medieval Scholastics, who had followed the Aristotelian fourfold schema of causation, Newton also wanted to maintain the existence of final causes, which

4. Cf. Jacques Brunschwig and David Sedley, "Hellenistic Philosophy," in David Sedley, ed., *Greek and Roman Philosophy* (Cambridge: Cambridge University Press, 2003), 151-83 at 155-63; Brian Inwood and L. P. Gerson, *The Epicurus Reader* (Indianapolis: Hackett, 1994).

5. Isaac Newton, *Opticks*, 3, query 28 (New York: Dover, 1952), 369.

had been expunged from physics by Descartes and others. In the General Scholium of the *Principia*, Newton's theological motivation is clear. We know God, he declares, "by the wisest and best construction of things and their *final* causes, and we admire him because of his perfections; but we venerate and worship him because of his dominion. For we worship him as servants, and a god without dominion, providence and *final* causes is nothing other than fate and nature."[6]

Like so many of his colleagues, however, Newton found himself attracted to Atomism as a more adequate philosophical basis for the concept of force in classical mechanics. In the *Principia* he distinguished between innate force and impressed force. "The *vis insita*, or innate force of matter, is a power of resisting by which every body, as much as in it lies, continues in its present state, whether it be of rest, or of moving uniformly forwards in a right line" (Def. III). Impressed force *(vis impressa)*, on the other hand, is "an action exerted upon a body, in order to change its state, either of rest, or of uniform motion in a right line" (Def. IV). Some readers thought this could be taken to imply that the force of gravity was an active principle inherent in matter itself. In one of his private letters, Newton pleads: "Pray, do not ascribe that notion to me; for the cause of gravity is what I do not pretend to know."[7] In the second edition he emphasized that he does not "affirm gravity to be essential to bodies: by their *vis insita* I mean nothing but their inertia."[8]

The theological significance of the laws of inertia can hardly be over-estimated. Up until the thirteenth century Christian theologians had almost unanimously operated within a cosmology that presupposed the need for inherent, vitalistic productive principles within matter to account for motion. Divine action played an essential role in the cosmos. Problems in the Aristotelian account led the fourteenth-century nominalist theologian John Buridan to propose a theory of impetus. If one body moves an-

---

6. Isaac Newton, *The Principia: Mathematical Principles of Natural Philosophy*, trans. I. Bernard Cohen and Anne Whitman (Berkeley: University of California Press, 1999), 940-41. Emphases added.

7. For a discussion of Newton's understanding of God's relation to gravity, see John Henry, "'Pray do not ascribe that notion to me': God and Newton's Gravity," in *The Books of Nature and Scripture: Recent Essays on Natural Philosophy, Theology, and Biblical Criticism in the Netherlands of Spinoza's Time and the British Isles of Newton's Time*, ed. James E. Force and Richard H. Popkin (Dordrecht: Kluwer, 1994), 123-48.

8. For discussion, cf. Max Jammer, *Concepts of Force* (New York: Dover, 1999), 137.

other by imparting to it an "impulse," then God's role could be limited to the initial provision of impetus at creation and the preservation of all things.[9] This opened up the possibility that cause and effect among bodies could be explained without appeal to active, living principles or entelechies. By the end of the seventeenth century, Newton found it utterly absurd to think that the force of gravity is innate, inherent, and essential to matter. In another letter, he insists that "Gravity must be *caused by an agent* acting constantly according to certain laws; but whether this agent be material or immaterial, I have left to the consideration of my readers."[10]

Newton's own views about this causal agent are clear. He does not believe that the inertia of bodies entails atheism. Quite to the contrary, the passivity of matter plays an apologetic role, pointing to the Creator. In the *Opticks* he asks rhetorically: "Does it not appear from phenomena that there is a being incorporeal, living, intelligent, omnipresent, who, in infinite space, as it were in his sensory, sees the things themselves intimately, and thoroughly perceives them; and comprehends them wholly by their immediate presence to himself?"[11] The idea of absolute space as the *sensorium dei* appealed to Newton because it provided a way of linking his natural philosophy and his theology. Divine immensity, which is the omnipresent agency of the Creator in space, is what causes bodies to move in a way that makes them appear to attract each other.[12] Newton's theory of the force of gravity was celebrated throughout the scientific community for its explanatory power; an explanation for gravity itself, however, is not provided from within his mechanical natural philosophy. A theological answer is offered in the *Principia*, where Newton concludes that the "most elegant system" of the astronomical world could not have arisen "without the design and dominion of an intelligent and powerful being. . . . He rules all things, not as the world soul but as lord of all. And because of his dominion he is called Lord God *Pantokrator*."[13]

---

9. Cf. Etienne Gilson, *History of Christian Philosophy in the Middle Ages* (London: Sheed and Ward, 1955), 511-16; Frederick Copleston, S.J., *A History of Philosophy*, 9 vols. in 3 (New York: Doubleday, 1985), 3:122-67.

10. Quoted in Jammer, *Force*, 139. Emphasis added.

11. *Opticks*, 3, query 28.

12. Cf. Richard S. Westfall, "The Rise of Science and the Decline of Orthodox Christianity: A Study of Kepler, Descartes and Newton," in *God and Nature*, ed. David C. Lindberg and Ronald L. Numbers (Berkeley: University of California Press, 1986), 218-37 at 233.

13. Newton, *The Principia*, 941.

The dominion of God over creation has been called the "emphatic regulative principle" that underlies all of Newton's work — not only his scientific proposals, but also his philosophy, theology, and even his politics.[14] In this sense Newton, whose anti-trinitarian views are now well known, exemplifies what we earlier called the *voluntarist* ideal in theology.[15] From his historical studies, Newton concluded that science had prospered only in strictly monotheistic cultures, and he found a consonance between the *unity* of God and the *universal* force of gravitation. If Atomism could be traced back to Moses,[16] as Newton believed, this provided yet another confirmation of the close relation between his scientific theory and his theology.

But how could the Lord God Pantokrator, an immaterial substance who dominates the world as a single subject with an omnipotent will, be more than merely the first efficient cause of the great world machine? When Newton suggested that God occasionally adjusts the orbits of the planets because they seem to be running down or getting off course, he was ridiculed by Leibniz for postulating an imperfect Creator who had poorly designed a machine that needed constant repair. Reflecting his preference for the intellectualist ideal, Leibniz's own solution was to argue that, on the basis of God's knowledge of all possible worlds, God willed to create this particular world, which is a pre-established harmony of the dynamic movement of monads and requires no repair. To Newton this God did not sound like an active personal *dominus* but a distant designer who is irrelevant to daily human existence. He saw deism in the wings.

Newton's concept of force, coupled with his view of absolute time, also complicated the question of the relation of an eternal God to a moving world of material bodies. If we ascribe "timelessness" to God, it is difficult

14. James E. Force, "Newton's God of Dominion: The Unity of Newton's Theological, Scientific, and Political Thought," in James E. Force and Richard H. Popkin, *Essays on the Context, Nature, and Influence of Isaac Newton's Theology* (Dordrecht: Kluwer, 1990), 75-102 at 95. In *The Religion of Isaac Newton* (Oxford: Clarendon, 1974), 17, Frank Manuel observes that Newton's personal writings are "the testament of a believer who feels deeply the power of a personal, not a metaphysical, God. A *dominus* has been bearing upon him."

15. "It is clear that God created the world by no other action than that of willing in the same way as we also by the sole action of willing move our bodies." Newton, *Unpublished Scientific Papers*, 107; quoted in Alexandre Koyré, *Newtonian Studies* (Chicago: University of Chicago Press, 1965), 93.

16. Cf. Danton B. Sailor, "Moses and Atomism," in *Science and Religious Belief*, ed. C. A. Russell (London: Open University Press, 1973), 1-19 at 18.

to make sense of God's relation to temporality. Such a view of eternity, negatively defined by its relation to time, reminds us of the problems with a spurious view of infinity. If the eternity of the divine life is defined strictly as timelessness, then it is not truly an all-embracing life. Newton believed that eschatology could help him link his scientific understanding of motion to his theology of time. He wrote extensively on the books of Daniel and Revelation, struggling to interpret the Book of Scripture as well as he had interpreted the Book of Nature. He wondered whether the Lord God Pantokrator would act in Newton's own lifetime to fulfill biblical prophecy and bring about the end of the cosmos. The passive matter of the world machine would fall apart without God's active rule. If the order of nature appeared to be decaying, this might indicate the imminence of the millennium reign, wherein God would reconstitute the heavens and the earth.[17]

§4.2. Eschatology in Early Modern Theological Projects

The connection between eschatological doctrine and the debates over divine causality may not be immediately evident. The term "eschatology" itself was introduced in seventeenth-century Protestant Scholasticism as a heading for theological treatments of the causal ordering of the "last things" *(eschata)*. The Lutherans described the *novissima* in various ways, but typically in the following order: the end of the world, the resurrection of the dead, the final judgment, and eternal life. The Reformed Scholastics also varied in their presentations but commonly focused on the ordering of events surrounding the Last Judgment and the identification of their causes. For example, Wollebius explains that the "principal efficient cause" of the Last Judgment is God, while angels are "instrumental" causes, all human persons are the "matter," and courtroom procedure is the "form."[18]

The fascination with the causal ordering of the *eschata* is connected to

17. For a treatment of Newton's view of biblical prophecy and his apocalytic hermeneutics, cf. two essays in Force and Popkin, eds., *The Books of Nature and Scripture:* Sarah Hutton, "More, Newton and the Language of Biblical Prophecy," 39-54; Matania Z. Kochavi, "One Prophet Interprets Another: Sir Isaac Newton and Daniel," 105-22. Cf. David Kubrin, "Newton and the Cyclical Cosmos," in Russell, ed., *Science and Religious Belief,* 147-69 at 168.

18. Johannes Wollebius, *Compendium Theologiae Christianae,* in *Reformed Dogmatics,* ed. and trans. John W. Beardslee III (New York: Oxford University Press, 1965), 183-84. Cf. the Heidelberg Catechism, Q. 52.

the debates over the causal ordering of the first things, namely the divine decrees. The doctrine of simplicity entails that the decrees are actually a single decree, and the doctrine of immutability that the decree is eternal — so the issue was one of logical rather than chronological order. One of the hottest debates was about the decree to damn the reprobate. Is it logically prior to *(supra)* or logically posterior to *(infra)* the decree to allow the fall *(lapsus)* of humanity? Not that it really matters to the reprobate, but a decision on this point did say something about the nature of God in relation to sin, evil, and human responsibility. Through these debates, the issue of the final eternal state of individuals was intimately tied to the articulation of the divine decree(s) as the *causa efficiens primaria* of all things.[19]

Initially the early modern resurgence of philosophical determinism and mechanistic science, which reduced motive force to *efficient* causes that push inert matter through linear time, appeared to be a boon for the voluntarists. They could argue that the power of God was still required to make sense of motion, although the *potentia dei* should be understood as the transcendent decree of the divine will rather than as the immanent creative fire of the Stoics. In the early Middle Ages, John of Damascus could still allow the more Platonic-sounding category of God as "Maker" to do most of the conceptual work in expositing the relation of the Creator to creation.[20] The renaissance of Aristotelianism in the high Middle Ages, however, led theologians to re-articulate the God-world relation in light of the Philosopher's understanding of causality. Along with this causal scheme came a medieval cosmology in which the heavenly orbs, which were moved by intelligent celestial beings, controlled the motions of material substances in the terrestrial sphere (e.g., Thomas Aquinas, *SumTh*, I.19.6). Most of the Protestant Scholastics adapted medieval Aristotelianism and developed the distinction between God as primary cause and creatures as secondary causes of all temporal events. In this scheme, too much emphasis on the power of secondary causes could be taken as a limitation on God's power, leaving a loophole for Pelagianism.

19. This is also connected to the Protestant Scholastic interest in the *ordo salutis*, the causes and ordering of the salvation of the individual (calling, justification, sanctification). I have examined the implications of the (re)turn to relationality for soteriology in F. LeRon Shults and Steven J. Sandage, *The Faces of Forgiveness* (Grand Rapids: Baker Academic, 2003), chap. 4.

20. *De Fide Orthodoxa*, I.3, NPNF2, 9:2-3. The Damascene does appear to be familiar with Aristotle's *On the Heavens*, which treats types of motion, but he does not use the more complex theories of causality in Aristotle's other writings.

When Zwingli insists in his sixteenth-century treatment of divine providence that "secondary causes are not properly called causes,"[21] he is not denying the Ptolemaic structure of the universe but implying that God is the *only* cause of all motion. In the seventeenth century the Roman Catholic theologian Malebranche makes this explicit. The tension between divine and creaturely agency is resolved by denying the latter; God is the sole agent, the only one who acts.[22] However, too much emphasis on divine agency as the primary (or sole) cause of all creaturely events can be (and was) taken to imply that God is the cause of evil. This objection is famously expressed in the eighteenth century in Hume's *Dialogues Concerning Natural Religion;* even if one accepts the idea of a (divine) first cause, all we can deduce about this cause from its effects (which include a great deal of evil as well as good) is that this cause does not care at all about us or perhaps is even hostile toward us.

The voluntarists were also faced with an intensification of the problem of human freedom and responsibility for sin, insofar as the early modern emphasis on efficient causation contributed to the popularity of materialism and determinism. As medieval cosmology slowly collapsed under the weight of the Copernican revolution, appeals to the Neoplatonic and Aristotelian categories of movement and causation became increasingly implausible. Some of the seventeenth-century Protestant Scholastics engaged Stoic categories as they struggled to explain the enigma of divine predestination and human freedom. Here they could appeal to Augustine who, after his shift toward the voluntarist ideal, adapted the Stoic idea of *rationes seminales,* arguing that God had created these invisible powers that unfold in temporal movement.[23]

When Turretin came to the question of reconciling the freedom of the human will (as a secondary cause) with divine concourse, he admits "I cannot understand how these can be mutually connected together" but insists that this connection must not be questioned or denied. He consistently maintains what he calls "Christian fate," arguing that the actual providence of God, which is the execution of the absolute decree of the divine will, determines the movement of the human will; yet, the latter may

21. Ulrich Zwingli, *On Providence, and Other Essays,* ed. William John Hinke (Durham, N.C.: Labyrinth Press, 1983), 138.

22. Nicolas Malebranche, *Dialogues on Metaphysics and on Religion,* trans. M. Ginsburg (London: Allen and Unwin, 1923).

23. Cf. *De Genesi ad litteram,* 5.4.7-9, 5.12.28; *De Trinitate,* 3.8.13.

still be said to "act spontaneously and from preference *(ek proaireseōs)*."[24] Here we find an appeal to the idea of *proairesis* to describe the motion of the human will — an idea which, as we saw at the beginning of Chapter 3, derives from the Stoic philosophy of Epictetus.

As we saw in our analysis of Ockhamist anxiety, the intellectualist ideal led many theologians to develop new distinctions within the divine intellect in their attempts to make sense of human freedom. The voluntarists adopted a parallel strategy. If God wills creatures necessarily, they are eternal objects and God is not free *not* to will them. The first distinction in the divine will, therefore, must be between *voluntas necessaria* and *voluntas libera* (analogous to God's necessary and free knowledge).[25] However, a similar problem arose. If God wills creatures freely, why did God "volunteer" to will a world with so much evil? This led the Reformed Scholastics to make a distinction within the "free" will of God between the *voluntas arcana* and the *voluntas revelata,* i.e., between the hidden and the revealed will of God. The actual ordering of the cosmos as it is revealed to creatures often seems evil, but its goodness is secured in the hidden will of God, which is inaccessible to us. Sometimes this is expressed as the good pleasure *(voluntas beneplaciti)* of God behind our experience of the signs of providence *(voluntas signi).*

However, if God's hidden will is the real cause of the very existence of all things, then it still seems that in some sense God causes evil to be. A further distinction was made between God's efficient and permitting will *(voluntas efficiens* and *voluntas permittens);* the former refers to God's directly accomplishing all things, the latter to God's not withdrawing divine concursus or primary causality. Because the objects of God's decree are twofold (the elect and the reprobate), another distinction had to be made within the revealed will, between the *voluntas evangelica,* which wills to save by the gospel, and the *voluntas legalis,* which demands obedience to the Law. All of these distinctions were overshadowed by the doctrines of simplicity and immutability, which implied that they did not refer to anything real in God. The apparent irrelevance of this focus on the causal ordering of a timeless divine will, rather than on the evocative and dynamic presence of God in religious experience, led many Christians to revolt

24. *Elenc.,* I.6.6.2, 8; 1:512-14.

25. For examples and analysis of these and the following distinctions in Reformed Scholasticism, cf. *PRRD,* 3:432-75; *RD,* 81-104. For illustrative quotes and discussion of the concept of causality in the Lutheran Scholastics, cf. *DTEL,* 127-29, and Preus, *Theology of Post-Reformation Lutheranism,* 2:197-203, 224-49.

against a perceived rationalism in Scholastic theology, a revolt that contributed to the emergence of Pietism and the Great Awakenings.

The main point for our purpose here is that all of these distinctions were based on the assumption that God is a single subject with an intellect and will, an immaterial substance whose essence is the first efficient cause of creaturely effects. These categories continue to structure many contemporary theological projects. Charles Hodge, who depended heavily on Turretin's theology, continued to emphasize the absolute divine decree, and relied on the scholastic notions of causality, including the distinctions between God's antecedent and consequent, decretive and preceptive, absolute and conditional will, etc.[26] Hodge's eschatology, which also maintained the focus on individual final states and their causal ordering, played an important role in mediating these early modern categories into American theology.

Rather than multiplying examples, let us illustrate the influence of these categories in the work of Millard Erickson. Questions about the divine decrees and their logical order structure Erickson's treatment of God's causal relation to the world. God "renders it certain" that persons act in the way they do, but they are free in the sense that they are not "under constraint."[27] The final chapters of his *Christian Theology* deal with "individual" eschatology, the second coming and its "consequents," the millennial and tribulational debates, and "final states." The emphasis here continues to be on individuals, causal ordering, and states; eschatology is about the last things that God has already rendered certain. In light of late modern philosophical and scientific insights into the nature of time and causality, as well as scholarship on the biblical concepts of promise and parousia, the need to rely on these early modern categories in the Christian doctrine of God has increasingly been challenged.

§4.3. Futurity in Late Modern Philosophy

The mechanical model of causation that came to characterize early modern science was undermined by several eighteenth-century philosophers who

---

26. Charles Hodge, *Systematic Theology*, 3 vols. (Grand Rapids: Eerdmans, 1981), 1:402-12; cf. Hodge's treatment of eschatology in 3:713-880.

27. Millard Erickson, *Christian Theology*, 2nd ed. (Grand Rapids: Baker, 1998), 383. Notice how this answer is structurally similar to the Stoic view of assent and *proairesis*.

worried that the reduction of movement to corpuscular collision implied an understanding of time that was alien to the qualitative human experience of process and continuity. The monadology of Leibniz and the dynamism of Wolff are examples of attempts to incorporate the human experience of harmonic interconnection into natural philosophy. Scientific reliance on the category of efficient causation was also criticized by David Hume, who argued that we cannot prove the necessity of causal relations between two motions. In his 1740 *A Treatise on Human Nature* (§I.3.12) and his 1748 *An Enquiry Concerning Human Understanding* (§7.2) he insisted that it is simply the habit of the human mind to associate (or conjoin) events, calling one "cause" and the other "effect."

Hume's critique built on the challenges to classical understandings of the ideas of duration and causation in the works of Locke (*Essay*, 1689) and Berkeley (*Principles*, 1710); both had struggled to explain the link between the ideas of cause and effect in the "world" and in the "mind." Kant's (in)famous limitation of the category of time to the transcendental structures of human reason in the first *Critique* (1787) represents another attempt to insist that the phenomena of quantitative change in the world cannot be divorced from the qualitative human perception of time. In Hegel's *Phenomenology of Spirit* (1807) the inherently relational movement of being is the self-actualization of the Absolute Spirit; this implies an orientation toward the future and reintroduces a form of teleology into cosmology.

Friedrich Schelling went even further in privileging the future. When he discussed God and time in *The Ages of the World* (1811) he suggested that the future plays a special role in understanding the whole or the totality of time: in a sense, "the whole of time is the Future."[28] Although the project of Karl Marx was to turn Hegel on his head, so that the dynamics of the world are explained through a "materialist" dialectic rather than a "spiritual" one, the importance of the *future* for the movement of history remains. The structures of government and society are developing in a particular direction with a specific and inevitable *telos*: the revolution of the proletariat and the establishment of an ideal communist state. In the twentieth century, followers of Marx expounded the importance of futurity for this dimension of human life in more detail, developing a philosophy of hope.[29]

---

28. "Die ganze Zeit aber ist die Zukunft." F. W. J. von Schelling, *Die Weltalter*, Ausgewählte Schriften, vol. 4 (Frankfurt: Suhrkamp, 1985), 294.

29. For Ernst Bloch, the recovery of the category of the Novum, the seriousness of "the

Anglo-American philosophy has also participated in the resistance to necessitarian conceptions of time that contradict the human experience of the future as an opening up of real possibilities. Writing in the late nineteenth century, after the development of Darwin's theory of evolution, C. S. Peirce challenged the "doctrine of necessity" on philosophical grounds. We must, he argued, postulate the prevalence of an element of absolute chance in the world.[30] For Peirce, the claim that meaning is related to consequences, which is the driving idea of pragmatism, requires an orientation toward (future) goals. William James was also critical of determinism, for which "the future has no ambiguous possibilities hidden in its womb."[31]

Many philosophers from the analytic tradition, which traces its lineage to Frege rather than Kant or Peirce, have pointed to the radical difference between propositions that are tensed with reference to the past and those tensed with reference to the future. This is particularly evident among modal logicians who have engaged the scientific theories of indeterminacy, the irreversibility of time, and the priority of the "possible."[32] Logical analysis of propositions that refer to future contingent events does not work in the same way as analysis of propositions dealing with the determinate past. The future resists the grasp of language more so than the past. For many philosophers this suggests that, among the modes of time, the future has a logical priority. As Georg Picht observes, the concept of "possibility" must be understood in the horizon of the future. The asym-

---

Front," are central for developing a "philosophy of hope." Being is understood out of its "Where from," but this is so "only as an equally tendential, still unclosed Where to." The Omega explains and interprets the Alpha, and not vice versa. "*The being that conditions consciousness, and the consciousness that processes being, is understood ultimately only out of that and in that from which and towards which it tends.* Essential being is not Been-ness; on the contrary: the essential being of the world lies itself on the Front." *The Principle of Hope,* 3 vols., trans. Neville Plaice et al. (Cambridge, Mass.: MIT Press, 1986), 1:18. Emphasis in original.

30. Cf. "The Doctrine of Necessity Examined," in *The Essential Peirce,* ed. N. Houser and C. Kloesel (Bloomington: Indiana University Press, 1992), 298-311.

31. Charles Sanders Peirce, "The Dilemma of Determinism," in *The Will to Believe and Other Essays in Popular Philosophy* (New York: Dover, 1956), 150.

32. Cf. A. N. Prior, *Past, Present and Future* (Oxford: Clarendon Press, 1967), especially chaps. 7 and 8; J. R. Lucas, *The Future: An Essay on God, Temporality and Truth* (Oxford: Blackwell, 1990).

metric structure of time is ordered by the priority of the future, and this asymmetry manifests what we call the modes of time.[33]

Process philosophy is another important manifestation of the resistance to past-privileging views of causality and time. One of Whitehead's major concerns in *Process and Reality* was to respond to the determinism that follows from the reductive use of the idea of efficient causation. He attempted to include the intuition of "final" causality within his concept of "subjective aim." God is causally related to every actual occasion by providing its subjective aim, the lure toward actualization. At the same time, every event has its own real causation as it actively prehends this luring.[34] For Whitehead, the determinate past is relevant, but not "creative." Past occasions are passive and achieve only "objective immortality" as they are prehended in the process of present occasions.

For most process thinkers it is enough to emphasize the present as the locus of causality; actual occasions are "caused" both by the multiplicity of finite prehending events and their incorporation into the primordial nature of God. Lewis Ford has pressed for a more radical view of "future causation." For Whitehead, all creativity is concentrated in the present, in the unity of prehending events; the future is as devoid of creativity as the past. Ford extends the locus of creativity to include the future as well. The future is "the still, small voice that calls the world into being out of practically nothing."[35]

Kierkegaard is a key figure in the philosophical (re)turn[36] to futurity. In *The Concept of Anxiety* he suggests "that the future in a certain sense signifies more than the present and the past, because . . . the future can in a cer-

33. Georg Picht, "Die Zeit und die Modalitäten," in his *Hier und Jetzt* (Stuttgart: Klett-Cotta, 1980), 370-74.

34. See especially Part V of *Process and Reality,* corrected edition, ed. David Ray Griffin and Donald W. Sherburne (New York: Free Press, 1978). For exposition and analysis, see the essays in David Ray Griffin, ed., *Physics and the Ultimate Significance of Time: Bohm, Prigogine, and Process Philosophy* (Albany: SUNY Press, 1986); cf. Robert Cummings Neville, *A Theology Primer* (Albany: SUNY Press, 1991), 79ff.

35. Lewis Ford, *Transforming Process Theism* (Albany: SUNY Press, 2000), 11, 18. Cf. also Ford, *The Lure of God* (Philadelphia: Fortress, 1978); "Creativity in a Future Key" in *New Essays in Metaphysics,* ed. Neville (Albany: SUNY Press, 1987), 179-97; "Nancy Frankenberry's Conception of the Power of the Past," *American Journal of Theology and Philosophy* 14, no. 3 (1993): 287-300. For a general critique of the process view of God and time see Robert Neville, *Creativity and God: A Challenge to Process Theology,* new ed. (Albany: SUNY, 1995).

36. As we will see in Chapter 7, the significance of the future for the constitution of time was an important theme for several classical philosophers and theologians.

tain sense signify the whole. This is because the eternal first signifies the future or because the future is the incognito in which the eternal . . . preserves its association with time."[37] For Kierkegaard this philosophical insight is linked to religious experience. "For an existing person, is not eternity not eternity but the future, whereas eternity is eternity only for the Eternal, who is not in a process of becoming? . . . where the *eternal* relates itself as the *future* to the *person in a process of becoming* — there the absolute disjunction belongs. In other words, when I join eternity and becoming, I do not gain rest but the future. Certainly this is why Christianity has proclaimed the eternal as the future, because it was proclaimed to existing persons."[38]

In his *Upbuilding Discourses* Kierkegaard discusses the relation of time and eternity with special reference to the future. To be a human person is to be expectant: "if there were no future, there would be no past, either . . . if there were neither future nor past, then a human being would be in bondage like an animal." Through the expectancy of faith a person dares to be occupied with the future, in which the present also appears. "The future is indeed everything, and the present is a part of it — how could we have conquered the whole before even coming to the first part of it?"[39] The religious experience of human persons occurs precisely in the ennobling struggle with the future. Perhaps Kierkegaard's most explicit statement is found in his *Works of Love*, where he speaks of eternity as "taking upon itself the form of the future, the possible [and] with the help of hope it brings up temporality's child [the human being]."[40]

The philosophical significance of the future is also a central theme in Heidegger's *Being and Time*, which is a phenomenological analysis of the appearance of the being of the self to its self in time. For Heidegger, the future "has a priority in the ecstatical unity of primordial and authentic temporality."[41] The meaning of existentiality *"is the future."* The "ahead-of-

---

37. S. Kierkegaard, *The Concept of Anxiety*, ed. and trans. Reidar Thomte (Princeton: Princeton University Press, 1980), 89.

38. Kierkegaard, *Concluding Unscientific Postscript*, ed. and trans. Howard V. and Edna H. Hong, 2 vols. (Princeton: Princeton University Press, 1992), 1:306-7.

39. Kierkegaard, *Eighteen Upbuilding Discourses*, ed. and trans. Howard V. and Edna H. Hong (Princeton: Princeton University Press, 1990), 17.

40. Ed. and trans. Howard V. and Edna H. Hong (Princeton: Princeton University Press, 1995), 252.

41. Martin Heidegger, *Being and Time*, trans. John Macquarrie and Edward Robinson (San Francisco: HarperCollins, 1962), 378.

itself" that makes Dasein (being-there) possible is "grounded in the future." For Heidegger this groundedness of temporality is not an explicitly theological phenomenon; Dasein lets *itself* be. Authentic human existence is characterized by "anticipatory resoluteness," which is "Being towards one's ownmost, distinctive potentiality-for-Being." The existence of Dasein *is* its coming towards itself. "This letting-itself-*come-towards*-itself in that distinctive possibility which it puts up with, is the primordial phenomenon of the *future as coming towards*." Dasein's Being-towards-death is possible "only as something *futural* [als *zukünftiges*]." By "futural" Heidegger does not mean simply a "now" that has not yet become actual, but "the coming [Kunft] in which Dasein, in its ownmost potentiality-for-Being, comes towards itself." In resolute anticipation Dasein is authentic in its relation to the future, in which it is always coming towards itself. "Only so far as it is futural can Dasein *be* authentically as having been. The character of 'having been' arises, in a certain way, from the future."[42]

This privileging of the future in the analysis of the experience of time had a profound effect on later twentieth-century philosophy.[43] Emmanuel Levinas expanded upon emphases within Kierkegaard and Heidegger in his description of the ethical relation to the other, in which the "I" journeys from its "at home" [*chez soi*] toward the alterity of that which is outside of itself [*hors-de-soi*]. This primordial relation is constituted by the presence of the transcendent Other, which is explicitly linked to the experience of the future, which represents the ultimate Other beyond our control.[44] Levinas does not want to collapse the idea of the future into mere possibility (as he interprets Heidegger). His interest is in the relation with a future that is "irreducible to the power over possibles," which he calls "fecundity." This future cannot be grasped but always confronts us as beyond, as the "absolute future."[45] Here

42. Heidegger, *Being and Time*, 372. Heidegger often hyphenates the German word for future (*Zukunft*) to emphasize its etymological connectedness to the idea of a coming-to (*zu-kunft*).

43. E.g., Gabriel Marcel, *Homo Viator: Introduction to a Metaphysic of Hope*, trans. Emma Craufurd (New York: Harper & Row, 1962); James Richard Mensch, *Postfoundational Phenomenology: Husserlian Reflections on Presence and Embodiment* (University Park, Pa.: The Pennsylvania State University Press, 2001).

44. Emmanuel Levinas, *Time and the Other*, trans. Richard A. Cohen (Pittsburgh: Duquesne University Press, 1987), 64, 70ff; cf. Levinas, *God, Death and Time*, trans. Bettina Bergo (Stanford: Stanford University Press, 2000).

45. Emmanuel Levinas, *Totality and Infinity: An Essay on Exteriority*, trans. Alphonso Lingis (Pittsburgh: Duquesne University Press, 1969), 268.

the relation to the future becomes explicitly theological. "The eschatological, as the 'beyond' of history, draws beings out of the jurisdiction of history and the future; it arouses them in and calls them forth to their full responsibility."[46]

Insofar as these and other late modern developments have challenged particular constructions of the concept of "first cause" that dominated early modern theology, they open up an opportunity for recovering the eschatological ontology of the New Testament. Before exploring this possibility, let us outline developments within natural science itself that have also undermined atomistic and mechanistic conceptions of space and time.

§4.4. Causality and Temporality in Contemporary Science

The replacement — or, better, incorporation — of Newton's conception of space and time by Einstein's special and general theories of relativity introduced a radically new way of thinking about temporality and causality. Already in the nineteenth century, the idea of bodies with Euclidean properties moving through absolute three-dimensional space was being challenged by the theory of electromagnetic fields and the slow demise of the "aether" hypothesis in physical cosmology. Einstein's special theory challenged the assumption in classical mechanics that both time-intervals and space-intervals are independent of the motion of bodies.[47] There is no universal "now" (simultaneity) that is experienced by all persons at the same "time," and the "size" (extension) of an object depends on its speed relative to each observer.

The general theory of relativity also suggests a non-Euclidean space-time of variable curvature; here gravitation is not so much a "force" (as it was for Newton) as a property of the space-time continuum.[48] The success of these theories raised objections to several key aspects of the early modern conception of the universe. Milič Čapek has argued that relativity theory requires us to give up static determinism and accept an open world in

46. Levinas, *Totality and Infinity*, 23.

47. Cf. Albert Einstein, *Relativity: The Special and the General Theory* (New York: Crown, 1961), 30-34; *Ideas and Opinions* (New York: Bonanza, 1954), 253-61.

48. Cf. Jammer, *Force*, 260.

which "genuine novelties come into being."[49] Even the concept of a "line of time" has been called into question by reflection on the implications of the Wheeler-DeWitt equation,[50] and the Newtonian model of an infinite static cosmos has been replaced by inflationary models of the universe.[51]

Developments in quantum mechanics and chaos theory have also challenged the early modern scientific dream of mathematically precise predictability, which presupposed a mechanistic view of the causation of bodies "through" space and time. Although Einstein himself resisted the implications of quantum theory,[52] Heisenberg's "uncertainty" principle and the Copenhagen interpretation of quantum phenomena indicate an irreducible "indeterminacy" in natural events. Reflecting on these scientific theories, Arthur Peacocke suggests an implication for the doctrine of God: "there just does not exist any future, predictable state of such systems *for* God to know."[53] On the basis of his interpretation of chaos theory, John Polkinghorne argues that Christian eschatology should take a more dynamic view of the consummation of the world.[54]

Scientists continue to debate the epistemological and metaphysical implications of both quantum mechanics and chaos theory, but the salient point here is that the certainty that once sustained the deterministic model of the cosmos has been undermined.[55] In light of current understandings

49. Milič Čapek, "Time in Relativity Theory: Arguments for a Philosophy of Becoming," in *The Voices of Time*, ed. J. T. Fraser, 2nd ed. (Amherst: University of Massachusetts Press, 1981), 434-54 at 454; cf. Capek, "Determinism in Western Theology and Philosophy," in *Religious Pluralism,* ed. Leroy Rouner (Notre Dame: University of Notre Dame Press, 1984), 54-74; *The Philosophical Impact of Contemporary Physics* (New York: Van Nostrand Reinhold Co., 1961).

50. Cf. Julian Barbour, *The End of Time: The Next Revolution in Physics* (Oxford: Oxford University Press, 1999), 35-57.

51. Cf. Alan Guth, *The Inflationary Universe: The Quest for a New Theory of Cosmic Origins* (Cambridge: Perseus, 1997).

52. Cf. Albert Einstein and Leopold Infeld, *The Evolution of Physics* (New York: Simon and Schuster, 1938), 293-97.

53. Arthur Peacocke, *Theology for a Scientific Age* (Minneapolis: Fortress, 1993), 155; cf. 122.

54. John Polkinghorne, "Eschatology: Some Questions and Some Insights from Science," in *The End of the World and the Ends of God,* ed. Polkinghorne and M. Welker (Harrisburg, Pa.: Trinity Press International, 2000), 29-41; "Chaos Theory and Divine Action," in *Religion and Science,* ed. W. Mark Richardson and Wesley Wildman (London: Routledge, 1996).

55. For representative analyses of the debate, cf. David Z. Albert, *Quantum Mechanics and Experience* (Cambridge: Harvard University Press, 1992); David Bohm, *Wholeness and*

of quantum entanglement and the behavior of nonlinear thermodynamic systems, this narrow concept of efficient causality no longer shapes most contemporary scientific discourse. Early modern models of time and causation were not necessary for patristic or medieval treatments of the doctrine of God, so why should they constrain contemporary theological discourse?[56]

Discoveries in the sciences of evolutionary biology have also led to fresh reflection on divine causality that moves beyond an emphasis merely on past determinism and present concurrence. One of the most influential scientists and theologians to thematize the future was the paleobiologist and priest Pierre Teilhard de Chardin. His concept of the "Omega Point" was an attempt to hold together the Future, the Universal, and the Personal. The Omega is supremely present, but as "Prime Mover ahead."[57] Teilhard impacted a whole generation of theologians, who were inspired to engage science positively and reflect upon divine causality in new ways, although few followed him in the material details. John Haught, for example, argues that evolution "seems to require a divine source of being that resides not in a timeless present located somewhere 'up above,' but in the future, essentially 'up ahead,' as the goal of a world still in the making."[58] He suggests that a metaphysics of the future can help theology overcome its fear of Darwinian biology and encourage us to imagine the novel informational possibilities that evolution has available to it as arising from the always dawning future. Haught argues that evolution is made possible by

---

the Implicate Order (London: Routledge, 1980); Ilya Prigogine and Isabelle Stengers, *Order Out of Chaos* (New York: Bantam, 1984); Wesley Wildman and Robert John Russell, "Chaos: A Mathematical Introduction with Philosophical Reflections," in *Chaos and Complexity: Scientific Perspectives on Divine Action,* ed. Russell et al., 2nd ed. (Berkeley: CTNS, 1997), 49-92.

56. Cf. my "A Theology of Chaos," *Scottish Journal of Theology* 45 (1992): 223-35; James Gleick, *Chaos: Making a New Science* (New York: Viking, 1987).

57. Pierre Teilhard de Chardin, *The Phenomenon of Man,* trans. Bernard Wall (New York: Harper & Row, 1959), 260-72. For the appropriation of the concept of the Omega among non-theologians, cf. Frank Tipler, *The Physics of Immortality: Modern Cosmology, God and the Resurrection of the Dead* (New York: Anchor, 1994), 216; Robert Wright, *Nonzero: The Logic of Human Destiny* (New York: Pantheon, 2000), 327-28; Errol E. Harris, *The Reality of Time* (Albany: SUNY Press, 1988), 158ff. For a review of theological responses, see Mark Worthing, *God, Creation and Contemporary Physics* (Minneapolis: Fortress, 1996), 168-75.

58. John F. Haught, *God after Darwin: A Theology of Evolution* (Boulder, Colo.: Westview, 2000), 84.

the "infinite generosity of God's futurity" and that "all things receive their being from out of an inexhaustibly resourceful 'future' that we may call 'God.'"[59]

The sciences that study the emergence of complexity in living organisms have also thematized the importance of the future for understanding causality. According to scientist Per Bak, the emergence of self-organized criticality cannot be reduced to or explained by other principles of physics, including chaos theory.[60] Theologian Niels Henrik Gregersen has explored the implications of theories of autopoiesis (self-organization) in natural systems for the doctrines of creation and providence. He proposes a model in which autopoietic processes are sustained by the "structuring causality" of God — divine providence involves the reconfiguration of the possibility spaces of self-productive systems. God's creative work is a creation of creativity, a "structuring" cause that graciously gives creation its own fecundity.[61] For Gregersen, the autopoiesis that can be observed throughout the systems of nature render problematic the idea of God's planning things deterministically from the past. Contemporary theories of emergent complexity suggest that "the classical claim of God's detailed knowledge of future contingents has hardly any constitutive importance for religious faith."[62] Other participants in the theology and science dialogue have responded in similar ways. In his discussion of the dynamics of genetic processes, Holmes Rolston borrows the metaphor of "attractors" from physics and suggests that, in reference to biological phenomena, we may think of God as "a sort of biogravity that lures life upward . . . [introducing] new possibility spaces all along the way."[63]

Questions like "why is the universe the way it is?" and "why is there a universe at all?" raise issues about the boundaries of the disciplines of cos-

59. Haught, *God after Darwin*, 97, 90.

60. Per Bak, *How Nature Works: The Science of Self-Organized Criticality* (New York: Copernicus, 1996).

61. Niels Henrik Gregersen, "From Anthropic Design to Self-Organized Complexity," in *From Complexity to Life*, ed. Gregersen (Oxford: Oxford University Press, 2003), 206-34 at 226.

62. Niels Henrik Gregersen, "The Idea of Creation and the Theory of Autopoietic Process," *Zygon* 33, no. 3 (Sept. 1998): 333-68 at 356; cf. Gregersen, "Beyond the Balance: Theology in a Self-Organizing World," in *Design and Disorder: Perspectives from Science and Theology*, ed. Gregersen and Ulf Görman (London: T&T Clark, 2002), 53-91.

63. Holmes Rolston III, *Genes, Genesis and God* (Cambridge: Cambridge University Press, 1999), 364.

mology and theology. From both sides of this interdisciplinary dialogue we find a growing interest in the significance of the future for understanding the human experience of temporality and causality. Interest in "teleology" does not require that we accept the Aristotelian concept of entelechies, the Neoplatonic vitalistic forces, or early modern theories of intelligent design. However, the dynamic structure and orientation of the cosmos itself suggest a more important explanatory role for the future than was allowed in the early modern linear view of space and time. The remarkably narrow margins for the initial conditions necessary for an environment that could lead to the emergence of intelligent life have led to the well-known cosmological "anthropic principle," which suggests that the concept of purpose or "telos" cannot easily be excluded from a general understanding of the universe. In chapter 8 we will revisit the task of reconstructing the teleological argument in late modernity.

Nancey Murphy and George Ellis have argued that these scientific discoveries provide an opportunity for incorporating intrinsically "moral" concerns into the fabric of an ultimate explanation of the cosmos,[64] a move that would have been extremely difficult within the context of seventeenth-century dualistic, mechanistic cosmology. Robert John Russell has explored the implications of contemporary physical cosmology, which suggests that the universe will eventually "freeze or fry," for the articulation of Christian eschatology. He encourages us to rethink the idea of the "beginning" of a finite universe, arguing that eternity is positively related to time, as its fully temporal source and goal.[65]

The renewed attention to the future in the sciences has helped to open conceptual space that facilitates the retrieval of biblical eschatology for theological engagement with late modern scientific discussions of human becoming. We will explore the concept of "Futurity" in more detail in Chapter 7, but it will be helpful here to outline the way in which biblical scholarship contributed to its theological renewal.

---

64. Murphy and Ellis, *On the Moral Nature of the Universe: Theology, Cosmology and Ethics* (Minneapolis: Fortress, 1996).

65. Russell, "Eschatology and Physical Cosmology," in *The Far-Future Universe: Eschatology from a Cosmic Perspective*, ed. George F. R. Ellis (Philadelphia: Templeton Press, 2002), 266-315, esp. 301-8; Russell, "Finite Creation without a Beginning: The Doctrine of Creation in Relation to Big Bang Quantum Cosmologies," in *Quantum Cosmology and the Laws of Nature*, ed. Russell et al. (Berkeley: CTNS, 1996), 291-325. Russell's interdisciplinary work engages several of the theologians who have emphasized the Futurity of God (cf. Chapter 7 below).

§4.5. Biblical Experiences of Futurity

As biblical scholarship rediscovered the significance of eschatological anticipation in the various genres of the Hebrew Bible and in the apostolic writings, the hermeneutical warrant for the dominance of the concept of "first
cause" in early modern theology was gradually weakened. Biblical scholars
became increasingly convinced that when causality became the ruling concept of Protestant Scholasticism it "became de-eschatologized and in this really lost contact with the message of the New Testament."[66] One of the most
significant developments that contributed to this renewal of interest in eschatology was Johannes Weiss's argument for the centrality of the "kingdom
of God" in the message of Jesus. In contrast to the present-oriented "ethical"
interpretations of this idea that dominated most of the nineteenth century,
in 1892 Weiss demonstrated the irreducibly future-oriented element of Jesus'
message.[67]

This instigated Albert Schweitzer's *Quest of the Historical Jesus* (1906)
and shaped the consequent debates about "realized" and "future" eschatology that continued throughout the twentieth century.[68] Rudolf Bultmann,
for example, argued that, while Paul still expects future events, John con-
ceives of the eschatological event as happening in the present.[69] Other scholars argued that Scripture consistently presents the kingdom as wholly in the
future. It became increasingly common, however, to hold in tension the dialectic between the "already" and the "not yet" of the inbreaking divine reign.
This was popularized by G. E. Ladd in his *The Presence of the Future*.[70] Inter-

---

66. James Martin, *The Last Judgment in Protestant Theology from Orthodoxy to Ritschl*
(Grand Rapids: Eerdmans, 1963), 26-27.

67. Johannes Weiss, *Jesus' Proclamation of the Kingdom of God*, trans. Richard Hyde
Hiers and David Larrimore Holland (Philadelphia: Fortress, 1971).

68. A. Schweitzer, *The Quest of the Historical Jesus*, trans. W. Montgomery (New York:
Macmillan, 1961). For a mid-century review, see T. F. Torrance, "The Modern Eschatological
Debate," *The Evangelical Quarterly* 25 (1953). For a thorough survey see Gerhard Sauter,
What Dare We Hope? Reconsidering Eschatology (Harrisburg, Pa.: Trinity Press International,
1999).

69. Rudolf Bultmann, *The Presence of Eternity: History and Eschatology* (New York:
Harper and Brothers, 1957), 47. This interpretation is difficult to maintain in light of 1 John
2:28. For another influential view, cf. Oscar Cullmann, *Christ and Time: The Primitive Christian Conception of Time and History*, trans. Floyd V. Filson, rev. ed. (London: SCM, 1962).

70. George Eldon Ladd, *The Presence of the Future: The Eschatology of Biblical Realism*
(Grand Rapids: Eerdmans, 1974).

est in the eschatological imagination of the New Testament has continued to lead biblical scholars to explore the relation between the redemptive experience of time and the arriving presence of the kingdom of God.[71] The theological issue here is not the causal order of the "last things" but the new understanding of temporal existence that emerged in the wake of transformative religious experiences of the promising presence of the biblical God.

One of the most significant developments in Hebrew Bible scholarship in the twentieth century was a fresh emphasis on the significance of the theme of "promise" for the ancient Israelites. The experience of YHWH as a promising presence was constitutive for their identity as a people, called to hope in the coming of the reign of divine peace. Gerhard von Rad argued that the Israelites' understanding of history was inherently open to a future: "in this connexion 'future' is always a future to be released by God."[72] Their memory of God's faithfulness and steadfast love oriented them in hope toward this future. The biblical texts cannot be understood apart from the eschatological anticipation that shaped the consciousness of their authors. This anticipation was not merely of an event further on the time-line, but of the absolute renewal of temporal experience; it was hope for and in a coming presence that is already making all things new.

In stark contrast to the philosophical fatalism of their neighbors,[73] the primary reality that constituted their communal identity was not a primordial myth, but a promised future. This is evident already in the call of Abram to a promised land; the Lord promises "I will make of you a great nation, and I will bless you, and make your name great, so that you will be a blessing . . . in you all the families of the earth shall be blessed" (Gen. 12:1-3). The link between blessing and promise is new in the religious experi-

71. Cf. James Alison, *Raising Abel: The Recovery of the Eschatological Imagination* (New York: Crossroad, 1996); Richard Bauckham and Trevor Hart, "The Shape of Time," in *The Future as God's Gift*, ed. D. Fergusson and M. Sarot (Edinburgh: T&T Clark, 2000); J. Louis Martyn, *Theological Issues in the Letters of Paul* (Nashville: Abingdon, 1997), esp. part II; and Greg K. Beale, "The Eschatological Conception of New Testament Theology," in *Eschatology in Bible and Theology*, ed. Kent E. Brower and Mark W. Elliot (Downers Grove, Ill.: InterVarsity Press, 1997), 11-52.

72. Gerhard von Rad, *Old Testament Theology*, 2 vols., trans. D. M. G. Stalker (Louisville: Westminster/John Knox, 2001), 2:361 (original German published 1957, 1960); cf. Walther Zimmerli, *Man and His Hope in the Old Testament* (Naperville, Ill.: Allenson, 1971).

73. Cf. Luther H. Martin, "Fate, Futurity and Historical Consciousness in Western Antiquity," *Historical Reflections/Réflexions Historiques* 17, no. 2 (1991): 151-69.

ence of ancient Mesopotamia; it breaks out of the magical-mythic view of the gods as providing immediate blessing (fertility, crops) through a determinate cultus, and opens up an endogenous experience of time oriented toward a wholly new future.[74]

Another significant aspect of the religious experience of the people of Israel was their anticipation of living in peace in the "promised land," a category that had both literal and symbolic meaning.[75] The liberating power of God in the Exodus orients them toward that land, a "place" where they would experience the fullness of the blessing promised to Abraham. However we interpret the bloody conquest of the taking of the land from the people of Canaan, an ambiguous history that continues to have political ramifications today, the important theological point is their longing for "place" — for an experience of space and time in community that would be characterized by *shalom*. Once they occupy the land, the people are called time and again to turn toward YHWH as the only source of their determination; their existence is rooted in the future that God brings.

On the one hand, the Israelites anticipated that this would occur in the actual political structures that concretely shaped their existence in that land; e.g., the year of Jubilee was intended to redistribute the land among the people of the community (Lev. 25–27). On the other hand, Israel's testimony also indicates an awareness that the divine reign cannot be reducible to political structures or even a specific plot of real estate, especially after the exile. Although they longed to return to the land, they came to recognize that the reign of God cannot be judged on the basis of which earthly powers currently dominate and control the "landedness" of the peoples (e.g., Dan. 4:17). The people of God are encouraged to look to the future: "Do not remember the former things, or consider the things of old. I am about to do a new thing; now it springs forth, do you not perceive it?" (Isa. 43:18-19a). They begin to anticipate the reign of God in terms of the creation of new heavens and a new earth (Isa. 65:17).

The experience of anticipation is expressed in various ways in the other genres of the Hebrew Bible. In the wisdom literature, those who pursue knowledge in the fear of the LORD will find a future; their hope will not

74. For analysis, see Wolfgang Achtner, Stefan Kunz, and Thomas Walter, *Dimensions of Time: The Structures of the Time of Humans, of the World, and of God* (Grand Rapids: Eerdmans, 2002), chap. 1.

75. Cf. Walter Brueggemann, *The Land* (Philadelphia: Fortress, 1977), 3.

be cut off (Prov. 23:18; 24:14). The Psalms are full of expressions of hope in the redemption of God not only *from* current enemies, but *into* the presence of the LORD forever (e.g., Ps. 41:12). The main function of the prophetic literature was not predicting events but mediating the divine address to the community, calling it to maintain hope and covenant faithfulness to the God of promise (e.g., Hos. 14; Zech. 8). The genre of apocalyptic literature generated significant research interest after the discovery of the Dead Sea Scrolls. Although the distinction between "prophecy" and "apocalyptic" is blurry, the use of otherworldly language to depict the presence of God in this-worldly events is more common in the latter. The imagery of Daniel's visions, for example, is shaped by the thought-world of Israel's captors.[76] The writing of all the biblical authors is shaped by (Calvin would say accommodated to) their cultural and cosmological context; in the postexilic period this included the belief in the astrological determination of earthly events by celestial movements. Like the rest of the Hebrew Bible, the main purpose of the apocalyptic literature is to orient Israel toward the promising presence of God, whose calling of them into an eternal future of blessing and peace already shapes their life together in the present.

Three themes in the Hebrew Bible are particularly relevant for the idea of the promising presence of God: the divine name, the divine reign, and the divine face. We will return to these themes in the context of our presentations of reformative concepts of divine knowing, acting, and being, but their significance for the concept of promising presence makes it important to introduce them here. First, the name of God revealed to Moses (Exod. 3:14) evokes a leaning into the future of this one who calls Israel to freedom: "I will be there; as who I am shall I be there" (cf. §8.2). J. B. Metz argues that this self-naming should lead us to link the transcendent to the future: "God revealed himself to Moses more as the power of the future than as a being dwelling beyond all history and experience. . . . [God's] transcendence reveals itself as our 'absolute future' . . . this future calls forth our potentialities to unfold themselves in history."[77] Second, the idea of the "kingdom of God" runs throughout Israel's religious experience,

76. Cf. Craig Hill, *In God's Time: The Bible and the Future* (Grand Rapids: Eerdmans, 2002); Christopher Rowland, *The Open Heaven: A Study of Apocalyptic in Judaism and Early Christianity* (New York: Crossroad, 1982), 80, 135, 189.

77. J. B. Metz, "The Church and the World," in *The Word in History*, ed. T. Patrick Burke (New York: Sheed and Ward, 1966), 76.

and is taken up in the message of Jesus and the apostles. The rule of the God of peace is the future of the world, but this reign is not like earthly kingdoms: it is "ahead" of the community in a way that breaks into and shapes its "now," calling it into a proleptic share in the arrival of the "new." Third, the experience of the "face" of God also bears on the idea of the divine presence. The longing for the divine countenance, which brings grace and peace (Num. 6:24-26), structures the religious desire of Israel throughout its ancient history. From the origin of the nation itself in the call of Abram and his family to a promised land, the religion of Israel orients the people to this coming future in which the glory of God will dwell with them forever.

In the New Testament, the promising presence of God is radically reinterpreted in light of the experience of the incarnation of Jesus Christ and the outpouring of the divine Spirit.[78] The word *parousia* is helpful as an organizing concept here because it means both "presence" and "coming." The concept of *parousia* suggests a "coming" that already bears upon the present, a "presence" whose coming opens up a new future.[79] This expression highlights the New Testament experience of the revealing *(apokalupsis)* and appearing *(epiphaneia)* of God in Christ and through the Spirit — of a real presence that evokes hope in the coming God. The New Testament authors experienced God's promising presence in a way that wholly oriented them to the reception of new being in relation to the divine *parousia* that makes all things new.

Paul's interest is not in the *eschata* ("last things") but in the *eschatos;* i.e., the *"eschatos Adam"* who became "a life-giving Spirit" (1 Cor. 15:45). What matters to Paul is the "new creation" (Gal. 6:15), which has already begun in the life of the community; "see, everything has become new" (2 Cor. 5:17). He is not held captive by deterministic "elemental spirits" [*stoicheia*] of the universe (Col. 2:8, 20); he rejects the philosophical fatalism of his contemporaries. Paul describes the "one thing" that shapes his

78. N. T. Wright traces the continuities and discontinuities between the hope of Israel expressed in the Hebrew Bible, post-biblical Judaism, and the New Testament in *The New Testament and the People of God* (Minneapolis: Fortress, 1992), chap. 10; *The Resurrection of the Son of God* (Minneapolis: Fortress, 2003), part I.

79. For a philological analysis of the Greek term *parousia* and its impact on eschatological interpretation in the twentieth century, cf. *New International Dictionary of New Testament Theology*, 3 vols., ed. Colin Brown (Grand Rapids: Zondervan, 1975-1978), 2:898-935.

ministry: "forgetting what lies behind and straining forward to what lies ahead, I press on toward the goal" (Phil. 3:13-14). He interprets reality in light of the experience of the resurrected Christ, through whom the Christian now lives in the Spirit; this experience is not of a static timeless immaterial substance, but of the "power of futurity."[80] Paul draws his readers' attention to the future that is breaking into the present, to the presence of the Promising One who is coming so that they may be glorified with him along with all of creation (Rom. 8:10-25). Christian believers were called to focus wholly upon the risen Lord, whose *parousia* was at the same time both anticipated as a final fulfillment in which God will be "all in all" (1 Cor. 15:28) and also already experienced proleptically through the indwelling Holy Spirit who is its "pledge" (Eph. 1:14).

The early church was not obsessed with proving God's existence as the first cause of the world; its concern was pointing all people to the One who is the source of future (eternal) life and whose presence *(parousia)* offers a share in that life. They were consumed by a passion for participating in the reconciling activity of the One who is "making all things new" (Rev. 21:5). As believers they "look forward" to the mercy of Jesus Christ that leads to eternal life (Jude 21). They "are receiving" salvation as life in hope, anticipating a *koinonia* in divine glory (1 Pet. 1:9; 5:1). The book of Hebrews orients its readers toward the hope in the promise (e.g., Heb. 6:19; 11:1-2); their spirituality was not a dualistic separation from the material world, but "a future stance towards the promises of God lived out in the hurly-burly of the relationalities of everyday life."[81] It was this radical placing of metaphysical hope in the eschatological coming of God that marked off the Christian from her religious neighbors. Jesus promised his disciples the outpouring of the Holy Spirit, and after his resurrection and the day of Pentecost, their interpretation of the being and becoming of the cosmos is wholly centered around their experience of this promising presence.

The Gospels had also focused the attention of their readers on the future. This is evident already in the message of John the Baptist, who proclaimed that the kingdom of heaven is near; all his formidable energy was spent calling his hearers to repent as he pointed them toward the coming

---

80. Cf. Rudolf Bultmann, *Theology of the New Testament* (London: SCM, 1952), 38, 330, 335-36.

81. Anthony Thiselton, "Human Being, Relationality and Time in Hebrews, 1 Corinthians and Western Traditions," *Ex Auditu* 13 (1997): 76-95 at 81.

of one who will baptize not only in water but in the Holy Spirit. Jesus urges his hearers: "Beware, keep alert; for you do not know when the time will come" (Mark 13:33). The dialectic between present arrival and future coming is also expressed in Luke: on the one hand, the kingdom "has come [*ephthasen*] upon you" (Luke 11:20), but on the other hand, the disciples must look toward the future: "stand up and raise your heads, because your redemption is drawing near" (Luke 21:28). Jesus speaks of the "hour" which is in some sense "now here" (John 4:23), but also "coming" (5:25-29); a future is promised in which he will draw all people to himself (12:32). Jesus is already "present" where two or three are gathered in his name (Matt. 18:20), yet the early Christian community still anticipates a future intensification of this presence (24:39). In his first epistle, John incorporates both elements in the same verse: "And now, little children, abide in him, so that when he is revealed we may have confidence and not be put to shame before him at his coming [*parousia*]" (1 John 2:28). As we will see in Chapter 7, reflection on these biblical themes has contributed to the renewal of eschatological ontology in systematic theology.

The biblical, philosophical, and scientific developments explored here do indeed challenge the early modern theological research project. The multiplication of qualifications (e.g., distinctions within the divine essence, intellect, and will) eventually sabotages rather than salvages the usefulness of the categories of God as an immaterial substance, single subject, and first cause. However, our brief historical overview has also shown that there has always been a reciprocity between theology and contemporary concepts of matter, person, and (space) time, which affect our understanding of God and creation. Challenging particular early modern formulations is not in itself an attack on the gospel, any more than the Reformer's critique of the medieval Aristotelian categories, Thomas's revision of Neoplatonic categories, or Augustine's antagonism toward ante-Nicene philosophical assumptions. The task of caring for the living tradition, to switch metaphors, sometimes requires pruning in order to promote fresh growth. This is the only way to remain faithful in our own context to the call to be the church — reformed, always reforming, and being reformed. Our first step was facing the de-constructive challenges that indicate where re-construction might be needed. Our next step is to identify resources in the theological tradition that can help us in this ongoing task.

· PART II ·

TRAJECTORIES IN THE DOCTRINE OF GOD

· 5 ·

RETRIEVING DIVINE INFINITY

In the following three chapters we outline three late modern trajectories in the Christian doctrine of God: the retrieval of an intensive understanding of divine Infinity, the revival of a robust doctrine of the Trinity, and the renewal of eschatological ontology. Each of these trajectories provides a theological critique of one of the early modern categories in the doctrine of God. The order in which we will examine these themes is not necessarily the order in which they come to be known in religious experience, and most emphatically not an order of being. However, the arrangement does follow a pedagogical logic. Struggling with the idea of Infinity is an initiation into the adventure of *theology*. Articulating the doctrine of the Trinity is what marks off a theology as *Christian*. Affirming the gracious Futurity of the biblical God is what makes Christian theology *evangelical* — essentially good news.

The chapters of Part II begin by tracing particular ways of thematizing these ideas in the Christian tradition, each of which runs like an Ariadnian thread through church history, offering us the opportunity to escape the conceptual labyrinth of rational causative substance. The second and third sections of each chapter outline the proposals of several leading Reformed and Lutheran theologians of the twentieth century who have contributed to the recovery of these strands of the biblical tradition. Fourth, the ecumenical and reformative appeal of each of these themes is illustrated in the work of Roman Catholic, Eastern Orthodox, feminist, and liberation theologians. Drawing from these resources in the last section of each chapter, we clarify the meaning and significance of the categories of intensive Infinity, robust Trinity, and absolute Futurity. In Part III we will attempt to weave together these themes within a presentation of the gospel of divine knowing, acting, and being. Outlining these trajectories separately, however, will help to clarify the way in which they attempted to overcome the early modern theological reliance on the categories of immaterial substance, single subject, and first cause.

In this chapter we trace the retrieval of divine Infinity in late modern theological discourse. The idea of the infinite has always played a crucial role in the Christian doctrine of God, but our interest here is in articulations of the idea that attempted to avoid the problem of a spurious infinity. As we will see, the intuition that late modern thinkers referred to with the phrase "true infinity" (cf. §2.4) was expressed in various ways throughout the history of Christian theology. We are also interested in recovering the way the term "infinite" was used in contemplative theology. The existential intensity of being confronted by a "different greatness" led St. Francis and his followers to run "barefoot before an infinite God." In his prayerful struggle with the idea of Infinity, Augustine confesses that he had once believed that God was an infinite corporeal reality, extended infinitely in space. However, experiences of intensive contemplation eventually led him to cry out: "I awoke in Thee, and saw Thee to be infinite, though in another way [*infinitum aliter*]."[1]

This "other" way of imagining divine Infinity moves beyond the idea of God as a being that is simply extensively greater than creatures. Such a being would be caught in the dialectic of "more" or "less," in the tension between transcendence and immanence — either far from or close to other beings. The difficulty in expressing doctrines like the incarnation and regeneration within the categories of substance metaphysics led many early Christian theologians to resist placing God under the constraints of "substance" or "being." As Gregory Palamas insisted, "if God is nature, then all other beings are not that; and if any other being different from God is nature, he is not that, just as he is not a being if the others are."[2]

---

1. *Confessions*, VII.14; cf. I.7. NPNF1, I:111. Cf. *De Trinitate*, V.2: God is "great without quantity."

2. Palamas, *Physical, Theological, Moral and Practical Chapters* 78 [*PG* 150.1176B], quoted and translated by John Meyendorff, *A Study of Gregory Palamas* (London: Faith Press, 1964), 162.

God is not just *sui generis,* but beyond "generic" definition altogether. This chapter commends the retrieval of an intuition about Infinity that emerges out of this experience of a qualitatively different difference in which all differentiation whatsoever lives and moves and has its being. The Christian tradition has significant resources that may be (and have been) recovered for a reconstructive presentation of the truly infinite God of the Bible.

§5.1. Traditional Resources

Here we arrive at a basic distinction between the Christian understanding of the relation between divinity and Infinity and the view that dominated ancient Greek philosophy. Plato and Aristotle had linked existence and "form," and so they maintained a distaste for the idea of the infinite *(apeiron),* which they defined as that which is *without* form or limit (*a-peras*).[3] For both philosophers, the divine *(theos)* was linked to "form" (over against matter). These assumptions rendered it inappropriate and even impious to describe God as "infinite" (form-less), since God was taken to be pure form.[4] Relatively early in the Christian tradition this "negative" view of the idea of Infinity was rejected. Through reflection on the biblical ideas of creation, incarnation, and regeneration, a "positive" view of the infinite emerged: a "perfect" Infinity that is qualitatively distinct from the finite, yet encompasses, permeates and draws the finite into existence.

---

3. Cf. L. Sweeney, "Presidential Address: Surprises in the History of Infinity," in *Infinity,* ed. D. O. Dahlstrom et al. (Washington, D.C.: The American Catholic Philosophical Association, 1981), 7, 18; A. M. Wilson, *The Infinite in the Finite* (Oxford: Oxford University Press, 1995).

4. Not all ancient Greek philosophers held a negative view of infinity. Anaximander viewed the infinite as the primal reality that is the eternal basis and source *(Archē)* of being, and even hinted at its positive relation to divinity. Cf. Dirk L. Couprie, Robert Hahn, and Gerard Naddaf, *Anaximander in Context: New Studies in the Origins of Greek Philosophy* (Albany: SUNY Press, 2003). In the third century A.D. Plotinus also developed a more positive understanding of Infinity. As we saw in Chapter 2, however, the negative view remained a constant temptation in Western theology.

Infinity in Patristic Theology

The main point of the doctrines of simplicity and immutability was to warn against the placement of the divine essence under the categories of finitude and temporality. Early in the Christian tradition it became clear that any description of God in relation to the world must recognize that God is not merely one reality in relation to another (creation) but an absolute fullness that "contains" all things. In the second century A.D., St. Irenaeus expressed the issue in this way:

> For how can there be any other Fullness or Principle, or Power, or God, above Him, since it is a matter of necessity that God, the Plēroma of all these, should contain all things in His immensity, and should be contained by no one? But if there is anything beyond Him He is not then the Plēroma of all, nor does he contain all. . . . But that which is wanting, and falls in any way short, is not the Plēroma of all things. In such a case, He would have both beginning, middle and end, with respect to those who are beyond Him.[5]

Here limitlessness (in-finity) is understood not simply as a lack of limit, or indefinite extension, but as a metaphysical reality whose "immensity" embraces all things.

This insight is emphasized by representatives of both the Alexandrian and Antiochene schools. For Athanasius all things have their being "in" God, and this does not mean that God is composed of extensive parts; reflection on the incarnation leads to an understanding of God as both present in the whole of creation and as containing all things.[6] Theophilus of Antioch describes God as "the place *(topos)* of all things" and "place to himself."[7] God is not "placed" in relation to other things, but is the absolute origin of all placement. A true (or positive) understanding of Infinity allowed them to claim that all things are "in" God without also claiming that creaturely things displace part of God or become parts of God. It is precisely the intensive experience of the divine presence through the Word and Spirit that led to the philosophical criterion of true Infinity in Christian thought.

5. *Against Heresies*, II.1; ANF, I:359.
6. Athanasius, *Against the Heathen*, NPNF2, IV:19; cf. *Incarnation of the Word*, §17; NPNF2, IV:45.
7. *To Autolycus*, 2.3; ANF, II:95.

One of the most valuable resources mined for the retrieval of divine Infinity has been the fourth-century Cappadocian theologian St. Gregory of Nyssa.[8] He fought particularly hard against the dominant "negative" understanding of the infinite as form-less (or in-definite) in Greek philosophy. According to this negative view, the infinite cannot be known, since human reason "knows" a thing by defining its genus and differentiae (form). On these assumptions, to say that God is "infinite" would imply that God is unknowable. In order to buttress their apologetic efforts with the Greeks, a few Christian theologians were willing to say that God is finite — and so knowable by human reason. For example, Origen had accepted the negative Greek idea of infinity and suggested that if God were infinite then God would not have the power to know God's self.[9] This conception of infinity was still being championed in Gregory's day by Eunomius, who (following Aristotle) argued that it made no sense to posit an "unlimited" entity protracted to infinity. Such an entity could not be knowable in any case; God is known and therefore not "infinite."

In his refutation of Eunomius, Gregory explicitly attacks his "extensive" conception of infinity. Eunomius's idea of "limit" refers to beings that are "circumscribed in some quantitative way," but the divine nature has no quantity or extension and cannot be measured.[10] When Gregory turns to the issue of theological predication and the divine attributes, he observes that his adversary "laboriously reiterates against our argument the Aristotelian division of existent things, has elaborated 'genera,' and 'species,' and 'differentiae,' and 'individuals,' and advanced all the technical language of the categories for the injury of our doctrines."[11] Gregory clearly sees the role that the philosophical assumptions of predication theory are playing in Eunomius's attack on the doctrine of divine Infinity.

Gregory's *positive* view of Infinity as the all-embracing divine reality is intrinsically connected to the "apophatic" way in theology, which recognizes an overarching *negation* that covers all theological language. This appears ironic until we realize that both of these are part of a broader mystical approach to knowing God. The often-misunderstood apophatic (or "negative") way does not mean that we have no knowledge of God, but

---

8. Cf. Sarah Coakley, ed., *Re-thinking Gregory of Nyssa* (Oxford: Blackwell, 2003).
9. *De Principiis*, II.9.1; ANF, IV: 289.
10. *Against Eunomius*, IX.3; NPNF2, V:215.
11. *Against Eunomius*, XII.5; NPNF2, V:247.

that we do not know God the way we know finite things — by conceptually grasping their genus and differentiae. In his refutation of Eunomius, Gregory insists "that it is not possible that that which is by nature infinite should be comprehended in any conception expressed by words."[12] No appellation has the force to enclose God; the power of language cannot speak the unspeakable. True knowledge of God involves being known by God in the intensity of mystical or contemplative experience. In his book on *The Life of Moses*, Gregory links the ineffability of the divine to true Infinity:

> The divine by its very nature is infinite, enclosed by no boundary. If the divine be perceived as though bounded by something, one must by all means along with that boundary consider what is beyond it. . . . In the same way, God, if he be conceived as bounded, would necessarily be surrounded by something different in nature.[13]

For this reason, we cannot use language to "differentiate" God from other things in the way we distinguish finite natures.

True Infinity and apophaticism go together in the Eastern tradition. In one of the most influential theological texts of this genre, the mystical theologian Pseudo-Dionysius says that God "is the boundary to all things and is the unbounded infinity about them in a fashion which rises above the contradiction between finite and infinite."[14] The criterion of true Infinity is evident here. Vladimir Lossky argues that the apophatic method is a way of recognizing that the God of Christian revelation "transcends the opposition between the transcendent and the immanent."[15] It is not simply that God is beyond knowing; God is beyond the distinction between knowing and not-knowing. The concept of "being" cannot be used of God

---

12. *Against Eunomius,* III.5; NPNF2, V:146; cf. VII.4; NPNF2, V:198.

13. *Life of Moses,* trans. E. Ferguson and A. J. Malherbe (New York: Paulist Press, 1978), 115-16. For additional analysis of Gregory's understanding of infinity, cf. Robert S. Brightman, "Apophatic Theology and Divine Infinity in Gregory of Nyssa," *The Greek Orthodox Theological Review* 18, no. 2 (1973): 97-114; Everett Ferguson, "God's Infinity and Man's Mutability: Perpetual Progress according to Gregory of Nyssa," *The Greek Orthodox Theological Review* 18, no. 2 (1973): 59-78.

14. Pseudo-Dionysius, *The Complete Works* [*The Divine Names*], trans. Colm Luibheid (New York: Paulist Press, 1987), 103.

15. Lossky, *In the Image and Likeness of God* (Crestwood, N.Y.: St. Vladimir's Press, 1985), 29.

even in the opposition of being and non-being, because "God is not opposed to anything. . . . God therefore remains transcendent, radically transcendent by His nature, in the very immanence of His manifestation."[16] Although creatures cannot ascend the ladder of being (or language) to know the *essence* of God, they are already embraced by and are called to participate within the *energies* of God.[17]

Western theologians sometimes worry that the "negative" way is really saying nothing at all, or pretending to say nothing while actually making negative assertions. However, negative propositions (just like positive ones) may or may not be "apophatic." As Denys Turner explains, apophaticism "is the linguistic strategy of somehow showing by means of language that which lies beyond language. . . . For there is a very great difference between the strategy of negative propositions and the strategy of *negating the propositional.*"[18] The negation of the propositional is counterintuitive for many Western Christians raised in ecclesial settings that emphasized the salvific importance of assenting to propositions. Apophaticism does not mean that we have no use for propositions; they serve by orienting us and others to attend to God. Ultimately they serve best when we give up our desire to grasp and control, leaving propositions behind as we experience the intensity of the divine embrace in worship.

Infinity in Medieval Theology

The idea of Infinity continued to have a significant function in the Latin theology of the Middle Ages. It is embedded within the so-called "ontological" argument of St. Anselm of Canterbury. Setting aside for now (cf.

16. Lossky, *Orthodox Theology: An Introduction*, trans. Ian and Ihita Kesarcodi-Watson (Crestwood, N.Y.: St. Vladimir's Press, 1989), 23.

17. The Eastern distinction between the divine essence and energies is an attempt to maintain both the intuition that humans really experience the reality of God in revelation and the intuition that they are not able to grasp that which is beyond grasping — the "superessence" [*huperousiotēs*] of God, to use the term preferred by St. Gregory Palamas. Cf. Lossky, *Image*, 56; Thomas L. Anastos, "Gregory Palamas's Radicalization of the Essence, Energies, and Hypostasis Model of God," *Greek Orthodox Theological Review* 38, no. 4 (1993): 338; Duncan Reid, *Energies of the Spirit: Trinitarian Models in Eastern Orthodox and Western Theology* (Atlanta: Scholar's Press, 1997).

18. Denys Turner, *The Darkness of God: Negativity in Christian Mysticism* (Cambridge: Cambridge University Press, 1995), 34-35. Emphasis added.

§10.4 below) the issue of the fecundity of this argument as a "proof" for God's existence, our interest here is the underlying philosophical assumption about Infinity that underlies the *Proslogion*, written around the turn of the twelfth century.[19] It is clear from the contemplative form of the text and from explicit references (e.g., III, XXIV, etc.) that Anselm is operating out of a conception of God as Creator. In other words, it is the absolute distinction between Creator and creature that is guiding his theological imagination. Anselm begins with the idea of "that than which nothing greater *(maius)* can be thought" (II). God is also the absolute Good, through whom all things exist (V) and in whom all things are contained (XIX), so also that than which nothing better *(melius)* can be thought. God and "all things" cannot be placed into an equation. One does not achieve a greater sum by adding the world to God. If the creation of the world added greatness (or goodness), then God would not be "that than which nothing greater can be thought," for then something greater (or better) than God could indeed be thought: namely, God and the world together (as a new "whole"). The idea of a truly infinite reality that is beyond the creaturely distinctions of existence and goodness, precisely as their origin, helps Anselm make sense of his religious experience.

Later medieval scholastic theologians began to develop theories of the intensive infinite, which for many of them was the only proper sense of the term "Infinity."[20] Here they were following but expanding upon Augustine's distinction between greatness measured in terms of bulk (quantitative extension) and greatness with reference to intensive phenomena (qualities like heat or holiness). God is not infinite by extension but rather is the metaphysically limitless perfection of all (good) qualities. As we saw in §2.1, Descartes vacillated between these senses of "infinity," and his substance dualism made it difficult for him to resolve the tension. His medieval predecessors had worked hard to avoid this problem. In the early thirteenth century, Alexander Nequam insisted that the greatness of God is an "infinity of immensity" that transcends both quantity and intensity. In the

19. "Proslogion," in *Confessions of a Rational Mystic,* Latin with English translation by Gregory Schufreider (West Lafayette, Ind.: Purdue University Press, 1994), 106ff.

20. For a comprehensive survey of the medieval development of this phrase, cf. Anne Ashley Davenport, *Measure of a Different Greatness: The Intensive Infinite 1250-1650* (Leiden: Brill, 1999), especially chaps. 1 and 6; and Leo Sweeney, S.J., *Divine Infinity in Greek and Medieval Thought* (New York: Peter Lang, 1992), esp. chaps. 18 and 19. The following paragraph relies heavily on these two sources.

middle of the century, however, Richard Fishacre moved beyond Nequam's linking of infinity and immensity because immensity suggested spatial imagery and the notion of extension. For Fishacre, it is appropriate to speak of God as "infinitely intense" *(infinitum intensa)* insofar as we mean that all "pure perfections" are infinite in God. For example, we cannot double or triple *(ad infinitum)* creaturely goodness and eventually reach the infinity of divine goodness. Both of these thinkers, as well as most who followed them, were careful not to immunize the term "infinity" from the natural limits of all human language. Nevertheless, they struggled to use language in a way that made sense of this limitation.

Thomas Aquinas's treatment of the doctrine of Infinity is particularly informative for our purposes, because it illustrates the significant role of the distinction between Creator and creature in the work of a theologian who is otherwise heavily dependent on Aristotle. In *SCG* (I.43) Thomas affirms the ancient philosophers' recognition of the importance of infinity as a first principle but rejects their interpretation of it in terms of quantity or extension. Instead, he argues that divine Infinity has to do with spirituality and perfection. For Thomas, divine limitlessness does not have to do with the limitlessness of extension *(SumTh, I.7.1)*, but with the limitlessness of perfection, which is all-embracing and contains the perfection of all existing things *(SumTh, I.4.2)*.

Thomas also follows the patristics in his insistence that "we cannot know what God is, but only what he is not" *(SumTh, I.2.3)*, and that God is not determined by inclusion "in any genus" *(SCG, I.43; cf. SumTh, I.3.5)*. David Burrell argues that Thomas's insight, through which he transcended the dilemmas of Ibn-Sina and Maimonides, was that the distinction between God as Creator and creatures must be articulated in a way that avoids treating the distinction as merely one more distinction *in* the universe, like the other distinctions we finite creatures make.[21] This means that God should not be construed simply as one being different from other beings — God "differs differently."[22]

---

21. Burrell, *Knowing the Unknowable God* (Notre Dame, Ind.: University of Notre Dame Press, 1986), 17. Cf. his "Distinguishing God from the World," in *Language, Meaning and God,* ed. B. Davies (London: Geoffrey Chapman, 1987). Cf. Burrell, *Freedom and Creation in Three Traditions* (Notre Dame, Ind.: University of Notre Dame Press, 1993), 61.

22. Burrell, "Reflections on 'Negative Theology' in the Light of a Recent Venture to Speak of 'God Without Being,'" in *Postmodernism and Christian Philosophy,* ed. Roman T. Ciapalo (Washington, D.C.: The Catholic University of America Press, 1997), 58-67 at 63.

Debates over the expression of divine Infinity continued throughout the Middle Ages. Unlike his Dominican counterpart, St. Bonaventure approached the issue of Infinity in a way shaped by his Franciscan tradition, focusing on the unlimited spiritual yearning that was evoked by the divine presence. The redemptive experience of the truly infinite led him (like the other "little brothers") to renounce the worldly commodification of finite goods. Duns Scotus attempted to prove the existence of God as "infinite Being" by appealing to our experience of the "grades" of perfection, which presupposes (he believed) an "infinitely good" being. This gradation is not extensive, but intensive — he offers the illustration of "intense whiteness" wherein the "intensity is an intrinsic grade of whiteness itself."[23] Not surprisingly, William of Ockham rejected the subtle doctor's optimism about natural reason, arguing that we cannot prove that God is intensively infinite either by way of causality or eminence, or by appealing to divine cognition or simplicity (*Quodlibets*, VII.11-15).[24]

In the fifteenth century, Nicholas of Cusa would express the intuition that the difference between God and creatures is not a difference between two "others" by speaking of God as "Not-other."[25] This does not mean "not" other or not "other" or even "not the other." God as "Not-other" is before and beyond all otherness, all quantity, all opposition, and even all substance. Creaturely others are not "Not-other," but this assertion cannot be symmetrically reversed; the otherness of creatures is defined by God as "Not-other" but not vice versa. Reading this text one gets a sense that the contemplative experience of the presence of the Creator is guiding Nicholas's reflections on the inadequacy of language to embrace the all-embracing divine Infinity. As we will see below (§5.3), Lutheran theologians have also found a resource in Luther's own reflections on God as Creator as well as his recognition that even as *deus revelatus* God is also *deus absconditus*.[26]

---

23. *Opus oxoniense*, I.3.1; quoted and translated in *Duns Scotus: Philosophical Writings*, trans. Allan Wolter (Indianapolis: Hackett, 1987), 27.

24. William of Ockham, *Quodlibetal Questions*, trans. Alfred J. Freddoso and Francis E. Kelley (New Haven: Yale University Press, 1991), 622-43. It is interesting that Ockham's nominalist separation of language from metaphysics opened up the possibility for the explorations that would eventually result in Cantor's view of the Absolute Infinite (cf. §2.4).

25. *De li non aliud*, in *Nicholas of Cusa on God as Not-Other*, trans. Jasper Hopkins (Minneapolis: University of Minnesota Press, 1979).

26. For a comparison of Luther and Cusa, cf. F. Edward Cranz, "A Common Pattern in

John Calvin, whose life and work illustrate the continuity and discontinuity between the late medieval and early modern periods, clearly saw the importance of the philosophical concept of Infinity for Christian theology. In the *Institutes,* I.13.1, he explicitly states that the idea of God's Infinity "ought to make us afraid to try to measure him by our own senses." The spirituality and Infinity of God protect not only against Seneca's pantheism, in which God is "poured out into the various parts of the world," but also against Manichean dualism, which restricts God's Infinity by imagining good and evil as eternally warring principles. The Christian understanding of Infinity maintains both that God is "incomprehensible" and also "fills the earth itself." This is the intuition of the criterion of true Infinity, which emerges out of biblical revelation and experience.

The primary function of this intuition for Calvin is to banish "stupid imaginings" and to restrain "the boldness of the human mind." The previous two chapters of the *Institutes* had been devoted to a rejection of idolatry of any kind, including a literal interpretation of figurative biblical language about God. Scripture uses anthropomorphism in the "manner of the common folk," but the authors take it for granted that "all we conceive concerning God in our own minds is an insipid fiction" (I.11.1, 4). It is also worth noting that the first biblical passage quoted by Calvin in the *Institutes* (I.1.1) is Acts 17:28 — *in* God we "live and move and have our being." Calvin alludes to this passage six times in the four subsections that follow, emphasizing that God is present to and in all things in such a way that all things are in and to God. Calvin's instincts about the idea of divine Infinity were an inspiration to several systematic theologians who contributed to its retrieval in the twentieth century.

§5.2. Reformed Reconstructions

In this section we explore the contributions of three leading Reformed theologians to this trajectory: Karl Barth, Colin Gunton, and Jürgen Moltmann. These are not the only twentieth-century Reformed thinkers who have struggled to retrieve divine Infinity but they are some of the most influen-

Petrarch, Nicholas of Cusa and Martin Luther," in *Humanity and Divinity in Renaissance and Reformation,* ed. John W. O'Malley, Thomas M. Izbicki, and Gerald Christianson (Leiden: Brill, 1993), 53-72.

tial.[27] To varying degrees, they have taken advantage of the opportunities that have arisen from biblical and historical scholarship as well as from late modern philosophical and scientific discourse. As we will see in §6.2 and §7.2, these theologians also attempted (in different ways) to integrate a robust understanding of the Trinity and an eschatological ontology into their presentation of the doctrine of God. Our goal here is not to provide an exhaustive exposition or critical evaluation, but simply to illustrate the prominence of the retrieval of divine Infinity in the work of these scholars.

Karl Barth

The significance of divine Infinity in Karl Barth's thought can be traced back to his early *Epistle to the Romans*. In the preface to the second edition he responds to critics by explaining, "if I have a system, it is limited to a recognition of what Kierkegaard called the 'infinite qualitative distinction' between time and eternity, and to my regarding this as possessing negative as well as positive significance: 'God is in heaven, and thou art on earth.'"[28] This infinite *qualitative* distinction is the root of Barth's well-known insistence that God is "wholly other." The later Barth admitted that his early emphasis on the diastasis between God and humanity too easily led to an abstraction of God from concrete human experience. He recognized that we also need to speak of the "humanity of God."[29]

The claim that God is "wholly other" should not be taken to mean that God is a being over against creation. Barth urged his readers not to think of God simply as "the infinite," which is bound by definition to "the finite"; rather God is "completely different,"[30] both beyond and within the

27. For example, we might also have included theologians like Emil Brunner, who argues that the biblical experience of the incomparable "Name" of God fortifies the theological insistence on the Infinity of God. Theology does not grasp God as one "object" among many; it is concerned with the Absolute beyond all creaturely reality, which is its origin and aim. Cf. Brunner, *The Christian Doctrine of God,* trans. Olive Wyon (Philadelphia: Westminster, 1949), 63, 117-18.

28. Barth, *Epistle to the Romans,* trans. Edwyn C. Hoskyns (first German ed., 1919; London: Oxford, 1933), 10. This is reflected in his exposition of Paul as well: "The Gospel proclaims a God utterly distinct from men," 28; cf. 331.

29. Barth, *The Humanity of God* (Richmond, Va.: John Knox, 1960), 44-45.

30. Stacey Johnson suggests this translation of *ganz anders* better captures Barth's intention (*The Mystery of God: Karl Barth and the Postmodern Foundations of Theology* [Louis-

distinction between infinite and finite. He emphasized that this theolo-goumenon derives from the revelation of the divine Word in Jesus Christ, through whom we come to know that God is "for" us and "with" us, and from life in the Spirit by whose power God is "in" and "among" us. The importance of relationality for Barth is clear in his ongoing critique of ap-proaches to the doctrine of God that begin with an *analogia entis* (analogy of being or substance). He argued that Christian theology ought to begin instead with the categories of relation revealed in the incarnation. Barth's preference for an *analogia fidei*, which is an *analogia relationis*, is one of the more obvious illustrations of the impact of the philosophical (re)turn to relationality in late modern theology.[31]

In the *Church Dogmatics*, Barth implicitly accepts the criterion of true Infinity: God "is infinite in a manner in which the antithesis and mutual exclusiveness of the infinite and the finite . . . do not enclose and imprison Him. . . . The infinity which as a concept stands in antithesis to finitude . . . is quite insufficient to describe what God is in relation to space and time" (*CD*, II/1, 467). Any use of the term "Infinity" for God, Barth argues, must be used in a way that recognizes that it "is *true infinity* because it does not involve any contradiction that it is *finitude as well.*" Yes, God is infinite, but "*He is also finite* — without destroying, but *in his infinity* — in the fact that as love He is His own basis, goal, standard and law."[32]

In this context, Barth is treating the unity and omnipresence of God, and is explicitly rejecting the view of infinity as a comprehensive attribute of God held by "the older theology" (seventeenth-century theologians such as Gerhard and Wollebius). Barth hints at the problematic undercur-rent of what we have called mathematical or extensive infinity in these thinkers when he suggests we must avoid the idea of finite things as "drops in the ocean" of the infinite, for then this ocean is constituted by these fi-nite drops. Here Barth notes that such a concept of the infinite, as drawn into the dialectic of the world's antithesis, opens the way for Feuerbach's critique. Moreover, such a concept of the infinite would limit God to the "sphere" of the time-less and non-spatial. He perceives this danger in the

---

ville: Westminster/John Knox, 1997], 20). See also the comparison between Barth's theologi-cal method and Derrida's economy of *différance* in Graham Ward, *Barth, Derrida and the Language of Theology* (Cambridge: Cambridge University Press, 1995).

31. For an exposition of the regulative function of relationality in Barth's theology, see my *Reforming Theological Anthropology,* (Grand Rapids: Eerdmans, 2003), chaps. 6 and 7.

32. *CD*, II/1, 467-68. Emphasis added.

Protestant Scholastics and wonders how such a God could be loving and free in relation to creation (*CD*, II/1, 466).

Earlier in that volume, Barth had outlined his own proposal for expressing the reality of God: "The Being of God as the One who loves in freedom" (*CD*, II/1, §28). He was critical of formulations like *actus purus*, which made it difficult to think of God as loving or free. Instead, Barth insisted that God's being and God's act be thought together. Understood in trinitarian terms, God's love and God's freedom are the being of God. Barth recognized the need to avoid a naive metaphysical dualism between God and the world; we should not imagine heaven and earth as two spheres side by side that can be spanned by human language or thought. Barth insisted that God is known only through God's self-revelation, and only by God's gracious granting and overcoming of the distinction between Creator and creation. God is "indissolubly Subject," and human knowing of God is first of all an acknowledgment of being addressed by the Word of God, not the identification of an "object" in worldly experience. In the early- to mid-twentieth century, Barth's context demanded a strong reaction to the tendencies of modern liberalism that emphasized God's immanence in the world (for which he blamed Schleiermacher). Although the emphasis in Barth's works may have alternated between transcendence and immanence during his career,[33] his overall intention was to hold them in dialectical tension.

Colin Gunton

Three themes in the work of Colin Gunton are particularly illustrative of the retrieval of divine Infinity in twentieth-century theology. First, Gunton is one of the many critics of the ancient Greek (especially Platonic) dualism between the material and the immaterial that shaped much Christian anthropology and cosmology. He contrasts this to the view of the ancient Hebrews, in which the "spirit" is not equated to "mind" or "unchanging immaterial substance" but is a dynamic force in concrete lived existence. God's Spirit permeates and (to use one of Gunton's favorite

---

33. The continuity of Barth's dialectical method is outlined by Bruce McCormack in *Karl Barth's Critically Realistic Dialectical Theology: Its Genesis and Development, 1909-1936* (Oxford: Clarendon, 1995).

verbs) "enables" all of creation to become what it is called to be.[34] The point in Scripture is not that the human (immaterial) "spirit" has some direct access to a different ontological realm separated from "matter." What makes the difference, according to Gunton, is "the mysterious reality of spirit, which in the Bible is not opposed to matter, but in some way represents a qualification of matter."[35]

In light of the incarnation, Christian theology should not portray God as simply distinct from the material world but as embracing the material as well. Gunton is particularly critical of the Platonic stream of the Christian tradition that tended to equate "created" things with "material" things.[36] Gunton is also critical of the *modern* dualism between God and the world as simply the mirror image of the *ancient* dualism of Greek philosophy. He believes that the dualisms of Descartes and Kant led to a crisis in theology, which denigrated the material in different ways; he finds resources for overcoming dualism not only in the doctrines of creation and Trinity, but Christology as well. Rather than beginning with the separation between finite and infinite (as in dualistic philosophy), the logic of divine love disclosed in Jesus compels us to understand God "as being eternally in himself that relatedness to the other which actualizes itself in our history."[37]

This brings us to Gunton's second contribution — his enthusiasm for what I have called the theological (re)turn to relationality. Gunton blames Augustine's acceptance of Aristotle's privileging of the category of substance over the category of relation for the loss of the theological power of relationality, which had guided the work of the Cappadocian fathers. In "Relation and Relativity" he observes that Augustine had rendered the concept of relation "effectively redundant in theology" but that it returned "to transform science in the nineteenth and twentieth centuries" with the emergence of the concepts of fields of force and relativity theory.[38] In addition to exploring the scientific use of the category of relationality,

34. *The Triune Creator: A Historical and Systematic Study* (Grand Rapids: Eerdmans, 1998), 10, 234. Gunton explicitly accepts the apophatic nature of theological language (92).

35. *The Christian Faith* (Oxford: Blackwell, 2002), 42.

36. *Act and Being: Towards a Theology of the Divine Attributes* (Grand Rapids: Eerdmans, 2002), 47.

37. *Yesterday and Today: A Study of Continuities in Christology* (Grand Rapids: Eerdmans, 1983), 135.

38. "Relation and Relativity: The Trinity and the Created World," in *Trinitarian Theology Today*, ed. Christoph Schwöbel (Edinburgh: T&T Clark, 1995), 92-112 at 107.

Gunton also engages the late modern philosophical interest in refiguring the debate over the one and the many in light of the category of the "other." In both antiquity and modernity, he argues that we find dualisms that play the one against the many or the many against the one. Gunton calls for a new way of conceiving and practicing relationality that both accounts for the relatedness of all things to God and attends to the particularity of the disappearing "other."[39] Gunton illustrates the openness of theologians in this theological trajectory to relational thought-forms that provide new ways of engaging late modern anthropology and metaphysics, with an emphasis on relation-to-other. This will become even more evident when we look at his role in the revival of trinitarian doctrine in Chapter 6.

Third, Gunton stresses the "absolute ontological distinction" between God and the world. Here we can see the impact of Barth's emphasis on the "wholly other," which was evident already in Gunton's early theological work.[40] Although he does not explicitly treat the criterion of true Infinity, Gunton expresses concern that God and the world not be imagined either as dualistically separated (as in deism) or as monistically fused (as in pantheism). The latter is the real enemy of contemporary theology, according to Gunton, and for this reason he is willing to stress "ontological otherness" rather than risk the blurring of the boundaries between God and the world.[41] Creaturely freedom requires real space and time for creatures. Following the lead of Coleridge and others, Gunton sees the danger in "a concept of a unitary being which, by swallowing everything else into itself, left room for nothing else," and searches for a model of God that allows for, and gives space to, "the being of the other."[42]

The results of this search are most clearly laid out in *The Triune Creator,* where Gunton's goal is to outline a doctrine of creation that adequately maintains the ontological distinction between God and the world

---

39. *The One, the Three, and the Many* (Cambridge: Cambridge University Press, 1993), chaps. 1 and 2.

40. Gunton's doctoral dissertation at Oxford was the basis of his book *Becoming and Being: The Doctrine of God in Charles Hartshorne and Karl Barth* (Oxford: Oxford University Press, 1978). Cf. idem, *The Actuality of Atonement* (Edinburgh: T&T Clark, 1998), 109-12, 178.

41. See "Immanence and Otherness: Divine Sovereignty and Human Freedom in the Theology of Robert W. Jenson," chap. 7 in Gunton's *The Promise of Trinitarian Theology* (Edinburgh: T&T Clark, 1991), 135.

42. *The One, the Three, and the Many,* 24.

without collapsing into deism. However, one can trace a slow shift in Gunton's authorship from his stress on the internality of God's relation to the world in his early work on Christology[43] to a willingness to emphasize the externality of God from the world in his later treatments of the doctrine of God. "There are two realities, God and the world he has made, each what they are in their own proper sphere."[44] Here Gunton is struggling to protect against the danger of blurring the distinction between Creator and creation, a danger he finds in the work of other theologians in this trajectory such as Jenson and Moltmann.

Jürgen Moltmann

While Gunton is worried about the loss of divine transcendence, Moltmann is more concerned about the loss of divine immanence. For him the real enemy of theology is a stark separation of God from the world, which has contributed to the exploitation of nature and human "others." The driving force of his *God in Creation* is his desire to maintain both the presence of God in the world and the presence of the world in God. The infinite God dwells in finite creation, and the finite creation finds space in God, who is the "dwelling place" of the world.[45] Moltmann is aware that this requires a different difference. "Without the difference between Creator and creature, creation cannot be conceived of at all; but this difference is embraced and comprehended by the greater truth which is what the creation narrative really comes down to, because it is the truth from which it springs: the truth that God is all in all."[46]

43. In his treatment of the incarnation, he speaks of a co-presence in space and time, the "spatial co-presence of the finite and the infinite" (*Yesterday and Today*, 116). "The world is what it is through the operation of the spatially omnipresent divine field of force. In Jesus Christ we see the outcome of the self-differentiation of the divine omni-spatiality" (118).

44. *The Christian Faith* (Oxford: Blackwell, 2002), 11. Cf. *Act and Being*, 47.

45. *God in Creation*, trans. Margaret Kohl (San Francisco: Harper & Row, 1985), 13, 148. Relationality is also central to Moltmann's understanding of creation itself. Against Leibniz's windowless monads, he argues that "every monad has windows. In actual fact, it consists only of windows" (17).

46. *God in Creation*, 89. Moltmann is aware of the dangers of pantheism but does not want this anxiety to hinder the insights of "true pan-entheism." Cf. "What God Would He Be Who Came Only from Outside . . . ?" in his *History and the Triune God* (New York: Crossroad, 1992), 164.

Moltmann recognizes the importance of the relation between the finite and the infinite for this discussion. Initially the concept of the infinite God suggests that *finitum non capax infiniti* (the finite cannot contain the infinite). This makes it difficult to think of God as "in" the world in any meaningful sense. Moltmann argues that the ancient Hebrews' testimony to the presence of the Shekinah glory in the temple and to the divine *ruach* among the people of Israel, as well as the New Testament witness to the outpouring of the Spirit on (and indwelling of) the community of believers, suggest that somehow the finite is able to contain the infinite *(finitum capax infiniti)*. In the broader context of a trinitarian and eschatological understanding of the God-world relation, Moltmann argues *infinitum capax finiti:* the infinite contains the finite. He believes this approach allows him to maintain both biblical intuitions: the world is in God and God is in the world.[47]

Moltmann's contribution to this trajectory is intimately connected to his Christology. The claim that the doctrine of God cannot be abstracted from the event of the cross, through which God is revealed as a suffering God, is the overriding concern of *The Crucified God.* If the death of Jesus really says something about God, this requires a "revolution" in the concept of God.[48] The cross is also connected to his acknowledgement of the apophatic nature of theological language; human knowing does not define God, for "a God understood conceptually would be a far-off God, an absent God, a dead idol which we 'grasped.'"[49] God is known through the Son and the Spirit because of the divine kenosis, which in Moltmann's view is a limiting of the omni-attributes. He believes the only options are either that the finite world sets a limit to the infinite God or that God limits Godself. The former makes no sense: "If this limit or frontier between infinity and finitude is already 'fore-given' to God, then God is not infinite."[50] For

---

47. Moltmann, "The World in God or God in the World?" in *God Will Be All in All: The Eschatology of Jürgen Moltmann,* ed. R. Bauckham (Edinburgh: T&T Clark, 1999), 35-42 at 39-40. The triune God is inherently living fellowship, and this life is "open for the uniting of the whole creation with itself and in itself." Cf. *The Trinity and Kingdom,* trans. Margaret Kohl (Minneapolis: Fortress, 1993), 96. The importance of Trinity and Futurity for understanding Infinity will become more clear in §6.2 and §7.2 below.

48. *The Crucified God: The Cross of Christ as the Foundation and Criticism of Christian Theology,* trans. R. A. Wilson and John Bowden (New York: Harper & Row, 1974), 201-2.

49. *Experiences in Theology* (Minneapolis: Fortress, 2000), 169.

50. "God's Kenosis in the Creation and Consummation of the World," in *The Work of Love: Creation as Kenosis,* ed. John Polkinghorne (Grand Rapids: Eerdmans, 2001), 145.

Moltmann, it is only by God's gracious self-limitation that the limit or frontier between infinite and finite exists. Elsewhere he spells this out in terms that are explicitly trinitarian — "the *outward incarnation* presupposes *inward self-humiliation*" of the trinitarian life.[51] His eschatology also shapes his linking of Infinity and the incarnation: in Christ we find a new paradigm for transcendence — the qualitatively new future that is present under the conditions of history but also alters these conditions. God is not merely "wholly other" but "what makes wholly other."[52]

Finally, the doctrine of the Holy Spirit is also central to Moltmann's way of understanding the relation between God and the world. The Spirit is the immanent source of life, but "source" in a sense that aims to uphold true Infinity: "the divine becomes the all-embracing presence in which what is human — indeed everything that lives — can develop fruitfully and live eternally."[53] Moltmann connects the Spirit to Israel's experience of the Shekinah — the glory of God that is present with God's people even in suffering and exile. Building on the kabbalist concept of zinzum, Moltmann argues that creation is the contraction or self-limiting of the infinite God; "God makes room for creation by withdrawing his presence."[54] This also affects his ecclesiology. On the basis of the biblical language of the mutual "indwelling" of the church and the Spirit, Moltmann describes the latter as the "broad place," the field of force, the reality in which the church exists and is given new life.[55] This understanding of the Spirit impacts his view of immanence and transcendence: "Christ's Spirit is our immanent power to live — God's Spirit is our transcendent space for living."[56] It is already clear that the ideas of Trinity and Futurity have shaped these Reformed reconstructions of the doctrine of divine Infinity. The convergence of these three trajectories is also evident in the proposals of leading theologians from other traditions.

---

51. *Trinity and Kingdom*, 119.

52. Moltmann, "The Future as a New Paradigm of Transcendence," in his *The Future of Creation* (Philadelphia: Fortress, 1979), 11.

53. *The Source of Life*, trans. Margaret Kohl (Minneapolis: Fortress, 1997), 12.

54. *God in Creation*, 87.

55. *The Church in the Power of the Spirit*, trans. Margaret Kohl (New York: Harper & Row, 1977), chap. 2.

56. *The Spirit of Life*, trans. Margaret Kohl (Minneapolis: Fortress, 2001), 43, 179. "In the experience of the Spirit, God is primal, all-embracing presence, not a detached counterpart" (195).

§5.3. Lutheran Reconstructions

While we could trace the theme of true Infinity in the work of several Lutheran theologians of the twentieth century,[57] we will limit ourselves to three: Robert Jenson, Eberhard Jüngel, and Wolfhart Pannenberg. These thinkers are particularly fruitful for our purposes, because each of them has contributed to all three of the late modern trajectories and has engaged in broader ecumenical dialogue on these issues.

Robert Jenson

The philosophical and theological criterion of true Infinity is explicitly affirmed by Jenson in his *Systematic Theology*: "the false infinite is that defined merely by negation of the finite, that is not-finite and so after all bounded by the finite, and so itself after all bounded, that is, finite. To be true, infinity must embrace also the finite."[58] In dialogue with Gregory of Nyssa and Thomas Aquinas, who in different ways stressed that God's essence and existence are identical, Jenson observes that "infinite-being cannot be something other than its own infinity, for were it *some*thing, it would just thereby be marked off from other things and would have a boundary, a *finis*, which is what 'infinite' denies" (*ST,* 1:215). Unlike Colin Gunton, Jenson is willing to use "language designed to blur the boundary between God and creature" (*ST,* 1:225). Although he worries about the way that nineteenth-century theology blurred that line (cf. *ST,* 2:41), he seems more worried that Barth's emphasis on transcendence threatens the real relation of God to, with, and in creatures. Leaning toward this side of the dialectic leads him to make statements that appear to threaten the "otherness" of cre-

---

57. For example, Paul Tillich argued that "Being-itself [the Being of God] is beyond finitude and infinity; otherwise it would be conditioned by something other than itself"; cf. *Systematic Theology,* 3 vols. (Chicago: University of Chicago Press, 1951-1963), 1:237. Humans are limited to finite categories such as substance and causation, and so cannot grasp the infinite — although like all creatures they participate in it as Being-itself (cf. 2:7). In *The Courage to Be* (New Haven: Yale University Press, 1952), Tillich insists that "theism" must be transcended insofar as its God is "a being beside others and as such a part of the whole of reality" (184).

58. *Systematic Theology,* 2 vols. (Oxford: Oxford University Press, 1997, 1999), 1:220 n. 64. Abbreviated as *ST* in the following paragraphs.

ation. For example, he approvingly quotes Jonathan Edwards' claim that all actual events are "done immediately by God" (*ST,* 1:44). Several contributors to his Festschrift expressed the concern that God and the world are linked too closely in his theology.[59] However, it is important to recognize that Jenson does want to claim (like the others in the trajectory) that there is a creaturely reality that is "really other" than God.[60] God presumably could have been God on terms other than in relation to the world, but about this sheer contrafactual "we can say nothing whatever" (*ST,* 1:65).

One of the most distinctive aspects of Jenson's doctrine of God is his appropriation and radical refiguring of Barth's linking of divine being to act or "event" rather than to "substance." His metaphysical revisioning articulates the infinite being of God in explicitly temporal terms; God's eternity is "*temporal* infinity." For Jenson, the statement "God is what happens between Jesus and his Father in their Spirit" is a "fundamental statement of God's being" (*ST,* 1:221). Both the appropriation and the refiguring of Barth are evident already in two of his early monographs. Jenson wants to speak of God as "an event, a happening," but he rejects the way in which Barth tries to maintain the freedom and transcendence of God "over against what he is for and with us."[61] He believes that Barth failed to follow through his own suggestion to its radical end. Jenson takes this up as his own project, developing the theme in *Story and Promise:* "By 'God,' the gospel means whoever and whatever it was that raised Jesus from the dead. Thus the specificity also of God is an historical specificity."[62] The focus on dynamic event rather than static substance continues in his *Systematic Theology.* In fact he describes "the whole argument" of that work as depending on moving "from the biblical God's self-identification *by* events in time to his identification *with* those events" (*ST,* 1:59). While Jenson ap-

---

59. See *Trinity, Time, and Church: A Response to the Theology of Robert W. Jenson,* ed. Colin Gunton (Grand Rapids: Eerdmans, 2000). This complaint is most explicit in Douglas Knight's chapter on the role of "time" in Jenson's theology, but also underlies the responses of Gabriel Fackre (on the Lutheran *capax*), Colin Gunton (on "mediation" in creation), and even James Buckley's overwhelmingly positive analysis of the character of Jenson's theology as "intimacy."

60. Jenson, "Aspects of a Doctrine of Creation," in *The Doctrine of Creation,* ed. Colin Gunton (Edinburgh: T&T Clark, 1997), 17-28 at 27.

61. *God After God: The God of the Past and the God of the Future, Seen in the Work of Karl Barth* (Indianapolis: Bobbs-Merrill, 1969), 153. Cf. Jenson's earlier analysis of Barth in *Alpha and Omega: A Study in the Theology of Karl Barth* (New York: Nelson, 1963).

62. *Story and Promise* (Philadelphia: Fortress, 1973), 6.

preciates the christologically oriented move toward an *analogia relationis,* it remains "analogy" and so is Barth's way of "leaving a loophole for God's transcendence."[63]

Jenson's understanding of divine Infinity is mutually implicated by other aspects of the doctrine of God, especially his attempts to reconstruct the theological ideas of Trinity and Futurity. For example, Jenson describes creaturely time and space as a "distention" within the triune God; they are created by God's making room for us in the eternal fugue of the trinitarian life. "To be a creature is to be in a specific way bracketed by the life of the triune persons" (*ST,* 2:25). Again, "the Son mediates the Father's originating and the Spirit's liberating, thereby to *hold open* the creatures' space in being" (27). We will explore these aspects of Jenson's doctrine of God in the following chapters, so it will suffice here to point to the way in which his event-oriented understanding of the God-world relation leads him to treat the "attributes" of God. At the heart of Jenson's method is an attempt to overcome the abstract definition of God apart from God's relations, and so it is understandable that he is critical of the seventeenth-century Lutheran distinction between "absolute" and "relative" attributes. He also recognizes that developments in the theory of language, which recognize its creative function, frees us from struggling with classical theology to find a precise number of definite attributes for the divine substance. For Jenson, Christian theology does make two types of "attributions," but both have to do with the claim of the gospel that "Jesus is risen." One type of attribute explains the meaning of the predicate while the other type clarifies the historicity of the subject of that claim.[64]

Eberhard Jüngel

In an influential 1969 essay Jüngel attempted to provide a philosophical and theological alternative to the Aristotelian distinction between potentiality and actuality as the metaphysical basis for the doctrine of God's relation to the world. In the Aristotelian scheme, the divine was on one side of the distinction between the actual and the not-yet-actual; i.e., pure actuality over

---

63. *God After God,* 154.

64. Jenson, "The Attributes of God," in *Christian Dogmatics,* 2 vols., ed. Carl Braaten and Robert Jenson (Philadelphia: Fortress, 1984), 1:184-91.

against the potential. Jüngel argued that a more fundamental distinction is disclosed by the event of justification and the resurrection of the dead — the distinction between the possible and the impossible. This distinction is more fundamental because it has to do with the distinction between being and nothingness; for this reason it concerns the relation between God and the world. However, even here God is not on one side of this distinction; rather, as "the one who distinguishes the possible from the impossible, God distinguishes himself from the world." God is beyond the distinction between possibility and impossibility; God is "equiprimordially both." In other words, "God *is* and his being is in becoming."[65] Thinking through the metaphysical implications of the doctrine of justification is a key part of Jüngel's theological project. In his book on *Justification,* he argues that the event that constitutes the justification relation between God and humanity cannot be separated from the question of the being of God.[66]

The implications for the doctrine of God are more expansively treated in Jüngel's *God as the Mystery of the World.* He argues that we should speak of God as "more than necessary" because the concept of necessity is tied to the concept of possibility. Here he is guided by the intuition of true Infinity. "Mere endlessness does not merit being called infinity, but rather that being which constantly overcomes its own end and its own boundaries should, with good reason, be called eternally unending being."[67] A simple distinction that sets God's being over against the world is unacceptable, for this would mean God's being is "another world," and the distinction would be merely between two (very) different worlds. Jüngel's goal is to make room for thinking and speaking of God in relation to the world in a way that maintains the distinction but overcomes the dualism. He observes that the rise of early modern atheism was made possible by Cartesian dualism. However, modern "theism" is not the answer, for it too was forged with the same philosophical categories.

65. "The World as Possibility and Actuality: The Ontology of the Doctrine of Justification," in Jüngel, *Theological Essays,* trans. J. B. Webster (Edinburgh: T&T Clark, 1989), 95-123 at 112. Cf. Jüngel, *God's Being Is in Becoming: The Trinitarian Being of God in the Theology of Karl Barth,* trans. John Webster (Grand Rapids: Eerdmans, 2001).

66. *Justification,* trans. J. Cayzer (Edinburgh: T&T Clark, 2001), 46.

67. *God as the Mystery of the World: On the Foundation of the Theology of the Crucified One in the Dispute between Theism and Atheism,* trans. Darrell L. Guder (Grand Rapids: Eerdmans, 1983), 223 n. 70. For an extended discussion of Hegel's treatment of and Feuerbach's response to "true" infinity, see 69ff.

Jüngel argues that to overcome this aporia we must speak (and think) of both "God" and "thought" in a new way. The point of *Christian* talk about God, he suggests, is not simply that God is *above* the contradiction between being and not being, but also that God is God "*in the midst* of this contradiction."[68] Rather than trying to use traditional forms of analogy to cross from the finite to the infinite, Jüngel proposes an "analogy of advent," which "expresses God's arrival among men [sic] as a definitive event." But when *God* is one of the members of the analogy, the relationship appears in a new light, "in a light which *makes* this world-relationship *new*, an eschatological light."[69] Speaking of God becomes possible as we recognize the presence of an absolute reality that cannot be manipulated by the human ego.

God is experienced in God's coming to the world, as an arrival into human life and language — the "*very great distance away* of the eschatological kingdom of God is surpassed by a *still greater nearness.*"[70] If God is simply above or beyond us, then God has nothing to do with us,[71] and so Jüngel emphasizes that the Infinity of God cannot be thought apart from the cross. He also appropriates Luther's emphasis on the dialectic between the *deus revelatus* and the *deus absconditus.* God is not simply invisible over against the visible, but present as the absent one. Conversely, God's apparent invisibility is not construed in terms of an absent God, "but as events in which God *as the absent One* is *present.*"[72] Through the history of the Crucified One, it becomes clear that God does not need an ontological theology to protect the divine being from "perishability"; in Christ's death God is subjected to death and overcomes it.

In the theistic metaphysics that has dominated some streams of the Christian tradition, God (the infinite) and perishability (the finite) are held in tension as opposites. Jüngel urges us to hold them together in a way that does not think of God's being "as infinite in contrast with every finitude." Rather, we should maintain the biblical intuition that God's being in

68. *Mystery,* 26, 35.

69. *Mystery,* 285. Here we begin to see how his understanding of God's infinite difference is mutually implicated in his understanding of Trinity and Futurity.

70. *Mystery,* 295. His emphasis.

71. Cf. Jüngel, "Quae supra nos, nihil ad nos," *Evangelische Theologie* 3 (June 1972): 197-240.

72. Jüngel, *The Freedom of a Christian,* trans. Roy A. Harrisville (Minneapolis: Augsburg, 1988), 32.

"heaven" does not preclude God's identification with the man Jesus on earth.[73] Jüngel regrets the unfortunate early Protestant distinctions between (for example) God's absolute and relative attributes. This approach to the doctrine of God is problematic because it obscures the claim that in God's relation to us we really have to do with the reality of God. He suggests that the analogy of "advent" can help us speak of *all* of God's attributes as shared (or communicable). Because speaking of God is made possible by God's arrival in the event of the justifying address of the divine promise, the ascription of attributes to God has no other function than giving expression as exactly as possible to the God who is love.[74]

Wolfhart Pannenberg

The concept of divine Infinity is an important theme for Pannenberg's overall theological project, which aims to understand God and all things under the aspect of their relation to God *(sub ratione Dei)*.[75] Like several others we have observed in this trajectory, his view of the Infinity of God is mutually implicated within a broader matrix of concerns that include the doctrines of Trinity and Futurity. In a discussion of the revival of trinitarian doctrine, Pannenberg explains that "God could not be conceived as *truly infinite* in distinction from His finite creatures, if He only were transcendent. In that case He would be limited by His being separate from the world and precisely by its distinction from God the world would then become constitutive of the very identity of His being God."[76]

Throughout his work, Pannenberg has also insisted that the relation between God and the finite (that which "exists") be expressed in terms of the coming divine reign. His (in)famous statement that in a sense "God does not yet exist" is found in this context: "The God of the coming rule is

---

73. *Mystery*, 209. Cf. his *Death: The Riddle and the Mystery*, trans. Iain and Ute Nicol (Philadelphia: Westminster, 1974), 108-9.

74. Cf. Jüngel, "Thesen zum Verhältnis von Existenz, Wesen und Eigenschaften Gottes," *Zeitschrift für Theologie und Kirche* 96, no. 3 (September 1999): 405-23 at 418.

75. For analysis of Pannenberg's *Grundprinzip*, see my book *The Postfoundationalist Task of Theology: Wolfhart Pannenberg and the New Theological Rationality* (Grand Rapids: Eerdmans, 1999), chap. 3.

76. Pannenberg, "The Christian Vision of God: The New Discussion on the Trinitarian Doctrine," *The Asbury Theological Journal* 46, no. 2 (Fall 1991): 35.

related to all that is finite and is the power determining the future of all that is present."[77] In some of his earliest articles, Pannenberg identifies the dangers of the ancient Greek definition of God over against the finite (material) world. He argues that the distinctively Christian understanding of God insists that divine freedom is beyond such distinctions: the biblical God is the "creative source of the ever new."[78] As we will see in the next two chapters, Pannenberg attempts to fill out the formal criterion of true Infinity materially by speaking of the trinitarian life of God, and by applying it also to the relation between eternity and time.

We will limit ourselves here to the two most significant treatments of true Infinity in his corpus. The first may be found in the essays within his *Metaphysics and the Idea of God*.[79] In "The Problem of the Absolute" Pannenberg traces the development of the philosophical concept of the finite and the infinite with special attention to Descartes, Kant, and Hegel. He agrees with Descartes that reflection on the finite presupposes the idea of the infinite, but this idea is initially unthematized — not "clear and distinct" (27). Pannenberg argues that Kant's understanding of infinity was too dependent on Aristotle, which made it impossible for him to think together the infinite and the divine (33). Pointing to patristic and medieval theologians like Gregory of Nyssa and Duns Scotus, for whom the infinite is that which has no other outside itself, Pannenberg hints that Enlightenment theology missed an opportunity to retrieve these resources. He agrees with Hegel's arguments about the criterion of "true" Infinity, which moves beyond the mathematical to the metaphysical, and about the importance of the concept of Spirit for its resolution. However, he disagrees with Hegel's way of using the concept in relation to a "Subject," suggesting instead that we spell out true Infinity in terms of the reciprocal relations among the eternal trinitarian persons (40).

---

77. *Theology and the Kingdom of God* (Philadelphia: Westminster, 1969), 56.

78. "The Appropriation of the Philosophical Concept of God as a Dogmatic Problem of Early Christian Theology," in Pannenberg, *Basic Questions in Theology II*, trans. George H. Kehm (Philadelphia: Fortress, 1971), 138. Essay originally published in 1959.

79. *Metaphysics and the Idea of God*, trans. Philip Clayton (Edinburgh: T&T Clark, 1990). Page numbers in this paragraph refer to this text. In addition to dealing with the philosophical turn to relationality, Pannenberg has also engaged the developments in physics and other sciences that open up new ways to overcome the ancient and early modern dualism between spirit and matter. For example, cf. Pannenberg, *Toward a Theology of Nature: Essays on Science and Faith* (Louisville: Westminster/John Knox, 1993), 65-66, 126ff.

Another essay in the same collection deals with the categories of "part" and "whole" and their significance for theology. For Pannenberg, God should not be conceived either as the "whole" of what exists finitely (i.e., the totality of finite parts), nor as one of the "parts" of the whole. In either case, God would be defined as a something in distinction to an "other." He argues that theology must think of God not as part of the whole or even as the unified unity of the whole, but rather as the "unifying unity" of the whole and its parts. "As the unifying unity of the world, God is distinct from the totality of the finite, though again not absolutely distinct. . . . God is indeed necessarily distinct from it [the totality]. Yet at the same time, he is just as necessarily immanent to the world of the finite . . . as the continuing condition of its unity" (143).

Pannenberg's major treatment of the idea of Infinity appears in volume 1 of his *Systematic Theology*.[80] He is critical of the early theological interpretation (by Origen among others) of the idea of God as Spirit in terms of mind. He argues that this is overly influenced by Platonic and Aristotelian conceptions of the divine (382). Pannenberg also wants to begin with the claim that "God is Spirit" (John 4:24), but spells this out both in terms of the divine essence as the infinite field of divine life and in terms of the "person" of the Holy Spirit who stands in relation to the Father and the Son. This allows him to account for another biblical assertion, "God is love" (1 John 4:8). By linking the two, Pannenberg aims to articulate the doctrine of God in a way that is consonant with the criterion of true Infinity.

Pannenberg organizes his treatment of all of the divine attributes around these two Johannine assertions: "the statement that God is love will prove to be the concrete form of the divine essence that is initially described as Spirit and in terms of the concept of the infinite" (396). In the case of divine "holiness," he argues that "the holiness of God is truly infinite, for it is opposed to the profane, yet it also enters the profane world, penetrates it, and makes it holy" (400). He would prefer to speak of God as "holy" other rather than "wholly" other. Pannenberg explicitly applies the criterion of true Infinity to the attributes of omnipresence and omnipotence as well, which means that they too are expressed in trinitarian terms. The perichoretic life of the persons of the trinitarian God manifested in the

---

80. *Systematic Theology*, 3 vols., trans. G. W. Bromiley (Grand Rapids: Eerdmans, 1991, 1994, 1998). Page numbers in the following paragraphs refer to volume 1.

economy of salvation "proves to be the true infinity of his omnipresence" (415). God's power (omnipotence) should not be construed as a power in antithesis to others who have power for then it would be finite. The almighty power of the Creator affirms "what is opposite to it in its particularity, and therefore precisely in its limits" — affirms it "unreservedly and infinitely," granting the creature the opportunity to "participate in infinity" (422).

§5.4. The Ecumenical and Reformative Appeal of Divine Infinity

Given the significant resources for retrieving divine Infinity in the patristic and medieval periods, it should not be surprising that some of the most important twentieth-century reconstructions of the doctrine have been produced by theologians deeply rooted in the Eastern Orthodox or Roman Catholic traditions. I have selected John Zizioulas and Karl Rahner as illustrations of reconstructive proposals from these traditions not only because of their influence within their own churches but also because they have both actively engaged in ecumenical dialogue. Further, most of the Protestant theologians we have just reviewed have also interacted with the work of these thinkers. This suggests that the retrieval of divine Infinity has an ecumenical appeal that may help us overcome some of the barriers that hinder Christian unity.

Liberation and feminist theologians who are interested in challenging the hegemony of particular (finite) political structures that control the life and thought of the church find an ally in the biblical intuition of the Infinity of God. The unmanipulable divine presence promises (or threatens, depending on one's perspective) to break into these structures and transform the way we measure "greatness." I argued in Chapter 1 that the process of reforming theology should include the attempt to articulate and practice theology in a way that *reforms* us. Reformation occurs not only in conceptual space, but also in the practical and liturgical space of lived Christian existence.

Karl Rahner

For Rahner the idea of divine Infinity is intimately connected both to Christology and to the doctrine of creation. The incarnation of the Logos reveals something about every relationship between God and creatures: "that closeness and distance, or being at God's disposal and being autono-

mous, do not vary for creatures in inverse, but rather in direct propor-
tion."[81] In other words, God's relation to the world is not based on the
contrast between close and far that characterizes extensive finite relations.
For creatures, God is present through a "mediated immediacy" that is unlike any other mediation or immediate relation. For this reason, Rahner
sees God's incomprehensibility and mystery not as something overcome
by revelation; rather, revelation *is* the experience of the "hidden God."[82]

Like many of his Protestant counterparts, Rahner resists the abstract
formalism of the division between the absolute (or metaphysically necessary) attributes of God and the attributes of God's redemptive and gracious relation to the world.[83] As with Calvin, the idea of Infinity also helps
Rahner avoid the forced options of pantheism or dualism. Pantheism fails
to recognize that the distinction between the ineffable infinite and the finite is not simply a distinction that we make, but the "*one and original* distinction that is experienced . . . the condition which makes possible all distinguishing." The problem with dualism, which underlies some popular
forms of "theism," is that it simplistically places God and creation as two
things alongside each other. According to Rahner, "the difference between
God and the world is of such a nature that God establishes and is the difference of the world from himself, and for this reason he establishes the
closest unity precisely in the differentiation."[84]

The regulative and constitutive function of true divine Infinity is also
clearly illustrated in Rahner's pneumatology and anthropology. In *Spirit in
the World,* Rahner appropriates and refigures Thomas Aquinas's understanding of the God-world relation. Along with Thomas, he insists that the
"darkness of ignorance" is the highest knowledge of God. However, Rahner
articulates the conditions for this knowledge in terms of the human experience of openness to the infinite, which is openness in and to the Spirit. Human spirituality exists as an orientation toward the absolute infinite; this
excessus to the Absolute *(esse)* is constitutive for human knowledge.[85] His

---

81. *Foundations of Christian Faith,* trans. William Dych (New York: Crossroad, 2000),
226. Cf. "On the Theology of the Incarnation," *TI,* 4:105-20 at 117.

82. "The Hiddenness of God," *TI,* 16:127-44.

83. "Observations on the Doctrine of God," *Theological Investigations,* 20 vols., trans. C.
Ernst et al. (London: Darton, Longman and Todd, 1961-1979), 9:127-44 at 136 (hereafter *TI*).

84. *Foundations,* 62.

85. Rahner, *Spirit in the World,* trans. W. Dych, S.J. (New York: Herder & Herder, 1968),
186-87.

reliance on the categories of phenomenology, such as intentionality, rather than the category of substance is evident in his attempt to overcome the simple dualism between material and immaterial that shaped early modern theology after Descartes. He argues that a sentient knower is a being that is "material" but expresses a "first and specific kind of immateriality" because its determination as an intention is linked to "its *intensity* of being."[86]

Rahner suggests that the Infinity of the divine Spirit is manifested in creaturely experience as the absolute "Whither" of human transcendence. Even if it is not consciously expressed, this dynamic experience of openness presupposes the "primordial distinction" between absolute being and all other beings; this is why God cannot be "defined" the way finite things are.[87] Human persons find themselves confronted with an infinite horizon. All of their conscious experience is grounded "in a pre-apprehension [*Vorgriff*] of 'being' as such, in an unthematic but ever-present knowledge of the infinity of reality."[88] As we will see in the next two chapters, Rahner also believes that the theological use of the concept of Infinity should be spelled out in relation to the doctrine of the Trinity and the idea of God as the absolute future.

John Zizioulas

"*God and the world cannot be ontologically placed side by side as self-defined entities.*"[89] This warning comes as part of John Zizioulas's summary of what he calls the "christological" approach of the Greek patristic theologians. For the Cappadocian fathers, especially Gregory of Nyssa, the emphasis on the *diastema* between God and the world is intended to signify the utter difference between the Creator's and creatures' modes of existence. Zizioulas also adopts the apophatic intuition of the tradition, which is based on the recognition that the difference between the truly infinite God and the finite world cannot be comprehended within the normal functioning of linguistic differentiation. Like many of the others in the trajectory, Zizioulas is concerned with the relation between humanity and the

86. *Spirit,* 371.

87. "The Concept of Mystery in Catholic Theology," *TI,* 4:36-73 at 51.

88. *Foundations,* 33.

89. John Zizioulas, *Being as Communion* (Crestwood, N.Y.: St. Vladimir's Press, 1997), 94; his emphasis.

rest of creation. He too has engaged the discoveries of natural science, embracing the radical relational implications of the theories of (for example) Darwin and Einstein, which have challenged the facile dichotomy between substance and event.[90]

Zizioulas's way of expressing the doctrine of creation, however, is shaped by the categories of his Eastern Orthodox tradition, especially the distinction between the divine "essence" and "energies," and the idea of creaturely participation *(theosis)* in the life of God. Orthodox theology aims to articulate doctrine in a way that remains intimately linked to the context out of which it emerges — liturgical participation within the life of God. In light of the experience of the Eucharist, the simple distinction between "supernatural" and "natural" is overcome; God is not merely "beyond" the world but present through the personal mediation of divine love.[91] For Zizioulas, the doctrine of God as truly infinite Creator serves to emphasize that the existence of created being is not a necessary emanation from the divine, nor a fashioning of the cosmos out of preexistent matter. All creaturely being is wholly dependent upon its infinite Origin, which is not an abstract "substance" but the "communion" of the trinitarian persons.

This is the driving intuition of his *Being as Communion*. For Zizioulas, the basis of God's relation to the world, and of God's very essence, is not an abstract "nature" (or "substance") but the personhood of the Father, who eternally shares the divine being in communion with the Son and the Spirit. If the source of all created being is the Father, whose identity is constituted through relations of communion with the Son and Spirit, this means that "to be" and "to be related" cannot be separated. Zizioulas credits St. Athanasius with the transformation of the idea of substance in light of the revelation of God in the Son. "To say that the Son belongs to God's

---

90. Cf. Patricia A. Fox, *God as Communion: John Zizioulas, Elizabeth Johnson, and the Retrieval of the Symbol of the Triune God* (Collegeville, Minn.: Liturgical, 2001), chap. 3. For a discussion of the resources of Eastern theology for dialogue with contemporary science, see Alexei V. Nesteruk, *Light from the East: Theology, Science and the Eastern Orthodox Tradition* (Minneapolis: Fortress, 2003). B. P. Vysheslavtsev argues that Christianity should respond to Marxist materialism not with an opposing spiritualism, but with its own unique view of the sublime, revealed in Christ, which elevates the material through its own humiliation (*The Eternal in Russian Philosophy,* trans. Penelope V. Burt [Grand Rapids: Eerdmans, 2002], chaps. 3 and 6).

91. Cf. Zizioulas, "La vision eucharistique du monde et l'homme contemporain," *Contacts: Revue française de l'orthodoxie* 19 (1967): 83-92 at 86-87.

substance implies that substance *possesses almost by definition a relational character.*[92] Elsewhere Zizioulas is explicit that Athanasius's contribution to Christian ontology involved an overcoming of the Aristotelian distinction between "primary" and "secondary" substance, which had hindered (and continues to hinder) coherent articulation of the doctrine of the Trinity.[93] As we will see in the next two chapters, Zizioulas's understanding of the doctrine of God is shaped not only by the revival of trinitarian voices but also by the renewal of eschatological ontology. Our purpose here has been simply to identify his retrieval and refiguring of the patristic emphasis on divine Infinity as one more resource for the contemporary task of reconstructing the doctrine of God in a way that engages the late modern philosophical turn to relationality.

Feminist and Liberation Reconstructions

The reformative force of the retrieval of divine Infinity has been evident throughout the preceding analysis, but it is important to make it explicit. This is most easily done by pointing to its appeal among theologians who challenge conceptions of divine transcendence that allow or support political oppression. In her book on *God and Creation in Christian Theology: Tyranny or Empowerment?* Kathryn Tanner distinguishes between "contrastive" and "non-contrastive" accounts of divine transcendence. In the former, God's transcendence and involvement with the world "vary inversely." When divinity is defined in direct contrast to "certain sorts of being" or to the world as a whole, God is "brought down to the level of the world and the beings within it in virtue of that very opposition: God becomes one being among others within a single order."[94] Non-contrastive accounts, she argues, open up space for understanding the divine presence as empowering rather than the tyranny of One against the others.

Elizabeth Johnson approaches the issue by exploring the nature of theological language about God. She attempts to retrieve the classical emphasis on the unobjectifiability of God, noting that sometimes exclusively

---

92. *Being as Communion*, 84; his emphasis. Cf. Athanasius, *Contra Arianos*, I.20, 33; II.2.

93. Cf. Zizioulas, "On Being a Person: Toward an Ontology of Personhood," in *Persons — Divine and Human*, ed. Colin Gunton (Edinburgh: T&T Clark, 1991), 33-46.

94. Kathryn Tanner, *God and Creation in Christian Theology: Tyranny or Empowerment?* (Oxford: Blackwell, 1988), 45.

male symbols for God have been reified in a way that inhibits an emphasis on God as incomprehensible mystery. "The experience of women today provides a powerful catalyst for reclaiming this classic wisdom as an ally in emancipating speech about God."[95] An emphasis on the true Infinity of God can have a prophetic function by challenging the privileging of particular linguistic idols among those who have a vested interest in controlling and "objectifying" the other, both human and divine.

Liberation theologians have expressed similar concerns. In *A Theology of Liberation* Gustavo Gutiérrez argues that the function of theology should no longer be limited by the early modern focus on rational knowledge, or even by the patristic emphasis on spirituality and contemplative wisdom. These dimensions of the theological task are important and necessary, but should be incorporated within an approach to theology as "critical reflection on praxis."[96] This formal concern, which is attentive to the power and limits of human language, is linked to material concerns in theology such as the doctrine of salvation. Although he does not use the term "true" or "intensive" Infinity, Gutiérrez believes that the biblical experience of the "intensity of the presence of the Lord" requires us to develop a *"qualitative and intensive* approach" to the doctrine of salvation, rather than a *"quantitative and extensive"* model.[97]

Resources for the retrieval of true divine Infinity may also be found in theologians who are working out of contexts that implicitly utilize communitarian and relational categories. For example, Timothy Njoya resists the aloof and irresponsible God of "missionary" Christianity and argues that the indigenous Christianity of Africa takes the incarnation more seriously. God's "finitization into a form of existence" reveals that God is distinct and free from "existence" but grants it its own "discontinuity" without losing God's "divine identity."[98] Another factor here is the importance of the experience of the Spirit in the emergence of Pentecostal churches worldwide, which tend to resist any attempts to control this incomparable presence — even through language, which may partially explain the enthusiasm for

---

95. Elizabeth Johnson, *She Who Is: The Mystery of God in Feminist Theological Discourse* (New York: Crossroad, 1997), 112.

96. Gutiérrez, *A Theology of Liberation* (Maryknoll, N.Y.: Orbis, 1988), 3-12.

97. *Theology of Liberation*, 84; his emphasis.

98. Timothy Njoya, "Conversion, Incarnation, and Creation: The New Context in African Theology," in *Revolution of Spirit: Ecumenical Theology in Global Context*, ed. Nantawan Boonprasat Lewis (Grand Rapids: Eerdmans, 1998), 171-86 at 182.

glossolalia. These developments open up opportunities for discourse across traditions and make room for the voices of many who have not been included in the conversation about the doctrine of God over the centuries. This suggests that the retrieval of divine Infinity will remain a trajectory that appeals to those concerned with the reformation of the church.

§5.5. Intensive Infinity

The adjective "intensive" has surfaced several times in our survey of the challenges to early modern categories and the retrieval of divine Infinity. All theological concepts have their limits, but the idea of intensive Infinity commends itself in our context for several reasons. First, it encourages us to avoid discussing the attributes of God merely in "extensive" terms, which so easily leads to the mathematical and quantitative conceptions that characterized the "negative" view of infinity in ancient philosophy. Moreover, it helps us to maintain the intuition that God is not reducible to material substance, which motivated the theological adoption of the category of immaterial substance, while providing a better safeguard against the temptation to grasp the Creator with creaturely definitions. The concept of intensive Infinity also serves to remind us of the intensity of religious experience out of which theological formulations arise and to which they attend. The exploration of the conceptual space of the doctrine of God ought not to be quarantined from the practical and liturgical space of lived Christian community.

The philosophical turn to relationality provides theology with the opportunity to liberate the idea of Infinity from its entrapment within substance metaphysics, which tries to force a choice between dualism (two substances) and monism (one substance). When the only options appeared to be Descartes or Spinoza, the Western tradition almost always leaned toward the former, stressing divine transcendence. If we accept the horns of this dilemma, any theological emphasis on divine immanence is then suspect of pantheism. The danger is real on both sides. A basic intuition of Christian faith is that God as Creator is distinct from and yet related to creation. On the one hand, if divine substance is really tied to creaturely substance, then God's freedom and majesty are threatened. On the other hand, protecting God's substance from the world by isolating it on one side of a harsh dualism might be too overprotective.

A God who is not intimately related to our time and space seems existentially irrelevant, unconnected to concrete religious praxis. Part of the problem may be the way in which the terms "transcendence" and "immanence," which became increasingly popular in English-speaking theology after the nineteenth century, are used to depict the God-world relation. On this model, the more one emphasizes God as transcendent immaterial substance, the less one can make sense of God's immanent relation to our substantive material lives.

Cartesian anxiety lives on in many Christians who cannot make sense of their redemptive experience of God within the confines of these early modern categories. Speaking of the intensive Infinity of God may help us escape this false dichotomy that hardened during the Enlightenment. However, the theological use of "intensive" should not be defined simply as the qualitative in opposition to the quantitative in the human experience of phenomena, as it was in Kant's first *Critique*. This would fail to uphold the criterion of true Infinity. The intensively infinite presence of God is "not" extensive, but we must go on to say that this non-extensivity is due to the divine encompassing and conditioning of all finite experience, quantitative and qualitative.

The resources we have outlined in this chapter may be critically appropriated as we respond reconstructively to the late modern philosophical interest in alterity as well as to postfoundationalist meta-mathematics and linguistics. As we have seen, the recovery of insights from the biblical tradition about true Infinity actually contributed to some of these late modern developments. However, our appropriation must be *critical*. Can we emphasize divine Infinity in a way that challenges substance dualism without falling into the opposite extreme of monism? In an attempt to avoid swinging the pendulum all the way to pantheism, several contemporary theologians have articulated versions of pan-*en*-theism: all things are *in* God. This view is particularly popular among participants in the global theology-and-science dialogue.[99] In this chapter we have observed several examples of orthodox Christian theologians who have emphasized the biblical idea that creatures are in some sense "in" God (cf. §2.5). However, the history of the use of the term panentheism is sufficiently ambiguous that we should hesitate before utilizing it in contemporary theological discourse.

---

99. Cf. Philip Clayton and Arthur Peacocke, eds., *In Whom We Live and Move and Have Our Being: Panentheistic Reflections on God's Presence in a Scientific World* (Grand Rapids: Eerdmans, 2004).

Perhaps the most serious theological concern about contemporary panentheist proposals is the common use of the relation between the mind and the body as an analogy for the relation between God and the world, which obscures the trinitarian nature of God. On this model, the early modern category of God as "single subject" continues to structure the discussion, further complicating theological engagement with a-theism. In Christian theology, the doctrine of the Trinity and divine Infinity must be intimately held together (along with Futurity). After setting out all three trajectories in Part II we will attempt to weave them together in Part III.

At this stage, the key point to observe is that the idea of true Infinity itself calls out for articulation in intrinsically relational terms. A true idea of Infinity would contain within itself the conditions for the differentiation of the finite from the infinite and their relational unification. We need a concept of the Absolute that is essentially relational, an eternal being-in-relation that constitutes the finite by distinguishing it from the infinite, incursively upholding the structures of the finite and evocatively opening up the finite to an intensification of its differentiated union with the infinite. This brings us to the doctrine of the Trinity.

· 6 ·

REVIVING TRINITARIAN DOCTRINE

W e turn now to another late modern trajectory in the doctrine of
God: the revival of the doctrine of the Trinity. Among the three trajectories, this is the most well-known and thoroughly documented.[1] In
Chapter 3 we outlined some of the developments in philosophy, science,
and biblical scholarship that have contributed to the surge of interest in
the doctrine of the Trinity. Our purpose in this chapter is to identify classical and contemporary resources for the ongoing reconstructive task of theology. Speaking of a "revival" of the Trinity is not meant to imply that the
doctrine had died. However, ancient and early modern concepts of "person" had so constricted the doctrine that it often appeared moribund. The
trinitarian imagination had certainly lost its generative power in some
streams of theological discourse during the Enlightenment. As we have
seen, the concept of God as a single subject, whose essence is identical to
the divine intellect and will, was increasingly subjected to philosophical
and theological challenges — in relation both to the internal coherence of
the idea and to its implications for God's relation to evil and the human

---

1. For an introduction to this revival see Ted Peters, *God as Trinity: Relationality and
Temporality in Divine Life* (Louisville: Westminster/John Knox, 1993); and Stanley J. Grenz,
Rediscovering the Triune God: The Trinity in Contemporary Theology (Minneapolis: Augs-
burg Fortress, 2004). For general introductions to the history of the doctrine see Roger
Olson and Christopher Hall, *The Trinity* (Grand Rapids: Eerdmans, 2002); Gerald O'Collins,
S.J., *The Tripersonal God: Understanding and Interpreting the Trinity* (New York: Paulist,
1999).

experience of freedom. These difficulties contributed to the rise of deism and a-theism.

After the turn to relationality, however, many theologians have responded to these challenges by allowing the doctrine of the Trinity to play a more robust role in the generative process of reconstructing theology. As with the retrieval of divine Infinity, the voices most commonly recovered in the twentieth-century revival of trinitarian doctrine have been theologians in the tradition who struggled to reconstruct dominant philosophical categories (like substance, person, and cause) in light of the relational forms of thought and practice essential to Christian faith. In most of the major contributors to the resurgence of the doctrine of Trinity we will find a preference for the Cappadocian fathers over Augustine, and for Luther and Calvin over the Protestant Scholastics. This trajectory has been guided by a growing sense that many classical trinitarian voices have not been sufficiently heard in Western theology.

§6.1. Traditional Resources

Risking oversimplification, we may observe several distinctions between the typically Eastern and typically Western approaches to the doctrine of the Trinity.[2] The early church had insisted that God is *three* persons and *one* essence. The orthodox theologians of every stream of the tradition have struggled to maintain both aspects of this doctrine. However, as we saw in §§3.1-2, the West preferred psychological analogies for the personhood of God. This way of buttressing the unity of the divine essence sometimes made it difficult to make sense of the claim that God is three persons. Eastern theologians, however, were often more comfortable with iconic and linguistic depictions of the sociality or communion of the three persons. Many Western theologians worried that this compromised the unity of God.

The East tended to emphasize the idea that the Father is the font (or

---

2. In the late nineteenth century, Théodore de Régnon developed what became an influential typology for differentiating between the classical treatments of the doctrine of Trinity in Eastern and Western theology. Cf. *Etudes de théologie positive sur la Sainte Trinité*, 3 vols. (Paris: Retaux, 1892-1898). Like any typology, it does not capture all of the intricacies and complexity of the differentiation between the East and West. Cf. Michel René Barnes, "Augustine in Contemporary Trinitarian Theology," *Theological Studies* 56 (1995:) 237-50. However, such distinctions can serve as a heuristically helpful starting point.

source) of divinity, a formulation that sometimes led to the charge of sub-ordinationism (the Son and Spirit not being fully divine). On the other hand, the heresy that tempted more Western theologians was modalism (God is one person, with three modes of appearing). Protecting divine unity by appealing to the idea of God as a single subject required the development of a conceptual formulation that could make distinctions among the three persons. One popular attempt to resolve this problem in the West was the doctrine of *appropriation:* all divine acts *ad extra* are undivided, but we may nevertheless "appropriate" particular acts to each of the persons (e.g., incarnation to the Son). The emphasis on the three persons in the East had to be balanced by a way of accounting for the unity of God. One popular way to accomplish this was with the doctrine of *perichoresis,* which claimed that the persons of the Trinity subsist in the unity of their dynamic relations in and through and to one another. Engagement with the East, which is not without its own conceptual problems, has played a significant role in the revival of the doctrine of the Trinity in the West.[3]

Patristic Voices

We can hardly overemphasize the centrality of the Trinity during the first millennium of the Christian church. Before the debates over trinitarian terminology that led to Nicea, most of the early church fathers were mainly concerned to express the relations between the Father, Son, and Holy Spirit in a way that made sense of the shape of salvation revealed in Scripture and experienced in Christian life.[4] This was the case in both their apologetic and their catechetical efforts, which were more integrated than they often are today. For example, Justin Martyr's (d. 165) arguments against the popular Greek philosophers of his time included discussions of the relations among the Father, Son, and Spirit, which were manifested in the structure of Christian worship and baptism.[5]

---

3. Duncan Reid traces the interaction between these traditions in several key twentieth-century theologians in *Energies of the Spirit: Trinitarian Models in Eastern Orthodox and Western Theology* (Atlanta: Scholars Press, 1997).

4. For a historical review of the development of the Christian doctrine of Trinity cf. J. N. D. Kelly, *Early Christian Doctrines* (San Francisco: HarperSanFrancisco, 1978); G. L. Prestige, *God in Patristic Thought* (London: Heinemann, 1936).

5. *First Apology,* 13, 61; ANF, 1:166, 183.

Irenaeus was more concerned about heretics than non-Christian philosophers. Like Justin, he was comfortable at this early stage with simply
referring to the one God as Father as Jesus himself did.[6] However, Irenaeus
clearly emphasized the eternal relationality of the Father, Son, and Spirit,
insisting that with the Father of all things "were always present the Word
and Wisdom, the Son and the Spirit, by whom and in whom, freely and
spontaneously, He made all things. . . ."[7] For Irenaeus all things are created,
upheld, and oriented by God — but this redemptive agency is always mediated by the two "hands" of God, the Son and the Spirit. This means that
his whole cosmology, soteriology, and anthropology are interpreted first
and foremost in trinitarian terms.

An important first step in the evolution of the terminology of the doctrine of the Trinity occurred in the work of Irenaeus's younger contemporary, Tertullian, who introduced the Latin term *trinitas* (to refer to God)
and applied the term *persona* to the Father, Son, and Spirit.[8] He also applied
the term *substantia* to the Godhead, and the orthodox formula for the
Christian doctrine of God became: three persons, one essence. Broadly
speaking, the Latin terms *substantia* and *persona* were reciprocally translated by the Greek terms *ousia* and *hypostasis*. The problem was that not everyone agreed on the meaning of these terms, and their semantic range
shifted during the debates that characterized the next few centuries. For our
purposes the important point is that many of the key contributors to the
doctrine of the Trinity worked hard to refigure these philosophical terms in
ways that expressed the divine essence as robustly relational. The divine essence *is* the dynamic relations of the persons in and through one another.

How to express this Christian doctrine was the driving question that
led to the formulation of the Nicene Creed (325 A.D.), which was expanded
at Constantinople (381 A.D.) and confirmed at Chalcedon (451 A.D.). "We
believe in one God, *the Father* Almighty, maker of heaven and earth. . . .
And in one *Lord Jesus Christ,* the only-begotten Son of God . . . of one substance *(homoousios)* with the Father, through whom all things were
made. . . . And in the *Holy Spirit,* the Lord and Giver of life. . . ." It is significant that the articles of this ecumenical creed are expressly trinitarian in
structure. Among its champions was Athanasius, who fought against the

---

6. *Adversus Haereses,* IV.1.2; ANF, 1:463.
7. *Adversus Haereses,* IV.20.1. ANF, 1:487.
8. *Adversus Praxeam,* 8, 12; ANF, 3:603, 606.

Arian heresy, which subordinated the *ousia* of the Son (and Spirit) to the *ousia* of the Father. For Athanasius, the one Godhead is "in a Triad" and as the perfect eternal divine essence this "must have been eternally so." The triadic relations are not added to the one divine essence; rather "we confess God to be one through the Triad."[9]

The voices of the fourth-century Cappadocian fathers are among the most important of those recovered in the twentieth-century revival of trinitarian doctrine. Although they disagree among one another and are often internally inconsistent, their value for our purposes is primarily in their willingness to engage and refigure the philosophical concepts of their culture as they struggled to articulate the intuitions of the New Testament and their experience of redemption. In this chapter our main interest is in the way in which the concept of "person" was understood relationally. Although the Latin term *persona* could mean "mask," this was not the case for the Greek term *hypostasis*, which simply meant a subsistent thing. As this latter term was connected to *prosōpon* (person, face) in the hands of the Cappadocians, it came to have an intrinsically relational meaning in the doctrine of Trinity. This contributed to an understanding of the Father, Son, and Spirit as perichoretically united in and through their dynamic mutual relations.

This relational, dynamic concept of "person" led Gregory of Nyssa to resist the use of Aristotelian substance-oriented categories in the doctrine of God. In Nyssa's *On 'Not Three Gods'* this is explicit. When he does use the categories of general and particular ("man" as common to "Luke" and "Stephen," etc.), his purpose is to get his readers *not* to think of the "Godhead" as a nature *(ousia)* with three particular instances *(hypostases)*, for this would entail tritheism (three "gods"). We cannot "name" the ousia or the hypostases of God in the same way we define and speak of creaturely essences and particulars. Our theological appellation signifies not "nature" but "operation," and this divine operation (which remains incomprehensible because of its true Infinity) in relation to creation "has its origin from the Father, and proceeds through the Son, and is perfected in the Holy Spirit."[10]

The concept of cause is also refigured in personally dynamic terms.

---

9. *Discourses against the Arians*, I.18, III.15; NPNF2, 4:317, 402.

10. *On 'Not Three Gods,'* NPNF2, 5:333-34. Gregory of Nazianzus and Basil of Caesarea are more willing than Nyssa to use the Aristotelian categories; cf. Nazianzus, The Third Theological Oration, *Orat.* 29.13, NPNF2, 7:305; and Basil, *Letter to Count Terentius*, NPNF2, 8:254.

Nyssa does not use the term cause *(aition)* to refer to the efficacious relation between substances, but to indicate a manner of existence — the essential communal *relations* among the persons of the Father, Son and Spirit. Divine "causation" is intensely personal and not abstracted from the relations of the persons of the Trinity.[11] In his Third Theological Oration ("On the Son"), Gregory of Nazianzus avoids the forced alternative of his adversaries, who want him to say that the name "Father" applies either to an essence or to an action. It applies to neither, "most clever sirs," he replies, but "it is the name of the *Relation* in which the Father stands to the Son, and the Son to the Father."[12] It is easy to see why so many twentieth-century theologians have found the Cappadocians to be valuable resources for the articulation of the doctrine of the Trinity after the philosophical turn to relationality, which shaped the contemporary social scientific understanding of persons as being-in-relation.

Medieval and Reformation Voices

The central significance of the doctrine of the Trinity is evident throughout the early Middle Ages. When John of Damascus summarizes the orthodox faith in the seventh century, he devotes most of the chapters in Book I to the exposition of the mystery of the Trinity and Unity of God, leaving a treatment of the divine attributes to the last chapter.[13] Distinguishing themselves from their interlocutors, whether Jewish, Muslim, or Arian, the theologians of the early Middle Ages continued to struggle against the logical implications of the claim that God is *a* person. The consensus that the Christian God is three persons and one essence is consistently affirmed. The question was not *whether* God is three persons but *how* the persons are relationally united. The generative power of the doc-

---

11. NPNF2, 5:336. Divine causality is personal and embraces creation dynamically. Cf. *On the Spirit*, 26.38; NPNF2, 8:23. We should think "of the original cause of all things that are made, the Father; of the creative cause, the Son; of the perfecting cause, the Spirit . . . the first principle of existing things is One, creating through the Son and perfecting through the Spirit."

12. NPNF2, 7:307; emphasis added. Nyssa, too, argues that "Father" signifies the "relation" to the Son in *Against Eunomius*, II.2; NPNF2, 5:102-3, and his Letter 38 (wrongly attributed to Basil); NPNF2, 8:140.

13. *De Fide Orthodoxa*, Book I; NPNF2, 9:17.

trine of the Trinity was so significant — conceptually, practically, and liturgically — that debates over its formulation led to the great schism of 1054 A.D. between East and West. This controversy was fueled largely by the debates over the Western addition of the *filioque* ("and the Son") clause to the original Nicene Creed: does the Spirit proceed only from the Father or also from the Son? Ecumenical dialogue on this point in the twentieth century has also contributed to the revival of trinitarian doctrine.[14]

The importance of the dialogue with Eastern Orthodoxy should not obscure the fact that Western theology also offers significant resources for the revival of trinitarian doctrine. In his twelfth-century treatment of the Trinity, Richard of St. Victor argued that a plurality of divine persons follows logically from the idea of divine goodness and charity.[15] If one divine person exists, who is absolutely good and loving, then this person must express this loving goodness in relation to another divine person, who in turn must be equal in worth (*De Trinitate,* III.2). This duality would not be supremely perfect, he argues, for the most excellent love, the fullness of goodness, must also share the excellent joy of its mutual love (III.11). We stop at three persons because of divine revelation (III.14). While Richard's argument has been criticized for the way it begins with an individualistic concept of person, the motivation behind his efforts provides us with a helpful model: his treatment of the Trinity is immersed within his broader concern for facilitating spirituality. As with his other writings, his purpose here is to invite his readers to share in the good, loving, and joyful life of the trinitarian persons through the contemplative life.[16]

In both the East and the West, some of the most important resources for the revival of trinitarian doctrine are found in mystical or contemplative theology. The dynamic life of the Trinity is implicit not only in the practice of following the way of Christ in the Spirit, but also in the Christian experience of prayer. For example, Pseudo-Dionysius's *The Mystical Theology* begins with this exclamation: "Trinity!! Higher than any being, any divinity,

14. For example, Ralph del Colle, *Christ and the Spirit: Spirit-Christology in Trinitarian Perspective* (New York: Oxford, 1994); David Coffey, *Deus Trinitas: The Doctrine of the Triune God* (New York: Oxford, 1999).

15. *Richard of St. Victor: The Twelve Patriarchs, The Mystical Ark, Book Three of the Trinity,* trans. Grover A. Zinn (New York: Paulist Press, 1979).

16. For additional examples of the resources of mystical theology for reviving the doctrine of Trinity, and reconnecting theology and spirituality, cf. Mark A. McIntosh, *Mystical Theology* (Oxford: Blackwell, 1998).

any goodness! Guide of Christians in the wisdom of heaven! Lead us up beyond unknowing and light." The mysteries of God, whom we name as three persons, ultimately lie "in the brilliant darkness of a hidden silence" and fill "our sightless minds with treasures beyond all beauty."[17] The trinitarian structure of the divine life is naturally linked to the way of contemplation, since knowledge of God occurs in the Spirit and through the Logos.

The trinitarian voice of the liturgy has never been completely silenced in the life of the church. This is due in part to the fact that the sacramental practices of the church, especially Baptism and the Eucharist, are implicitly trinitarian. Even in the seventeenth century, when the doctrine of the Trinity was not always at the center of theology, it was at the heart of worship. It may have seemed to be "bones to philosophy" but it was "milke to faith."[18] The doxology sung today in many Reformed churches, "Praise God, from whom all blessings flow. . . . Praise Father, Son and Holy Ghost," was derived from the 1674 hymn "Awake, My Soul." In most of the liturgical forms of the Roman Catholic church, the focus is on calling worshippers into the relational life of the triune God.[19] In Eastern Orthodoxy, many icons unabashedly represent a tri-personal God, and the trinitarian shape of salvation is expressed in the liturgy itself.[20]

In spite of the problems we have observed in the formulations of Augustine and Thomas Aquinas, particular emphases within their treatments of the Trinity may also be recovered for a contemporary relational doctrine of God. Both of these theologians were deeply influenced by Greek substance metaphysics, but seemed to realize that ultimately these categories broke down in reference to the persons of the Trinity. For example, in *On the Trinity* (V.5.6), Augustine makes it clear that things said about God "according to relation" are not "accidental." He recognizes the dissimilarity

---

17. Pseudo-Dionysius, *Complete Works* (New York: Paulist, 1987), 135.

18. For a historical overview and liturgical examples, cf. Philip Dixon, *Nice and Hot Disputes: The Doctrine of the Trinity in the Seventeenth Century* (London: T&T Clark, 2003), chap. 1.

19. Cf. Cyprian Vagaggini, O.S.B., *Theological Dimensions of the Liturgy*, trans. L. J. Doyle and W. A. Jurgens (Collegeville, Minn.: The Liturgical Press, 1976), 191ff.

20. For an introduction, cf. Boris Bobrinskoy, *The Mystery of the Trinity: Trinitarian Experience and Vision in the Biblical and Patristic Tradition* (Crestwood, N.Y.: St. Vladimir's, 1999); Kallistos Ware, *In the Image of the Trinity* (Crestwood, N.Y.: St. Vladimir's, 2004); Leonid Ouspensky and Vladimir Lossky, *The Meaning of Icons* (Crestwood, N.Y.: St. Vladimir's Press, 1999).

between the psychological analogies and the three persons of the Trinity; it is not that these three "belong" to one God, but "they are one God, and these are three persons, not one" (XV.23.43). Thomas Aquinas is also willing to acknowledge that a divine "person" signifies a "relation as subsisting," although this relation in God is not an "accident" but the divine essence itself (*SumTh*, I.29.4). Because affirming the triune revelation of the biblical God was not negotiable for these theologians, they resisted the claim that there are no real relations in the divine substance. As we saw in §3.1, however, it was primarily the categories of substance metaphysics that shaped their formulation of other aspects of the doctrine of God, such as simplicity, immutability, and the divine attributes.

Although the surge of scholarly interest in the work of the Protestant Scholastics may reveal additional resources[21] for the contemporary task of articulating a robust doctrine of the Trinity, the twentieth-century revival has relied more heavily on the earlier Reformers. Luther and Calvin may not have sufficiently worked through the philosophical problems they inherited along with the Augustinian psychological analogies, but their emphasis on the experience of justification by faith began to challenge the bifurcation between the divine essence and the economy of salvation. For example, Luther insisted in the 1518 Heidelberg Disputation that true theology is the "theology of the cross" and that knowledge of God should not be abstracted from the relations between the three persons in the history of Jesus Christ. Another resource taken up by twentieth-century Lutheran theologians is his emphasis on the Holy Spirit[22] as the real presence of God who draws us into relation to the Father through the Son. Calvin for the most part followed Augustine in his material presentation of the Trinity, although he worried about those who spend too much time trying to render the Trinity intelligible by using analogies from human existence (*Inst.*, I.13.18). What makes Calvin a resource is the way in which his emphasis on salvation by faith is expressed within an overarching trinitarian structure. What is of the "highest degree of importance," according to Calvin, is the "mystical union" of believers and Christ, which occurs through the Spirit: "Christ, having been made ours, makes us sharers with him in the gifts with which he has been endowed" (III.11.10).

21. Cf. Muller, *PRRD*, IV, "The Triunity of God."

22. For an analysis of Luther's pneumatology, cf. Regin Prenter, *Spiritus Creator*, trans. John M. Jensen (Philadelphia: Muhlenberg, 1953).

§6.2. Reformed Reconstructions

The revival of trinitarian doctrine among Reformed theologians has involved the recovery of biblical and traditional testimony to the robust relations of the Father, Son, and Spirit, as well as engagement with developments in the social scientific understanding of personality, and the philosophical revolt of a-theism against the idea of an absolute single subject. While the "robustness" of the reconstructions varies, we will observe a common desire to hold together an emphasis on both the three persons and the unity of God. As T. F. Torrance points out, the 1991 "Agreed Statement on the Holy Trinity," which was developed through an official dialogue between the Orthodox Church and the World Alliance of Reformed Churches, does not start either with the unity or with the three persons, and then work toward the other, but tries to account for them at one and the same time.[23] While many Reformed theologians might be called in as witnesses to this revival, not least Torrance himself,[24] for the sake of continuity and comparison we will limit ourselves to the same thinkers we reviewed in the previous chapter: Barth, Gunton, and Moltmann.

Karl Barth

Barth's most significant contribution to the twentieth-century revival of trinitarian doctrine was his formal restructuring of the presentation of dogmatics. As we saw in Chapter 3, most systematic treatments of the doctrine of God in the Western tradition (after Thomas Aquinas) outlined the essence and attributes of God before discussing the three divine persons. In reference to this approach, Barth asks, why would they treat the "That" and the "What" of God first, as though these could be separated from the "Who?" (*CD*, I/1, 301). He was critical of the Protestant Scholastics for following and hardening this formal distinction, which opened the way for modern liberalism to push the Trinity further into the background or, as in

---

23. T. F. Torrance, *Trinitarian Perspectives: Toward Doctrinal Agreement* (Edinburgh: T&T Clark, 1994), 126.

24. Cf. Torrance, *The Trinitarian Faith* (Edinburgh: T&T Clark, 1998); *The Christian Doctrine of God: One Being, Three Persons* (Edinburgh: T&T Clark, 1996).

the case of Schleiermacher, into a "conclusion" that does not belong "immediately" to Christian dogmatics.[25] Barth explicitly breaks with tradition by placing the Trinity at the head of dogmatics rather than at the end of the doctrine of God.

In the first volume of his *Church Dogmatics,* "The Triune God" is the first material topic after he argues for the "Word of God as the Criterion of Dogmatics." For Barth, precisely this criterion leads to a reconsideration of the place of the doctrine of the Trinity in dogmatics, for the root and ground of the doctrine of Trinity is God's self-revelation in and through the Word. However, even putting Trinity first is not enough — its content must be "decisive and controlling for the whole of dogmatics" (303). Barth acknowledges that the *mysterium trinitatis* must remain a mystery, and cannot be objectified by human reason; however, theology should engage in a rational wrestling with the manifestation of this mystery or we will not even know what we are saying when we talk about God's mystery (368). Throughout the remaining volumes of the *Church Dogmatics,* Barth attempted to interpret the various theological loci in light of this distinctively Christian understanding of God.

Barth applied the personalist concept of "I-Thou" not only to human persons but also to God. "the *tertium comparationis,* the analogy between God and man, is simply the existence of the I and the Thou in confrontation" (*CD,* III/1, 185). The image of God is the fellowship of I and Thou: "God exists in relationship and fellowship. As the Father of the Son and the Son of the Father He is Himself I and Thou, confronting Himself and yet always one and the same in the Holy Ghost. God created man in His own image, in correspondence with His own being and essence. . . . God is in relationship, and so too is the man created by Him. This is his divine likeness" (III/2, 324).[26] Barth's trinitarian proposal is summarized by the claim that "God reveals himself as Lord." The three "modes" of God's being are manifested in this self-revelation. It is the Lord who is the subject of revelation, the revealing and the revealed. Barth is hesitant to use the term

---

25. See F. D. E. Schleiermacher, *The Christian Faith,* trans. H. R. MacKintosh and J. S. Stewart (Edinburgh: T&T Clark, 1989), 738-51. Barth's influence can be seen in several more recent Reformed treatments of the doctrine of God. For example, Shirley Guthrie's *Christian Doctrine,* rev. ed. (Louisville: Westminster/John Knox, 1994), organizes the themes in the doctrine of God so that the Trinity is treated before the divine attributes.

26. For a critical analysis of Barth's proposal, see my *Reforming Theological Anthropology* (Grand Rapids: Eerdmans, 2003), chap. 6.

"person" with reference to the three in God because "what we to-day call the 'personality' of God belongs to the one unique essence of God" (*CD*, I/1, 350). Barth is even willing to say that God as the revealing Lord is "person, i.e., an I existing in and for itself with its own thought and will" (358). Later Barth will refer to God as a single divine Ego (*CD*, III/1, 205).

It is at this point that Barth remains dependent on the early modern concept of God as a single subject, and this is where his proposal has been most often criticized. It appears overly reliant on the traditional Western privileging of psychological analogies for the Trinity. Several scholars have argued that Barth has not escaped the philosophical presuppositions of the logic of German idealism, in which the individual subject as "I" finds itself in the reflection of consciousness.[27] For example, Michael Menke-Peitzmeyer argues that Barth's exposition of the Trinity as an interpretation of the absolute self-determination of God indicates that Hegel's speculative idea of God as an Absolute Subject is the ground of his doctrine of God, rather than the revelation of God in Jesus Christ. Because God (as subject) is "Lord," and this Lordship is inherently linked to divine predestination (of both God and creatures), then Barth's desire to uphold both divine and human freedom fails. This leaves Barth open to the Feuerbachian projection critique.[28]

Despite these problems, several aspects of Barth's material presentation proved helpful for those who took up the cause of the trinitarian revival. In his initial exposition of the doctrine of Trinity, Barth argues that we should speak of the "triunity" of God, which involves the movement of two mutually related thoughts that are in dialectical union — "unity in trinity" and "trinity in unity" (*CD*, I/1, 369). Either thought alone is one-sided and dangerous. On the one side lies the danger of subordinationism, which denies that the *Revealer* is God. Here Barth insists that the one God really is the indissoluble Subject of revelation. On the other side, modalism denies that *God* is the Revealer. Barth insists that in the triune revelation

27. Cf. my *Reforming Theological Anthropology*, chap. 6.

28. Michael Menke-Peitzmeyer, *Subjektivität und Selbstinterpretation des dreifaltigen Gottes: Eine Studie zur Genese und Explikation des Paradigmas "Selbstoffenbarung Gottes" in der Theologie Karl Barths*, Münsterische Beiträge zur Theologie 60 (Münster: Aschendorff, 2002). Alan Torrance urges a move beyond Barth's "revelational" model and toward a "doxological" and "communion" model that makes more sense of participation; see *Persons in Communion: An Essay on Trinitarian Description and Human Participation* (Edinburgh: T&T Clark, 1996).

we are dealing with "God Himself" (380-82). Later Barth suggests a rule for the doctrine of God: "statements about the divine modes of being antecedently in themselves cannot be different in content from those that are to be made about their reality in revelation. All our statements concerning what is called the immanent Trinity have been reached simply as confirmations or underlinings or, materially, as the indispensable premises of the economic Trinity."[29] As we will see below, this "rule" is generally followed by most of the other leading theologians in this trajectory and is given its best-known formulation by Karl Rahner. By thrusting the doctrine of the Trinity into the center of theological discourse and placing it at the head of dogmatic presentation, Barth opened up space for the creative material reconstructions that came after him.

Colin Gunton

Although he embraces Barth's emphasis on the doctrine of the Trinity as a generative force in theology, Gunton moves beyond him materially in several important ways. First, he more explicitly expresses his preference for the Cappadocians over St. Augustine, and this leads him to a stronger emphasis on the robust relations of the divine persons. In fact Gunton has been one of the most vocal critics of the Augustinian influence on the doctrine of God. In *The Promise of Trinitarian Theology* he describes the "theological crisis of the west," the responsibility for which must largely be laid at the door of St. Augustine. He argues that the Bishop of Hippo's conceptions of materiality and substance, along with his psychological analogies and weak pneumatology, all contributed to a state of affairs in which the "unity" of the unknowable divine essence is separated from the "trinity" of biblical revelation.

This is why so much Western theology views the task of upholding Christian orthodoxy as facing the logical "problem" of the Trinity rather than as "glorying in the being of a God whose reality as a communion of persons is the basis of a rational universe in which personal life may take

---

29. *CD*, I/1, 479. However, earlier in the same volume Barth maintains the need for a "deliberate and sharp distinction between the Trinity of God as we may know it in the Word of God revealed, written and proclaimed, and God's immanent Trinity" (*CD*, I/1, 172). Here he is interested in protecting the transcendence and freedom of God against any necessity.

shape."[30] Gunton points to the Cappadocian fathers, especially Basil of Caesarea, as resources for solving this crisis. Their relational view of God allows us to think of divine being as essentially the shared communion of the three persons of the Father, Son, and Spirit. God's being is not primarily understood as immaterial substance but as "personal space" in which the personal being of God is their conferring on and receiving from each other particularity and freedom.[31]

A second contribution is Gunton's attempt to offer an account of creation as "the mediation, through Son and Spirit, of a world that is genuinely other than God while yet remaining in relation with him."[32] In his book on *The Triune Creator,* he turns to Irenaeus as a resource for this task. As we saw above, for Irenaeus the relation between God and the world must be understood as mediated by the Son and Spirit who are the "two hands" of God. Gunton is critical of William of Ockham who, unlike Irenaeus, explained the God-world relation in non-trinitarian terms, primarily focusing on the divine "will" — this easily leads to a view of God as simply juxtaposed to a particular world (124). In the Irenaean model, however, the mediation of the relation between infinite Creator and finite creation does not require "intermediate" beings or "secondary" causes. The very nature of all created things, their constitution as they take shape in time and space, is mediated through the Son, who is the principle of the world's unity in its distinction from God, and through the Spirit who enables the particularity of creaturely things in their relation to God (143). Gunton's stress on this constitutive mediation is usually qualified by his insistence on a strong ontological distinction between God and the world. This may explain his resistance to the equation of the "immanent" and "economic" Trinity,[33] which might be interpreted as a dangerous fusion of God and the world.

---

30. Gunton, *The Promise of Trinitarian Theology* (Edinburgh: T&T Clark, 1991), 31. Throughout this book, the Cappadocians are a source for the remedial work of trinitarian theology; e.g., 9, 39-42, 52-54, 204-5.

31. Gunton, *Promise,* 94. Cf. Gunton, "Trinity, Ontology and Anthropology: Towards a Renewal of the Doctrine of the *Imago Dei,*" in *Persons, Divine and Human,* ed. C. Schwöbel (Edinburgh: T&T Clark, 1991), 47-61 at 56. For his special interest in Basil, cf. Gunton, "Between Allegory and Myth: The Legacy of the Spiritualising of Genesis," in *The Doctrine of Creation,* ed. C. Gunton (Edinburgh: T&T Clark, 1997), 47-62 at 58-60.

32. *The Triune Creator* (Grand Rapids: Eerdmans, 1998), 156. Page numbers below refer to this text.

33. Cf. *Promise,* xvii-xviii.

A third way in which Gunton moves beyond Barth is his willingness to engage contemporary anthropology, especially the relational concept of person that has emerged in late modern philosophy and social science. He is careful not to begin with the modern idea of human personhood as self-consciousness or autonomous subjectivity, and then to speak of God as three "persons." This would indeed be the dread heresy of tritheism. Instead Gunton argues that personal beings "have their being in their personal relatedness: their free relation-in-otherness."[34] This is true for both divine and human persons; however, the trinitarian persons are eternally related in their perichoretic being while for human creatures "person" is an eschatological concept, an ideal that calls us forward. Gunton is well aware of Feuerbach's charge that the idea of the Trinity is a projection of the human ideal of "participated life," but he suggests that we may in fact make a historical argument that the dependence goes the other way: the anthropological concept of "person" emerged within and was shaped by Christian theological reflection on the revelation of God in Jesus Christ whose very life is personal participation in the Spirit.[35] Building on the relational philosophy of Samuel Coleridge and others, Gunton argues that the idea of the Trinity can actually help us make sense of our own longing for personal being.

Jürgen Moltmann

The relations among the three persons of the Trinity are thematized in more strongly "social" terms in Moltmann's theology. One of the driving concerns here for Moltmann is providing a response to protest atheism's critique of the modern "theistic" idea of God as an all-determining single subject, who seems more like an impassible dictator than a God of love. These antagonists share the same understanding of the divine and are mutually defined by their negation of each other. Assuming that God is an absolute single subject, modern theism embraces divine subjectivity at the expense of human freedom, while modern a-theism expends with God for the sake of human dignity. In light of the impasse between these opposing options, Moltmann argues that Christian theology should respond not by

34. *The One, the Three and the Many* (Cambridge: Cambridge University Press, 1993), 229.

35. *Promise*, 90-91.

buttressing theism but by articulating the hope in the trinitarian God revealed in the cross and resurrection of Christ.

European atheism makes a valid point to which theology must respond; it is driven by the desire to liberate human beings "from this superego in the soul and in heaven, which does not really deserve the name of Father at all."[36] In its response to the evil and suffering in the world (especially after Hiroshima and Auschwitz), Christian theology must acknowledge the a-theist critique. In *The Crucified God* Moltmann proclaims: "For Christ's sake I am an atheist" and "Only a Christian can be a good atheist."[37] Bare "atheism" is not the answer of course, but a further explication of the doctrine of the Trinity, which "protects faith from both monotheism and atheism because it keeps believers at the cross." Insofar as contemporary atheism is parasitic on early modern theism, Moltmann asks: "if metaphysical theism disappears, can protest atheism still remain alive?"[38]

Moltmann's interest in the Trinity has also been shaped by his passion for responding to the concerns of those who have suffered from oppression in its various forms. Besides the problems it creates for Christology and Pneumatology, a "strict" monotheism may also be used politically to support earthly monarchies. Sometimes this connection is explicit (as in Hobbes' *Leviathan*), but usually it takes a subtler form by reinforcing the structures through which particular persons maintain power over others on the basis of race, gender, or class.[39] For Moltmann, the Trinity is the key for overcoming conceptions of God that have been used to condone or support such domination. In this sense, a trinitarian understanding of God also motivates his "social program." Moltmann regrets that even Barth allowed "Lordship" to trump the loving relations of the trinitarian

36. J. Moltmann, *The Trinity and the Kingdom,* trans. Margaret Kohl (Minneapolis: Fortress, 1993), 163.

37. *The Crucified God: The Cross of Christ as the Foundation and Criticism of Christian Theology,* trans. R. A. Wilson and John Bowden (New York: Harper & Row, 1974), 195. Moltmann discusses this claim in more detail elsewhere; cf. "Where There Is Hope, There Is Religion (Ernst Bloch)," in his *History and the Triune God: Contributions to Trinitarian Theology,* trans. John Bowden (New York: Crossroad, 1992), 143-55.

38. *Crucified God,* 246, 221.

39. Moltmann explores each of these forms of oppression, as well as others, in his *Experiences in Theology,* trans. Margaret Kohl (Minneapolis: Fortress, 2000). Cf. "I Believe in God the Father: Patriarchical or Non-Patriarchical Talk of God?" in his *History and the Triune God,* 1-18; *God for a Secular Society: The Public Relevance of Theology,* trans. Margaret Kohl (Minneapolis: Fortress, 1999).

persons as the heartbeat of the doctrine. He argues that Barth's idealist heritage (Fichte, Hegel) led him to replace the "one substance" of deism with the "one subject" of theism. When the reflection logic of an Absolute Subject is applied to the Father and the Son, "the Son is nothing other than the self of the divine 'I,' the counterpart, the other, in whom God contemplates himself, finds himself. . . ."[40] Moltmann insists that the divine revelation in the economy of salvation demands that we not separate the interpersonal relations of the persons of the Trinity from the divine essence.

Moltmann is critical of both the Western and the Eastern models of the Trinity, insofar as both privileged the personhood of the Father in a way that left room for subordinationism. He argues instead that we think of each of the three persons as having their personhood in their relations to the others. The unity of the Trinity is not secured by the Father alone because all of the interpersonal relations are reciprocal or "genetically connected." For Moltmann, the unity of the Trinity is "constituted" by the Father, but this cannot be understood apart from the way in which the unity is "concentrated" around the Son and "illumined" through the Holy Spirit. This also suggests that we should not think of the Father, Son, and Spirit as "persons" in exactly the same sense.[41] However, the way in which they mutually share power is the model (and the hope) for human social relations. The biblical idea of the "kingdom" or "rule" of God must not be conceptualized as domination, but as the manifestation of the shared love of the Father and the Son in and through the Spirit.[42] In the cross and resurrection of Jesus Christ and the outpouring of the Spirit, God is revealed as "passionate," suffering with and for us, promising us an eschatological victory over evil and suffering. As we will see in our treatment of the Futurity of God, Moltmann believes that this victory has already broken into the world and continues to take shape as the church shares in God's liberative activity in the power of the Spirit.[43]

40. *Trinity and Kingdom,* 143.

41. *Trinity and Kingdom,* 178, 189. Cf. Moltmann, *God in Creation,* trans. Margaret Kohl (New York: Harper & Row, 1985), 97.

42. *Trinity and Kingdom,* 71, 122ff.

43. "The economic Trinity completes and perfects itself to immanent Trinity when the history and experience of salvation are completed and perfected. When everything is 'in God' and 'God is all in all,' then the economic Trinity is raised into and transcended in the immanent Trinity" (*Trinity and Kingdom,* 161). Cf. *The Church in the Power of the Spirit,* trans. Margaret Kohl (New York: Harper & Row, 1977), 54.

§6.3. Lutheran Reconstructions

As with the other trajectories, we could point to several leading Lutheran theologians who have contributed to the twentieth-century revival of trinitarian doctrine. Ted Peters, for example, not only formally places "God the Trinity" at the beginning of his exposition of Christian theology but also differentiates the trinitarian understanding of God from "classical theism."[44] Because our purpose in these sections is primarily to illustrate the trajectories and to point toward ways in which they might be integrated, we will limit ourselves to the same three scholars.

Robert Jenson

The theological importance that Jenson places on the idea of God as event shapes his understanding of the doctrine of the Trinity. God is identified by the triune narrative. Jenson argues that a story always has more than one agent; he depicts the "persons" of God's identity as the *dramatis dei personae* — the "characters of the drama of God."[45] He resists the temptation to speak of the essential identity of God apart from this narrative. God is "one with himself just by the dramatic coherence of his eventful actuality," and this actuality coheres around the story of the resurrection of Jesus (*ST*, 1:64). The Father, Son, and Spirit are identified in and with the events in which God and creatures are mutually emplotted. For Jenson, "the Trinity is simply the Father and the man Jesus and their Spirit as the Spirit of the believing community."[46]

God's being (identity) has to do with the mutual emplotment of God's people and God (*ST*, 1:110). For Jenson, the Trinity is directly linked to our other trajectories: "God is eternal or infinite, in the sense that suits him, *because* he is triune" (218). He argues that when we think of the doctrine of the Trinity in these terms, it may be seen as consonant with, and as the fulfillment of, the faith of Old Testament Israel. The Son and the Spirit are already present as agents in the drama in the Hebrew Bible. The "word" of

---

44. Ted Peters, *God — The World's Future,* 2nd ed. (Minneapolis: Fortress, 2000), 86ff.

45. Jenson, *Systematic Theology,* 2 vols. (Oxford: Oxford University Press, 1997, 1999), 1:75. Identified as *ST* in the text below.

46. Jenson, *The Triune Identity* (Philadelphia: Fortress, 1982), 141.

the Lord is a "Shekinah-phenomenon," indicating that the subject of the speaking is both within Israel and beyond Israel. The Spirit is also a *persona* in the Old Testament narrative — the *ruach* of the Lord is a "historical agency through Israel's leadership" and the "agent of prophecy" (86). These phenomena are manifested more clearly in the New Testament through the history of the incarnation and the sending of the Paraclete.

Like so many in this trajectory, Jenson has been heavily involved in ecumenical dialogue, and this has shaped his contribution to the revival of trinitarian doctrine. In *The Unbaptized God: The Basic Flaw in Ecumenical Theology,* he argues that a relational and dynamic doctrine of God (and other theological loci) will be required if we hope to overcome some of the key debates between East and West (including issues surrounding sacramentology and the *filioque* clause).[47] In his *Systematic Theology,* Jenson takes over the Cappadocian "rule" as articulated by Gregory of Nyssa: "All action that impacts the creature from God . . . begins with the Father and is actual through the Son and is perfected in the Holy Spirit. *Therefore* the attribution of the action is not divided among the plurality of actors" (*ST,* 1:110).

Jenson insists that Pentecost is a peer of Easter, that Pneumatology and Christology must be held together. He is willing to acknowledge that the Father is the *archē* of deity, but he also wants to say that the Spirit is the End of all God's ways. The Spirit is the one as whom God is future to himself, and thereby "liberates God the Father from himself . . . to be the actual *archē* of deity" (*ST,* 1:158). This is not abstracted from the agency and identity of the Son in relation to the Father and the Spirit. Jenson summarizes his proposal: "the Father begets the Son and freely breathes his Spirit; the Spirit liberates the Father for the Son and the Son from and for the Father; the Son is begotten and liberated, and so reconciles the Father with the future his Spirit is" (*ST,* 1:161).

Although Jenson prefers the Cappadocians and is critical of Augustine (e.g., *ST,* 2:29), he wants to argue that there is a sense in which we may rescue the "psychological" explication of trinitarian being. His proposal for doing so is spread out within three chapters (*ST,* 1, chaps. 7-9) in which he treats the "patrological" problem (whether there is a divine "personal"

---

47. Jenson, *The Unbaptized God: The Basic Flaw in Ecumenical Theology* (Minneapolis: Fortress, 1992), esp. chap. 10. Cf. *Visible Words* (Philadelphia: Fortress, 1978), 25: "For indeed, God is a person; and that means that he is Spirit *and* Body."

unity behind the three persons), the "christological" problem (whether God suffers), and the "pneumatological" problem (whether the Spirit is really a person or merely a bond between Father and Son). In response to all three problems, he appeals to "what Kant taught us to call the 'transcendental unity of apperception,' the sheer *focus* of consciousness that constitutes a consciousness as *a* consciousness" (*ST,* 1:120).[48] The Father, as *a* person of the Trinity, is a consciousness that "finds his 'I' in the Son, just thereby becoming himself a focused locus of experience, and in such a fashion that the Son and the Father are free for each other in the Spirit" (122). The Son "finds his 'I' and is free in the same way that other human beings do — or , rather, that other humans find their 'I' and are free as does he" (137). Like the Father, the Spirit finds his "I" in the Son but in a different way: "just insofar as the Son is the *totus Christus,* insofar as the Son includes and is included in his community. And the Spirit him*self* is nothing other than the Freedom that occurs in these relations" (160). On this model of "person," identity and personality are not correlated one to one, which means that there are various *ways* to be personal. Jenson believes this allows us to say that, while in one way the Father, Son, and Spirit are each fully personal, in another way they may be interpreted as "poles in the Trinity's personal life."[49]

Eberhard Jüngel

The significance of the doctrine of Trinity for Jüngel was already evident in his early book *God's Being Is in Becoming: The Trinitarian Being of God in the Theology of Karl Barth,* originally published in 1964. Much of the book is an exposition of Barth's understanding of the Trinity in the context of mid-century debates about divine "being," but Jüngel's major contribution is his philosophical analysis of the way in which the category of "relation" shapes the doctrine. He critiques theology's reliance on the cate-

---

48. Cf. Jenson's treatment of this issue in a chapter titled "Thinking Consciousness," in his *On Thinking the Human: Resolutions of Difficult Notions* (Grand Rapids: Eerdmans, 2003), esp. 27ff.

49. This means that we may also address the Trinity as personal, but only insofar as we understand that "The Father of the Son and breather of the Spirit, only as such himself a unity of consciousness, knows his 'I' exactly as the *archē* of Son and Spirit, as the oneness of the one Trinity" (*ST,* 1:123).

gories of "substance" and "accident," which has created so many difficulties in articulating the God-world relation. Jüngel engages what I have called the philosophical turn to relationality (cf. §1.2), and insists that theology should conceive of God's being as essentially relational. "God's being is thus *self-related* being. As being it is relationally structured . . . the modes of God's being which are differentiated from each other are related to each other in such a way that each mode of God's being *becomes* what it *is* only *with* the two other modes of being."[50]

For Jüngel, God's being must be thought of as "pure relation," in the sense that "as self-relatedness God's being is a being in becoming."[51] This impacts the link between the "immanent" and "economic" Trinity. Jüngel is not particularly fond of this terminology, and his main concern is to ensure that any mediation between the two concepts is mediated christologically (and soteriologically). Because God's being is "in" becoming, God is able to "reiterate" Godself; the relations of God *ad extra* (economic Trinity) "correspond" to the relations *ad intra* (immanent Trinity).[52] For him, the real identity of the immanent and economic Trinity can be maintained only in light of the freedom of divine grace in the event of God's being.[53]

In his later book, *God as the Mystery of the World*, Jüngel further explains this correspondence: "The self-relatedness of the deity of God takes place in an unsurpassable way in the very selflessness of the incarnation of God. That is the meaning of talk about the humanity of God. It is not a second thing next to the eternal God but rather the event of the deity of God."[54] After outlining the crisis of theological uncertainty about how to talk about God in Part I, Jüngel sets out in Part II to trace the historical emergence of the problem and its significance in light of the modern talk of the "death of God." Part III shows that the root of the problem is a metaphysical dualism that separates God's being from perishability. He argues that only through the cross can we think of God's existence in relation to our experience of perishability, and the cross leads us to speak of the re-

---

50. Jüngel, *God's Being Is in Becoming: The Trinitarian Being of God in the Theology of Karl Barth*, trans. John Webster (Grand Rapids: Eerdmans, 2001), 77.

51. *Becoming*, 116; cf. 104f.

52. *Becoming*, 119.

53. "Das Verhältnis von 'ökonomischer' und 'immanenter' Trinität," *Zeitschrift für Theologie und Kirche* 72, no. 3 (September 1975): 353-64.

54. *God as the Mystery of the World*, trans. Darrell Guder (Grand Rapids: Eerdmans, 1983), 372.

lations between the Father, Son, and Spirit. God's "being" must not be abstracted from the event of God's identification with, and overcoming of, perishability. Jüngel suggests in Part IV that we think and speak of God as the mystery of the world that confronts the world by differentiating the impossible from the possible (cf. §5.3 above). The basis of such speech is the analogy of "advent," which relies wholly on the trinitarian God who enters the event of human speech about God. In Part V, Jüngel exposits the claim that God is love by arguing that this statement requires us to think of God's being first and foremost as triune, as the differentiation between the Father and the Son as the event of the Spirit.

Jüngel also contributes to this trajectory in the doctrine of God by attempting to move beyond the impasse between atheism and theism. He notes that "perhaps the end of theism had to begin in order to disclose the existential relevance of a doctrine of the Trinity which must be grounded and explicated anew."[55] He is critical of much of the tradition, which he sees as privileging abstract metaphysics, focusing on the "essence" of God without considering God's concrete trinitarian subsistence. Theology must respond to non-Christian atheism but also leave behind the alternative of non-Christian theism.[56] Jüngel recognizes the challenge of Feuerbach and Nietzsche, but argues that their negations presuppose the "theistic" (non-trinitarian) metaphysical tradition they are attacking.

The subtitle of *God as the Mystery of the World* is telling on this point: *On the Foundation of the Theology of the Crucified One in the Dispute between Theism and Atheism*. Rather than choose one side against the other in this dispute, Jüngel attempts to revive the trinitarian thought forms in the Christian theological tradition that have been suppressed. Here he calls for a recovery of resources in the theology of Luther, for whom the triune action of justification is crucial for understanding the being of God. For Jüngel the category of relationality helps clarify both the doctrine of God and theological anthropology, as well as the relation between them. The "relational riches" that are God's own life are disclosed as Christ takes our "relationlessness" on himself so that we can share in the relational life of God.[57]

55. *Mystery*, 371.

56. For discussion and analysis, see John Webster, *Eberhard Jüngel: An Introduction to His Theology* (Cambridge: Cambridge University Press, 1986), 80-81.

57. Jüngel, *Justification: The Heart of the Christian Faith*, trans. Jeffrey F. Cayzer (Edinburgh: T&T Clark, 2001), 88; cf. 46, 113.

Wolfhart Pannenberg

The centrality of the doctrine of the Trinity is already evident in Pannenberg's early works. For example, in *Theology and the Kingdom of God,* he argues that trinitarian doctrine is no mere Christian addition to a philosophical (monotheistic) idea of God, but the ultimate expression "for the one reality of the coming God whose Kingdom Jesus proclaimed."[58] In his *Jesus — God and Man,* he argues that Jesus' revelational unity with God, which is constituted by his self-distinction from the Father, is the starting point for the doctrine of the Trinity.[59] In 1981 Pannenberg indicated that when he did produce a systematic theology it "will be more thoroughly trinitarian than any example I know of."[60] The three volumes of his *Systematic Theology*[61] show clear evidence of his attempt to fulfill this promise. In §1 of the first volume, Pannenberg insists that Christian theology as the science of God must deal comprehensively with the relation between the eternal trinitarian life and God's presence in history, i.e., the "economic" Trinity (*ST,* 1:6). The third volume concludes with the claim that divine love is manifested as the coming forth of the immanent divine life as the economic Trinity, which incorporates creatures into that life. "The distinction and unity of the immanent and economic Trinity constitute the heartbeat of the divine love, and with a single such heartbeat this love encompasses the whole world of creatures" (*ST,* 3:646).

Pannenberg's material understanding of the doctrine is spelled out in the most detail in chapter 5 of *Systematic Theology,* "The Trinitarian God." Like Barth, he places his treatment of the Trinity prior to his presentation of "The Unity and Attributes of the Divine Essence" (chapter 6). Pannenberg suggests that the decay of the doctrine of the Trinity in the seventeenth and eighteenth centuries was due to the lack of an inner connection between the unity of God and the relations of the triune persons (*ST,* 1:291). To remedy this bifurcation, he argues that the doctrine of the Trinity

58. W. Pannenberg, *Theology and the Kingdom of God* (Philadelphia: Westminster, 1969), 71.

59. Pannenberg, *Jesus — God and Man,* 2nd ed., trans. Lewis L. Wilkins and Duane A. Priebe (Philadelphia: Westminster, 1977), chap. 4.

60. Pannenberg, "God's Presence in History," *The Christian Century,* March 11, 1981, 263.

61. Pannenberg, *Systematic Theology,* 3 vols., trans. G. Bromiley (Grand Rapids: Eerdmans, 1991, 1994, 1997). Identified as *ST* in the text below.

should be an "exposition of the relation of Jesus to the Father and the Spirit" (305), but in such a way that the reciprocal self-distinction of each of the persons constitutes the unity of the divine life (321). For help in this task Pannenberg explicitly calls for "a concept of essence that is not external to the category of relations," which then allows us to say that the "unity of the essence may be found only in their concrete life relations" (335).

He argues that we cannot derive the threeness from a unity that is either based on the Father (a common Eastern approach) or on the divine substance (a common Western approach), because these lead to forms of subordinationism or modalism. Instead, we must think of the unity as such as manifest in the mutual relations. Distinguishing his position from Barth and others, Pannenberg insists that the trinitarian persons ". . . are separate centers of action [*selbständige Aktzentren*] and not just modes of being of the one divine subject" (336). It is important to note that he does not say three centers of "consciousness." Pannenberg wants to avoid projecting the reflection logic of self-consciousness onto the persons of the Trinity. Instead, he aims to take advantage of the introduction of the category of relation into the concept of essence, especially as it impacts the concept of "person."[62] The logic of the trinitarian relations is then spelled out in the remaining two volumes as he exposits the other theological loci.

We alluded in §5.3 to the way in which Pannenberg connects the Trinity to the criterion of the true infinite.[63] He argues that concepts of the divine that define God merely over against the world have inadvertently made God a correlate to the world. The trinitarian God, however, "without blotting out the *difference* between creator and creature, transcends while preserving [*hebt auf*] this opposition by means of the idea of the reconciliation of the world."[64] Avoiding a spurious concept of the infinite requires that the unity of God (as the Absolute) be conceived as a differentiated unity, which is precisely what the doctrine of Trinity affirms. The conditions for distinction and unity in God's relation to the world are not dependent on God's relation to the world because God is eternally unity in distinction.

---

62. Cf. his treatment of the concept of person in *Anthropology in Theological Perspective,* trans. Matthew J. O'Connell (Philadelphia: Westminster, 1985), chaps. 4 and 5.

63. For a more detailed analysis of this connection, see my *The Postfoundationalist Task of Theology: Wolfhart Pannenberg and the New Theological Rationality* (Grand Rapids: Eerdmans, 1999), 92ff.

64. Pannenberg, "Problems of a Trinitarian Doctrine of God," *Dialog* 26, no. 4 (1987): 256; emphasis added.

The doctrine of the Trinity enables us "to do justice to the unity of transcendence and immanence with regard to God's relation to the world of His creation. . . . The Christian trinitarian doctrine can be considered as determining the question of how these [immanent] forms of God's presence in the world are related to His transcendent existence. The answer is that they cannot be different from God Himself, if the unity of the one God is to be preserved."[65] In his *Systematic Theology*, Pannenberg argues that this is connected to the Christian claim that "God is love." It will not suffice to say that God eternally loves Godself, for love rises above persons and "gives them their selfhood," binding them together in their reciprocal relations (*ST*, 1:426-27). Love can be conceived as identical with the divine essence only if we think of it as the power that manifests itself in the mutual relations of the trinitarian persons.

§6.4. The Ecumenical and Reformative Appeal of Trinitarian Doctrine

The revival of trinitarian doctrine has been fueled not only by ecumenical dialogue between East and West, but also by the growth of Pentecostal and charismatic churches worldwide, for whom the implications of the experience of the person of the Spirit for the doctrine of God ought not to be ignored. The significance of trinitarian symbols in Christian spirituality and praxis is increasingly coming to the fore in theological discussions of the doctrine of the Trinity.[66] This has contributed to a growing recognition that the doctrine is inherently connected to our pastoral praxis and worship life as Christians, as well as to our desire for unity as the body of Christ.

---

65. Pannenberg, "The Christian Vision of God: The New Discussion on the Trinitarian Doctrine," *The Asbury Theological Journal* 46, no. 2 (Fall 1991): 35.

66. E.g., Elizabeth Johnson, "Trinity: To Let the Symbol Sing Again," *Theology Today* 54, no.3 (October 1997): 299-311; Ellen Charry, "Spiritual Formation by the Doctrine of the Trinity," *Theology Today* 54, no. 3 (October 1997): 367-80; Philip Sheldrake, *Spirituality and Theology: Christian Living and the Doctrine of God* (Maryknoll, N.Y.: Orbis, 1998); Michael Downey, *Altogether Gift: A Christian Spirituality* (Maryknoll, N.Y.: Orbis, 2000); David S. Cunningham, *These Three Are One: The Practice of Trinitarian Theology* (Oxford: Blackwell, 1998); Paul S. Fiddes, *Participating in God: A Pastoral Doctrine of the Trinity* (Louisville: Westminster/John Knox, 2000); James J. Buckley and David Yeago, *Knowing the Triune God: The Work of the Spirit in the Practices of the Church* (Grand Rapids: Eerdmans, 2001).

Karl Rahner

Rahner was one of the most influential Roman Catholic theologians in the twentieth-century revival of trinitarian doctrine. His 1967 book *The Trinity* deeply affected the theological conversation by introducing the axiom, "The economic Trinity is the immanent Trinity, and the immanent Trinity is the economic Trinity."[67] The *economic* Trinity refers to how God is revealed in the outworking of the history of salvation; the *immanent* Trinity has to do with God's eternal being as distinct from creation. Rahner's point is that we should not think of these as two wholly *separate* things. The eternal God *is* the God revealed in Christ by the Spirit. On the other hand, if the economic and immanent Trinity are simply identical, then God eternally depends on the world to be what or who God is. This axiom did not answer the question of *how* to speak of the distinction *and* unity of the economic and immanent Trinity, but it did shape much of the later twentieth-century debate as we have seen.

Rahner's aversion to abstract formal discussions of the metaphysical attributes of God and his deeply pneumatological imagination contributed to his own interest in the doctrine of the Trinity. For Rahner, however, as for Barth, the focus on God's *self*-communication sometimes diminishes the traditional emphasis on the *three* divine persons. Rahner is well aware of the problems in the history of the concept of "person," yet he still wants to assert that in some sense "God is a person,"[68] though not in the way that human individual persons are (i.e., defined over against others). For God cannot "experience himself as defined in relation to another." Like Barth, he resists applying "personal" to all three "subsistences" of the Trinity; there is only "one real consciousness" in God.[69] For Rahner, "There is real difference in God as he is in himself between one and the same God insofar as he is — at once and necessarily — the unoriginate who mediates himself to himself (Father), the one who is in truth uttered for himself (Son), and the one who is received and accepted in love for himself (Spirit) — and insofar as, *as a result of this,* he is the one who can freely communi-

---

67. K. Rahner, *The Trinity,* trans. J. Donceel, with an introduction by C. M. LaCugna (New York: Crossroad, 1997), 22. Originally published in 1967.

68. Rahner, *Foundations of Christian Faith,* trans. William Dych (New York: Crossroad, 2000), 74. For a sense of Rahner's ambiguous attitude toward the concept of "person," which he seems more willing than Barth to use to indicate distinctions in God, see *Trinity,* 44.

69. *Trinity,* 107.

cate himself."[70] Although Rahner's trinitarian model (like Barth's) is still characterized by an emphasis on God as single subject, his reflections have inspired other Roman Catholic theologians to pursue more relationally robust proposals.

John Zizioulas

For Western theologians interested in the trinitarian revival, Zizioulas has been one of the most prominent recent dialogue partners from the Eastern Orthodox tradition. In his *Being as Communion*, Zizioulas sets out the rationale for the Eastern emphasis on God's relational being, which he traces especially back to the Cappadocians, but also to others in that tradition. The key for the Cappadocians is that the ontology of God is not based in an "ousia" but in a person, namely, the Father. For the East, this helped to emphasize that the very being of God is relational. The Father is the "source" or "font" of divinity not in a way that makes the other persons subordinate, but as the person of the Trinity who makes room for the sharing of the essence. As Lossky puts it: these expressions "do not mean that the divine essence is subject to the person of the Father, but only that the person of the Father is the basis of common possession of the same essence, because the person of the Father, not being the sole person of the Godhead, is not to be identified with the essence."[71] This relationality is spelled out in terms of the doctrine of Trinity, and so "participating in the divine nature" does not mean sharing in the "substance" of God but in God's personal existence.[72] This takes shape for human creatures through becoming like Christ, sharing in the Son's personal relation to the Father. As Panayiotis Nellas has made clear, "the real anthropological meaning of deification is Christification."[73]

Perhaps Zizioulas's most important contribution has been his explica-

---

70. *Trinity*, 101-2. His emphasis.

71. V. Lossky, *In the Image and Likeness of God*, ed. and trans. J. H. Erickson and T. E. Bird (Crestwood, N. Y.: St. Vladimir's Press, 1985), 82. This is one of the reasons why the Orthodox resisted the filioque.

72. John Zizioulas, *Being as Communion* (Crestwood, N.Y.: St. Vladimir's Press, 1997), 50.

73. Panayiotis Nellas, *Deification in Christ: The Nature of the Human Person*, trans. Norman Russell (Crestwood, N.Y.: St. Vladimir's Seminary Press, 1987), 39.

tion of the relations among the key concepts of person, ontology, and *koinonia*. He is critical of both Barth and Rahner for linking the "economic" and "immanent" Trinity in a way that either introduces time into God or allows the concept of revelation to determine the *ontological* structure of the theology of Trinity.[74] Zizioulas tries to show that the Greek idea of the "ecstasis" of God, i.e., God's existence on the basis of the person of the Father, offers a different ontology that protects against a common "horizon" of manifestation shared by the three persons in a parallel coexistence. Rather than emphasizing the common *ousia* as the basic ontological claim about the unity of God, the Cappadocians stress the eternal origin of divine unity in a person, namely the Father.[75]

It is important to emphasize that for the Cappadocians (and Zizioulas) the divine persons are named in ways that indicate *schesis* or relationship.[76] Zizioulas argues that this opens up a new ontology of personhood, both for human and divine persons, so that personal identity is recognized and posited through a relationship, not through an isolated identity. It is "in Christ" and "in the Spirit" that creaturely personhood is fully realized,[77] and this affects his understanding of the communion that constitutes the church. "This hypostatic fullness as otherness can emerge only through a relationship so constitutive ontologically that relating is not consequent upon being but is being itself. The hypo-static and the ek-static have to coincide."[78] The ontological condition for personhood is relation to other, and this has reformative ramifications for ecclesial life.

Feminist and Liberation Reconstructions

For many people in contemporary culture, the dominant psychological analogies for God in Western theology evoke images of a powerful man

---

74. Zizioulas, *Communion*, 45.

75. Zizioulas, *Communion*, 88.

76. Gregory Nazianzus, Oration 29 (*PG* 36, 96). Cf. Zizioulas, "The Doctrine of the Holy Trinity: The Significance of the Cappadocian Contribution," in *Trinitarian Theology Today*, ed. C. Schwöbel (Edinburgh: T&T Clark, 1995), 44-60 at 50.

77. Zizioulas, "Human Capacity and Human Incapacity," *Scottish Journal of Theology* 28 (1975): 401-48 at 441-42.

78. Zizioulas, "On Being a Person: Toward an Ontology of Personhood," in *Persons — Divine and Human*, ed. Colin Gunton (Edinburgh: T&T Clark, 1991), 33-46 at 46.

who thinks about himself constantly and loves himself completely. It is no surprise that this does not sound like good news to feminist and liberation thinkers. Feminist theologians have contributed significantly to the revival of trinitarian doctrine, noting that some formulations of the doctrine of God have been used to condone the domination of women. One of the best-known proposals was offered by Catherine Mowry LaCugna in *God for Us,* where she argued for an inherent link between the doctrine of the Trinity and the practical experience of salvation.[79] LaCugna outlined ways in which a relational ontology grounded in the doctrine of God can illuminate our shared life together. She also addressed the practical implications of understanding "doxology" as the appropriate mode of doing theology, arguing for a vision of living trinitarian faith in which the trinitarian life of God *is* our life. The Trinity becomes for her a criterion by which we judge the way in which we arrange our lives together — are we exclusive and competitive or inclusive and communal? The general willingness among many feminist theologians to acknowledge the implicitly relational nature of the human experience of God and neighbor is a major resource for the ongoing revival of trinitarian doctrine.

Several Latin American theologians have also emphasized the importance of a robust doctrine of the Trinity, arguing that the idea of God as a single absolute ruler and the political oppression of the poor are more than simply conceptually related. The affirmation that God is essentially trinitarian communion can contribute to a move away from domination and toward shared self-giving love as the ideal for human relations.[80] The sense that a fresh trinitarian emphasis can transform the way in which we act and think about the nature of the church and salvation has increasingly shaped the consciousness of African and Asian theologians as well.[81]

The growth of the Pentecostal movement of the twentieth century, as well as the "charismatic" renewals that influenced both Roman Catholi-

79. LaCugna, *God for Us: The Trinity and Christian Life* (San Francisco: HarperCollins, 1991); cf. her "God in Communion with Us," in *Freeing Theology: The Essentials of Theology in Feminist Perspective,* ed. LaCugna (San Francisco: HarperCollins, 1993).

80. See, e.g., Leonardo Boff, *Holy Trinity, Perfect Community,* trans. Phillip Berryman (Maryknoll, N.Y.: Orbis, 2000).

81. E.g., A. Okechukwu Ogbonnaya, *On Communitarian Divinity: An African Interpretation of the Trinity* (New York: Paragon House, 1994); Jung Young Lee, *The Trinity in Asian Perspective* (Nashville: Abingdon, 1996).

cism and most traditions within Protestantism,[82] took on proportions that eventually could not be theologically ignored. Increased attention to the Spirit leads naturally to reflection on the Trinity. The explanatory power of the doctrine of the Trinity has spilled over from ecumenical discussions, and has become a significant theme in interreligious dialogue.[83] These developments help to fuel ongoing attempts to articulate a *reformative* doctrine of the trinitarian God of the Bible.

§6.5. Robust Trinity

The purpose of this chapter has been to commend the late modern revival of interest in the doctrine of the Trinity, which has rediscovered the generative power of this uniquely Christian understanding of God. The threat of tritheism is sometimes raised as a potential objection to this revival. In Chapter 3 we observed how defining "person" as an individual substance of a rational nature or as an autonomous subject can indeed lead to tritheism, if the term thus defined is applied to the three persons of God. Fear of this specter has too often led Western theology to settle for a frail doctrine of the Trinity. After the (re)turn to relationality, however, we are no longer constrained by medieval or early modern concepts of person. The early modern defense of the idea of God as a single subject was an attempt to uphold the Christian intuition that God is not an impersonal power; a robust doctrine of the Trinity can serve the same purpose while also accounting for the New Testament emphasis on being drawn into the relationality of eternal life.

Understanding personality as being-in-relation, which is more consistent with biblical anthropology and contemporary social science, opens up

---

82. Cf. Richard Shaull and Waldo Cesar, *Pentecostalism and the Future of the Christian Churches* (Grand Rapids: Eerdmans, 2000); Veli-Matti Karkkainen, *Toward a Pneumatological Theology: Pentecostal and Ecumenical Perspectives on Ecclesiology, Soteriology and Theology of Mission,* ed. Amos Yong (Lanham, Md.: University Press of America, 2002), esp. chap. 7: "Trinity as Communion in the Spirit."

83. See, e.g., Mark Heim, *The Depths of Riches: A Trinitarian Theology of Religious Ends* (Grand Rapids: Eerdmans, 2001); Kevin J. Vanhoozer, ed., *The Trinity in a Pluralistic Age: Theological Essays on Culture and Religion* (Grand Rapids: Eerdmans, 1997); Gavin D'Costa, *The Meeting of Religions and the Trinity* (Maryknoll, N.Y.: Orbis, 2000); Raimundo Pannikar, *The Trinity and the Religious Experience of Man* (Maryknoll, N.Y.: Orbis, 1973).

new possibilities for articulating trinitarian doctrine. We do not have to think of the three "persons" of the Trinity as three repetitions of the same kind of rational individual, who happen to take different roles. The "personality" of the eternal Son was manifested in the life of Jesus of Nazareth — facing the eternal Father in faithful, loving, and hopeful dependence on the eternal Spirit — and this is the way in which human creatures are called to be "persons." We still speak of the perichoretic being-in-relation of the Father and the Spirit as "personal," but the way in which they are mutually present to, in, and for one another and the Son is the eternal *ground* of the evocation of the human experience of personality — not simply two more examples of it. True *human* personhood is participation in the robustly relational divine nature that takes shape as a sharing in the Son's way of being-in-relation to the Father and the Spirit.

The attempt to articulate a "robust" doctrine of the Trinity is guided by a desire to privilege rather than problematize the intense vitality of the *relationality* of the Father, Son, and Holy Spirit. After all, this was the approach of the New Testament authors, as we saw in §3.5. The good news that we are called to participate in this powerful relationality is well illustrated in the overarching story of Luke-Acts. Setting aside the question of how to calculate the unity of three divine substances, let us notice how the empowering *relations* of divine life structure the narrative. Mary is told that the Spirit of the Lord God will come upon her and that her child will be called the Son of God (Luke 1:31-35). During Jesus' baptism the Holy Spirit descends upon him like a dove, and the voice from heaven calls out: "you are my Son" (3:21-22). After his baptism Jesus is "full of the Holy Spirit" and experiences forty days of temptation prior to beginning his formal ministry; the focus of this struggle is coming to terms with his relation to the Father (4:1-13).

Filled with the power of the Spirit (Luke 4:14), Jesus begins to teach in the synagogues, and when he arrives in Nazareth he reads from the scroll of Isaiah: "The Spirit of the Lord is upon me . . . to proclaim the year of the Lord's favor" (4:18-19). Jesus' ministry and teaching continue to focus on the gift of the Spirit from the heavenly Father (e.g., 11:13), and his last words on the cross are "Father, into your hands I commend my spirit" (23:46). The story picks up in the Book of Acts where the resurrected Jesus tells his disciples that the kingdom will be restored by the authority of the Father, but that they will receive power through the outpouring of the Holy Spirit (Acts 1:6-8). After Pentecost the message of the gospel spreads, namely, "how God anointed Jesus of Nazareth with the Holy Spirit" (10:38) and now the gift of the Holy Spirit is poured out "even on the Gentiles" (10:45). The narrative of redemption identifies the robustly relational agency of the Father, Son, and Spirit, whose gracious presence invites creatures to share in eternal life.

Our attitude toward the late modern resources in the revival of trinitarian doctrine must be one of *critical* appropriation. The diversity of the proposals in itself requires discernment among them. We have observed some of the concerns that have been raised against these proposals, such as Barth's reliance on idealist reflection logic, which leads him ultimately to collapse back into a single subject model. Similarly, Gunton's use of Irenaeus's "two hands" model may insufficiently emphasize the real personality of the Son and the Spirit. By proposing a "robust" doctrine of the Trinity, I am not suggesting we develop new "social" analogies, which can be just as problematic as "psychological" analogies. Moltmann's attempt to use the relations of the divine persons as a model for democratic political human relations is just as susceptible to the charge of projection as the single subject model. Pannenberg's use of the phrase "separate centers" of action to refer to the three persons of the Trinity is misleading at best, disintegrating at worst.

Part of the problem may be the way in which the distinction between an "immanent" and an "economic" Trinity functions in the discussion. Even when the distinction is employed for the sake of overcoming the distinction, it brings with it an implicit danger. Insofar as the immanent Trinity and the economic Trinity are dialectically defined concepts, we are too easily forced back into another false dilemma: either they are substantially the same or substantially separate. This way of framing the debate makes it difficult to avoid these pitfalls. In Part III we will explore other linguistic practices that aim to conserve the intuition that lies behind both the distinction and its negation — God's freedom in relation to the world.

We must not forget our first trajectory: we cannot step back from our relation to the *infinite* trinitarian God and compare this divine object to other objects. However, *all* theological statements must submit to the apophatic intuition that human language cannot grasp the reality of God. Singling out the Trinity as more "mysterious" than other doctrines simply reinforces the bifurcation between faith and reason, and makes it seem incidental to the gospel and Christian life. Rather than a confusing contradiction or enigma, we may find that the mystery of the triune divine life, which is "made known" (Eph. 3:5; 6:19) through the presence of the Spirit of Christ, actually illuminates the conditions of our finitude. Rather than placing the Trinity at the end of the doctrine of God, we will weave it together with Infinity and Futurity into the very heart of our presentation of divine knowing, acting, and being. I will argue that the life of the trinitarian persons may be understood as the origin, condition, and goal of the noetic, moral, and aesthetic desire that constitutes human personality.

Just as we cannot construct a "model" of Infinity, our goal here should not be to develop a "model" of the Trinity by analogy to some finite reality, but to be modeled after Christ, participating in his relation to the Father through life in the Spirit. Through this process we come to realize that the Trinity is beyond analogy not simply because it is "unlike" finite things, but because it is the absolute condition for the differentiation and unification that make all analogizing possible. We cannot prove the doctrine of Trinity or secure our knowledge of the trinitarian God on the foundation of any finite analogy. However, we may identify ways in which the biblical experience of the trinitarian God illuminates the human experience of longing for truth, goodness, and beauty. This experience of "longing" raises the question of time. Before moving more explicitly to the task of reconstruction, we need to identify resources for articulating the Christian doctrine of the infinite trinitarian God in a way that makes sense of the creaturely experience of temporality.

· 7 ·

RENEWING ESCHATOLOGICAL ONTOLOGY

The relation between the eternal God and temporal being is at the heart of our third late modern trajectory. Broadly speaking, "eschatological ontology" involves the metaphysical claim that in some sense creaturely *being* is constituted by the *coming* of God. Twentieth-century proposals on the ontological significance of the future have more often been met with confusion than critique. While the epistemological and ethical importance of the future (e.g., the anticipation of ideals) is commonly acknowledged, theological eyebrows are suspiciously raised upon hearing proposals for the *ontological* priority of the future. As the renewal of interest in divine Futurity crossed the Atlantic from Germany to North America in the 1960s, Carl Braaten commended it heartily but acknowledged that this conceptual exercise "threatens hernia of the mind."[1] This is surely due in part to several infelicitous formulations of the idea. However, if braided together with intensive Infinity and robust Trinity, the idea of absolute Futurity may very well provide us with the generative power to do some of the conceptual heavy lifting that seemed impossible under the constraints of early modern categories. Part III will explore this possibility in detail; our purpose in this chapter is simply to trace the factors that contributed to this ongoing trajectory and to begin the process of clarifying the concept of "Futurity."

In Chapter 4 we observed shifts in philosophical and scientific under-

1. Carl Braaten, *The Future of God* (New York: Harper & Row, 1969), 16.

standings of causality and temporality since the seventeenth century that have challenged theological formulations that rely heavily on the category of past efficient causation in their depictions of the relation between Creator and creature. Like the other trajectories, we saw that the surge of interest in eschatological ontology was not simply a response to philosophical and scientific developments, however, but a *renewal* of the emphasis on the irreducibly eschatological experience of the presence of God. In this chapter we explore some of the resources in the Christian tradition that have fueled this renewal, searching for insights that can be woven together with the other trajectories, for the sake of presenting the gospel of the biblical God in late modern culture.

The early modern use of the concept of first cause was partly aimed at protecting the Christian intuitions that God is the origin of all things and that God is not susceptible to the decay associated with the creaturely causal nexus. These intuitions should continue to guide the Christian doctrine of God, even as we struggle to overcome the early modern dependence on the category of *causa efficiens primaria*. The late modern renewal of eschatological ontology provides resources for this task, opening up conceptual space for an articulation of the Futurity of God as the origin, condition, and goal of all creaturely temporality and causality.

§7.1. Traditional Resources

The tendency to emphasize God as first efficient cause was more dominant in Western theology than in Eastern theology. It will be no surprise that several of the most influential resources for renewing eschatological ontology derive from the Eastern Orthodox tradition. St. Irenaeus was one of the first and most influential of the patristic theologians who emphasized the ontological importance of the future. In his late-second-century *Against Heresies,* he argued that the first humans were created with an orientation toward a future in which they would be united with Christ, becoming the image and likeness of God.[2] The concept of the future *anakephalaiōsis* or *recapitulatio* of all creation in Christ was central not only for Irenaeus's theological anthropology, but for his whole theology.[3]

---

2. *Adversus Haereses,* IV.33.4, V.16.2; ANF, 1:507, 544.

3. Cf. Gustaf Wingren, *Man and the Incarnation: A Study in the Biblical Theology of*

This Irenaean theme was an important contribution to later developments in the doctrine of creation that emphasized that all things are from the Father *and* to the Father. The origination of creation in relation to God is intrinsically an orientation *to* God, which suggests that temporality itself is conditioned by its relation to the Eternal.

For Gregory of Nyssa, an emphasis on God's presence as the eschatological reality that evokes human desire toward the future flows naturally from his view of divine Infinity. In *The Life of Moses* he observed that God is unlimited and infinite Good: "since this good has not limit, the participant's desire itself necessarily has no stopping place but stretches out with the limitless . . . the perfection of human nature consists perhaps in its very growth in goodness."[4] As we saw in Chapter 4, the inherently future-oriented nature of the cosmos was also recognized by several ancient Greek philosophers. When Plotinus treated the issue of time and Eternity, he explicitly related the human experience of the latter to futurity: Eternity is the fullness of Life, and what future "could bring to that Being anything which it now does not possess?" (*Enneads,* III.7.3). The existence and movement of all (generated) things require the future. Eliminating futurity would destroy their being; their movement "seeks perpetuity by way of futurity" (III.7.4). The "will be" (τὸ ἔσται) cannot be predicated of the Eternal; rather, all temporal things have their "going to be" (μέλλοντος) in relation to their orientation toward the Eternal. Insofar as the mystical tradition emphasized the human longing for union with God as an orienting reality, we may speak of the critical appropriation of this Neoplatonic insight for theological reconstruction.

Engagement with Greek patristic theologians has been an important factor in the thought of most of the Lutheran and Reformed proposals we will outline below. As we will see, however, these scholars also appeal to the eschatological imagination that drove the work of the early Reformers themselves. The heuristic force of the concept of God's promising presence was never lost in the West, although its generative power was constrained in the early modern period. The idea of Futurity is probably less familiar to most Protestant readers than Infinity or Trinity, so we will devote more

Irenaeus, trans. R. MacKenzie (Philadelphia: Muhlenberg, 1959). Cf. Douglas Farrow, *Ascension and Ecclesia: On the Significance of the Doctrine of the Ascension for Ecclesiology and Christian Cosmology* (Grand Rapids: Eerdmans, 1999).

4. *Life of Moses,* trans. A. J. Malherbe and E. Ferguson (New York: Paulist Press, 1978), 31.

space to Luther and Calvin here than we did in §5.1 and §6.1. Although both were voluntarists,[5] their theological projects were also shaped by powerful emphases on the creative power of God's promising presence. I do not claim that they explicitly anticipated the strong accent on the ontological priority of the future that emerged in the late twentieth century. Nevertheless, it seems fair to say that emphases in their writings prepared the way for later theologians to liberate the illuminative power of eschatological ontology once science and philosophy moved away from the past-privileging determinism that dominated early modern views of temporality and causality.

Martin Luther

One of the significant insights of the renewal of Luther scholarship in the twentieth century was the recognition of the centrality of eschatology for his theological project. According to Regin Prenter, Luther's whole theological vision was focused on God's presence in, to, and for us, not as a transcendent impersonal causality, but as a present reality mediated through the Spirit of Christ — this reality "is the living and acting God himself who draws us into his all-embracing, eschatological saving act."[6] Winfried Vogel suggests that Luther's emphasis on the future consummation was so pervasive that his whole work should be labeled "eschatological" theology.[7] Luther argued that all of creation is granted being through the word of promise; this led to the eschatological saturation of his treatment of every theological theme. The eschatological goal of creation was at the heart of Luther's understanding of the faith, for without belief in the article of the resurrection and the future life, he argued that all the other articles "and the entire Christ are lost or preached entirely in vain. For after all, that is the goal of our faith in Christ, of Baptism, of sermon, and of

5. For Luther, "What God wills is not right because He ought, or was bound, so to will; on the contrary, what takes place must be right, because He so wills it" (*Bondage of the Will*, 196). For Calvin, nothing can finally alter the will or power of God (*Inst.*, I.18.1, 2).

6. Regin Prenter, *Spiritus Creator: Luther's Concept of the Holy Spirit*, trans. John M. Jensen (Philadelphia: Muhlenberg, 1953), 171.

7. Winfried Vogel, "The Eschatological Theology of Martin Luther — Part I: Luther's Basic Concepts," *Andrews University Seminary Studies* 24, no. 3 (Autumn 1986): 249-64 at 250.

Sacrament, that we hope for a new life, that we come to Christ, that we rule eternally with Him, delivered from sin, devil, death, and every evil."[8]

Although the later Lutheran Scholastics maintain a formal orientation toward eschatological themes,[9] it is the general consensus of scholars that they materially diverge from Luther here. This divergence may be perceived in at least three important areas. First, as Paul Althaus suggests, seventeenth-century theology involved more reliance on medieval discussions of a metaphysical doctrine of the soul.[10] A review of the Lutheran Scholastics seems to confirm this judgment. Most of the energy in their eschatological analysis is devoted to arguments for the immortality of the soul, relying on a mixture of Platonic and Aristotelian anthropological models.[11] Luther was naturally interested in the salvation of the soul, but he was less apt to rely on the medieval categories that had shaped the Roman Catholic articulation of these doctrines.

Second, in the systematic organization of themes, the Scholastics tended to separate the material treatment of the idea of *Eternity* as a divine attribute from their discussions of the trinitarian God. For Luther, however, the Eternity of God's triune life is present already in a way that justifies and makes new. Finally, the Scholastics allowed the medieval debates over *causality* (newly figured in light of the early modern mechanistic science) to structure their analyses of the transition to final states. Eschatology was about the determination and interpretation of the sequence of the "last things" *(eschata)* to occur at the end of linear time, things that had already been determined by God as the "first cause." For Luther, on the other hand, examination of what later came to be called the "last things" was not the main theme of his eschatology, but only one consequence of his whole essentially eschatological theology.[12]

---

8. *LW,* 28.60.

9. Cf. Erhard Kunz, *Protestantische Eschatologie: Von der Reformation bis zur Aufklärung* (Freiburg: Herder, 1980), 44.

10. Paul Althaus, *The Theology of Martin Luther,* trans. Robert C. Schultz (Philadelphia: Fortress, 1966), 417.

11. This holds true at least for J. Gerhard (1582-1637), C. Brochmann (1585-1682), D. Hollaz (1646-1713), and J. A. Quenstedt (1617-1688), though perhaps less true for L. Hutter (1563-1616) and A. Calov (1612-1686). Cf. Schmid, *DTEL,* 624-33.

12. Cf. Ulrich Asendorf, *Eschatologie bei Luther* (Göttingen: Vandenhoeck & Ruprecht, 1967), 280-94. This had been emphasized earlier by Althaus, *The Theology of Martin Luther,* 404-5.

Several factors contributed to Luther's eschatological emphasis, including his reaction to the this-worldliness of the papacy and his sense of an imminent judgment on the decaying society around him. Eschatological and "scatological" language about the pope and the devil are sometimes intimately linked for Luther.[13] The significant theological factor, however, was his rigorous scriptural exegesis, which led to his discovery of an emphasis on the future throughout the Bible. This eschatological dynamism is built into his understanding of the doctrine of justification by faith. The eschatological aspect of the process of justification allows Luther to maintain both the *simul* and the *initium*, which belong directly together.[14] Luther's assertion that the believer is *simul iustus et peccator* (at once righteous and a sinner) is complemented by the idea of the divine *initium* — the gracious initiative of God through which the believer already begins to experience a relation to God that will be fulfilled eschatologically.

This idea is spelled out in various ways in his treatment of the life of those whose justification by faith has been initiated. In the case of baptism, we can see the regulative role of the eschatological initiative. Although death "is not yet entirely swallowed up in us, the victory gained by Christ is already present, and through Gospel, Baptism, and faith it has become our victory" — although the sacrament of baptism is quickly over, "the spiritual baptism, the drowning of sin, which it signifies, lasts as long as we live and is completed only in death."[15] Lutheran theologians have increasingly recognized the importance of eschatology for Luther and its impact on distinctive Lutheran doctrines such as justification by faith,[16] the classic distinction between law and gospel,[17] and the doctrine of the two kingdoms.[18]

---

13. Cf. Heiko Oberman, "Teufelsdreck: Eschatology and Scatology in the 'Old' Luther," *The Sixteenth Century Journal* 19, no. 3 (Fall 1988): 435-50.

14. Asendorf, *Eschatologie*, 42.

15. *LW*, 28.206; 35.30.

16. Martin Seils, "Luther's Significance for Contemporary Theological Anthropology," in *Luther's Ecumenical Significance*, ed. P. Manns et al. (Philadelphia: Fortress, 1984), 183-202 at 196-97.

17. Gerhard Forde, "The Formula of Concord Article V: End or New Beginning?" *dialog* 15, no. 3 (Summer 1976): 184-91 at 189.

18. Asendorf, *Eschatologie*, 248ff.

John Calvin

The popular linking of Calvin's name to views that stress divine predetermination might lead us to dismiss his theology as a potential resource for the renewal of eschatological ontology. Such a judgment would be premature. The significant emphasis on the future that pervaded Calvin's writings has too often been obscured by some of his followers. In addition to a "push-view" of history, Calvin also had what has been called a "pull-view" of history. David Holwerda argues that some "Calvinists" have not been fully attentive to "the dynamic, active pulling into the future stemming from the renewal already possessed in hope" that characterized Calvin's own theology.[19] After the hardening of mechanistic science in the seventeenth century many later Reformed Scholastics attended primarily to the past-oriented aspects of Calvin's thought, in a way that was not characteristic of his earlier followers such as Zanchi.[20] Erhard Kunz has suggested that Calvin's eschatology permeates so many of his doctrinal presentations because his very understanding of God itself is characteristically eschatological.[21]

The dynamic nature of the "future life" captured Calvin's imagination early in his career as a reformer. *Psychopannychia* was his first theological work, written in 1534, although it was not published until 1542.[22] His concern in this book was to defend against the Anabaptist teaching that the soul sleeps after death. For a believer, Calvin insists, to die is to be united with Christ, who by his death and resurrection has already initiated the kingdom of God. Therefore, it makes no sense to postulate an intermediate state of sleep.

Calvin's eschatology is christologically driven. In *De Meditatio vitae futurae* (*Inst.*, III.9) he emphasizes the importance of becoming aware of one's relation to Christ, which is still future but already participated in

19. D. Holwerda, "Eschatology and History: A Look at Calvin's Eschatological Vision," in *Exploring the Heritage of John Calvin,* ed. Holwerda (Grand Rapids: Baker, 1976), 110-39 at 138.

20. John L. Farthing, "Christ and the Eschaton: The Reformed Eschatology of Jerome Zanchi," in *Later Calvinism: International Perspectives,* ed. W. Fred Graham (Kirksville, Mo.: Sixteenth Century Journal Publishers, 1994), 332-54.

21. E. Kunz, *Protestantische Eschatologie: Von der Reformation bis zur Aufklärung* (Freiburg: Herder, 1980), 31.

22. For background on this early work, see George H. Tavard, *The Starting Point of Calvin's Theology* (Grand Rapids: Eerdmans, 2000).

through the Spirit of promise. This christological mediation of the believer's future is also clear in his *Commentaries*. In the prayer at the end of his comments on Daniel 12:1-4, Calvin asks that Christ "may ever admit us into alliance with himself in that conquest which he has procured for us."[23] Earlier he had spoken of Christ as eternal in himself, but also as the one who "communicates his eternity to" those who hope so that they are "now not mortal only" but "bear within them heavenly life."[24] This is life in the tension between the initiation and the consummation, between the ascension and return of Christ.

Calvin privileged *hope* alongside faith and love in a way that set him apart from many other Reformers. T. F. Torrance argued that, in distinction from Luther's eschatology of faith and Bucer's eschatology of love, Calvin's view may be described as "the eschatology of hope."[25] Heinrich Quistorp even went so far as to apply this not merely to his eschatology but to his whole theology: Calvin may be characterized as the *theologian of hope*. Eschatology is the center and aim of the whole of Calvin's theology: "all his declarations are, so to speak, concerned with the future."[26] Calvin did not have a separate section on "last things" in the *Institutes*, but his theology was wholly eschatological — focused on the source of new being and life. Not only humanity, but all of creation is moved by this hope. In his commentary on Romans 8:20, Calvin spoke of natural movement, including the alacrity of the sun's shining and the sedulity of the earth's fruitfulness, as springing *from hope*, for God "implanted inwardly the hope of renovation" in the universe itself.[27]

Another resource is Calvin's preference for dynamic, personal, fellowship-oriented depictions of God's redemptive relation to humanity. In contrast to the more abstract volitional causality typical of many medieval theologians (and some of Calvin's own followers), Calvin himself empha-

---

23. *Commentaries*, XIII, 380. The original French sounds more dynamic, personal, and participative than the English translation: "Jésus Christ, ton Fils ne combatte tellement pour nous qu'il nous recevra tousjours en la compagnie et participation de la victoire qu'il nous a acquise."

24. *Commentaries*, XII, 188.

25. T. F. Torrance, *Kingdom and Church: A Study in the Theology of the Reformation* (London: Oliver and Boyd, 1956).

26. H. Quistorp, *Calvin's Doctrine of Last Things*, trans. H. Knight (London: Lutterworth, 1955), 15.

27. *Commentaries*, XIX, 304.

sized the more dynamic metaphors of personal agency and fellowship. While much Western medieval theology articulated the relation of God to the world through the concept of "causality," linked to the will of a single divine subject, Calvin more strongly emphasized the personal mediation of creation through the agency of the Son and the Spirit. Yes, the sovereign God is the cause of all things, including salvation, but Calvin makes it clear that the form and goal of this sovereign causality are personal and relational (e.g. *Inst.*, III.9.10).

Calvin's eschatology and his Christology are intertwined: "as Christ begins the glory of his body in this world with manifold diversity of gifts, and increases it by degrees, so also he will perfect it in heaven" (*Inst.*, III.10). Pneumatology is also woven into the fabric of his understanding of God's redemptive relation to creatures. The "way" in which we receive the grace of Christ by the secret working of the Spirit and the "means" by which God invites us into the society of Christ and holds us therein (*Inst.*, IV) are mediated through the triune God's providential care for creatures. Although Calvin inherited (and never fully escaped) a past-oriented causal concept of predestination, he consistently emphasized the personal, dynamic, and future-oriented relation of creation to God. For Calvin, Eternity's relation to time should be understood not in terms of the passing of hours, but as "la présence ou l'absence de Dieu" to which humans respond in faith or impiety.[28] The divine presence orients creatures toward the future by presenting them with the promise of new being; this aspect of Calvin's theology is an important resource for the late modern renewal of the eschatological ontology in Reformed theology.

§7.2. Reformed Reconstructions

The eschatological emphasis in twentieth-century Reformed theology is certainly not limited to Barth, Gunton, and Moltmann. For example, we might have included Emil Brunner's description of the life of the Christian in the church as the present reality of the future, made possible by the personal presence of the One who makes all things new.[29] For the sake of con-

28. Cf. Oliver Fatio, "Remarques sur le temp et l'éternité chez Calvin," in *Temps et Eschatologie: Données bibliques et problématiques contemporaines*, ed. Jean-Louis Leuba (Paris: Cerf, 1994), 161-72 at 172.

29. E. Brunner, *Eternal Hope* (Philadelphia: Westminster, 1954), 59-66.

tinuity and showing the connections between Infinity and Trinity, we will limit ourselves to the same Reformed representatives.

Karl Barth

At least three aspects of Barth's theology contributed to the renewal of eschatological ontology. First, Barth makes eschatology more central to his theology than did many of his Reformed predecessors, and links it to Christ in a new way. In the second edition of *The Epistle to the Romans,* Barth argued, "If Christianity be not altogether thoroughgoing eschatology, there remains in it no relationship whatever with Christ."[30] He explicitly rejected the idea that human conduct could be traced to the will of God as its efficient cause. Who would dare, Barth asks, speak of God and humanity as "links in a chain of causality"?[31] He clearly has some of the Protestant Scholastics in mind.

For Barth, God confronts humanity not as a first cause *(Ursache),* but as primal origin *(Ursprung).* Eschatology and Christology are inherently linked because reflecting on the incarnation of the divine Word in Jesus Christ leads us to speak of divine Eternity as a true Eternity that "includes this possibility, the potentiality of time . . . [that] has the power to take time to itself" *(CD,* II/1, 617). Barth attempted to root the Reformed doctrine of predestination or "gracious election" *(Gnadewahl)* in Christology and eschatology, both of which are essential for understanding the being of God. While the link between God's electing activity and Christology was not new to the Reformed tradition, Barth refigured the link in a way that drew eschatology closer to the center of the doctrine of God.

A second Barthian contribution was the recovery of Calvin's emphasis on hope. In the last completed volume of the *Dogmatics,* he returns to the intimate connection between Christology and eschatology. The expectation of the *parousia* of Jesus Christ as the "end, and therefore the dawn of eternal light," permeates the Christian life in hope *(CD,* IV/3.2, 934). It is ironic that this subsection, which is titled "The Holy Spirit and Christian Hope," hardly mentions the Spirit; this is indicative of his weak

30. K. Barth, *The Epistle to the Romans,* 2nd ed., trans. Edwyn Hoskyns (Oxford: Oxford University Press, 1968), 314.
31. Barth, *Romans,* 356.

pneumatology. Even if Barth has not done full justice to the topic, we may still appreciate his insistence that the idea of Christian hope ought to be brought into the center of theological discourse. His *Evangelical Theology* includes a chapter on hope and its role in the task (and being) of the theologian. Barth insists that in faithfulness to its character as a *theologia crucis,* theology will also be a *theologia gloriae* because it is the cross that gives rise to hope.[32] In his monograph on *Ethics,* Barth also elevates hope in relation to faith and love. After treating the latter two ideas, he notes that when we come to the concept of hope, we have entered the "innermost eschatological circle of ethical reflection." This hope in God alters our understanding and experience of time in relation to Eternity: "in hope, we are citizens of the future world in the midst of the present . . . faith and love and hope are in and with each other the obedience that is required of us. But if faith does it with respect and love with hot necessity, hope does it with what has already secretly become the present felicity."[33]

Barth's third and perhaps most important contribution to the renewal of theological interest in Futurity was his way of describing Eternity as *positively* related to time. For Barth, Eternity embraces time in three "forms," which he calls pre-temporality, supra-temporality and post-temporality. He notes that the Reformers (and many of their predecessors) showed a dangerous one-sided interest in *pre*-temporality; under this model the doctrines of election and providence often appeared fatalistic. Barth thought that most Protestant liberal theology in the nineteenth century (and especially Schleiermacher) was too focused merely on God's *supra*-temporality — the emphasis fell too heavily on the "now" of human consciousness and its dependence on the divine in each moment. In contrast to both of these tendencies, the early Barth sought to emphasize the *post*-temporality of God. Later, in the *Church Dogmatics,* Barth recognized that in his own early writings his enthusiasm for thinking "with new seriousness about God's futurity" (II/1, 636) had led him to risk reducing divine Eternity to its post-temporal form. To avoid this he argued that the three forms of Eternity are equally God's Eternity and "therefore the living God Himself."[34] Barth's argument for a

---

32. K. Barth, *Evangelical Theology: An Introduction,* trans. Grover Foley (Grand Rapids: Eerdmans, 1963), 155.

33. K. Barth, *Ethics,* trans. G. W. Bromiley (New York: Seabury, 1981), 513-14.

34. *CD,* II/1, 638. Ingolf Dalferth provides insight into this important aspect of his thought in "Karl Barth's Eschatological Realism," in *Karl Barth: Centenary Essays,* ed. S. W.

positive "embracing" relation between Eternity and time led to a reconsideration of the Reformed reliance on the idea of God as first cause.

Colin Gunton

Gunton also insists that Eternity and time should be expressed in terms of a positive relation rather than a simple opposition. In fact, he was critical of Barth for vacillating between these two ways of expressing the relation, arguing that his view of analogy ultimately led him to neglect the Futurity of God.[35] For Gunton, Christology is the impetus for bringing eschatology into the heart of theology: we must learn from "the fact that the New Testament is more interested in the ontological than the noetic significance of Jesus's futurity."[36] While modern thought (e.g., Kant) denies the possibility of knowing Eternity and focuses on the temporal, and ancient thought (e.g., Plato) denigrates the temporal and focuses on knowledge of the eternal, they share the same presupposition: a dualism between time and Eternity in which these realms are mutually and negatively defined.[37]

Gunton calls for a return to the explicitly Christological way of dealing with this relation. For theologians like Athanasius, Eternity and time are positively related. In the history of Jesus of Nazareth, we have the "good news of the movement into time of the eternal," which allows Christian theology to speak of time as the "positive creation of the eternal love." The eternal is conceived as a "time-embracing and not a time-denying reality."[38] In his later work, *The Triune Creator*, Gunton is particularly critical of Augustine's view of time and Eternity and argues for a retrieval of the Cappadocians, especially Basil of Caesarea.[39]

Sykes (Cambridge: Cambridge University Press, 1989), 14-45. Dalferth's own attempt to link eschatology and ontology may be found in his *Existenz Gottes und christlicher Glaube: Skizzen zu einer eschatologischen Ontologie* (Munich: Kaiser, 1984).

35. C. Gunton, *Becoming and Being* (Oxford: Oxford University Press, 1978), 183-85.

36. C. Gunton, *Yesterday and Today: A Study of Continuities in Christology* (Grand Rapids: Eerdmans, 1983), 131.

37. Gunton, *Yesterday*, 111.

38. Gunton, *Yesterday*, 128-30.

39. C. Gunton, *The Triune Creator* (Grand Rapids: Eerdmans, 1998), 68-69, 79-80. For his interest in Basil, see Gunton's essay "Between Allegory and Myth: The Legacy of the Spiritualising of Genesis," in *The Doctrine of Creation*, ed. Gunton (Edinburgh: T&T Clark,

Gunton is partial to Irenaeus's view of creation as an eschatological project. He argues that an adequate articulation of the doctrine of the Tri-une Creator requires this rigorous eschatological orientation.[40] His view of Futurity in his later works, however, becomes less ontological and more focused on the epistemological and the ethical. For example, in his treatment of revelation he speaks of the future as validating the tradition, but distances himself from those who want to speak of the "priority of the future."[41] Not only human knowing, but also human acting must be conceptualized in light of the positive relation between Eternity and time, which orients persons toward the future. If humans are intrinsically relational beings, we may think of God's gracious action as "that whereby he realizes forms of relationality which can be described as free."[42]

For the later Gunton, particular creatures are each directed *to* rather than *from* "their particular future end, their God-given *telos* or goal."[43] This means that the same tensions we found in the early modern projects resurface in Gunton's theology. If the project of creation is directed toward a determinate future, how can humans really be free? If the project of creation is determined by a wholly good God, why do we experience the existence of sin and evil, which appear to imperil this future? While the early Gunton chastised Barth for insufficiently emphasizing Futurity, the later Gunton was wary of the proposals of Moltmann, Pannenberg, and others, who he believed overemphasized Futurity.[44]

1997), 47-62 at 58-60. Augustine is the target of a crucial chapter in Gunton's *The Promise of Trinitarian Theology*, 2nd ed. (Edinburgh: T&T Clark, 1997): "Augustine, the Trinity, and the Theological Crisis of the West," 30-55. Throughout the latter work, the Cappadocians are a source for the remedial work of trinitarian theology (e.g., 9, 39-42, 52-54, 204-5).

40. Gunton, *Triune Creator*, 212.

41. C. Gunton, *A Brief Theology of Revelation* (Edinburgh: T&T Clark, 1995), 88. Similarly, "The question of systematic theology is the question of eschatology, of how far our intellectual constructions may anticipate such eschatological perfections of knowledge as may one day be granted us" (*Intellect and Action* [Edinburgh: T&T Clark, 2000], 36).

42. C. Gunton, "God, Grace and Freedom," in *God and Freedom*, ed. Gunton (Edinburgh: T&T Clark, 1995), 119-33 at 131.

43. C. Gunton, "Dogmatic Theses on Eschatology," in *The Future as God's Gift*, ed. D. Fergusson and M. Sarot (Edinburgh: T&T Clark, 2000), 139-43 at 142.

44. For a more detailed critique of Pannenberg and Moltmann, see his *Triune Creator*, 216-24. Yet Gunton speaks of the "strength of recent theologies like that of Pannenberg which speak of things being created from the future" because they suggest a completion that is "destined, but not fully determined, in advance" (p. 184).

One of Gunton's most significant contributions to the incorporation of eschatology into the doctrine of God was his campaign against the dominance of the category of first cause in the doctrine of creation. In his article "The End of Causality?" Gunton traces the development and use of the concept of divine causality in the Middle Ages, arguing that the focus on the divine will led to an abstract concept of God's causal relation to the world and intensified the problem of creaturely freedom. The antinomy is not solved by the distinction between primary and secondary causality, he argues, because the latter is either too strong (making God's causality redundant) or too weak (not causal in a robust sense).[45] For Gunton, the problem is the lack of emphasis on the personal mediation of creation through the agency of the Son and the Spirit. He argues that the Reformers began the process of replacing abstract concepts of causality with concepts that connote more personal and loving agency. Rather than focusing their attention on proofs for the existence of a single first cause, Luther and Calvin emphasized a trinitarianly mediated understanding of God's creative and providential agency in the world.

In his own final systematic proposal, *The Christian Faith*, Gunton discusses the eschatological agency of God with special reference to the Holy Spirit. The work of the Spirit has an "eschatological force" as the "perfecting cause" of creation, and this shapes his understanding of the eternal being of God. "In eternity the Spirit is the one who . . . perfects the being of God, so as first to enable the relation between the Father and the Son to be properly described as one of love; and second to provide the basis for God's movement out into the world in his Son to create and redeem."[46] In this way Gunton aims to integrate eschatology and Trinity within the doctrine of God.

Jürgen Moltmann

The theme of the Futurity of God pervades all of Moltmann's work.[47] We will attend to three general aspects of his contribution to the renewal of eschatological ontology. First, in his *Theology of Hope*, which gave a name to

45. C. Gunton, "The End of Causality?" in Gunton, ed., *The Doctrine of Creation*, 63-82 at 74 n. 36.

46. C. Gunton, *The Christian Faith* (Oxford: Blackwell, 2002), 185-86.

47. The significance of this concept for Moltmann is indicated by the title chosen for his German Festschrift: *Gottes Zukunft: Zukunft der Welt*, ed. H. Deuser et al. (Munich: Kaiser, 1986).

a theological movement that intensified in the 1960s, Moltmann called for a hermeneutic of "hope seeking understanding." This grew out of his desire to articulate an understanding of God that is not abstracted from Christology and Pneumatology. The coming consummation of God's kingdom through the Spirit is already present in the promises of Jesus, whose gospel "proclaims the present breaking in of this future, and thus *vice versa* this coming future announces itself in the promises of the gospel."[48] Those who follow Jesus interpret the world in light of God's future for the world; they are "placed in the midst of a history which is instituted and determined by the mission of Jesus and by his future as revealed and made an object of hope in the fore-glow of Easter."[49]

In several early articles, he stressed the New Testament category of the "new" and its importance for the early church's understanding of the present and coming Christ.[50] Moltmann's concern is not primarily with the "end" of the world but with the "goal" of the world, with the Future that has already begun — the Christian and the church find their being in active participation in the breaking-in of the new creation that is transforming and will finally transfigure the "old." One of the most controversial aspects of Moltmann's theology is his insistence that the history of the Son and the Spirit in relation to the world brings something "new" even for "God himself within the Trinity."[51] Perhaps with Jüngel in mind (see §7.3 below), he observes that "God's being is in his coming, not in his *be*coming. . . . If God and the future are linked together theologically in this way, God's being has to be thought of eschatologically; and then the future has to be understood theologically . . . in this way the future becomes the paradigm of transcendence."[52]

48. J. Moltmann, *Theology of Hope,* trans. James Leitch (Minneapolis: Fortress, 1993), 139. Originally published in German 1965.

49. Moltmann, *Theology of Hope,* 202.

50. J. Moltmann, "'Behold, I make all things new': The Category of the New in Christian Theology," in *The Future as the Presence of Shared Hope,* ed. Maryellen Muckenhirn (New York: Sheed and Ward, 1968), 9-33; "Religion, Revolution and the Future," in *The Future of Hope,* ed. Walter Capps (Philadelphia: Westminster, 1971), 102-26; "Hope and the Biomedical Future of Man," in *Hope and the Future of Man,* ed. Ewert H. Cousins (Philadelphia: Fortress, 1972), 89-104.

51. J. Moltmann, *The Church in the Power of the Spirit,* trans. Margaret Kohl (New York: Harper & Row, 1977), 62. Cf. Moltmann, "Is the World Coming to an End or Has Its Future Already Begun?" in Fergusson and Sarot, eds., *The Future as God's Gift,* 129-38.

52. J. Moltmann, *God in Creation,* trans. Margaret Kohl (New York: Harper and Row, 1985), 133-34.

A second contribution derives from Moltmann's engagement with scientific and philosophical reflection on the priority of the future, which he believes can help liberate theology from its dependence on past-privileging models of causality. Already in the 1960s, Moltmann was engaging natural scientific descriptions of causality that were moving away from the idea of a transition from *causa* to *effectus*, and toward the concept of a transition from possibility to reality.[53] His later constructive proposals build on the work of philosophers such as Picht, Luhmann, and von Weizsäcker, who have argued that it is not the past but the future that has priority in the experience of human freedom. These new philosophical theories of time justify considering the "future" to be the "transcendental condition for the possibility of time in general."[54] Moltmann rejects the reduction of God's creative power to the category of a *causa prima* that uses *causae secundae*. To the question, "what moves time in the complex networking of our experience of the modes of time?" Moltmann answers, the "eschatological future," which is not simply future history, but the future *of* history, which transcends "all remembered, experienced and still-to-be experienced presents."[55]

For Moltmann, the early modern view in which God pre-programs a redemptive "plan" cannot finally be distinguished from historical Deism. The cosmological arguments of classical theism, which moved backward from effect to cause, did not answer the atheistic protest about suffering and evil, but in fact *provoked* it.[56] Theism and a-theism share the presupposition that God must be thought of as the first cause of the world. If God is "pure causality," wholly unmoved, then the suffering of the cross has no relevance for the divine life. Instead Moltmann proposes that theology begin with the future of God manifested in the sign of the crucified Christ; God is revealed as the One who raises the dead.[57]

If God's being is thought eschatologically, and the future is thought

---

53. Moltmann, *Theology of Hope*, 243.

54. J. Moltmann, "The Bible, the Exegete, and the Theologian," in *God Will Be All in All: The Eschatology of Jürgen Moltmann*, ed. R. Bauckham (Edinburgh: T&T Clark, 1999), 228.

55. Moltmann, *God in Creation*, 129. Moltmann also suggests that evolutionary theory fits better, not with a unilinear chain of causality, but as a fanning out and open extending of new structures (202).

56. J. Moltmann, *The Crucified God*, trans. R. A. Wilson and J. Bowden (San Francisco: Harper & Row, 1974), 221.

57. Moltmann, *Crucified*, 221, 214, 187-88.

theologically, then past and future are no longer reduced to the same *linear* temporal concept, but are related by the qualitative difference between "old" and new."[58] Moltmann does not intend to imply that the past is unimportant, but rather that the history of Christ must be understood in terms of both its origin and its future. This future is mediated not only christologically but also pneumatologically. He describes the Spirit as "the power of futurity," for it is through the power of the Spirit that creatures are "opened up and urged on by the future of the thing that is entirely new."[59]

In *The Coming of God*, Moltmann pulls together previous emphases and develops new ones.[60] He distinguishes between the Latin terms *futurum*, the "future" that develops out of the past and present, and *adventus* as that which is "coming." When the New Testament speaks of the coming one, it has *adventus* in mind — which is why this term is used to translate the Greek word *parousia*. For Moltmann, "the future is God's mode of being in history . . . the power of the future is his power in time" (24). God's coming to the world and making of all things new is the "source" of time. "The essence of its [the world's] time is *futurity*, as indeed its beginning too was the future" (283). Moltmann also stresses the categories of beauty and the aesthetic, with special reference to the imagery of feasting in the final reign of God. In the final sections of *The Coming of God*, he deals with the question of *divine* eschatology, or the meaning "for God himself" of the glorification of the world. He is critical of attempts to use the distinction between God's essence and will (Scholasticism) or the idea of the self-realization of the Absolute (Hegel) to answer this question because both lead to the self-glorification of a *single* divine subject. Instead Moltmann argues for a trinitarian understanding of the consummation of the world, which brings about a "new" experience *for* God — the eschatological "handing over of the kingdom" by the Son to the Father is "evidently an inner-trinitarian process too" (335).

58. Moltmann, *God in Creation*, 134.

59. Moltmann, *The Church in the Power of the Spirit*, 34.

60. J. Moltmann, *The Coming of God*, trans. Margaret Kohl (Minneapolis: Fortress, 1996). Page numbers in the text refer to this edition. For an exposition and analysis of this book, see Richard Bauckham, ed., *God Will Be All in All: The Eschatology of Jürgen Moltmann*.

§7.3. Lutheran Reconstructions

Several Lutheran theologians played a role in the renewal of eschatological ontology in the twentieth century. Carl Braaten, for example, contributed many provocative and memorable phrases to the discussion. He depicted the rule of God's power as "present in Jesus through advance symptoms of its futurity," described Jesus as the "fulcrum of the future," and spoke of Christian disciples as those who "look to the hills of God's future for redemption" and as "partisans of the future."[61] For the sake of continuity and comparison, however, we will limit ourselves once again to illustrating this renewal in the work of Jenson, Jüngel, and Pannenberg.

Robert Jenson

The concept of the Futurity of God runs like a thread through Jenson's works. Already in his early books, it was clear that for him divine Futurity bears not only on issues of authentic knowledge and agency but also on metaphysics. While *The Knowledge of Things Hoped For* focused on the epistemic and ethical implications of Futurity,[62] his essays in *The Futurist Option* emphasized the ontological significance of the eschatological presence of God.[63] A basic theme in *Story and Promise* is the claim that through the word of promise God incorporates creatures into the divine

---

61. Carl Braaten, "God and the Idea of the Future," *Dialog* 7 (Autumn 1968): 252-59 at 255-57. Braaten argued that a prioritization of the future is implied by biblical belief that in Jesus of Nazareth the end of history has appeared, yet without ceasing to be future. "In his very being God is the future of the world. He is the common future and unifying force of all contingent events in nature and history. . . . If God is not his own future, there would be some other future beyond him, and this would have to be thought of as God. The very idea of God requires that we think of him as the ultimate future" (C. Braaten and R. Jenson, eds., *The Futurist Option* [New York: Newman Press, 1970], 28-29). Jesus "made present the reality of God's future in a concentrated way" (Braaten, "The Recovery of Apocalyptic Imagination," in *The Last Things: Biblical and Theological Perspectives on Eschatology*, ed. C. Braaten and R. Jenson [Grand Rapids: Eerdmans, 2002], 14-32 at 20). For additional examples, see Gerhard Sauter, *What Dare We Hope?* (Harrisburg, Pa.: Trinity Press International, 1999); Hans Schwarz, *Eschatology* (Grand Rapids: Eerdmans, 2000).

62. R. Jenson, *The Knowledge of Things Hoped For* (Oxford: Oxford University Press, 1969), 168-69.

63. Jenson, *The Futurist Option*, esp. 147ff. and 166-67.

story by giving the world its future.[64] In his book on Barth, which is sub-titled "The God of the Past and the God of the Future," Jenson is critical of Barth's unwillingness to take seriously the priority of the future. Jenson argues that the Futurity of God is the very structure of the trinitarian life and is present to the world as the condition for human freedom.[65]

God is not a causal power over against creatures, but rather the life of the triune God is "the condition of the subsistence of any reality that intuition will let us call time. . . . created time must be the *accommodation* God makes in his own life for persons other than the three he himself is."[66] In his chapter on the Being of God in *Christian Dogmatics,* Jenson describes God as "the event by which the world has a future, to *be* a world of time."[67] In his later *Systematic Theology,* Jenson maintains this emphasis: God is "primally future to himself and only thereupon past and present for himself." It is Futurity that determines divine Infinity: God is *temporally* infinite "because 'source' and 'goal' are present *and* asymmetrical in him."[68]

Jenson's linking of eschatology and ontology is both pneumatologically and christologically grounded. He finds a connection between Barth's insufficient attention to Futurity and his weak pneumatology. Jenson's attempt to overcome the simple opposition between Eternity and time leads him to claim that God does have a real future. However, it is a future in which God confronts himself: "the Spirit is God as the Power of his own and our future; and it is that the Spirit is God as the Power of his own future, as the Power of a future that is truly 'unexpected' and yet connected, also for him, that the Spirit is a distinct identity of and in God."[69] The temporal infinity of God is the "unsurpassibility" of the event of the Spirit as God who comes to us from the last future. The Spirit is "at the End of all God's ways because he *is* the End of all God's ways. The Spirit is

64. R. Jenson, *Story and Promise: A Brief Theology of the Gospel about Jesus* (Philadelphia: Fortress, 1973).

65. R. Jenson, *God After God: The God of the Past and the God of the Future* (Indianapolis: Bobbs-Merrill, 1969), 173, 189.

66. R. Jenson, "Does God Have Time?" in *Essays in Theology of Culture* (Grand Rapids: Eerdmans, 1995), 199.

67. R. Jenson, "The Triune God," in *Christian Dogmatics,* 2 vols., ed. Carl Braaten and Robert Jenson (Philadelphia: Fortress, 1984), 1:167.

68. R. Jenson, *Systematic Theology,* 2 vols. (Oxford: Oxford University Press, 1999), 1:216, 217. Hereafter referred to in the text as *ST.*

69. R. Jenson, "What Is the Point of Trinitarian Theology?" in *Trinitarian Theology Today,* ed. C. Schwöbel (Edinburgh: T&T Clark, 1995), 31-43 at 41.

the Liveliness of the divine life because he is the Power of the divine future" (*ST,* 1:157; cf. *ST,* 2:26).

Jenson's appreciation of Jonathan Edwards' privileging of the category of beauty[70] plays a significant role in his presentation of the relation between the world and divine Futurity (cf. *ST,* 1:234-36). God's life is a divine fugue, in which space and time are made for creatures. In "Telos," the final chapter of his *Systematic Theology,* Jenson concludes that the redeemed will be appropriated into God's own being: "In the conversation God is, meaning and melody are one. The end is music" (*ST,* 2:369).

For Jenson, the "futurist option" in theology must be rooted in an appeal to the Person of the future, who is risen and coming.[71] The gospel is summarized in the claim that *"Jesus* is *risen* from the *dead."* The future the Spirit brings is the triumph of Jesus as a definite individual (*ST,* 1:165, 219); this transforms our understanding of divine causality. Jenson does have a place for *narrative* causation, which is real for God and creatures; however, it is not a reality determined beforehand by a first cause, but the unfolding of the story of God, in which creatures are included: "God the Spirit is God's own future and so draws to and into the triune converse those for whom the Trinity makes room. . . . God can himself be the purpose of his own act to create without absorbing his creation, in that God who is God's own future is another person than God as the one who has this future" (*ST,* 2:26).

Jenson uses this insight to reinterpret the prefix "pre" as it appears in words like predestination and the preexistence of Christ; for the New Testament authors the "post-existence" of Christ interprets the "preexistence" of Christ, not the other way around (*ST,* 1:142). For Jenson, the Spirit is "the postdestining God," through whose power is manifested "the freedom of Jesus's future to transform and renew all previous events whatever."[72] The theological meaning of "pre" indicates God's anteriority to creation, but this should be understood as "primally the priority of God's futurity to all being" (*ST,* 2:177).

---

70. R. Jenson, *America's Theologian: A Recommendation of Jonathan Edwards* (Oxford: Oxford University Press, 1988); cf. Jenson's chapter "Beauty," in *Essays in Theology of Culture.*

71. R. Jenson, "Appeal to the Person of the Future," in Braaten and Jenson, eds., *The Futurist Option,* 147-58.

72. R. Jenson, "The Holy Spirit," in *Christian Dogmatics,* 2:139.

Eberhard Jüngel

The ontological significance of eschatology is clear in Jüngel's under-standing of the relation between God and the world. He argues that the human experience of time (and freedom) is granted by God, who gra-ciously distinguishes the possible from the impossible: "such a distinction comes out of the future . . . the world's possibility is not within but exter-nal to its actuality. And its being is external to its futurity."[73] God's cre-ative relation to the world is not a "making" that depends on the past and present. God allows possibility to arise *ex nihilo;* in the event of the word of God, "that which God's love makes possible from outside, and not from a future which arises out of the past, is the ultimate concern of the world's actuality."[74] This distinction is manifested in the resurrection of the Crucified, which brings to light "the ontology of the doctrine of justi-fication." Jüngel distinguishes between a "final future" that illuminates the meaning of all history and a humanly constructed future which "pre-cedes" this last future.[75]

He challenges Augustine's understanding of time, in which temporal-ity is distended and held together in the human soul, arguing instead that time is constituted by "the occurrence of something new which remains *new for all time*."[76] For Jüngel, "the concept of an *eternal future* is not a mere paradox but rather an indication that there is not only a *temporal succession* of the modes of time, but also an *eternal interpenetration* of the modes of time." This leads him to an ontological view of the eschaton as the divine reality that "also *generates* what it determines; it also *effects* the judgment which it presents. As that which remains new, the eschaton is known by its effect, which consists in *making new. . . . As that which renews* it is that which remains new."[77]

In *God as the Mystery of the World*, Jüngel explains that God's being as "love" implies "the eternal newness according to which the eternal God is

73. E. Jüngel, "The World as Possibility and Actuality," in Jüngel, *Theological Essays,* trans. J. B. Webster (Edinburgh: T&T Clark, 1989), 116-17.

74. Jüngel, "Possibility," 117.

75. E. Jüngel, "Zukunft und Hoffnung," in *Müssen Christen Sozialisten sein?* ed. W. Teichert (Hamburg: Lutherisches Verlagshaus, 1975), 16.

76. E. Jüngel, "The Emergence of the New," in *Theological Essays II*, ed. J. B. Webster, trans. A. Neufeld-Fast and J. B. Webster (Edinburgh: T&T Clark, 1995), 53.

77. Jüngel, "Emergence," 54, 55.

always his own future. God and love never grow old. Their being is and remains one that is coming."[78] God's love lets our being *become*. The divine address to the human ego encounters it as an "eschatological outdistancing," in which humans experience a newness that surpasses the here-and-now, an "eschatological presence" (174-75). This eschatological newness that is created by the word of God relates us not to an ambiguous future, but to the God who has come in the past to humanity through the word. Those who anticipate the coming of the Crucified live in relation to God's presence as that which brings with it an eschatological distance: this must be understood "with regard both to the past in which God came and to the future out of which God is coming" (184).

Jüngel argues that the "*ontological primacy* of possibility" allows us to affirm the thinkability of God in the dispute with atheism. Rather than thinking of God on the analogy of cause and effect, which resulted in the atheistic response to scholasticism, Jüngel proposes an *"analogy of advent"* in which God's "coming" to the creation *"makes* this world-relationship *new"* (285). This coming is expressed in explicitly pneumatological terms: "as the Spirit of love, God gives himself eternal future, in which God is eternally his own origin and his own goal" (388). As a personal power that "opens up the future," the Spirit gives a share of God's own life; we are "oriented to the future out of which God is coming" (389) in faith, love and hope.

Jüngel's willingness to challenge traditional ways of formulating the relation between Eternity and time is evident in the title of his book on Barth's view of the trinitarian being of God: *God's Being Is in Becoming.* God's essential self-relatedness must be understood as "being in act." However, the "becoming" that is proper to God's being "is not constituted by temporality; rather, temporality is constituted through God's becoming."[79] This view of divine being is derived from his Christology. In the crucifixion of Christ, God's being in becoming is swallowed up in perishing, but the resurrection reveals that "perishing was itself swallowed up in the becoming," so that God's being *"remains* a being in becoming."[80]

Like many of the other theologians in this trajectory, Jüngel also places special emphasis on the Holy Spirit for our experience of God as an orien-

---

78. E. Jüngel, *God as the Mystery of the World,* trans. Darrell Guder (Grand Rapids: Eerdmans, 1983), 375. Page numbers in the following paragraphs refer to this book.

79. E. Jüngel, *God's Being Is in Becoming: The Trinitarian Being of God in the Theology of Karl Barth,* trans. John Webster (Grand Rapids: Eerdmans, 2001), 115 n. 151.

80. Jüngel, *Becoming,* 122.

tation toward the future.[81] Jüngel's understanding of the event of the address of God's word as the origin of the world's possibility has ramifications for his doctrine of the "attributes" of God (cf. §5.3 above). An analogy of advent allows him to understand all the divine attributes as God's sharing of the divine Love that God is with creatures.[82] The doctrine of justification, which for Jüngel is the heart of the Christian faith, is also interpreted in an eschatological light; the new being of the Christian is "defined by the future as it comes from God."[83]

Wolfhart Pannenberg

Pannenberg's interest in the ontological priority of the future emerged out of his struggle with the idea of human freedom, which had been the basis of the atheist attack against the theistic conception of God as single subject whose will is the first cause of all things. He argued that we should think instead of the absolute future of freedom as the very nature of God.[84] This approach allowed Pannenberg to describe human subjectivity not in terms of the faculty of an existing substance, but as a gift that is received in relation to others and that must be developed through openness to the future.[85] If to "exist" is to be determinate in the past or present, and if God is personal and absolutely free, then this means "in a restricted but important sense, God does not yet exist."[86] For Pannenberg, "God is in himself

81. "Indem Gott als Vater in besonderer Weise sich selber Herkunft, als Sohn in besonderer Weise sich selber Gegenwart und als Geist in besonderer Weise sich selber Zukunft." Cf. E. Jüngel, "Thesen zur Ewigkeit des ewigen Lebens," *Zeitschrift für Theologie und Kirche* 97 (2000): 80-87 at 84.

82. E. Jüngel, "Thesen zum Verhältnis von Existenz, Wesen und Eigenschaften Gottes," *Zeitschrift für Theologie und Kirche* 96, no. 3 (September 1999): 405-23 at 417.

83. E. Jüngel, *Justification*, trans. J. Cayzer (Edinburgh: T&T Clark, 2001), 225.

84. W. Pannenberg, "The Significance of Christianity in the Philosophy of Hegel," in *The Idea of God and Human Freedom*, trans. R. A. Wilson (Philadelphia: Westminster, 1973), 174.

85. W. Pannenberg, "Speaking about God in the Face of Atheist Criticism," in *Idea of God*, 112ff.

86. W. Pannenberg, *Theology and the Kingdom of God* (Philadelphia: Westminster, 1969), 56. In a later article, Pannenberg makes explicit that this is "from a finite point of view." Cf. "A Theological Conversation with Wolfhart Pannenberg," *Dialog* 11 (Autumn 1972): 286-95 at 294.

the power of the future. The reason for this is that the very idea of God demands that there be no future beyond himself. He is the ultimate future."[87]

This is intrinsically linked to Pannenberg's understanding of the trinitarian being of God, for it is the ministry of Jesus in the power of the Spirit that manifests the Futurity of the reign of God as a reality that appears in the present.[88] Pannenberg outlined the implications of this radical claim in several early works, calling for an "eschatological ontology" to support christological reflection,[89] suggesting that we think of God "with futurity as a quality of being,"[90] and describing human imagination as hoping for that which is "hidden in the womb of the future."[91] He was willing to describe the future as the "mode of God's being,"[92] as well as to speak of the future of God as the parousia of his Eternity.[93]

The idea of the Futurity of God plays an important role throughout Pannenberg's three-volume *Systematic Theology*.[94] In the first volume, he argues that the traditional formulations of the divine essence and attributes are dead ends because their "basis in every form is the idea of God as the first cause of the world" (*ST*, 1:364; cf. 343). Either God's essence is conflated with the idea of first cause (leading to God's eternal dependence on the world) or God's essence is separated from the relational causes in the world (challenging the possibility of real divine revelation). Instead of the category of causality, Pannenberg suggests that we follow Gregory of Nyssa and Descartes and begin with the category of Infinity. When combined with the Plotinian definition of the totality of life (*Enneads*, 3.7), the criterion of true Infinity

87. Pannenberg, *Theology and the Kingdom of God*, 63.

88. Cf. Pannenberg, *Theology and the Kingdom of God*, 71, 133.

89. W. Pannenberg, *Jesus — God and Man*, 2nd ed., trans. L. Wilkins and D. A. Priebe (Philadelphia: Westminster, 1977), 410; cf. 367.

90. W. Pannenberg, *Basic Questions in Theology*, vol. 2, trans. G. H. Kehm (Philadelphia: Fortress, 1971), 242.

91. W. Pannenberg, *What Is Man?* trans. D. A. Priebe (Philadelphia: Fortress, 1970), 42.

92. W. Pannenberg, "The God of Hope," in *Basic Questions in Theology*, vol. 2, trans. G. H. Kehm (Philadelphia: Fortress, 1971), 242.

93. W. Pannenberg, "Zeit und Ewigkeit in der religiösen Erfahrung Israels und des Christentums," in *Grundfragen systematischer Theologie II* (Gottingen: Vandenhoeck & Ruprecht, 1980), 202. For a comprehensive exposition of the role of the ontological priority of the future in Pannenberg's theology, see Christiaan Mostert, *God and the Future: Wolfhart Pannenberg's Eschatological Doctrine of God* (London: T&T Clark, 2002).

94. W. Pannenberg, *Systematic Theology*, 3 vols., trans. G. W. Bromiley (Grand Rapids: Eerdmans, 1991, 1994, 1998). Identified as *ST* in the text that follows.

leads to a recognition that only "in terms of the future could the totality be given to time" (*ST*, 1:408). The primacy of the future is not understood (as in Heidegger) as the being of *Dasein* in relation to death, but as the opening up of each being to participation in Eternity.[95] For Pannenberg, "God is eternal because he has no future outside of himself." God is God's own future and the future of all creatures; as such God is perfect freedom. "The eternal God as the absolute future, in the fellowship of the Father, Son and Spirit, is the free origin of himself and his creatures" (*ST*, 1:410).[96]

In his treatment of the doctrine of creation in volume 2, Pannenberg speaks of the form of duration that characterizes the existence of creatures as constituted by their being referred to "eternity as the future of the good" that grants them their existence (*ST*, 2:96). The future is the "field of the possible" for creatures, the expression of the dynamic of the divine Spirit as the arrival of the eschatological future (98). "The working of the Spirit constantly encounters the creature as its future, which embraces its origin and its possible fulfillment" (102).[97] Pannenberg does not separate creation from eschatology; the eschaton is the creative beginning of the cosmic process. This way of thinking about temporality is disclosed through the resurrection of Jesus by the life-giving Spirit: "creation itself is set in the light of the eschatological future" (145) because in this event the future of creation has already come (396).

When he turns to the theme of "eschatology" proper in volume 3, Pannenberg argues that God's Eternity comes into time as the eschatological future that is creatively present to all things (*ST*, 3:531); the work of the Spirit plays a central role in this dynamic (551). We can resolve the conceptual problem of thinking of an "end" of time (after which we still have "life") only if we consider "that *God and not nothing is the end of time*" (594). This requires thinking of God's Eternity as the condition and not as the antithesis of time. Pannenberg concludes that the future of God "is

95. W. Pannenberg, *Metaphysics and the Idea of God*, trans. P. Clayton (Edinburgh: T&T Clark, 1988), 88.

96. Pannenberg summarizes the trinitarian dynamics of this shared eternal, in which the persons are the future of one another, in "Eternity, Time and the Trinitarian God," in *Trinity, Time, and Church*, ed. C. Gunton (Grand Rapids: Eerdmans, 2000), 62-70.

97. In this context, Pannenberg engages the scientific developments that led to the prioritizing of the future among the modes of time. Cf. his *Toward a Theology of Nature: Essays on Science and Faith*, ed. Ted Peters (Philadelphia: Westminster/John Knox, 1993), and "God as Spirit — and Natural Science," *Zygon* 36, no. 4 (2001): 783-93.

constitutive for what we now are and already have been" because "God is the future of the finite from which it again receives its existence as a whole as that which has been" (607).

§7.4. The Ecumenical and Reformative Appeal of Eschatological Ontology

Most of these Lutheran and Reformed theologians have been heavily engaged in ecumenical dialogue, and some of them have interacted with the contributions of feminist and liberation theology. In fact one of the key factors driving the early theological turn to Futurity was an interest in the reformative power of the idea.[98] We can illustrate this broader appeal of the concept of Futurity with reference to some of the same theologians who contributed to the other late modern trajectories.

Karl Rahner

The idea of God as "absolute future" plays a central role in Rahner's theology. In his book on *The Trinity* he links the future and transcendence; however, the future is not simply "that which is still to come," but a "modality" of God's self-communication. "Transcendence arises where God gives himself as the future," and this transcendence derives from grace "as the possibility of accepting an absolute future which is in fact presented."[99] The idea of absolute future also shapes his discussion of divine Infinity. Instead of the scholastic emphasis on the "infinite being" of God, Rahner suggests that we articulate the intuition of divine transcendence "with reference to the incomprehensibility of our divinely inspired hope in the absolute future."[100] While Rahner sometimes wrote of Eternity primarily as a present

---

98. For example, Carl Braaten argued that union will be possible only when the churches "think back to their past and their present in light of that absolute future which God has promised." Cf. "The Reunited Church of the Future," *Journal of Ecumenical Studies* 4, no. 4 (Fall 1967): 611-28 at 628.

99. K. Rahner, *The Trinity*, trans. J. Donceel (New York: Crossroad, 2003), 97. For a discussion of the idea of "absolute future," see Rahner, *Theological Investigations*, 6:77-88; hereafter referred to as *TI*.

100. "Hiddenness," in *TI*, 16:243.

dimension of time, most of his work used the category of the future in a theological way to speak of God's transcendence as a real future reality.

What marks off Christianity from other political (e.g., Marxist) engagements with the future and from other religions, argues Rahner, is that it is the "religion of the absolute future" — Christianity "keeps open the question of God as the absolute future."[101] Rahner distinguishes between the "this-worldly future" and God as the absolute future. The Christian message calls persons to maintain openness in relation to the absolute future as God's gracious self-bestowal, which is mediated through (but not reducible to) our experience of "this-worldly" future.[102] Rahner believes this can help us overcome our reliance on cause-effect categories in describing the relation between God and the world. The notions of cause and effect are mutually dependent and dialectically defined; Christian theology explicitly denies that this applies to the God-world relation.[103]

The idea of God as absolute future also shapes Rahner's treatment of other theological loci. The incarnation and resurrection of Jesus are understood in faith as the "definitive beginning of the coming of God," a coming that is "the absolute future of the world and of history."[104] His Pneumatology is also explicitly connected to the human openness to the future. In *Spirit in the World*, Rahner works hard to reconstruct the Thomistic understanding of causality, especially "efficient" causality, and emphasizes the *excessus* toward the Absolute as that which constitutes human spirituality in relation to God as Spirit.[105] The role of the concept of Futurity is particularly evident in Rahner's anthropology. For him, the "presentness" of human being is a being "referred to futurity." But this future is that which "remains the future as such," not simply that which will become the present and fade into the past; "it is an inner moment of man and of his actual being as it is present to him now."[106] Human persons ex-

---

101. "Marxist Utopia and the Christian Future of Man," in *TI*, 6:59-68 at 60-61.

102. "The Question of the Future," *TI*, 12:181-201 at 188. For analysis, see Peter C. Phan, *Eternity and Time: A Study of Karl Rahner's Eschatology* (London: Associated University Presses, 1988), 57ff., 201ff.

103. Cf. K. Rahner, *Foundations of Christian Faith*, trans. William Dych (New York: Crossroad, 2000), 78.

104. "The Universality of Salvation," *TI*, 16:224.

105. K. Rahner, *Spirit in the World*, trans. W. Dych (New York: Herder and Herder, 1968), 186, 355-56, 394-95.

106. "The Hermeneutics of Eschatological Assertions," *TI*, 4:331.

ist in their openness to the transcendent future. For Rahner this means that Christian anthropology is Christian eschatology; human persons are those creaturely beings who are "open to the absolute future of God himself." He concludes that the "absolute future" of humanity and human history is "God himself as the origin of its dynamism and as its goal."[107]

In the wake of the treatment of *Gaudium et spes* in Vatican II, several Roman Catholic theologians began to engage the issues of eschatology in a fresh way, attending to its implications for the being of God and the world.[108] Two examples will suffice. Edward Schillebeeckx urges that we replace Barth's emphasis on the "wholly Other" with the conception of God as the "wholly New." In his *God, the Future of Man*, he describes the transcendent God as the "One who is to come," the God who "is *our* future."[109] Schillebeeckx speaks of God not only as "new each day," but "absolutely new." God is the constant source of new possibilities and as such the "absolute source of freedom."[110] Hans Urs von Balthasar's five-volume *Theo-Drama* is permeated by an emphasis on the future, in the sense that the drama of creation is movement from and toward God. In *The Last Act* von Balthasar depicts a trinitarian drama that makes possible human participation in the divine life. Creatures are invited to share in the "time" of Jesus Christ, through which "earth moves heavenward." The eschaton is not so much an end-time closing of a horizontal future, but the insertion of the earthly future "into an ever-new 'now' that is a gift of divine grace."[111] As with their Protestant counterparts, the renewal of interest in eschatological ontology among these (and other) Roman Catholic theologians arose alongside a recovery of biblical and traditional emphases on the coming reign of the God of peace, manifested in Christ through the Spirit.

---

107. Rahner, *Foundations*, 431, 446.

108. For an overview, see Zachary Hayes, O.F.M., *Visions of a Future: A Study of Christian Eschatology* (Wilmington, Del.: Michael Glazier, 1992).

109. Edward Schillebeeckx, *God, the Future of Man*, trans. N. D. Smith (New York: Sheed and Ward, 1968), 181-82; cf. 72-77.

110. Edward Schillebeeckx, *God Is New Each Moment*, trans. David Smith (Edinburgh: T&T Clark, 1983), 29.

111. Hans Urs von Balthasar, *The Last Act* (*Theo-Drama*, vol. 5), trans. G. Harrison (San Francisco: Ignatius Press, 1998), 187.

John Zizioulas

Among contemporary Orthodox theologians, Zizioulas has been one of the most active in the ecumenical discussions. With reference to the renewal of eschatological reflection in the twentieth century, he acknowledges that this is largely a fruit of Protestant theology.[112] The Eastern tradition has a long history of emphasizing the future orientation of creation, however, reaching back at least to Irenaeus. A central aspect of Zizioulas's project is to show that the Cappadocians are also a resource for the (re)turn to Futurity. Building on these and other thinkers within his tradition, he argues that "the truth of history lies in the future, and this is to be understood in an ontological sense: history is true, despite change and decay, not just because it is a movement *towards* an end, but mainly because it is a movement *from* the end, since it is the end that gives it meaning."[113] This is revealed not through analysis of cause and effect, but through the manifestation of the openness of the Father to the Son in the Spirit, which is the basis of the Christian claim that ontology must be understood in terms of "communion." For human creatures, this means that being is oriented toward a future in which they share in this communion. This shapes Zizioulas's anthropology and ecclesiology. *"The truth and the ontology of the person belong to the future, are images of the future."* The church "has its roots in the future and its branches in the present."[114]

The sacramental event of the Eucharist is crucial to the Orthodox understanding of the relation between time and Eternity. In addition to *anamnesis* (remembering Christ), the liturgy of the Eastern Orthodox church includes an *epiclesis,* an invocation of the Holy Spirit. Following St. Chrysostom, Zizioulas speaks of the "memory of the future" at the Eucharist. The Spirit brings the "eschata into history" in this liturgical event, but this is a new creation made possible precisely by this personal presence that calls persons into communion.[115] This eschatological dimension of

112. J. Zizioulas, "Déplacement de la perspective eschatologique," in *La chrétienté en débat,* ed. G. Alberigo et al. (Paris: Éditions du Cerf, 1984), 89-100 at 93.

113. J. Zizioulas, *Being as Communion* (Crestwood, N.Y.: St. Vladimir's Press, 1997), 96.

114. Zizioulas, *Communion,* 62, 59; his emphasis. For his critique of the Platonic and Aristotelian conceptions of causality in relation to God, see "On Being a Person: Toward an Ontology of Personhood," in *Persons, Divine and Human,* ed. C. Schwöbel and C. Gunton (Edinburgh: T&T Clark, 1991), 33-46 at 38.

115. Zizioulas, *Communion,* 180.

the Eucharist should not be seen as a natural part of historical evolution or development but as "grâce ontologique," an eschatological penetration that transforms the community into a new creation. In this way, the Hellenistic opposition between time and Eternity is overcome; time and history are "sanctified" by the presence of the Eternal Spirit whose "pénétration eschatologique" transfigures the present.[116] As it celebrates the resurrection of the Crucified, the church interprets the ultimacy of being "from the angle of the Parousia" — the experience of history and time are oriented toward a transfiguration of the cosmos in which persons find their ultimate being in communion.[117]

These eschatological, eucharistic, and ecclesiological emphases may be found in several leading twentieth-century Orthodox theologians. Building on the Irenaean language of "recapitulation," Vladimir Lossky points to Christ as *ho eschatos Adam,* who finally realizes the unity of human nature; "this eschatological reality is not some kind of ideal 'beyond' but the very condition of the existence of the Church."[118] This leads to a dynamic and future-oriented ontology; "the created universe appears as a dynamic reality tending towards a future plenitude which for God is always present. The unshakable foundation of a world created out of nothingness consists in the fulfillment which is the end of its becoming."[119] For Alexander Schmemann, the centrality of the Eucharist in this tradition lends itself to a new understanding of time; the celebrant affirms and confesses that the "new time," the time of God's kingdom, has entered into the time of the present world.[120] This experience should not be understood in terms of the categories of "sacred" and "profane," but as based on the distinction of "old" and "new" (Rev. 21:5). More recently David Hart has urged the appropriation of resources found in theologians like Gregory of Nyssa and Maximus the Confessor for articulating a Christian understanding of be-

---

116. J. Zizioulas, "La Vision eucharistique du monde et l'homme contemporain," *Contacts: Revue française de l'orthodoxie* 19 (1967): 83-92 at 87, 91.

117. J. Zizioulas, "Human Capacity and Human Incapacity: A Theological Exploration of Personhood," *Scottish Journal of Theology* 28 (1975): 401-48 at 443-44.

118. V. Lossky, *In the Image and Likeness of God* (Crestwood, N.Y.: St. Vladimir's Press, 1985), 184.

119. V. Lossky, *The Mystical Theology of the Eastern Church* (Crestwood, N.Y.: St. Vladimir's Press, 1998), 241.

120. A. Schmemann, *The Eucharist,* trans. P. Kachur (Crestwood, N.Y.: St. Vladimir's Press, 2000), 48.

ing. "Both our being and our essence always exceed the moment of our existence, lying before us as gratuity and futurity, mediated to us in the splendid eros and terror of our *in fieri.*"[121]

Feminist and Liberation Reconstructions

It is often those theologians who are responding to real crises with visions for emancipatory praxis in the church who are most open to reconstructing theology through a fresh thematization of eschatology and hope.[122] Among feminist theologians this has taken shape in the anticipation of a future in which the present oppression of women is overcome. As Anne Carr observes, "to envision God as future, as ahead, rather than above and over against the human and natural world, is a reorientation that helps women to see the feminist dilemmas in the church as a temporary one."[123] This eschatological vision should not lead to a passive longing for a far-distant future. Sallie McFague argues that eschatology should not deal merely with "last things" but with "the breaking in of new possibilities, of hope for a new creation. It can mean living from a vision of a different present based upon a new future."[124] The single divine subject of early modern theology was often depicted as the ideal "man of reason," an all-sufficient male dictator, whose rule (and that of "his" earthly ministers) should be obeyed without question. This way of articulating the doctrine of God is rooted in psychological and sociological presuppositions that are deeply problematic.[125] For many feminist theologians, this suggests that Christian eschatology must move beyond an emphasis merely on the state of individuals after death, and work toward a holistic and even ecological

121. D. Hart, *The Beauty of the Infinite: The Aesthetics of Christian Truth* (Grand Rapids: Eerdmans, 2003), 244.

122. Cf. Rebecca S. Chopp and Mark Lewis Taylor, "Introduction: Crisis, Hope and Contemporary Theology," in *Reconstructing Christian Theology*, ed. Chopp and Taylor (Minneapolis: Fortress, 1994), 1-24.

123. Anne Carr, *Transforming Grace* (New York: HarperCollins, 1990), 153. Cf. idem, "The God Who Is Involved," *Theology Today* 38, no. 3 (October 1981): 314-28.

124. Sallie McFague, *The Body of God* (Minneapolis: Fortress, 1993), 110.

125. Cf. Sarah Coakley, "Gender and Knowledge in Western Philosophy: The 'Man of Reason' and the 'Feminine' 'Other' in Enlightenment and Romantic Thought," in *The Special Nature of Women?* ed. Anne Carr and Elisabeth Schüssler Fiorenza (London: SCM, 1991), 75-83.

approach to understanding and transforming the painful structures of life within oppressive political systems and an entropic cosmos.[126]

Many liberation theologians have also worked hard to reconstruct the relation between eschatology and the doctrine of God. For Gustavo Gutiérrez eschatology is not just one element of theology but the key to understanding the Christian faith. He argues that the Bible does not oppose time and Eternity but witnesses to an experience of transcendence in which "God is revealed as a force in our future and not as an ahistorical being." Christian hope is not like the Marxist hope that relies on human effort; rather, it opens us up "to the gift of the future promised by God." The hopeful relation to the gift, however, "makes us radically free to commit ourselves to social praxis."[127] The fact that so many feminist and liberation theologians have participated in the renewal of eschatological ontology suggests that the idea of divine Futurity may play a significant role in *reforming* theology.

The contribution of "liberation" theology is not limited to South America. Gabriel Fackre's *The Rainbow Sign: Christian Futurity*[128] emerged out of his own concern with the turbulence of the civil rights movement led by Martin Luther King, Jr.; his argument was that the telling of the Christian story ("narrative") orients us toward hope and is a good connecting point for dialogue with "modern hopers." His goal was to show that the Christian understanding of the future is not divorced from social action but intimately connected to it. Building on the work of René Girard, James Alison argues that sharing Jesus' eschatological imagination and being led by the Holy Spirit involve overcoming the structures of society that try to build peace by sacrificing scapegoats, i.e., by blaming and annihilating victims.[129] These theological contributions encourage the church to remember that hope is not merely patiently waiting for utopia, but a way of relating to the future that transforms reality now.

The work of Ted Peters provides a good place to end our brief review

126. Cf. Rosemary Radford Ruether, *Sexism and God-Talk: Toward a Feminist Theology* (Boston: Beacon, 1983), 235-58.

127. Gustavo Gutiérrez, *A Theology of Liberation,* trans. and ed. Sister Caridad Inda and J. Eagleson, rev. ed. (Maryknoll, N.Y.: Orbis, 1988), 95, 139.

128. Gabriel Fackre, *The Rainbow Sign: Christian Futurity* (Grand Rapids: Eerdmans, 1969).

129. James Alison, *Raising Abel: The Recovery of the Eschatological Imagination* (New York: Crossroad, 1996).

of the renewal of eschatological ontology because his theological contributions have incorporated most of the concerns that have shaped this trajectory. Much of his early work focused on human hope and the renewed cultural consciousness of the future in terms of ecological issues and doomsday hypotheses. In various articles and books in the 1970s, he suggested that these developments call for a theological evaluation and response.[130] Peters explicitly tries to provide this response, building on the work of Pannenberg and others. Many of his articles over the years have addressed the theme of the future, whether in relation to the debates over the resurrection, or to broader ontological issues in eschatology. In regard to the latter, he calls for a "futuristic ontology" that recognizes that the "power of being comes from the future, God's future." As the ground of being, God "cedes" being to the world, i.e., "grants the world a future."[131] For Peters, this futuristic ontology sheds light on all of the theological loci; even the title of his magnum opus suggests this approach: *God — The World's Future: Systematic Theology for a New Era*. Peters challenges the modern Western view of causality, which is tied to a linear concept of time. Instead of a "bowling ball" theory of creation, Peters proposes a "proleptic" conception — Futurity is God's gift to the world. Peters argues that "God creates from the future, not the past," bestowing the future by opening up the possibility of the world's becoming. Without a future the world would be nothing; Peters uses the phrase *creatio ex nihilo* to refer to "God's first gracious gift of futurity."[132]

§7.5. Absolute Futurity

Of the three late modern trajectories, the renewal of eschatological ontology may be the most difficult to understand for many Western readers.

130. See, e.g., "Future Consciousness and the Need for Theology," *dialog* 13 (Autumn 1974): 251-57; *Futures — Divine and Human* (Atlanta: John Knox Press, 1978); *Fear, Faith and the Future* (Minneapolis: Augsburg, 1980).

131. T. Peters, "Eschatology — Eternal Now or Cosmic Future?" *Zygon* 36, no. 2 (June 2001): 349-56. Cf. Peters, "Resurrection: The Conceptual Challenge," in *Resurrection: Theological and Scientific Assessments,* ed. T. Peters, R. J. Russell, and M. Welker (Grand Rapids: Eerdmans, 2002).

132. T. Peters, *God — The World's Future: Systematic Theology for a New Era* (Minneapolis: Fortress, 1992; 2nd ed. 2000), 142, 143.

This is due in part to the way in which our experience of time has been shaped by our culture's framing of temporal experience in terms of the linear and mechanistic measurements of clock and calendar. Although philosophical reflection on the phenomenology of time consciousness and scientific discoveries in complexity theory and quantum cosmology have challenged this way of understanding time, most of our efforts to frame concepts operate unconsciously within this conceptual frame. Breaking out of this frame will require a kind of effort that is qualitatively different from replacing one concept with another. It may require a new way of ordering consciousness itself.[133] The remainder of this book will be devoted to facilitating this shift by inviting the reader to explore the integration of the idea of Futurity (along with Infinity and Trinity) into the basic themes of the doctrine of God.

Because this trajectory is so susceptible to misunderstanding, however, it will be helpful to provide a few clarifying comments about the concept of *absolute* Futurity. One of the most common objections brought against some of the reconstructive proposals outlined above is that the idea of divine Futurity simply replaces predeterminism with post-determinism. For example, Lewis Ford is concerned that Pannenberg's model collapses into a kind of "futuristic deism" or "eschatological pantheism."[134] Luco van den Brom argues that Moltmann's approach spatializes time as well as Eternity, presupposing an already realized transcendent Eschaton, which turns out to be "more deterministic than any traditional doctrine of decrees has ever been."[135] In this way of interpreting Futurity, however, "the future" is defined over against the past and the present. In such a case we are led to imagine that the "Future" of God is defined *relatively* to the other modes of time. If we think of divine Eternity as essentially "the future" in this sense, we have defined God as one part of the temporal process. In such a case, we are confronted with a view of Eternity that is spuriously infinite. If God was the "realm of the possible" or a

133. Cf. my *Reforming Theological Anthropology* (Grand Rapids: Eerdmans, 2003), chap. 2.

134. L. Ford, "The Nature of the Power of the Future," in *The Theology of Wolfhart Pannenberg*, ed. P. Clayton and C. Braaten (Minneapolis: Augsburg, 1988), 85; cf. Ford, "God as the Subjectivity of the Future," *Encounter* 41, no. 3 (1980): 292.

135. Luco van den Brom, "Eschatology and Time: Reversal of the Time Direction?" in *The Future as God's Gift: Explorations in Christian Eschatology*, ed. D. Fergusson and M. Sarot (Edinburgh: T&T Clark, 2000), 159-67 at 165.

"set of future times," the divine would be limited in its dialectical relation to the past and present.

If such a God were all-powerful, we would indeed be faced with determinism in reverse; the mightiness of God as the future would overpower the weakness of the present and the past. This is why it is crucial that we speak of the *absolute* Futurity of God, which embraces all the modes of time. Initially this may seem to indicate an even more strongly fatalistic vision of the relation of Eternity to time. The way in which the term "Futurity" evokes images of one of the modes of time might lead us to reject it outright. However, similar objections obtain in the case of Infinity and Trinity, which also require careful qualification. Acknowledging the limitations of all theological language, I will nevertheless commend the idea of Futurity for its fecundity in illuminating the dynamic asymmetry that structures Christian religious experience. As we articulate the way in which Eternity identifies itself and time in the gracious arrival of absolute Futurity, we must avoid simply absolutizing one aspect of our experience of time (the future) and identifying it with God; this would fail the criterion of true Infinity. If the truly infinite embracing of time by Eternity is itself the *condition* of temporal experience precisely as the *goal* that *constitutes* creaturely becoming, then we may think of the presence of God in relation to the world as the gracious liberation of creation in and to the possibility of sharing the eternal life of the trinitarian persons.

The way in which Trinity is integrated with Futurity is also crucially important. An anomaly in Jenson's approach provides us with a warning. Jenson correlates the three persons of the Trinity with the three modes of time in a way that links the Spirit to the power of the future, in contrast to the other persons. This pneumatological identification of Futurity is hard for Jenson to maintain. On the one hand, the Spirit is "the very Power of futurity," but on the other hand, "to be God is to be the power of the future to transcend what is. . . . To be God is to be Eschatos."[136] On the one hand, "The Spirit is God as his and our future *rushing upon him and us*," but, on the other hand, "*nothing* in God recedes into the past or *approaches from the future*."[137] This inconsistency derives from Jenson's linking of the Spirit in particular to Futurity; if God is "primally future" and "to be God is to be

---

136. Jenson, *The Triune Identity* (Philadelphia: Fortress, 1982), 166-67.

137. Jenson, *Systematic Theology,* 1:160, 218. Emphases added.

the power of the future," then the Son and the Father are subordinate to the Spirit.

Rather than tying the eschatological orientation of creation to any one of the persons, I will suggest that it is the relationality of the shared life of the trinitarian persons that constitutes the human experience of absolute Futurity. As we will see, in this way of thinking the presence of the eternal God does not threaten human freedom but is the very condition of its coming-to-be. This experience of being confronted by the coming of the new creation must be materially filled out as the arrival of the trinitarian life of God. If the goal of creaturely temporality were an eternal relation to a singular rational substance, then eschatological imagery would once again be forced into a dichotomy between dualism and monism. Either we would statically behold God forever or we would become assimilated into divine thought. However, if the truly infinite Futurity of God *is* the eternal life of the trinitarian persons into which creatures are dynamically being-called into relation, we may imagine eschatological transformation as the eternal intensification of the human desire to know, love and belong in fellowship with God and neighbor.

The purpose of the chapters of Part II has been to outline trajectories in the doctrine of God that have responded to the philosophical, scientific, and biblical challenges to the early modern categories we explored in Part I. In each case, we found resources in the writings of classical and Reformation theologians that have been taken up and refigured by leading thinkers from a variety of Christian traditions. The great theologians of each generation have realized that merely repeating particular formulations inherited from previous generations would only preserve the gospel by petrifying it. Fear can easily drive us to treat our theological propositions as fossils, unearthed from a privileged period in church history and placed in an ecclesiastical museum, quarantined from the polluted air of cultural anxiety that might contribute to its deterioration. Such a paleo-constructive fettering of the gospel is precisely that against which the Reformation responded so violently, demanding that theological reflection engage the categories of the social and cultural lived world in which it operates. With resources in hand from all three of the late modern trajectories we turn now to the task of reforming the doctrine of God in a way that conserves the biblical intuitions of the gospel by liberating them for dialogue within contemporary culture.

• PART III •

REFORMING THE DOCTRINE OF GOD

· 8 ·

OMNISCIENT FAITHFULNESS

The three chapters of Part III outline a presentation of the gospel of divine knowing, acting, and being. I organize these topics around the New Testament themes of faith, love, and hope. If only these three "remain" or "abide" (1 Cor. 13:13)[1] it makes sense to use them as guides for understanding the nature of the eternal God. I link these themes to three classical issues in the doctrine of God: omniscience, omnipotence, and omnipresence. Presenting divine knowing, acting, and being in successive chapters carries the danger of implying that these are three separate attributes of God. This would run afoul of the theological criteria of simplicity and immutability, which were meant to uphold the intuitions that God is not divided into parts or susceptible to dissolution like creatures. I will attempt to show how these intuitions may be conserved by weaving together the insights of intensive Infinity, robust Trinity, and absolute Futurity. Together these theological trajectories open up conceptual space for reconstructing the doctrine of God in our late modern culture.

These chapters are correlated to Chapters 8-10 of my *Reforming Theological Anthropology*. In that context, I presented a theology of *human* knowing, acting, and being, organized around the classical loci of human nature, sin, and the image of God. I argued that, while the philosophical

---

1. In this context Paul's panegyric on love leads him to list it last. However, my presentation here will follow the more common pattern of faith, love, hope (Col. 1:4-5; 1 Thess. 1:2-3; 5:8).

turn to relationality challenges some traditional formulations of theological anthropology, it also provides opportunities for reconstructively articulating the biblical intuitions that guide these doctrines. In *The Faces of Forgiveness,* I also organized my presentation of redemptive forgiveness as sharing in divine grace around the religious experience of faith, love, and hope. I linked these themes to the epistemic, ethical, and ontological dimensions of human anxiety that inhibit forgiveness. In the current context, my goal is to outline in more detail the understanding of divine knowing, acting, and being that was already implicitly (and explicitly) operative in those presentations.[2] Organizing the themes in this way is intended to shed light on conceptual patterns within theology that have been obscured by some of the formal and material decisions that structure presentations of the doctrine of God in many early modern theological projects.

The contemporary debate in North American theology over the ideas of divine knowing, acting, and being is often shaped by the following questions: Does God's mind contain some or all future contingents? Does God's will control some or all creaturely events? Does God exist inside of time or outside of time? As we saw in Part I, the meaning of these terms and the structure of the debate in Protestant theology were hardened in the context of early modern science and philosophy. These ways of framing the questions are overly dependent on the categories of God as an immaterial substance, single subject, and first cause. In the first subsection of each of the following chapters, we will observe the way in which these categories lead to antinomies in discussions of divine foreknowledge, predestination, and timelessness, restricting the available options for explicating divine knowing, acting, and being. After the philosophical turn to relationality, with its impact on the concepts of matter, person, and force, we now have the opportunity to refigure the way in which we formulate questions (and answers) in the doctrine of God.

Our goal is "reforming" theology — not only "reconstructing" doctrine but also attending to its "reformative" power. Our interest is not merely in shuffling around ideas in conceptual space, therefore, but in opening ourselves up to the transformation of the practical and liturgical space in which we find ourselves — a transformation wholly dependent on the grace of

---

2. Because the loci of systematic theology mutually implicate one another, the following presentation will often overlap themes treated in these other contexts. This matrix of theological inquiry is outlined in more detail in the Epilogue.

God. For this reason, the second subsection of each chapter will acknowledge the trembling delight that characterizes the biblical testimony to being known, loved, and held in being by God. The Christian experience of divine knowing, acting, and being is primarily mediated by sharing in the way of Jesus Christ and by intensification in the Spirit of life, and so it seems counterproductive to begin with philosophical and scientific categories that problematize these intuitions, especially when we have good reasons to leave them behind. In the third subsections, therefore, I bring christological and pneumatological insights immediately into the presentation of the doctrine of God. Rather than treating the "arguments" for the existence of God prior to and abstracted from Christian religious experience, they are reconstructed in the fourth subsections of each chapter in the conceptual light of inherently relational categories. This is not an escape from reason by appealing to faith but a rational appeal from within the context of a faith that seeks understanding. I will conclude each chapter by demonstrating how braiding the late modern trajectories can help us articulate the knowing, acting, and being of the biblical God as real gospel.

In this chapter we attend to a constellation of themes related to divine *knowing*, including omniscience, foreknowledge, wisdom, and the teleological argument. These issues are connected to a deep Christian intuition: *God's knowing embraces all things.* In other words, nothing escapes divine knowing.[3] This intuition has been maintained by the vast majority of theologians throughout the history of the Christian tradition. The biblical writings testify to an experience of knowing and being-known by an all-embracing faithful presence, a personal reality that calls creatures to share in intimate communal relation. God is faithful (*pistos ho theos,* 1 Cor 1:9) Moving beyond the issue of the propositional content of a single divine intellect, we may seek to conserve this intuition about the biblical God by linking *omniscience* to the evocative *faithfulness* of the infinite trinitarian God.

Divine knowing and faithfulness were connected in ancient Israel's testimony about YHWH. When the psalmist prays for the LORD to "know" his thoughts (Ps. 139:23), this is grounded in his experience of the One who has

---

3. Irenaeus expressed this intuition by insisting that "not one of the things which have been, or are, or shall be made, escapes the knowledge of God." *Adversus Haereses* II.26.1; ANF 1:397.

knit him together (v. 13) and holds him fast (v. 10). In Genesis 18:19, the LORD describes the covenant with Abraham, saying, "for I have chosen [*known*] him, that he may charge his children and his household after him to keep the way of the LORD by doing righteousness and justice, so that the LORD may bring about for Abraham what he has promised him." For the Israelites "knowing" was not about the contemplation of abstract eternal forms or the neutral assent to objective propositions, but about being faithfully oriented in concrete relations.[4] Being known by God is an experience of intimate embrace, of being called and "consecrated" (Jer. 1:5). The term "knowing" is even translated as "feeding" in relation to the LORD's care of the Israelites in the wilderness (Hos. 13:5-6). It is not that God knows "things" and then is faithful; God's faithful omniscience is an intimate knowing that binds and holds and calls into relation.[5]

The concept of "faith" in the New Testament *(pistis)* also suggests a binding of oneself and being-bound in relation to the other. For example, Jesus refused to "entrust" *(episteuen)* himself to the crowds of people who "believed" *(episteusan)* in him, because their believing was an attempt to bind him to their own political ends (John 2:23-24). Faithfulness has to do with personal and relational fields of intentionality, in which we know and are truly known. The term *epignōsis,* which connotes a fuller, more intimate sense of knowing than *gnōsis,* is commonly used in the New Testament to emphasize this relational character of being faithfully bound to God (e.g., Eph. 1:17; 2 Pet. 1:2). Faith and knowledge, then, primarily have to do with relationships, with "bindings," and not with the power of an individual intellectual faculty. Our task is to identify and outline the use of categories that can help us articulate a Christian understanding of the good news of divine knowing in a way that avoids the impasse forced upon us by the early modern categories of rational causative substance.

4. The semantic range of the word for knowing *(yada')* even covers sexual intercourse, a connection that is carried over into English in the King James Version: "Now the man *knew* his wife Eve, and she conceived" (Gen. 4:1). This intimate commitment is obscured by a narrow focus on cognitive knowledge as justified true belief.

5. The Hebrew language does not have an abstract noun that correlates precisely to the English term "faith." The word *emunah* means faithfulness (or faithful), and is typically used of persons whose trustworthiness is demonstrated in communal relations.

§8.1. Beyond the Antinomy of Divine Foreknowledge

Does God's mind infallibly know the truth value of all or only some propositions concerning future events? When the question of God's knowing is posed in this way, a tension arises between the capacity of the divine intellect and the possibility of human freedom. It seems that one is forced to choose between limiting God's foreknowledge on the one hand or limiting the freedom of creatures on the other. If human actions really surprise God, then divine knowledge does not seem to embrace all things. Yet if God knows the truth value of all propositions concerning future (contingent) events, then it seems that human actions are already determined.

Understanding the Impasse

This debate is often framed in terms of a continuum, upon which we may imagine those positions that emphasize creaturely freedom on the left and those that stress exhaustive divine foreknowledge on the right. The attempted resolutions of the antinomy in *Divine Foreknowledge: Four Views* fall along this spectrum. Each of the contributors accepts the formulation of the question in the introduction of the book about the "nature and content of God's foreknowledge."[6] The four authors defend (respectively) open theism, simple foreknowledge, middle knowledge, and the "Augustinian-Calvinist" view. Those on the left side of the continuum tend toward the intellectualist ideal, while those on the right prefer the voluntarist ideal. The biblical aspect of the debate focuses on how to interpret anthropomorphic passages about God's changing or not changing "his mind" (Num. 23:19; 1 Sam. 15:29; 1 Chr. 21:15; Jer. 18:4-10), most of which occur in the Hebrew Bible. Rather than attending to the knowing and being known of the trinitarian God of the New Testament, most of the theological and philosophical analysis is focused on defeating or defending early modern theological positions on the nature of the divine intellect such as "middle knowledge."

The failure of each contributor to resolve the logical and existential problems of the antinomy is helpfully clarified by the other contributors in the "Objections" sections that appear after each chapter. However, the pos-

6. J. Beilby and P. Eddy, eds., *Divine Foreknowledge: Four Views* (Downers Grove, Ill.: InterVarsity, 2001), 10.

sibility that this failure is rooted in the very construction of the spectrum of options is not explored. The assumption that the only options are those available on this continuum pervades the discussion in much conservative theology.[7] Here I am not interested in taking one position against (or between) the others, but in interrogating the validity of the theological and philosophical assumptions that force the debate into this particular shape, which is still sometimes described as a choice between early-seventeenth-century opponents: the "Arminians" and the "Calvinists."

If we can see how the horns of this dilemma are set upon a deeper set of categories that are philosophically and scientifically implausible, as well as underdetermined by the biblical tradition, we may be able to escape the antinomy. In the early patristic tradition, when the intellectualist ideal was dominant, some theologians attempted to avoid the impasse by claiming that the operation of the divine intellect is logically prior to that of the divine will. Irenaeus is even willing to argue that human merit was pre-known by God and that this conditioned predestination.[8] Commenting on Romans 8:29, Ambrose insisted that God "did not predestine them before He foreknew them, but he did predestine the rewards of those whose merits he foreknew."[9] John of Damascus meant to capture the consensus of the tradition when he explained that God "knows all things beforehand, yet He does not predetermine all things . . . predetermination is the work of the divine command based on fore-knowledge."[10]

The primary source of the voluntarist solution to the problem of fore-knowledge is Augustine. Although he originally agreed with the consensus,[11] the debates with the Pelagians over free will and human merit even-

---

7. Cf. William Hasker, "The Openness of God," *Christian Scholar's Review* 28, no. 1 (Fall 1998): 121; David Hunt, "On Augustine's Way Out," *Faith and Philosophy* 16, no. 1 (January 1999): 3-26 at 19; Bill Craig, "Middle Knowledge: A Calvinist-Arminian Rapprochement?" in *The Grace of God, the Will of Man,* ed. Clark Pinnock (Grand Rapids: Zondervan 1989), 141-164. Craig tries to reduce the chasm from Calvin vs. Arminius to Molina vs. Suarez, but this shrunken continuum is still based on the same assumptions.

8. *Adversus Haereses* IV.39.4 (ANF, 1:523). Cf. Origen, *Against Celsus* II.20 (ANF, 4:440); Athanasius, *Incarnation of the Word* 1-6 (NPNF2, 4:36-39).

9. *De fide,* 5:83. For similar quotations, cf. James Jorgenson, "Predestination according to Divine Foreknowledge in Patristic Tradition," in *Salvation in Christ: A Lutheran-Orthodox Dialogue,* ed. John Meyendorff and Robert Tobias (Minneapolis: Augsburg, 1992), 159-83 at 166-67.

10. *Exposition of the Orthodox Faith,* III.30 (NPNF, 9:42).

11. Augustine explains to Evodius: "As you remember certain things that you have done

tually led him to emphasize the divine will as the basis of all future events. Many of the leading Western theologians from Augustine onward recognized that the very idea of divine *fore*-knowledge is inherently misleading and inconsistent with other key theological intuitions. Properly speaking, Augustine says, we should speak only of God's knowledge, and not of foreknowledge, since God does not know "before."[12] To say that God knows something "ahead of time" would place God under the constraints of time and jeopardize divine timelessness. The main proponents of the voluntarist tradition have followed Augustine here. Even Thomas Aquinas, who leans toward the intellectualist ideal, admits that not even God can know future contingent events *as* future; rather than saying that if God knows something, then it *will be,* it is better to say that if God knows something, then it *is* (*De Veritate,* II.12.7; cf. *SCG,* I.70-71; *SumTh,* I.14). This denial of divine *fore*-knowledge follows from the immutability of the divine intellect, as Boethius, Ockham, Luther, and Calvin all observe.[13]

As we saw in Part I, this tension between the intellectualist and voluntarist ideals was heightened in the early modern period under the pressure of changing conceptions of matter, person, and force. Each position on the spectrum of responses to the antinomy of foreknowledge begins with a conception of God as a single immaterial subject and inquires about the "content" of the divine intellect in relation to creation. This approach naturally lends itself to expressions that describe God in terms of "extensive" infinity, so that the knowledge of the Creator and that of creatures are compa-

---

and yet have not done all the things that you remember, so God foreknows all the things of which He Himself is the Cause, and yet *He is not the Cause of all that He foreknows*" (*On Free Choice of the Will,* trans. Anna S. Benjamin and L. H. Hackstaff [Indianapolis: Bobbs-Merrill, 1964], 94-95). Emphais added.

12. *De diversis quaestionibus ad Simplicianum,* II.2.2. Cf. *The City of God* (XI.21; NPNF1, 2:216): "nor does His present knowledge differ from that which it ever was or shall be, for those variations of time, past, present, and future, though they alter our knowledge, do not affect His."

13. Cf. Boethius, *Consolation of Philosophy,* trans. Joel C. Relihan (Indianapolis: Hackett, 2001), 146. Teturo Shimizu, "Time and Eternity: Ockham's Logical Point of View," *Franciscan Studies* 50 (1990): 283-307 at 302, outlines Ockham's view that God's cognition is simultaneous with future action, which is present to God. Cf. Luther's Commentary on Romans (*LW,* 25:432) and *Bondage of the Will,* trans. J. I. Packer and O. R. Johnston (Grand Rapids: Baker, 2003), 80. For Calvin's treatment of *fore*-knowledge, cf. *Concerning the Eternal Predestination of God,* trans. J. K. S. Reid (Louisville: Westminster/John Knox, 1997), 115, and *Inst.,* III.21.5; CC, XIX:318.

rable in quantitative terms.[14] Divine and human knowing are two things set side by side and measured by the same scale. Moreover, both the intellectualist and voluntarist models treat God as a single subject, rather than beginning with the trinitarian relations of knowing and being known revealed in the New Testament. Finally, the formulation of the debate as a question of *fore*-knowledge easily allows the idea that God is "before" time as the first cause in a series of events to slip unobserved into the discussion.

The options forced by the continuum upon which the antinomy is based often do not seem like good news. Both the assertion that an absolute divine intellect timelessly contains all true propositions (even those about future contingent events), and the view that the divine mind is dependent upon and changes in response to (surprising) creaturely events that are beyond God's control, lead to serious problems for upholding key intuitions about the biblical gospel, as opponents on both sides of the spectrum admit. However, these are not the only options for articulating a doctrine of divine knowing. In light of the challenges to early modern categories (Part I) and of the recovery of other streams of the biblical tradition (Part II) we may now aim for a dissolution (rather than a resolution) of this theological antinomy. The conceptual space opened up by the philosophical turn to relationality and the late modern trajectories allows us to move beyond the impasse, and reconnect the doctrine of divine knowing to the reformative praxis and worship of lived Christian experience.

God and Intentionality

Speaking of God's knowing as a *scientia* that embraces all *(omnia)* things makes more sense if we weave together the insights of Infinity, Trinity, and Futurity. If divine knowing is imagined in terms of an "intention" in relation to creatures, we may think metaphorically of the "stretching out"[15] of the eternal trinitarian knowing and being known as the origin, condition,

14. For example, William Hasker asserts that "God has a *vast amount* of knowledge," and "God knows an *immense amount* about each of us — *far more*, in fact, than we know about ourselves," in "A Philosophical Perspective," in Clark Pinnock et al., *The Openness of God* (Downers Grove, Ill.: InterVarsity, 1994) 151; emphasis added.

15. In the Middle Ages, the Latin word *intentio* (a stretching out) was often used to translate the Arabic word for "concept" in the engagement with Muslim philosophical interpretations of Aristotle.

and goal of creaturely knowing. As the eternally full life of the trinitarian God, divine omniscience originates, upholds, and orients human temporal experience. It is important to avoid applying intentionality to God in a way that is simply "more" than human intentionality. In human cognition, *intentio intendens* (knowing) is dependent upon its relation to the *intentio intenta* (the thing known). If the eternal God were essentially a single subject, divine intentionality would require the object of intentionality (creation) to be eternal. Divine intentionality has to be thought of in robustly trinitarian terms, so there is no "intention" abstracted from the concrete faithful relations of Father, Son, and Spirit. The Father intends (knows) the Son and the Son intends (knows) the Father, and this knowing and being known is an eternal intentionality with(in) and through the Spirit.

Yes, God knows everything — God knows all creaturely being. But God's knowing of all is a *trinitarian* "knowing," an intimate faithful grasping of creatures, a holding all things close while granting all things space and time to become what they are called to be. Because the trinitarian persons are related faithfully in their shared Eternity, divine omniscience is not dependent upon creaturely objects. The trinitarian God *is* this faithfulness of the persons to and for and in one another; their triunely structured dynamic faithfulness *is* intensive Infinity. The religious experience of omniscient faithfulness is the experience of the manifestation of the eternal knowing and being-known of the trinitarian God, which holds together the plurality of finite creatures and calls them into Eternity. As the infinitely intimate faithful presence of the trinitarian God, divine knowing grants the temporal asymmetry of human self-conscious experience, calling creatures into a share in the peace and joy of divine life.

The omniscient faithfulness of the trinitarian God is the inescapable fiduciary of the world's emergence. God's knowing in relation to the world is *constitutive* — it grants creatures their existence. This granting of existence, however, is not merely a setting apart of creation over against God as an object of knowledge. God's faithful creativity is both *incursive* and *evocative*. Divine knowing constitutes *as* it moves incursively in faithfulness toward and addresses creatures. This constitutive incursion is also evocative, for as it grants existence and moves toward creatures it calls them toward fellowship in the trinitarian life. As humans we experience this being-called as the absolute Futurity of divine intentionality, which evokes in us a desire to know and be known — a longing for God.

God's setting of the "boundaries of our habitation" orients this longing, so that we might "grope" after God (Acts 17:26-27). This infinite divine "setting" does not limit the way finite things limit, but creatively liberates the known into a dynamic ek-stasis oriented toward the eternal fullness of trinitarian life. Rather than construing divine foreknowledge and human free will as two "things" that are either compatible or not compatible, we may imagine divine knowing as the infinite creative presence of the trinitarian God that makes the experience of freedom possible. We turn now to the exploration of biblical categories that can help us spell out this understanding of divine knowing.

§8.2. A Trembling Delight in the Name of God

The delightful terror of being known and named by God is a thread that runs throughout Scripture. The name of YHWH is the focus of worship and the basis of hope in the Hebrew Bible, and New Testament believers signify their trust in God by being baptized into the name of the Father, the Son, and the Holy Spirit. Attention to this biblical experience may help us reconstruct the idea of divine knowing in a way that is conceptually, practically, and liturgically "reformative."

The Hebrew Bible

When God says to Moses "I know you by name" (Exod. 33:17), the point is not the propositional content of the divine intellect but the faithful intentionality of the divine promise. The name of the LORD indicates an intimate presence: "Behold, the name of the LORD comes from far" (Isa. 30:27); "The LORD answer you in the day of trouble! The name of the God of Jacob protect you!" (Ps. 20:1). The name of the LORD is a "strong tower" (Prov. 18:10; cf. Ps. 20:1) into which the righteous run. God's blessing is described as "putting" the divine name on the Israelites (Num. 6:27; cf. Deut. 12–16; 2 Chron. 20:9). To be "called" by God's name is to belong to God (Isa. 4:1; 43:1; Jer. 14:9; 15:16; 1 Kings 8:43). It is "for the sake" of constituting the identity of Israel in redemptive relation to God that the divine name is faithfully called out over the people, binding them together in hope (cf. Pss. 9:10; 23:3; Isa. 48:19; Ezek. 20).

Our interest here is not in the various divine names that Israel used for

God, which were based on their experiences of God's blessing and redemption, but in the relation between God's naming of Israel and divine faithfulness. Being named by God is an experience of the intensive Infinity of divine faithfulness, and the unspeakability of *the* divine name came to signify this infinite qualitative difference between Creator and creature. In ancient Israel, naming and control were connected. It is God who names all things, and although creatures are called to share in this naming,[16] the people of God eventually learn that only God names God. The tension between the divine naming of creatures and the human desire to name God is illustrated in the story of the renaming of Jacob. A "man" wrestles with Jacob all night near Jabbok and then asks for his name (Gen. 32:27). When he answers "Jacob," the man names him anew — "Israel," which means "one who strives with God." Jacob asks for the name of the man, who refuses to give his name but blesses him.[17] Some of their ancient neighbors attempted to control their gods by invoking their names through rituals, but the Israelites came to understand that the one true God could not be manipulated or named as finite objects are named.[18] Their reverential attitude toward the divine name is connected to the prohibition against graven images; they were aware that the impulse toward idolatrous representation of God could take both sculptural and linguistic forms.

Although the Israelites had many "names" for God, which were based on their experience of God's saving faithfulness in history, they came to understand that ultimately God is beyond the reach of human naming.[19]

---

16. In the first account of creation, God's creating involves the naming of the sky, the earth, and the seas (Gen. 1:6-10). In the second creation story, the man's naming of the animals is a sign of his rule over them (Gen. 2:19-20). God's powerful faithfulness in relation to creation is described in Ps. 147:4 as the provision of names to all the stars. A negative example of creaturely naming and controlling is found in Ps. 49:11, where the ungodly "call out their names over [new] property," taking possession of more and more land.

17. Similarly, when the angel of the LORD appeared to Manoah, he did not know who it was and so asked for his name, "Why do you ask my name? It is too wonderful" (Judg. 13:17-18).

18. At later stages in Israel's history, the scribes who made handwritten copies of the sacred scrolls would leave gaps in the copy text when they came to the tetragrammaton (YHWH); only after special rites of purification would they go back and fill in the gaps. In order not to utter the name, the Israelites would say Adonai (LORD) when they came to the name YHWH in the text. The common English practice of translating the name "the LORD" is a result of this substitution.

19. For an analysis of this historical development, see Tryggve Mettinger, *In Search of God: The Meaning and Message of the Everlasting Names* (Minneapolis: Fortress, 1998), 14-49.

In Exodus 3:14, God utters the name in the first person (*'ehyeh 'asher 'ehyeh*), but in the next verse Moses is told to communicate the name in a way that appears to be connected to the third person form of the verb "to be" (YHWH, Yah'weh; the One who is — see discussion of translation below). When Moses later asks to see God's glory, he is not allowed to see the face of God but he hears the LORD proclaim "the name" (Exod. 34:5). The pronouncement of the name (in the first person) is the manifestation of the divine presence. This is what the righteous Israelite longed for above all, in fear and trembling. Throughout the Hebrew Bible, trusting and living "in" the divine name are described as the goal of the Israelite religion (e.g., Ps. 33:21; Jer. 7:14; Mic. 4:5). Because God cannot be (properly) "named" in the same way that finite existent entities are "named," our "naming" of God can only be our doxological opening up of ourselves in trust to this Naming Presence that evokes a delightfully reformative terror. Divine knowing constitutes us (as creatures) and evokes in us a longing to name and be named in faithful communion.

This experience of being known and named by God is inseparable from the experience of the promising presence of divine Futurity. Although the name revealed to Moses is often rendered "I am who I am," several versions (including the NRSV) point out in the footnotes that this can be translated "I will be what I will be." The growing consensus among Hebrew scholars is that this latter translation more likely communicates the meaning that would have been understood by the original audience.[20] As J. B. Metz suggests, "God revealed Himself to Moses more as the power of the future than as a being dwelling beyond all history and experience."[21] The proclamation of the divine name offers a promising presence: I will be there for you as who I am and as who I am will I be there for you. After all, Moses was seeking the name of God not in order to acquire a metaphysical definition of the divine, but to receive assurance that the One who was calling him to lead the Israelites would remain faithfully present.

Warrant for a future-oriented and promise-providing understanding of divine naming is also suggested by the structural similarity between *the*

20. For discussion of this translation see the analysis of John Murray, S.J., *The Problem of God* (New Haven: Yale University Press, 1964), chap. 1. Cf. Richard Kearney, *The God Who May Be: A Hermeneutics of Religion* (Bloomington: Indiana University Press, 2001), 24-25.

21. Metz, *Theology of the World* (London: Burns & Oates, 1969), 88. Cf. his essay "The Future in the Memory of Suffering," in J. B. Metz and J. Moltmann, *Faith and the Future* (Maryknoll, N.Y.: Orbis, 1995).

name and the first-person promises of God that permeate the story of Moses' calling to lead Israel. The revealing of the divine name is preceded by the promise: "I will be with you" (Exod. 3:12). After Moses returns to Egypt, God declares: "I will free you. . . . I will redeem you. . . . I will take you as my people and I will be your God" (Exod. 6:6-7). After the golden calf incident, Moses' commitment to leading the Israelites begins to waver, and God again tells Moses that he knows him by name. In the context of proclaiming "the name" before Moses, God promises: "I will be gracious to whom I will be gracious, and will show mercy on whom I will show mercy" (Exod. 33:19). The very name of God, which is the divine naming of all things, opens up creatures into a future of knowing and being-known. The hope of the ancient Israelites was oriented toward that coming infinite presence that promises to name them in a way that eternally secures them in intimate relation.[22]

The New Testament

In the New Testament, the intensive Infinity and absolute Futurity of the divine naming continue to be held together, but they are refigured and clarified through the invitation to share in the robustly relational mutual naming of the trinitarian God. As in the Hebrew Bible, we find the idea that God's name is "invoked" over the community (Jas. 2:7; cf. Acts 15:17). The name also represents the presence and power of God; e.g., Peter insists that it is the "name itself" that heals the crippled beggar at the Beautiful Gate of the temple (Acts 3:16). What is radically different, however, is the claim that it is through the name of the man Jesus that salvation comes. The community experiences the divine presence as it meets "in" his name: "for where two or three are gathered in my name, I am there among them" (Matt. 18:20). This broader, dynamic understanding of divine naming may help us understand why the gospel is precisely the "good news about the kingdom and the *name* of Jesus Christ" (Acts 8:12).

The claim that the name of Jesus now manifests the redemptive presence hoped for in the Hebrew Bible is often expressed in the Pauline litera-

---

22. The ancient Hebrews' interest in genealogies was related to the desire to be "named" in the future, to "belong" in the community even after death (e.g., Jer. 11:19). In the apocalyptic imagery of the Book of Revelation, this is expressed as hope for a new transformed experience of being named in the new community (3:12).

ture. God's resurrection of Christ from the dead seated him "far above all rule and authority and power and dominion, and above *every name that is named,* not only in this age but also in the age to come" (Eph. 1:20-21). A name that is "above every name" is beyond the finite categories of naming, and this "name" was reserved for YHWH in the Hebrew Bible. In the New Testament, however, it becomes clear that the Father shares the divine name with the Son. "Therefore God also highly exalted him and gave him the name that is *above every name,* so that at the name of Jesus every knee should bend" (Phil. 2:9-10). However, the Son does not exploit the name but places all things under the authority of the Father (1 Cor. 15:24-28). The Father is still the one "from whom every family in heaven and on earth takes its name" (Eph. 3:15). After the resurrection of Christ, however, the redemptive experience of being named by the truly Infinite divine presence is spelled out in trinitarian terms. Paul tells the Corinthians, "you were washed, you were sanctified, you were justified in the name of the Lord Jesus Christ and in the Spirit of our God" (1 Cor. 6:11).

The mutual naming and being named of the trinitarian God is especially clear in the Gospel of John. Like the "strong tower" of Proverbs 18:10, the disciples are protected in the name of God, but this is precisely the name that the Father has "given" the Son (John 17:11). Jesus comes in the name of the Father (5:43). He makes the name of the Righteous Father known to his disciples in a way that is inextricably linked both to knowledge and intimate salvific love: "I made your name known to them, and I will make it known so that the love with which you have loved me may be in them, and I in them" (17:26). The good shepherd calls his sheep "by name" (10:3), and this calling orients them toward their entry into abundant life, which is knowing and being known by God (cf. 17:3). Jesus promises that the Advocate, "the Holy Spirit, whom the Father will send *in my name,* will teach you everything" (14:26). The teaching (or "naming") of the Spirit will be oriented toward the glorification of the Father and the Son (16:12-15). The whole Gospel aims at convincing the reader that the presence of the divine name, which is wholly dependent on God's grace, is now mediated through the name of Jesus who is present through the Spirit — calling her into a community that shares in the eternal knowing and being known of the trinitarian God.

Our naming of God as "Abba, Father" (Rom. 8:15) is a participation in Jesus' naming, into which we are invited by the Spirit. This naming does not control God, but is our response to God's naming of us. In light of the trembling delight evoked by the presence of the One who names all things, and our recognition of the incapacity of our appellations to control the absolute Futurity of the divine presence, an appropriate humility should accompany all of our "namings," both of God and of one another. Although masculine metaphors for God are more common in Scripture, we also find feminine imagery for the intimate faithfulness of divine knowing (e.g., Isa. 49:15; 66:12-13). This does not mean that God is a female, any more than "Father" means God is a male. The gods (and goddesses) of Israel's ancient neighbors were sexually differentiated, but one of the functions of the name YHWH was to indicate that the true God is beyond distinctions like gender. We may call God "Abba" as we share in Jesus' way of naming and being named by God in the Spirit. However, our naming of God depends on our being named, and this should lead us (like Jesus) to use our own power of naming our neighbors in ways that are liberating rather than oppressive.

In the experience of Christian Baptism, God's name is called out over believers as a signification that they belong to God. But the name "in" which they are baptized is the "name of the Father and of the Son and of the Holy Spirit" (Matt. 28:19). This being named represents entry into the divine fellowship, which is the mutual knowing of the Son and the Father in the Spirit. The eternal life of the trinitarian God is this knowing and being known, and Baptism is our immersion into this life — in the Spirit who draws us to Christ's way of naming and being named by the Father. The experience of the Christian Eucharist also signifies our participation in this life. As we remember the gift of Jesus in whose name we are gathered, and invoke the Holy Spirit through whom we are named as the children of God, we are convicted of our own selfish attempts to name and manipulate our neighbors. We receive anew our calling that orients us toward practices of table fellowship that manifest the promising presence of divine naming.

§8.3. Jesus Christ and the Spirit of Wisdom

As we have seen, abstracting the idea of divine knowing from the omniscient faithfulness of the trinitarian God revealed in the intentional relations between the Son and the Father in the Spirit has been largely responsible for the antinomy of foreknowledge. The focus on the content of the divine intellect has also obscured the importance of the biblical category of the wisdom of God. In the message of Jesus and the proclamation of the apostles, divine knowing is not a philosophical problem for which one needs a logical "way out." The way in which Jesus found his own identity in relation to the Father in reliance on the Spirit of wisdom is not a conceptual enigma, but the answer to the human longing for infinitely faithful intimacy. If we give up the early modern abstract formulation of the question, and begin with(in) the concrete relational categories of the Christian community, we may humbly attempt to articulate the gospel of divine knowing in public discourse in a way that invites exploration of its illuminative and reformative power. Although filling out the details of such a theological proposal will need to be outlined in more detail in the context of reforming Christology and Pneumatology, it is important to show how these categories may be integrated into the very heart of a presentation of the doctrine of God.

In the New Testament, divine knowing is a mutual affair: "No one knows the Son except the Father, and no one knows the Father except the Son" (Matt. 11:27), and "No one comprehends what is truly God's except the Spirit of God" (1 Cor. 2:11). The possibility of participating in this emperichoretic mutuality of divine knowing is opened up to believers as they share in the way of Jesus Christ through intensification in the Spirit of wisdom. Second Peter 1:3-4 offers its readers the promise of becoming "partakers of the divine nature" *(genēsthe theias koinōnoi physeōs)*. It is important to recognize that the whole epistle is anchored by the phrase "in the knowledge" [*en epignōsei*] of Jesus Christ, which serves as an *inclusio* for the letter (1:2, 8; 3:18).[23] The way we understand our entry into a fellowship *(koinōnia)* of relational unity with God will depend on how we conceptualize the divine nature *(physis)*. If the nature of God is the infinite trinitarian knowing and being known, which was revealed in Jesus' faithful dependence on the absolute promise of the divine Spirit, then we may be able to move beyond some of the impasses forced upon us by early modern categories. The late modern trajectories can help us articulate a reformative understanding of God's intimate faithful knowing of creatures, which is mediated in Christian experience by entering into the Son's knowledge of the Father in the Spirit.

If we believe that God's knowing of creation is manifested ultimately in

23. James M. Starr, *Sharers in Divine Nature: 2 Peter 1:4 in Its Hellenistic Context,* Coniectanea Biblica New Testament Series 33 (Stockholm: Almqvist & Wiksell, 2000), 27.

the revelation of Jesus Christ, then Christological categories should not be accidental or optional for the doctrine of God. We begin with the fact that Jesus himself "increased in wisdom and in years, and in divine and human favor" (Luke 2:52). His whole life was oriented toward finding his identity in relation to the Father, entrusting himself to God (1 Pet. 2:23), so that he was ultimately able to offer himself through the Eternal Spirit (Heb. 9:14). The experience of the resurrected Christ led the apostle Paul to declare that Jesus Christ "became for us wisdom from God, and righteousness and sanctification and redemption" (1 Cor. 1:30). The omniscient faithfulness of God revealed in Jesus Christ is good news because now we too may grow in knowledge as we receive the gracious "spirit of wisdom and revelation" from "the God of our Lord Jesus Christ, the Father of glory" (Eph. 1:17). Jesus' way of knowing and being known reveals the eternal triune self-identification as an omniscience that faithfully tends to creatures, calling them to share in the intimate intentionality of trinitarian life.

It is important to indicate the sense in which this "identification" of God is "mystery." In the New Testament, the idea of divine mystery is not a confusing enigma, or a contradiction that comes at the end of an argument. It is a powerful reality that has been set forth in Christ (Eph. 1:9) and is now being *made known* (Eph. 3:9-10; 6:19). The mystery that has now been revealed is "Christ in you, the hope of glory" (Col. 1:26-27). Yet even the intimate experience of being known by God remains "mysterious" — beyond our manipulative control. As the gracious arriving presence of trinitarian self-identification, the intensive Infinity of God cannot be grasped by human cognition. As creatures we are always and already bound up and oriented toward the self-identification of the Creator, which we experience as the absolute Futurity that evokes our desire to identify and be identified. We cannot escape our creatureliness and compare creaturely and divine "identities" from some higher or neutral vantage point. The Infinity of the trinitarian God is experienced by us as an absolute Futurity that incursively creates any and all creaturely vantage points.

A Christian doctrine of divine knowing ought to account for the way in which the wisdom literature of ancient Israel related the idea of divine wisdom to the Spirit of God. In the early chapters of Proverbs, "Wisdom" is personified and linked to divine creation and guidance. Wisdom was "beside" God like a master worker during the establishment of the cosmos (Prov. 8:30) and now calls human beings to knowledge of the Holy One. The *ruach* (Spirit) of the Almighty is the basis of all creaturely life, and its presence makes possible the gaining of wisdom and understanding (Job 32:8; cf. Exod. 31:3). The divine Spirit is the source of both the natural tension of creaturely life and the gracious intensification of human life. God does not make us wise by giving us more of an immaterial substance but by calling us toward a redemptive intensification of the relations in which our lives are already bound together and enlivened by the Spirit.

This personification of Wisdom is also evident in the apocryphal literature, where it is explicitly connected to the concept of the *ruach* of God: "For wisdom is more mobile than any motion; because of her pureness she pervades and penetrates all things. For she is a breath [*ruach*, Spirit] of the power of God, a pure emanation of the glory of the Almighty . . . though she is but one, she can do all things, and while remaining in herself, she renews all things; in every generation she passes into holy souls and makes them friends of God, and prophets" (Wis. 7:24-27).[24] This passage articulates the idea of divine wisdom in a way that is suggestive for the concepts of intensive Infinity and absolute Futurity. God's wisdom is not depicted as an unmoved substance that externally "causes" material substances to move; she remains "in herself" precisely as she "pervades all things." Wisdom is not susceptible to temporal decay as creatures are, but this is because she is "more mobile than any motion" — a truly infinite mobility, so to speak. This is why we experience her as an absolute Futurity whose motivation of creaturely mobility is a renewal of all things, orienting us toward faithful prophetic friendship with God.

The idea of divine knowing also raises the question of the relation between God and "truth." In the Hebrew Bible, truth (*'emet*) is that which is disclosed in history as dependable, reliable, and faithful. The Song of Moses links God's faithfulness to truth: "The Rock, his work is perfect, and all his ways are just. A faithful God, without deceit, just and upright is he" (Deut. 32:4). For the Psalmist, truth has to do with being in faithful relation to the One who saves: "lead me in your truth, and teach me, for you are the God of my salvation" (Ps. 25:5; cf. Ps. 86:11; Dan. 4:37). The semantic range of the term includes what we would call the "truth value" of propositions, but even interest in the latter is oriented toward discerning whether the truth is "in" a person, whether he or she is faithful and trustworthy (e.g., Gen. 42:16). In the New Testament too, "truth" is not primarily about assertions

---

24. Later the "Word" is also linked to Wisdom (Wis. 9:1-2) and similarly personified: "Your all-powerful word leaped from heaven" (Wis. 18:15). Cf. Sirach 43:26 and Col. 1:17.

but is an unveiling *(alētheia)*, a disclosure that invites into relation. When the author of Ephesians urges his readers to speak "the truth in love" (4:15), the Greek term indicates a "holding-on-to-truth" *(alētheuontes)* that is oriented toward binding the community in faithful relations. The experience that "the truth is in Jesus" (Eph. 4:21) is the basis of this being bound together and learning to live truthfully with one's neighbors.

In the Gospel of John, "truth" has to do with the transforming faithfulness of God. John writes that truth (and grace) "came through Jesus Christ" (1:17), and those who accept Jesus' testimony acknowledge that "God is true" (3:33). However, truth here refers not primarily to propositional accuracy but to a faithful personal presence that liberates human beings. Jesus tells his disciples that they will know the truth "and the truth will make you free" (8:32). He declares: "I am the way, the truth, and the life" (John 14:6). The "truth" is not simply a message to which one gives cognitive assent. Those who "do what is true" (3:21) are those who are in the light of the gospel. The promised "Spirit of truth" (16:13) will guide the disciples into all truth, and Jesus longs for them to be "sanctified" in the truth (17:16-19). John explains in his first Epistle that it is through the Spirit, who "is the truth" (5:6), and through the Son of God, who "has given us understanding," that we "know him who is true" and "we are *in him* who is true, in his Son Jesus Christ" (5:20).[25] The biblical understanding of truth is clearly "reformative."

If truth and knowing in Scripture primarily have to do with intimate loving, with relational faithfulness, so too might the idea of *fore*-knowing. James D. G. Dunn argues that *proginōskō* in Paul's writing is not simply about knowledge before the event; "It has in view the more Hebraic understanding of 'knowing' as involving a relationship experienced and acknowledged."[26] The three times the form *proginōskō* is used in relation to

---

25. While this dynamic, relational understanding of truth may seem foreign to Western ears accustomed to thinking about "justified belief," it is quite common among other cultures. For examples, see G. Gutiérrez, *The Truth Shall Make You Free* (Maryknoll, N.Y.: Orbis, 1990); Kwok Pui Lan, "Discovering the Bible in the Non-biblical World," *Semeia* 47 (1989): 28; Abe Masao, "The Japanese View of Truth," *Japanese Religions* 14, no. 3 (December 1986) — "makoto" means both truth and faithfulness; Constantine N. Tsirpanlis, "What Is Truth: An Orthodox Response," *The Patristic and Byzantine Review* 5, no. 2 (1986): 85-90.

26. *Romans 1–8*, Word Biblical Commentary 38A (Dallas, Tex.: Word Books, 1988), 482. C. K. Barrett suggests that the "slightly ambiguous phraseology" of Rom. 8:29-30 "may serve as a warning that we are not dealing here with a rigidly thought out and expressed determinist philosophy, but with a profound religious conviction" (*A Commentary on the Epistle to the Romans* [New York: Harper & Row, 1957], 170).

God it primarily has to do with salvation in Christ by the Spirit, not divine knowledge of future contingent propositions. Divine knowing has to do with God's faithful binding of believers to Christ. First Peter speaks of Christ as "destined [*proegnōsmenou*] before the foundation of the world," emphasizing that his revelation was oriented toward evoking trust in God (1:20-21). When Paul uses the verb in Romans his interest is in assuring his readers of God's faithfulness in calling them into salvation in relation to Christ. Those whom God foreknew *(proegnō)* God destined *(proōrisen)* to "be conformed to the image of his Son" (8:29). Three chapters later Paul applies the same term to God's faithful relation to the people of Israel, whom God has not rejected (11:2).[27]

It is important to realize that this term is also applied to *human* knowers. For example, those who know beforehand *(proginōskontes)* ought to guard themselves so that they might grow in the knowledge of Jesus Christ (2 Pet. 3:17-18). Paul in his defense to Agrippa applies the term to "the Jews," especially those in Jerusalem, who could testify on his behalf since they "have known [*proginōskontes*] him for a long time" (Acts 26:5). The paucity of the biblical usage of this term suggests that its interpretation and dominance in much seventeenth-century theology were underdetermined by the biblical data. Stoic epistemology, which was revived during the Renaissance, emphasized the importance of propositions and their pre-determined truth.[28] In the Pauline literature that was written in polemic with this epistemology, however, readers were urged into a relational knowing that was not dependent on a philosophy of the "elementary principles" of the world but on life "in Christ" (e.g., Col. 2:6-8; cf. 2:20; Gal. 4:3, 9). We may think of God's pro-gnosis, then, as an acknowledging embrace of human creatures, calling them to a new life of knowing and being known in the Spirit of Christ.

A reformative understanding of divine knowing (and revelation) is also evident in the biblical experience of prophecy. The mode of prophetic expression changed over time, but for the most part what marks off the

---

27. The noun form is used of God the Father; the *prognōsis* of the Father destines believers into a life of salvation, which involves being sanctified by the Spirit in relation to Jesus Christ (1 Pet. 1:2). Acts 2:23 speaks of Jesus the Nazarene as part of the purpose and *prognosis* of God, who raised him up from death.

28. Cf. R. J. Hankinson, "Stoic Epistemology," in *The Stoics,* ed. Brad Inwood (Cambridge: Cambridge University Press, 2003), 59-84; Suzanne Bobzien, "Logic," ibid., 85-123; Troels Engberg-Pedersen, *Paul and the Stoics* (Louisville: Westminster/John Knox, 2000), 95.

prophet (or "seer") was his or her deeper vision of divine intentionality, which is materially expressed in terms of God's faithfulness. Some of the "apocalyptic" aspects of the message of the classical prophets shared the predictive element of that literary genre, especially in texts written after the Israelites' interaction with Babylonian astrology.[29] Given the theological problems with anthropomorphically attributing "foreknowledge" to God, it makes sense to think of prophecy primarily as a signification of the divine intention expressed in a way that calls the community into faithful relations with God and neighbor. The late modern recovery of the insights of Infinity, Trinity, and Futurity can help us recognize that we are not bound by the assumptions of ancient cosmological models of time and space as we seek to make sense of the human experience of an absolute *telos* that faithfully orients all things.

§8.4. Reconstructing the Teleological Argument

The categories opened up by the (re)turn to relationality also provide an opportunity for reforming the "teleological" argument, which is aimed at upholding the Christian intuition that God is the ultimate ground of the irreducible sense of purposiveness in human experience. Insofar as it deals with divine intentionality, this argument has to do with the nexus of concerns related to divine knowing. In the early modern theological project this argument functioned as an objective and foundational "proof" of a single intelligent causative substance. Isolated from a treatment of the knowing and being known of the infinite trinitarian God, it easily became divorced from the gospel and irrelevant to the praxis of the church. This approach is also subject to the same philosophical, scientific, and biblical challenges we outlined in Part I. The late modern trajectories of Part II, however, open up conceptual space for a reconstructive presentation of the argument.

Our goal is to articulate this theme in a way that emphasizes the reformative power of attending to the divine intentionality that orders the world by presenting an absolute *telos* that evokes noetic desire and transforms the practical and liturgical space of human becoming. In this postfoundationalist approach, the teleological argument is not part of an

---

29. Cf. Craig C. Hill, *In God's Time: The Bible and the Future* (Grand Rapids: Eerdmans, 2002).

apologetic prolegomenon, but is sublated into the very heart of a presentation of the divine knowing of the biblical God. Beginning with the categories that emerge out of the context of the living Christian tradition is not meant to immunize them from critique. We begin where we are — in faith seeking understanding — and reach out transversally in dialogue as we struggle to make sense of our experience of purposiveness in the world.

Classical and Contemporary Formulations

The idea that God's existence and intelligence, and so divine "knowing," are somehow made known through the ordering of the universe was common in the early patristic tradition. For Athanasius, creation is a revelation of God "especially in the order and harmony pervading the whole. . . . For often the artist even when not seen is known by his works . . . so by the order of the Universe one ought to perceive God its maker and artificer, even though He be not seen with the bodily eyes."[30] Augustine is aware that the world is not always beautiful or designed the way we would like, yet with respect to the nature of things, we say that they glorify the Artificer (*City of God*, XII.4).

It is important to recognize that these arguments are embedded in assumptions about the nature of God, even when they are intended as rationally objective proofs. This may be illustrated in Thomas Aquinas's "fifth way" of proving the existence of God, which was developed after Aristotelian categories had come to play a more significant role in Christian theology. Thomas's formulation is based on the "guidedness" [*gubernatione*] of nature. He notes that "an orderedness of actions to an end is observed in all bodies [*corpora*] obeying natural laws, even when they lack awareness [*cognitione*]." Corporeal substances lack the intelligence of immaterial substances and therefore their movement toward specific goals must be caused "by someone with understanding [*aliquis intelligens*], and this we call 'God'" (*SumTh*, I.2.3).

Several things may be observed about the implicit understanding of God and the world embedded in Thomas's formulation of the argument. First, God is linked to the world by way of "causality," filling a specific gap within the overall explanation of the ordered movement of nature.[31] This

---

30. *Against the Heathen*, NPNF2, 4:22-30.

31. Cf. David Burrell, *Knowing the Unknowable God* (Notre Dame: University of Notre

view of movement presupposes medieval cosmology, which explained the forces in the world with a mixture of Neoplatonic and Aristotelian categories. Second, the teleological argument in this classical form has to do with proving the existence of an intelligent (immaterial) being as the only explanation for the movement of *non-intelligent* (material) things. This dualism, which was hardened by Descartes in the seventeenth century, has increasingly lost its scientific plausibility as the concept of "matter" itself has undergone significant alteration. Finally, God is described as a "someone with understanding," i.e., a single subject with an intellect. Later in the *Summa,* Thomas treated the idea of the unity of God as an intelligible substance and single subject (with an intellect and will) separately from (and prior to) his treatment of the doctrine of the Trinity. As we have seen, the projection of this ancient "faculty psychology" onto God as *a* person has been challenged for biblical, scientific, and philosophical reasons.

These aspects of Thomas's way of construing divine "knowing" continue to shape some contemporary forms of the teleological argument, including many of those proposed by what has come to be called the "Intelligent Design" (ID) movement.[32] Although this movement has been met with enthusiasm in some conservative North American circles, the typical responses from the scientific community have ranged from reserved judgment to outright ridicule.[33] Our concern here is not with the value or status of ID as a scientific research program, but with the reasons for the considerable resistance this movement has faced in the broader *theological* guild. For some, the whole idea of "proving" God's existence from science is inappropriate, and ID represents the worst kind of proof — introducing a "God of the gaps" to fill in for what science cannot (yet?) explain. For others, the reliance on the metaphor of "design" implies the idea of God as

Dame Press, 1986), 5-6, 17, on the logic of the proofs for articulating the God-world relation in Thomas.

32. Cf. William Dembski, *Intelligent Design: The Bridge Between Science and Theology* (Downers Grove, Ill.: InterVarsity, 1999); idem, ed., *Mere Creation: Science, Faith and Intelligent Design* (Downers Grove, Ill.: InterVarsity, 1998); Michael Behe, *Darwin's Black Box* (New York: Simon and Schuster, 1998).

33. For examples of the former, see John Marks Templeton, ed., *Evidence of Purpose: Scientists Discover the Creator* (New York: Continuum, 1994); and Neil A. Manson, *God and Design: The Teleological Argument and Modern Science* (London: Routledge, 2003). For examples of the latter, see R. Pennock, *Intelligent Design and Its Critics* (Cambridge, Mass.: MIT Press, 2001); and Barbara C. Forrest and Paul R. Gross, *Creationism's Trojan Horse: The Wedge of Intelligent Design* (Oxford: Oxford University Press, 2003).

a great mechanical Engineer, which obscures the relational and dynamic agency of God to which Scripture attests. Insofar as the argument relies on the imagery of a divine blueprint or plan that God "designed" *before* the world was set in motion, it places the God-world relation under the constraints of time. Moreover, given the evil and suffering evident in nature, such a Designer appears to be blind or apathetic (at best) — as Hume already observed in the eighteenth century.

Articulating the Christian belief in the wisdom (and goodness) of God is extremely difficult within these conceptual constraints. If God is a single subject who foreknows and mechanically foreordains all temporal events from an untouchable timelessness, the teaching of Jesus and our experience of freedom in the Spirit make little sense. However, we are still faced with the irreducible experience of purposiveness in the world. The fact that contemporary science has given us a better understanding of the physical and biological roots of this experience does not require us to deny the real emergence of a more complex awareness of a temporal orientation at the level of human life and consciousness. However, responding to these developments will require a theological utilization of the ideas of divine purpose and wisdom that is not bound to early modern categories.

The Origin, Condition and Goal of Noetic Desire

We can begin by outlining the claim that the omniscient faithfulness of the trinitarian God of the Bible is the origin, condition, and goal of the *noetic* desire of creatures. We are dealing here with the basic *desiring* that structures all of our searching for intelligibility and meaning in the world, not simply the criteria by which we adjudicate claims about the value of particular goals. In the first sentence of the *Metaphysics,* Aristotle observed that all people by nature desire to know. This does not mean that all people are good students, nor that all people seek knowledge for altruistic reasons, but that being a person naturally involves this desire to render the world intelligible. How are we to make sense theologically of this longing to know? Paul argues in Acts 17:27 that we were created so that we might "grope" after God, and insists in Romans 11:36 that all things are from, through, and to God. Within this conceptual space we may say that the world receives its purposiveness as its very being in becoming from, through, and to the intensively infinite trinitarian life of God.

The Eternity of trinitarian life is the goal of noetic desire, but precisely as its origin and condition — the *telos* of creation is originated by the truly infinite Futurity of God, whose presence calls creatures toward a share in the fidelity of divine life. This origination incursively opens us up to ourselves, quickens our conscience, and calls us toward intimacy. Our longing for wisdom, our thirst for healthy intimate trust in communion, is constituted by the evocative presence of the Spirit who invites us into the intensively infinite mutual knowing of the Father and the Son. The God of promise whose arriving reign of peace is mediated through the Logos and the Spirit constitutes creaturely intentionality, creating the conditions for the emergence of complexity and the experience of purposiveness. These conditions are always and already "gift" as a being-originated from God, which is also a being-oriented toward God.

Explicating the relation of divine knowing to the world should not be isolated from the reformative concerns of Christian life. Making sense of the purposive dimension of the universe is connected to the religious experience of searching for ultimate meaning, of finding one's identity within the world. This occurs within the dynamic relationality of knowing and being-known by God. It is important not to obscure the deeply existential concern that ultimately drives our interest in "teleology." How am I related to the intentionality of God? How are you? The issue of the content of a divine intellect may be philosophically interesting, but our real concern is whether our knowing and being known will be secured in the future. Imagining God as a single subject who designed the order of the world and set it in motion does not solve the existential question but further complicates it. In Christian experience the ultimate teleological significance of creaturely existence is discovered by knowing and being-known in the presence of the infinite life-giving *telos* that calls us toward a share in the trinitarian life of God. Our natural desiring — our purposive orientation — is created by this infinite gracious presence. We are invited to participate in the knowledge of Jesus Christ, who trusted the Father as he experienced the intensification of life in the Spirit of wisdom, which freed him for non-anxious intimacy in relation to his neighbors.

The emergence of intentional purposive bio-cultural creatures is not the result of a "design" of a highly intellectual Engineer in the past. It is creation's becoming wise in response to the evocative presence of the trinitarian God. The condition for creaturely noetic desire is trinitarian intentionality, the fullness of knowing and being known that is Eternity.

The intensely infinite stretching-out *(intentio)* of the divine life makes space and time for creatures to participate in the omni-intimate faithfulness of the trinitarian persons. Creatures are not simply "objects" of a divine intellect, components of a complex design. Their objectivity is contingent upon the intentional faithfulness of the triune Creator, who creates them by calling them into the Son's knowing of the Father in and through the Spirit. God does not add *entelechies* to order creaturely bodies and make them move. The emerging order that is creation is constituted by the very *eschatological* presence of the trinitarian God — from, through, and *to* whom all things are (Rom. 11:36). In the omniscient faithfulness of this God we live and move and have our knowing.

§8.5. The Gospel of Divine Knowing

In the Christian Scriptures divine knowing is good news. The experience of being known by God is the delight of the Psalmist: "O Lord, you have searched me and known me. You know when I sit down and when I rise up; you discern my thought from far away . . . such knowledge is too wonderful for me; it is so high that I cannot attain it" (139:1-2, 6). The Lord's knowing of Jeremiah comforts him and gives him hope for deliverance (15:15). Scripture makes clear that being known by God also evokes trembling, for the penetrating intimacy of divine knowing has a convicting, judging, purging power — but this too is part of the gospel because it calls us toward deeper intimacy. The omniscient divine searching-out may be terrifying, but as the intensively infinite faithful promising of the trinitarian God, it also evokes a delight in being called into an eternal life of knowing and being-known.

Saving Knowledge

When John writes that God "knows everything" (1 John 3:20), the context is his reassuring the hearts of his readers that God's love abides in them by the Spirit as they believe in the name of his Son Jesus Christ and love one another. Jesus' message about divine knowing is one that alleviates anxiety: "do not worry" because the heavenly Father *knows* our needs (Matt. 6:31-33). Paul rejoices that the Galatians "have come to know God," but immediately qualifies himself — "or rather to be *known by* God" (Gal. 4:9). Part of the gospel is that "anyone who loves God is *known by* him" (1 Cor. 8:3). The biblical authors are not primarily interested in the objects of the divine intellect, but in witnessing to the One by whom and through whom and in whom they know and *are known*. The saving knowledge of the trinitarian God — the knowledge *of* the God who saves — is inherently good news.

Our noetic desire is permeated by anxiety. On the one hand, we long to become wise so that we can meaningfully relate to our neighbors in community. On the other hand, this desire is also driven by a fear that we will ultimately not be able to find the meaning of our existence through these relations. The fact that we do not know what is beyond the boundaries of our current comprehension — which is a condition for the dynamism of noetic desire itself — leads to an anxiety about the nature of our boundedness and the mystery beyond it. Our desire to know and be known revolts against the inevitable finality of death, which threatens an absolute end to our identity. Trying to secure one's own identity by blocking intimacy or forcing intimacy through one's own epistemic power leads to the dissolution or isolation of the self. We cannot get our minds around everything, and this incapacity incites both fear and fascination. We are terrified by our inability to secure our identity in relation to others through our own noetic power, and yet we cannot escape our desire for an intimate knowing and being-known by others.

This searching for intelligibility has to do with our very *identity* as human beings, for it is through our intentional making-meaning that we are formed as persons. The revelation of our impotence as we strive to secure truth on our own is part of the gospel, for as we come to face the epistemic anxiety that haunts our experience of finitude we also become aware of our existential dependence on God as the origin, condition, and goal of our noetic desire. Human knowing cannot "grasp" divine knowing in the way that it comprehends finite concepts, for the temporal experience of grasping is itself constituted by the faithful presence of divine intentionality. Nevertheless, we may experience this being-grasped within the truly infinite life of God as a call toward a share in the eternal communion of the trinitarian persons, which evokes our own self-disclosure.

Divine knowing is good news because it opens us up to the promise of finding our identity upheld within the infinitely faithful relations of the trinitarian God. This is revealed to us in the way of Jesus Christ. In the Gospel of John, Jesus describes his own intimate relation to God the Father: "I and the Father are one" (10:30) and "the Father is in me and I am in the Father" (10:38). Jesus found his identity as he trusted in the Father's faithfulness and relied on the life-giving Spirit of wisdom. He described this as abiding in God and as God abiding in him. The invitation to the disciples to share in this mutual abiding is made clear in Jesus' prayer: "As you, Father, are in me and I am in you, may they also be in us. . . . I in them and you in me, that they may become completely one" (17:21, 23).

On the basis of his experience of the saving knowledge of God through the resurrected Christ, Paul comes to a new awareness of his own identity: "it is no longer I who live, but it is Christ who lives in me. And the life I now live in the flesh I live by faith in the Son of God" (Gal. 2:20). His experience of the intimate presence of the Spirit of wisdom leads him to insist that "anyone united to the Lord becomes one spirit with him" (1 Cor. 6:17). This dialectical identity (the relational union of I and not-I) is not based on a fusion or cooperation between two types of substances that can be measured extensively or defined over against each other. It is a reception of the gift and task of finding our identity "in" Christ and "in" the Spirit as we are embraced by the omniscient faithfulness of the trinitarian God of the Bible.

The Creative Revelation of God

The late modern trajectories may also help us overcome the harsh dichotomy between "creation" and "revelation" that often characterizes the doctrine of God. This dualism sometimes leads to a sharp distinction between "general" and "special" revelation. On this model, God once created (and now upholds) nature, which provides knowledge to all, but God also (occasionally) communicates propositional truths to some. The intuition here is that not everyone experiences divine knowing in the same way, and that the biblical witness to events such as the exodus and the incarnation discloses the wisdom of God in significantly unique ways. Recognizing the need to avoid conflating these concepts, we can link them within a broader understanding of divine knowing as the omniscient faithfulness of the trinitarian God. We must first recognize that *all* creaturely knowledge of God is based on God's knowing of and faithful tending to creatures. God is known only through God and only God identifies God; however, creatures are invited to participate in this triune mutual knowing and identification. This is how God's creative revelation "reforms" us.

All human knowing (and so all theology) is made possible by and is responsible to divine revelation, which *is* God's faithful upholding of nature in its tensional becoming. All revelation is trinitarianly shaped, including the appearance of the "natural" world, which is upheld by the Logos and enlivened by the Spirit. The creative revelation of God is mediated by the intensively infinite presence of the Spirit of wisdom who calls creatures into existence and invites them into fellowship with God by sharing in the knowledge of Jesus Christ. What we call "special" revelation does not sneak around the natural conditions of human knowing, which are already upheld by the gracious intentionality of God. The intensity of our experience of this revelatory creativity in Christ through the Spirit graciously transforms our "general" experience of the intensively infinite divine intentionality that we cannot control.

Divine revelation is the faithful creative incursion of the trinitarian God "in" and "to" our historical finite existence, in response to which we worship and *about which* we formulate propositions.[34] Divine revealing is mediated through the symbol systems of human language, but we do not simply "have" revelation in the form of propositions that can be manipulated as linguistic idols. God's revelation "has" us, although human creatures respond to this experience of being-had in radically different ways. We are not saved by assenting to propositions alone, but our use of them can mediate the divine invitation to participate in the intimate intentionality of the trinitarian life.

The omniscient faithfulness of the biblical God is good news for those whose epistemic anxiety has suffocated their noetic desire to know and be known in faithful intimacy. Jesus' ministry was the display of God's intimate knowing of those who are sick and weary, of the Father's gracious faithfulness and the Spirit's provision of liberating truth. The noetic desire of those who find their identity by following in the way of Christ through life in the Spirit is freed from anxiety. Even death no longer threatens the believer whose life is "hidden with Christ in God" (Col. 3:3), for her partic-

---

34. *Could* God have decided to create a different world? *Might* God have designed things differently? These questions fail to recognize that the truly infinite trinitarian God is not susceptible to the subjunctive mood. Divine intentionality is the absolute origin, condition and goal of all creaturely linguistic differentiation, which mediates noetic desire but cannot ultimately control or satisfy it. The idea of absolute divine Futurity helps us make sense of the human experience of not-knowing, of our inability to grasp that which is essentially ahead of us and evokes our noetic groping with all its subjunctive moodiness.

ipation in the knowing and being-known that is eternal life has already begun. The Christian knows God as she is known by God, and calls others to respond to the infinitely faithful tending of the trinitarian embrace. Responding to this ever-new evocation into the intensification of mutual identification takes shape as we share in Jesus Christ's knowledge of the Father through the Spirit of wisdom. The gospel is that we are called to participate in the eternal intimacy of divine knowing, and this is that good news than which none better can be conceived.

OMNIPOTENT LOVE

D ivine knowing cannot be separated from God's active presence, and so our outline of a presentation of the doctrine of God must also explore the implications of the late modern trajectories for our interpreted experience of divine acting and being. In this chapter we turn to a cluster of ideas that surround the concept of divine *acting,* including omnipotence, predestination, providence, and the cosmological argument. The intuition of the Christian tradition that guides theological discussion of these themes is the belief that *God's agency embraces all things.* That is to say, nothing escapes the power of God. The first sentence of the Nicene Creed — "We believe in God the Father Almighty *(pantokrator, omnipotens)*" — underlines the importance of this theologoumenon. However, the Johannine insistence that "God *is* love" (1 John 4:8) and the Pauline claim that nothing is able to separate us from the love of God (Rom. 8:39) compel us to link divine power and love; holding these together within a coherent understanding of divine acting has been a perennial task for Christian theology.

One of the most significant issues that drives this discussion is the so-called "problem of evil." If God is both all-powerful and all-loving, then why does evil exist? Many contemporary debates on "theodicy" — justifying God in light of evil — presuppose the idea of God as a single subject, who is the immaterial first cause of the world. Beginning with these categories leads to answers that fall somewhere on a continuum between human libertarianism (evil is explained wholly in reference to free will) and divine determinism (God causes everything, including evil). The horns of this dilemma are set upon the bull of the early modern concept of God as rational causative substance. The very construction of the continuum assumes that God is a single subject, *a* person of a certain sort. But what sort? Is God a person who is wholly good but acts with (self-)limited power in the world, or a person who is wholly powerful but whose causality does not seem good (or loving) to us? It seems that either God's power or God's love must be limited. This way of framing the debate also assumes an "extensive" view of infinity, in which creaturely and divine power are measured on the same quantitative scale and so are capable of mutual limitation. Insofar as proponents of the early modern theological project accept the harsh dualism between immaterial and material substance, they are also faced with the difficulty of explaining how an unchanging God "acts" in or on a changing world.

The conceptual problems forced upon us by these philosophical categories make it difficult to articulate a doctrine of divine acting in a way that upholds the intuition that God *is* Good, that than which nothing "better" can be conceived (Anselm). Finite acting is conditioned by objects of desire, in relation to which the agent uses his or her *power* in an attempt to secure that which is *loved*. Applying this concept of "acting" to God as *a* person implies that God is in time, looking forward to *goods* that God does not (yet) have. This would entail that the power of God is distinct from those goods, that the life of God does not (yet) encompass all good. Not only does this way of separating God from the Good deny the very idea of divine Eternity, it also raises the specter of a Manichean cosmology in which the mightiest (good) actor in the world is a God at war with metaphysical evil. Moreover, the very coherence of the idea of a *single* absolute divine agent has increasingly been brought into question, as we observed in Chapter 3.

However, if we believe that the agency of the trinitarian God is most clearly displayed in the eschatological arrival of the reign of God through the ministry of Christ and the outpouring of the Spirit, why begin our doctrine of divine acting with categories that obscure these biblical intuitions? The intimate relation between divine power and love is expressed throughout the New Testament. Divine power is disclosed ultimately in the cross and resurrection of Jesus Christ, which manifests God's love for the world. Paul encourages the Romans by insisting that it is precisely because God's power is "for us" that nothing can separate us from the love revealed in Christ (8:31, 35). This love is "poured into our hearts through the Holy Spirit" (5:5), and God "proves his love for us" (5:8) through the manifestation of the divine power over death itself. The nature of divine love is disclosed in the suffering of the Crucified, which empowers us to share in that love: "We know love by this, that he laid down his life for us; and we ought to lay down our lives for one another" (1 John 3:16). If we begin within the relational and dynamic categories of the arriving reign of the trinitarian God, we may be able to articulate the good news of the infinite agency of God in a way that overcomes some of the conceptual impasses that have plagued the doctrine of divine acting.

§9.1. Beyond the Antinomy of Divine Predestination

If God really has *all* power, then how can human beings have *some* power? How can we maintain both God's *omni*-potence and the sufficient potency of human persons to act responsibly? This brings us again to the issue of human freedom, which has to do with the power of finite agents to act as they seek to secure the goods they love. The problem of creaturely freedom is intrinsically related to the problem of evil: if God's power is the cause of all things, including human free acts that result in evil and suffering, then on what basis can we claim divine power is all-loving? On the other hand, if God's loving agency does not encompass all creaturely activity, then how can we claim that divine love is all-powerful? This antinomy leads to the temptation either to limit God's power (to particular acts) or God's love (to particular creatures). In some streams of the Christian tradition, articulating the doctrine of "predestination" has become one of the primary means for describing divine acting in relation to the world. Along with most Reformed theologians, I believe that the intuition that God destines all of creation ought to be central to a reformative doctrine of divine agency.

Understanding the Impasse

However, we are not necessarily dependent on the categories of early modern philosophy and science for our articulation of this intuition. Reconstructing this aspect of the doctrine of God will require that we challenge the assumptions that hold up the horns of the "predestination vs. free will" dilemma. As we saw in Chapter 4, this way of structuring the debate typically presupposes a model of the divine "will" as the absolute power that ordains all things, which then must somehow be related to the divine "intellect." In addition to the presumption of faculty psychology projected onto God, which leads to a lack of attention to the trinitarian dynamics of divine agency, this way of framing the question often implicitly suggests an extensive view of divine infinity. The debate is over the "extent" to which limitations are posed on God's "control." On this model, the more control humans have the less control God has (and vice versa). Finally, the emphasis on *pre*-destination buttresses a reliance on the category of God as first efficient cause, which easily leads to the depiction of God as an agent moving through time and anticipating a better future.

The way in which these early modern categories continue to structure the debate is illustrated in *Predestination and Free Will: Four Views of Divine Sovereignty*. All four contributors accept the following way of asking the question about divine acting: "To what extent does human freedom pose limitations on God's sovereign control over earthly affairs?"[1] We can imagine their answers being placed on a spectrum that reflects the tension between the intellectualist and voluntarist ideals. The view that "God ordains all things" is quite obviously on the voluntarist side of the spectrum; the author defends a form of compatibilism in which human actions are "free" although causally determined by the divine will (appealing to Hodge, among others). Moving toward the middle of the continuum, we find a greater openness to the intellectualist ideal in the claim that "God knows all things"; the author tries to show how God's predetermination of all things is in *accordance* with divine foreknowledge. The third view, that "God limits his power," represents a clear preference for the intellectualist ideal, and is supported by classically Arminian arguments. Finally, the position that has come to be called the "open" view appears in this context under the heading "God limits his knowledge." This approach implicitly depends on the intellectualist ideal — it is *because* God's knowledge is limited that divine power to resist evil is also limited.

The editors of the volume point out the importance of the practical implications of these positions and require each author to respond to specific pastoral case studies. In every case, the other authors do not see the views of their colleagues as good news for those confronting real life choices. If God ordains all things, what choice do they really have? The idea

---

1. David Basinger and Randall Basinger, eds., *Predestination and Free Will: Four Views of Divine Sovereignty* (Downers Grove, Ill.: InterVarsity, 1986), 10.

that God's timeless foreordaining is in conjunction with God's timeless fore-knowing still leaves us wondering how our temporal experience can really be free. If God's power is really limited, can we be sure that God has sufficient control over the world to work efficaciously in our lives? Our hope in God's saving power is further complicated if the divine intellect is surprised by each new creaturely action in the world. The logical impasse is intensified by our existential experience of moral freedom and our longing for the good life. Insofar as providing a coherent resolution to the antinomy seems to entail either denying human responsibility for sin or making God the direct cause of evil, many theologians would rather live with the impasse and appeal to mystery. Each author's proposal is followed by three "Responses," in which the others show the logical, biblical, and existential problems that follow if one takes that author's position on the continuum. The legitimacy of the continuum itself, however, is not challenged.

The first step toward reconstruction is acknowledging the genealogy of the antinomy. Although most theologians realized that it threatened the theological criteria of simplicity and immutability, the tendency to describe God's will as a power in the past that pushes toward the future was a recurrent temptation during the early modern period. The deterministic and materialist worldview of Hobbes and his contemporaries intensified the problem of divine and creaturely agency. If one begins with these categories, compatibilism and incompatibilism seem to be the only choices — either our intuitive sense of being free is compromised to make it fit in a deterministic world or there are gaps in the causal chain of the material world that leave room for human free will. This problem was further complicated by the rise of Newtonian science, and the role of divine causality in the effects of the world of space and time increasingly became one of the key issues that drove theological discourse.[2] Prior to the early modern period, the idea of the divine as first (or higher) cause often served to emphasize the inability of creaturely reason to place the experience of loving divine agency under the constraints of human language.[3] In the wake of

2. E.g., when Newton's friend Samuel Clarke published *A Demonstration of the Being and Attributes of God* (ed. Ezio Vailati [Cambridge: Cambridge University Press, 1998]) in 1705, five of the twelve major sections had headings with the term *cause* in the title, and most of the other sections engaged the issue of causality to some extent.

3. Clement of Alexandria, e.g., notes that "The first cause is not then in space, but above both space, and time, and name, and conception" (*Stromata* [or Miscellanies], V.11; ANF, 2:461). Augustine generally used the term "cause" to emphasize that nothing has any

Newtonian anxiety, however, debate over the *power* of God could be carried out without significant reference to the *love* of God.

As we saw have seen, the tension between the intellectualist and voluntarist ideals had its roots in the patristic and medieval period. In the view of John of Damascus, who privileged the divine intellect, the contingency of events caused by intelligent creatures is God's concession to "freewill."[4] Although the voluntarist stream gained momentum in the work of those who followed Augustine, the relation between the divine faculties continued to structure the debate in the Middle Ages. For example, although Thomas Aquinas follows Augustine in his treatment of predestination (*SumTh*, I.23.5), one finds both intellectualist and voluntarist tendencies in his work (I.14; I.19). Voluntarism came to the fore in the writings of Scotus and Ockham, but the intellectualist ideal resurfaced with a vengeance in the work of sixteenth-century Catholic theologians like Suarez and Molina.

The early Protestant Reformers preferred the voluntarist ideal. Against the intellectualist tendencies of Erasmus, Luther insists that it is "fundamentally necessary and wholesome for Christians to know that God foreknows nothing contingently, but that he foresees, purposes, and does all things according to his own immutable, eternal and infallible will. This bomb-shell knocks 'free-will' flat, and utterly shatters it."[5] For Calvin, nothing can finally alter the will or power of God (*Inst.*, I.18.1, 2). In his *On the Eternal Predestination of God*, Calvin concludes that "of all the things which happen, the first cause is to be understood to be His will, because He so governs the natures created by Him, as to determine all the counsels and the actions of men to the end decreed by Him."[6] However, if God's will causes *all* things then God seems to be an unfair tyrant and responsible for

---

other origin besides God; cf. *De Trinitate*, III.2-4; NPNF1, 3:57-59. For Pseudo-Dionysius, and the tradition that followed him in positing the *via causalitatis* as the basis for the *via negationis* and the *via eminentiae*, the language of divine causality was not tied to serial efficacy but served to emphasize that the "supreme" or "unique" cause of all things is beyond all finite control and conception. Cf. "The Mystical Theology," in *Pseudo-Dionysius: The Complete Works*, trans. Colm Luibheid (New York: Paulist, 1987), 134-41.

4. *On the Orthodox Faith*, II.29; NPNF2, 9:42.

5. *Bondage of the Will*, 80.

6. *Eternal Predestination*, 178. He also followed Augustine by refusing to give in to the temptation to resolve the antinomy by privileging divine foreknowledge, an approach championed by those who preferred the intellectualist ideal (115).

sin and evil. This drove some seventeenth-century theologians like Arminius back to the intellectualist ideal; God's will (and power) must be limited in some sense in order to protect divine love.

In order to protect the intuition that God's will is all-powerful, many Reformed Scholastics who defended voluntarism were willing to limit God's love to only some creatures or to appeal to the inscrutability of divine judgment. As we have seen, classical mechanics contributed to the displacement of the human experience of love from the "real" (quantitatively measurable) world; motion and causality came to be explained in terms of the inertial force of colliding bodies extended in absolute time and space. Predestinarian models embedded within a mechanistic, deterministic world view were tempted to depict divine causality as the initial cause that started a domino effect, and now somehow concursively effects the motion of bodies along the line of time. However, this is not how the power of love works. Love is a force that does not simply push; it also pulls, draws, unites, enlivens, engages, reorders, and evokes. Contrary to the popular stereotype, the seventeenth-century debates on predestination were not wholly abstracted from Christology.[7] However, their reliance on the concept of God as a single subject complicated their task of articulating the role of the Son (and the Spirit) in divine agency.

God and Causality

The early modern dichotomy between power and love made it difficult to articulate the biblical experience of the omnipotent love of the trinitarian God. We can begin healing this conceptual bifurcation by speaking of divine acting in terms of God's constitutive, incursive, and evocative relation for, to, and in the world. Divine acting is constitutive of creation; all things are from, through, and to God (Rom. 11:36). As the empowering love of God that grants existence to all things, divine determining holds all things in be-

---

7. Richard Muller shows the way in which predestination is linked to Christ in the Reformed Scholastics in *Christ and the Decree: Christology and Predestination in Reformed Theology from Calvin to Perkins* (Durham, N.C.: Labyrinth Press, 1986); cf. idem, *God, Creation and Providence in the Thought of Jacob Arminius* (Grand Rapids: Baker, 1991), 162-63. F. Stuart Clarke provides an overview of the role of Christ in the doctrine in "Christocentric Developments in the Reformed Doctrine of Predestination," *Churchman* 98, no. 3 (1984): 229-45.

ing and calls all things toward new being. As the intensive Infinity of trinitarian love, the agency of God embraces all things. However, the power of the promising God of the Bible is not like a finite force that pushes created objects along. The determining of the trinitarian God provides the "terms," the conditions, for the becoming of creaturely space and time.

God's power is not like the power of a pagan god who causes things in the world the same way that finite human agents do, moving through time and competing with creatures for space in the world. Through the incursion of the intensively infinite agency of the trinitarian God, creatures are called into existence toward love. This evocation is not simply "from" a future point in time, but is the all-conditioning embrace of the eternal God whose active presence creates the asymmetric experience of temporality. God's agency calls creatures out of nothing in(to) love. If God is essentially the omnipotent love of the trinitarian life, then we may think causality and God together without collapsing into the problems of a conditioned and spuriously "infinite" god, who is defined as the "cause" of an "effect."

If divine power *is* divine love and vice versa, then the eternal life of the trinitarian God *is* a mutual sharing of truly infinite power, and divine agency *is* the mutually shared love of the three persons of the Trinity. The distinction between acting-on-the-other and being-acted-upon does not constrain the eternally perichoretic agency of the trinitarian God of love. The question of what God was doing (causing) "before" time is also refigured. If divine causality *is* love, then the eternal life of the trinitarian God is this mutual "causing." There was no time when God was not causing, so long as we interpret this eternal causing in terms of mutual love. This shared love is the power of the trinitarian persons in their relational unity. The conditions for the plurality of differentiated creatures, for the emergence of personal finite agents, and for their being called into fellowship with(in) divine love, originate in the Eternity of the biblical God.

God does not "have" power and then use (some of) it to do loving things. God *is* love, and this is manifested in creation as the intensively infinite all-powerful agency of the trinitarian God. Creaturely agency is not simply an effect that comes "after" the cause, but rather a dynamic becoming-in-love, oriented toward the fullness of Eternity. Divine goodness is the shared eternal life of the Father, Son, and Holy Spirit, which empowers creatures as the presence of absolute Futurity. The omnipotent love of God is the constitutive incursion of Eternity in(to) time that calls all things — including human freedom — toward redemption. Nothing escapes God's power, but this is the power of trinitarian love that holds the other in being and calls the other (in)to being — truly omnipotent love. The categories opened up by the (re)turn to relationality and the late modern trajectories can help us present the doctrine of divine acting in a way that conserves the biblical intuitions about the power and love of God by liberating their illuminative and reformative force in dialogue with contemporary culture. We begin with the biblical experience of seeking the kingdom of God.

§9.2. A Trembling Delight in the Reign of God

Divine acting is not described in Scripture merely as a generic force but as a ruling agency, as a personal reality that salubriously forms human acting, ordering the community toward the truly Good. The idea of a divine "kingdom" might not initially appear to be a good candidate for presenting the doctrine of divine acting in late modern culture. However, the biblical understanding and experience of the reign of omnipotent love are inherently reformative.

The Hebrew Bible

The trembling evoked by the idea of a divine reign may begin as an anxiety about being told what to do, producing stress about our capacity (or willingness) to follow the rules.[8] However, as we recognize our inability to secure the good life with our own finite power, this trembling may become a hopeful fascination in the arriving reign of infinite divine love that promises to empower us to live in right relations with our neighbors. Because Scripture was written over a long period of time, it is not surprising that we find several different political images and metaphors used to speak of the reign of God. However, we may still identify a basic theme: divine act-

8. The Israelites were called to obey the voice of the LORD so that they might become a "priestly kingdom" (Exod. 19:6); they trembled at the prospect and preferred that the rule of YHWH be mediated through Moses and the tablets of the law. After the people of Israel settled in the promised land, later generations preferred a king like the other nations (1 Sam. 10:19).

ing encompasses all things (including nature and human society), and the mighty acts of God call human persons into a way of acting in relation to one another that is just and good.[9] The provision of the law is for the "well-being" of the people (Deut. 10:13), and is grounded in the fact that "the LORD set his heart in love" on Israel (10:15). The psalmist uses the metaphor of "king" to draw attention to the justice of God in relation to the people: "The LORD is king! The world is firmly established. . . . [God] will judge the peoples with equity" (Ps. 96:10).

The mediation of the divine reign, whether through the law or an earthly king, was oriented toward the creation of a community of justice. The monarchical formula "The LORD your God is God of gods and Lord of lords, the great God, mighty and awesome" is materially filled out in terms of God's execution of justice for the orphan, widow, and stranger (Deut. 10:17-18). "You shall fear the LORD your God" (10:20), ". . . you shall love the LORD your God" (11:1) — a trembling delight in God is the relational context within which obedience emerges and out of which justice flows. God's reign is over all things, including the elements of nature and all creaturely life (Exod. 15:1-17; Job 41; Judg. 5:4, 21). The promised reign of God does not exclude the rest of the natural world; the wolf and the lamb will live together in peace (Isa. 11:6).

The Israelites come to learn that the reign of YHWH is not like the power of earthly kings; it is the intensively infinite power of the promising divine presence. God does not use power to force the people into obedience like a dictator. The kingdom of God does not compete with human kingdoms, as they compete with each other. It is not simply a much larger kingdom that uses quantitatively more power to secure its rule. Human reigning (or governing) is about the use and monitoring of power in order to control the goods in a community, but the reign of the biblical God is not based on finite commodification. The reign of God convicts and discloses the powerlessness of such human "lording" over one another to bring about the good life in community. The infinite power of divine love embraces the community and reorients its finite power so that it shares in the manifestation of the rule of divine peace. God's kingdom is not chal-

---

9. For an overview of the theme of the kingdom in various genres, see Dale Patrick, "The Kingdom of God in the OT," in *The Kingdom of God in Twentieth-Century Interpretation,* ed. Wendell Willis (Peabody, Mass.: Hendrickson, 1987), 67-80; John Bright, *The Kingdom of God* (New York: Abingdon, 1953).

lenged by the waxing and waning of human commitment to its rule, or by the vicissitudes of struggling human kingdoms.[10] For the Israelites, trust in YHWH was grounded in an experience of a promising presence that is already forming the hearts of the righteous toward a peaceful and just community.

As we saw in §4.5 and §§7.1-4, the biblical experience of the kingdom of God suggests an eschatological ontology. On the one hand, the dominion of God is present (2 Chron. 19:11; Ps. 145:11-13; Isa. 6:3-4) and always has been established (Ps. 93:1-2). On the other hand, it is anticipated as a dynamic reign in which the people of God will share in the future. This is expressed in the vision of Daniel 7:27; when "one like a Son of Man" comes to the "Ancient of Days" and is given dominion and glory and kingship — then the "holy ones" will gain possession of an everlasting kingdom. It is the anticipation of the promised kingdom that will establish the community in a new way that characterizes Isaiah's prophecies. The coming righteous reign of peace is described by Isaiah as mediated through a child, "a son given to us . . . he is named Wonderful Counselor, Mighty God, Everlasting Father, Prince of Peace." His authority will grow continually and "there shall be endless peace"; he will establish a kingdom and "uphold it with justice and with righteousness" (Isa. 9:6-7).

The New Testament

In the last few decades, biblical scholars have increasingly pointed to the significant appropriation of Isaiah's promise as a leitmotif in the Gospels and Acts, which is interpreted as a "new exodus" mediated through Christ and the Spirit.[11] The Gospels are saturated by the application of the title "son of man" to Jesus, which is particularly significant given the importance of the Jewish anticipation that this "son of man" would bring in a new political order.[12] G. E. Ladd argued that the Israelites' experience of the tension between the "already" and the "not yet" is maintained but

10. Habakkuk illustrates the experience of hope in the power of YHWH, who *is* his strength, who evokes joy and exultation even though the wicked prosper and "though the fig tree does not blossom, and no fruit is on the vine" (3:17-18).

11. E.g., Rikki E. Watts, *Isaiah's New Exodus and Mark* (Tübingen: Mohr Siebeck, 1997); David W. Pao, *Acts and the Isaianic New Exodus* (Grand Rapids: Baker Academic, 2000).

12. Cf. N. T. Wright, *Jesus and the Victory of God* (Minneapolis: Fortress, 1996).

refigured in the New Testament: "for Jesus, the Kingdom of God was the dynamic rule of God which had invaded history in his own person and mission to bring men in the present age the blessings of the messianic age, and which would manifest itself yet again at the end of the age to bring this same messianic salvation to its consummation."[13] As we saw in §4.5, the idea of the kingdom of God became a significant organizing theme in twentieth-century biblical scholarship for interpreting the message and ministry of Jesus.[14] The New Testament authors take over the Israelites' belief in the almighty power of the divine reign, but reinterpret the "kingdom of God" in explicitly trinitarian terms.

The Infinity of the divine reign is also implicit in the New Testament. The kingdom of God cannot be measured in the same terms that human political power is measured. In response to the Pharisees, Jesus insisted that "the kingdom of God is not coming with things that can be observed; nor will they say, 'Look, here it is!' or 'There it is!' For, in fact, the kingdom of God is among you [within you, or within your reach]" (Luke 17:20-21). The kingdom of God is beyond us precisely as a power that is closer to us than we are to ourselves; this intensively infinite presence opens us up to ourselves and others, calling us to share in the empowering rule of love. When asked if he was a king, Jesus answered Pilate, "My kingdom is not from this world. If my kingdom were from this world, my followers would be fighting to keep me from being handed over to the Jews. But as it is, my kingdom is not from here" (John 18:36). The reign of God is not "signified" in the same way that we interpret the power of earthly kingdoms. It is not one kingdom among many, but the arriving presence of the infinite power of divine love. The parables about the kingdom are also suggestive here. Entering into the reign of God is beyond finite creaturely calculation; the householder does not reward laborers as we have come to expect (Matt. 20). The reign of God is like a treasure hidden in a field, or a pearl of great price — one gives everything for it (Matt. 13).

The kingdom of God is not simply a message but a powerful manifestation of divine love that is arriving through Jesus' ministry. "But if it is by the Spirit of God that I cast out demons, then the kingdom of God has

13. George Eldon Ladd, *The Presence of the Future* (Grand Rapids: Eerdmans, 1974); *The Gospel of the Kingdom* (Grand Rapids: Eerdmans, 1959), 307.

14. Cf. Robert Morgan, "From Reimarus to Sanders: The Kingdom of God, Jesus and the Judaisms of His Day," in *The Kingdom of God and Human Society,* ed. Robin Barbour (Edinburgh: T&T Clark, 1993).

come [*ephthasen*] to you" (Matt. 12:28). The kingdom has arrived and is arriving. We often emphasize "going to heaven," but Jesus teaches us to pray, "thy kingdom come" (Matt. 6:10). The reign of divine love graciously comes to us. Jesus encourages his hearers, "Do not be afraid, little flock, for it is your Father's good pleasure to give you the kingdom" (Luke 12:32). The kingdom of God is not far off: we "are receiving" a kingdom that cannot be shaken (Heb. 12:28). John writes to the churches that he is their brother "who shares with you . . . the kingdom" (Rev. 1:9). The ministry of Jesus makes clear that God's reign is an empowering love that embraces the other in justice. After the resurrection of Christ and the outpouring of the Spirit, this becomes a common theme in the writings of the apostles. "Has not God chosen the poor in the world to be rich in faith and to be heirs of the kingdom that he has promised to those who love him?" (Jas. 2:5).

Jesus also linked love intrinsically to the power of the divine reign. He came not to abolish the law (or rule) of God but to fulfill it (Matt. 5:17). The fulfillment of the law, however, is precisely a sharing in divine love. The greatest commandments are to love God and neighbor (Matt. 22:36-39). Jesus calls his disciples to follow his commands, which is to abide in his love "just as I have kept my Father's commandments and abide in his love" (John 15:10). This theme is echoed later in the New Testament. "Owe no one anything, except to love one another; for the one who loves another has fulfilled the law" (Rom. 13:8). For the whole law is summed up in a single commandment, "You shall love your neighbor as yourself" (Gal. 5:14; cf. Jas. 2:8). Dwelling in love and submitting to the divine reign go together, because the rule of the trinitarian God reforms creatures by empowering them to share in the redemptive agency of divine love.

The way in which believers are called to receive the kingdom of the trinitarian God by sharing in the power of divine love is further spelled out in the Pauline literature. The reign of God is not about a single subject, a dictator who timelessly decrees to cause all events by force, but about the omnipotent love of God that calls creatures into a share in the empowering righteousness of the triune life. Jesus called his hearers into the reign of the Father, but the book of Colossians indicates that the Father "has rescued us from the power of darkness and transferred us into the kingdom of his beloved Son, in whom we have redemption, the forgiveness of sins" (Col. 1:12-14). First Corinthians 15:24-28 describes the sharing of the divine reign. God the Father has put all things under the subjection of the Son, but we look toward a future in which the Son will hand over the kingdom to the Father "so that God may be all in all." The Christ hymn in Philippians calls believers to have "the same mind" that was in Christ, who, having emptied himself, was highly exalted by God "so that at the name of Jesus every knee should bend . . . to the glory of God the Father" (Phil. 2:10-11). Furthermore, the reign of God is inseparable from life in the Spirit: "For the kingdom of God is not food and drink but righteousness and peace and joy in the Holy Spirit" (Rom. 14:17). Sharing in the inheritance of the kingdom with the Son is made possible by the Spirit who makes us heirs; "for all who are led by the Spirit of God are children of God" (Rom. 8:14).

If the kingdom of God is the reign of omnipotent love, why do we find so much disorder and suffering in the world? A theological response to this question should begin with the observation that the biblical texts are not obsessed with theodicy, nor do they try to absolve God of the responsibility for the ordering of the world. Jesus did not try to justify God to the poor and the oppressed, but actively confronted them with the love of God and invited them into the good life of the kingdom. In Romans Paul exclaims that "the creation was subjected to futility not of its own will but by the will of the *one who subjected it* in hope" (8:20). All things are from, through, and to God (11:36) and among all things we experience evil and suffering. Similarly, the Hebrew Bible does not shrink from the implications of the almighty power of divine agency.[15]

This lack of defensiveness is bothersome on the assumptions of early modern theology; for if God is a single subject whose intellect knows ahead of time what will happen, and whose will is the efficient first cause of all events, then God seems like an evil agent. Part of the problem may be in the way in which the debate was structured in the early modern period, during which the term "theodicy" emerged. Linking *omnipotence* and *love* within the conceptual space opened up by the late modern trajectories may help us reach out from within our interpreted experience as Christians into dialogue with late modern culture. Our understanding of the reign of the God of peace should not be abstracted from the manifestation of divine activity in the suffering Christ and the justifying Spirit, for it is

---

15. In Deut. 32:39, God announces: "I kill and I make alive; I wound and I heal." In response to his wife, Job (2:10) asks "shall we receive the good at the hand of God, and not the bad?" Isaiah prophesies: "I form light and create darkness, I make weal and create woe [evil]; I the LORD do all these things" (Isa. 45:7; cf. Jer. 18:6, 11; 45:4-5; Amos 3:6; Job 9:12; Eccl. 7:13).

precisely the experience of *this* agency that provides us with a new way of interpreting and responding to finite goods and evils.

§9.3. Jesus Christ and the Spirit of Justice

The Christian experience of divine acting is mediated through the love operative in the ministry of Jesus Christ, who is the *power* of God (1 Cor. 1:1–2:5), and interpreted through life in the Spirit, in whom God's *love* is poured out into the community (Rom. 5:5). Therefore, a Christian understanding of the relation between divine acting and "the Good" should not be abstracted from Christ, through whom "the righteousness of God has been disclosed" (Rom. 3:21-22), or from the Spirit of holiness whose manifestations in the community are for "the common good" (1 Cor. 12:7). For Jesus, the reign and justice of God are intimately connected: "seek first the *kingdom* of God and his *righteousness* [*dikaiosyne*]" (Matt. 6:33). Several scholars have challenged the popular translation of the Hebrew term *tsedeq* and the Greek term *dikaiosyne* as "righteousness," arguing that "justice" better captures the communal aspect of this term in the political and religious life of Israel and the early church.[16] While "righteousness" easily lends itself to an individualistic (and inner-oriented) view of salvation, "justice" reminds us that the agency of God grants us life in the Spirit by orienting us outward to our neighbors.

Jesus insisted that God alone is good (Luke 18:19; Matt. 19:17). God's goodness, however, makes others righteous by granting a share in divine holiness. Divine goodness has been revealed so that in Christ "we might become the righteousness [*dikaiosyne*] of God" (2 Cor. 5:21). The arriving kingdom is good news because it is the justifying agency of the Spirit, the presence of empowering divine love that invites creatures to share in the infinite goodness of trinitarian life. God's gracious power was revealed through the appearance of Jesus Christ "who abolished death and brought life" (2 Tim. 1:8-10) and now gives life to believers through the indwelling

16. Cf. Jason J. Ripley, "Covenantal Concepts of Justice and Righteousness, and Catholic-Protestant Reconciliation: Theological Implications and Explorations," *Journal of Ecumenical Studies* 38, no. 1 (Winter 2001): 95-108. Steven M. Voth, "Justice and/or Righteousness: A Contextualized Analysis of sedeq in the KJV (English) and RVR (Spanish)," in *The Challenge of Bible Translation,* ed. Glen G. Scorgie, Mark L. Strauss, and Steven M. Voth (Grand Rapids: Zondervan, 2003), 321-45.

Spirit (Rom. 8:11). The goodness of those who receive this gift is a manifestation of the fecundity of this justifying agency (Gal. 5:22). The experience of the Spirit is connected to the real transformation of political power structures, a loving force that holds the embodied community together.[17]

Framing the issue simply as the "problem of evil" misses the broader biblical understanding of human and divine agency. Already in the story of the Garden of Eden, eating from the forbidden tree signifies the acquisition of "the knowledge of good *and* evil" (Gen. 2:17). The problem in Jesus' ministry is not merely the evils that threaten the poor but the goods (wealth, oppressive power) that seduce the rich. To those who had been crushed by the evils of social injustice, Jesus brought healing and wholeness. The resistance to divine agency in the ministry of Jesus was strongest among those who had the "goods" of earthly life. This means that Christian theology must also speak of "the problem of the good."

The doctrine of *justification* is not about abstract decrees that occur apart from concrete human existence, but about the intensification of life in the justifying Spirit who reforms our agency in relation to our neighbors. Salvation is not primarily about an *ordo salutis,* the order of causes that effect the final state of individual souls, but about a *salutary ordering*[18] that calls into being a just community. Already in the Hebrew Bible, the righteous Israelite's experience of trembling delight in the divine reign pointed to the irreducibly social dimension of the human experience of good and evil.[19] The Christian community is called to participate in the redemptive fellowship of divine goodness, which moves (in)to the world as the infinite power of love, giving itself for the other.

We interpret divine acting in light of our experience of being called to share in this divine agency through a life of *cruciformity.* We are fellow heirs with Christ, "provided we suffer with him in order that we may also be glorified with him" (Rom. 8:17). Paul prays that he "may know him and the power of his resurrection, and may share his sufferings, becoming like him in his death, that if possible I may attain the resurrection from the dead" (Phil. 3:10-11). First Peter urges its readers to "rejoice insofar as you

---

17. Cf. Michael Welker, *God the Spirit,* trans. John F. Hoffmeyer (Minneapolis: Fortress, 1994), 74, 227, 330.

18. Cf. F. LeRon Shults and Steven J. Sandage, *The Faces of Forgiveness: Searching for Wholeness and Salvation* (Grand Rapids: Baker Academic, 2003), chap. 4.

19. Walter Brueggemann, "Theodicy in a Social Dimension," *Journal for the Study of the Old Testament* 33 (1985): 3-25.

are sharing [*koinōneite*] Christ's sufferings" because whoever has suffered in the flesh (in the way Christ did) "has finished with sin" (4:1, 13). The idea that those who would follow Christ must deny themselves and "take up the cross" is found in all three of the Synoptic Gospels (Matt. 10:38-39; Mark 8:34-35; Luke 9:23-24; cf. John 12:25). Galatians describes being "crucified with Christ" (2:19-20), living united with him in faith that is "made effective through love" (5:6). For those who belong to Christ "have crucified the flesh with its passions and desires" (5:24). The call to share in the suffering of Jesus Christ does not initially appear to be good news — until we realize that it opens us up to an intimate fellowship with and in the infinite goodness and love of the trinitarian God.

Christians participate in divine acting as they become like Christ, who saw his own ministry as fulfilling the prophecy of the suffering servant: "The spirit of the Lord GOD is upon me, because the LORD has anointed me; he has sent me to bring good news to the oppressed, to bind up the brokenhearted, to proclaim liberty to the captives and release to the prisoners . . . to provide for those who mourn in Zion" (Isa. 61:1-3; cf. Luke 4:18). The suffering of Jesus is not a passive acquiescence to oppression, but an active bearing of the burdens of the weak, offering them liberation from the crushing agency of destructive political structures. This liberation is mediated through the all-powerful agency of the Father whose Spirit grants new life in the divine love. This love is absolutely beyond the threatening seduction of the finite world, which is passing away. Those who are being formed together as the body of Christ do not accept the suffering of the poor and the abused as a necessary part of the world, but actively confront the finite causes of their suffering — which are almost always dialectically related to the hoarding of finite "goods" — with the healing power of God's love. The justifying agency of the Spirit creates a community of agents who are not seduced by finite goods because these do not provide that for which they truly long — righteous relations within loving *koinōnia*.

In Romans 8:18, Paul indicates that his suffering is "not worth comparing" with the coming glory of God. Suffering and glory cannot be placed on the same extensive scale.[20] The push and pull of finite goods and

---

20. For a discussion of the incommensurability of God's goodness and finite goods, see Marilyn McCord Adams, *Horrendous Evils and the Goodness of God* (Ithaca: Cornell University Press, 1999); Robert M. Adams, *Finite and Infinite Goods* (Oxford: Oxford University Press, 2002); Simone Weil, *Gravity and Grace* (London: Routledge, 2002); Søren Kierkegaard, *Purity of Heart Is to Will One Thing*, trans. D. V. Steere (New York: Harper & Row, 1956).

evils are conditions for the creaturely longing for justice, but the truly infinite Goodness of the loving agency of God offers liberation from the power of this finite tension. No suffering that threatens, nor any worldly good that lures, disrupts Paul's contentment (Phil. 4:11) because his contentment is grounded in an experience of a dynamic agency that cannot be extensively measured or compared to worldly goods or evils. In 2 Corinthians 4:17, he indicates that "this slight momentary affliction is preparing us for an eternal weight of glory *beyond all measure.*" This way of understanding the relation between divine acting and the evils and goods of the world does not downplay their real metaphysical power to shape the agony and ecstasy of human existence, but it does offer a new way of actively responding to these finite forces.

When Jesus teaches us to pray "Our Father . . . your kingdom come, your will be done" (Matt. 6:9-10), he is calling us to attend to a dynamic presence whose arrival orients us toward hopeful participation in a redemptive, forgiving agency. Jesus himself did not experience the divine will as a force that pushed him deterministically from the past, but as a personal agency that invited him into obedient love. Jesus understood his own activity as dialectically related to the activity of the Father: "I seek not to do my own will but the will of him who sent me" (John 5:30b). What is this "will"? It is calling others into the eternal life and love of God (5:39-42). The divine will was a relational reality that called him to share in the Father's love, mercy, and compassion for his neighbors (cf. John 6:9-13). Jesus invited others to share in this dynamic activity: "not everyone who says to me, 'Lord, Lord,' will enter the kingdom of heaven, but only the one who does the will of my Father in heaven" (Matt. 7:21). As the other New Testament authors repeatedly emphasize, our participation in that loving will is possible only through dependence on the life-giving Spirit of love.

Like foreknowledge, the word predestination does not occur often in the New Testament. When it does, it is bathed in trinitarian language. In Romans 8:28-30, Paul is assuring those who love God that their destiny, which is being conformed into the image of his Son, is secured by the empowering agency of the Spirit. These verses come in the midst of a chapter devoted to describing the power of the One whose Spirit raised Christ from the dead (8:11) so that we might become children of God. The emphasis is not on tracing creaturely effects back to a pre-programming causality, but on encouraging believers to remember that their own agencies are embraced by a power that cannot be compared (8:18) with finite powers, for even death cannot separate them from divine love (8:38-39). In Ephesians, it is the "God and Father of our Lord Jesus Christ" (1:3) whose destining of the saints "in" (1:4) and "through" Christ (1:5) is a blessing that is sealed in the Holy Spirit (1:13) and experienced as an adoption into a new loving fellowship.

The main point of divine "destining" is not the pre-selection of individuals but the shaping of the community that is called to share in this blessing of the Spirit for the sake of the world.[21] First Corinthians describes God's destining (2:7) as now revealed through the Spirit (2:4, 10) and oriented toward bringing the community to an understanding of the power of God revealed in Christ (1:23; 2:2, 16). In Acts 4:28, the testimony to God's destining power emerges out of the apostles' experience of the Father's "holy servant Jesus" (4:27) and their being filled with the Holy Spirit (4:31). These passages naturally use the term in a way that appropriates the cosmological understanding of the first century, but they should be read in the context of the broader Pauline polemic against the Stoic view of pre-programmed divine governance.[22] We can try to understand the author's expression of his experience of God without accepting the validity of the cosmological models of space and time within which it is embedded. As Calvin emphasized, the biblical texts are "accommodated" to the cultural and scientific views of its original hearers. The main point of these passages is reformative — orienting the life of the community in a way that shares in the loving activity of God through the Spirit of Christ.

Rather than beginning with the idea of the all-powerful will of a single divine subject, and then *later* trying to make sense of Scripture and religious experience, I am suggesting that we instead attempt to illuminate the issue of divine agency from within the categories that structure our lived experience in community, reaching out in a transversal dialogue that is always open to being reformed. Our theological concern should not be focused on identify-

21. Cf. Shirley C. Guthrie, "Romans 11:25-32," *Interpretation* 38, no. 2 (April 1984): 286-91; G. B. Caird, "Predestination — Romans 9–11," *The Expository Times* 68 (Oct. 1956–Sept. 1957): 324-27; Jean-Pierre Arfeuil, O.P., "Le dessein sauveur de Dieu: La doctrine de la prédestination selon saint Thomas d'Aquin," *Revue Thomiste* 74 (October-December 1974): 591-641.

22. Cf. Abraham J. Malherbe, "Determinism and Free Will in Paul: The Argument of 1 Corinthians 8 and 9," in *Paul in His Hellenistic Context*, ed. Troels Engberg-Pedersen (Minneapolis: Fortress, 1995), 231-32; Anthony Thiselton, *The First Epistle to the Corinthians* (Grand Rapids: Eerdmans, 2000), 242; C. K. Barrett, *The Acts of the Apostles* (Edinburgh: T&T Clark, 1994), 248; Charles S. Cosgrove, "The Divine δεῖ in Luke-Acts," *Novum Testamentum* 26, no. 2 (1984): 168-90 at 184.

ing the causal joint or mechanism by which God as a single immaterial substance effects the movement of material bodies in the world, but on the unconditioned gracious agency of divine love that empowers creatures to participate in the truly infinite goodness of God. While a full presentation of these themes will require more detailed treatments of specific issues within Pneumatology and Christology, my goal here has been to outline the intrinsic function of these categories within a Christian doctrine of divine acting.

§9.4. Reconstructing the Cosmological Argument

The philosophical turn to relationality and the late modern theological trajectories also open up conceptual space for reforming the cosmological argument, which is intended to support the intuition that the whole cosmos depends upon God as Creator for its being and becoming. As Romans 11:36 says, all things are from, through, and to God. Insofar as this argument deals with God's causal power in relation to the *cosmos*, it bears on our treatment of the theme of divine acting. This proof has a complex history, not only because the form of the argument shifted along with developments in cosmology but also because many of its versions incorporated elements of the teleological and ontological arguments. Generally speaking, the teleological argument infers the existence of God from the *order* of the world, while most forms of the cosmological argument begin with the sheer *existence* of the world and deduce the necessity of a first cause or sufficient reason for this cosmos. The question before us is whether using the philosophical categories that have shaped many formulations of this argument in Western theology is the best way to articulate this Christian intuition in contemporary culture.

Classical and Contemporary Formulations

The cosmological arguments of medieval Arabic philosophers appropriated the Aristotelian tradition[23] in various ways; some stressed the impossibility of

23. Plato argued for the existence of an ideal Soul from the motion of bodies *(Laws)*, the existence of the Good from the human pursuit of justice *(Republic)*, and the existence of a Demiurge from the structure of the cosmos *(Timaeus)*. However, Aristotle's discussion of the four types of "causality" and his inference to an unmoved mover (cf. Chapter 4 above) have been more influential in the history of the cosmological argument.

a temporal regress (e.g., Al-Ghazali), while others emphasized the importance of the distinction between necessary and possible being (e.g., Ibn Sina). These debates are behind the first four of Thomas Aquinas's "five ways" of proving the existence of God (*SumTh*, I.2.3). The first way argues from the process of change to a first cause of change that is unchanged; the second from the nature of efficient causation to a first efficient cause; the third from the existence of things that need not be (contingent being) to something which must be (necessary being); the fourth from the gradation of qualities like goodness observed in things to the existence of a being that possesses these qualities most fully and "causes" them in all other things. It is important to notice that Thomas, along with most medieval Muslim philosophers, assumed the basic validity of Aristotelian cosmology, in which causality is explained by the movement of the four elements of earth, water, wind, and fire toward their proper place, and by the turning of the celestial spheres.[24]

Duns Scotus's treatment of the argument begins with the observation of efficient causality among created things; from the impossibility of an infinite regress of efficient causes he argues for the necessary existence of a first efficient cause, which is uncaused.[25] Scotus's explicit insistence on a univocal concept of "being" that embraces both creatures and Creator, and his incorporation of the tension between the intellectualist and voluntarist ideals into the heart of the argument, had a profound effect on the history of the proof. The growing emphasis on mechanistic force and efficient causality in seventeenth-century physics led Spinoza and Leibniz to embrace determinism in order to shore up the cosmological argument, although in quite different ways. Spinoza argued that an infinite self-causing substance must exist, which he called "God or Nature." His version of the cosmological argument in the *Ethics* opened the way for philosophers to consider the possibility that Nature is itself infinite; we do not need a "reason" beyond Nature — it *is* itself necessary being.

Leibniz's version of the cosmological argument, however, relies heavily on his principle of sufficient reason: "nothing ever comes to pass without there being a cause or at least a reason determining it."[26] For

---

24. Thomas explicitly acknowledges his dependence on Aristotle both in his outline of the five ways in *Summa Theologiae* and elsewhere, e.g., *SCG*, I.9; I.13.

25. *Opus oxoniense*, I.2; reprinted in *Philosophical Writings*, ed. and trans. A. Wolter (London: Nelson, 1962). For a more concise argument see Scotus's *De primo principio*, 4.

26. G. W. Leibniz, *Theodicy: Essays on the Goodness of God, the Freedom of Man and the Origin of Evil*, ed. E. M. Haggard (LaSalle, Ill.: Open Court, 1985), 147.

Leibniz, God is the substance that is the *necessary* reason for the existence of the world, which is the assemblage of *contingent* things. Further, this causative substance must be intelligent, and have had epistemic access to all possible worlds, before fixing upon one with an act of the will.[27] Such a substance would also be absolutely perfect since it relates to all that which is possible, so it would fix upon the best of all possible worlds, which must be the actual world. Later in the eighteenth century David Hume attacked this argument by challenging both the inference from the world to a wholly good God *(Dialogues Concerning Natural Religion)* and the assumption that our experience of movement could be explained by the categories "cause and effect" *(Enquiry Concerning Human Understanding)*. Kant outlined the antinomy that flows from theological reliance on these categories and claimed to demonstrate the "Impossibility of a Cosmological Proof of the Existence of God," in his *Critique of Pure Reason*.[28] In the nineteenth century, Schleiermacher would speak of God as the "Whence" of the feeling of absolute dependence, but refused to speculate on the substance of this Cause apart from the world. Most nineteenth-century theologians discussed God's relation to the cosmos more in terms of ethical agency rather than ontological causality.

The medieval and early modern approach to the cosmological argument continues to capture the interest of some contemporary philosophers of religion. For example, Bill Craig has returned to the "kalam" argument developed by Arabic philosophers such as Al-Ghazali, emphasizing the impossibility of an infinite temporal regress. Craig constructs the argument in this way: (1) whatever begins to exist has a cause; (2) the universe began to exist; (3) therefore, the universe has a cause. From his analysis of "what it is to be cause of the universe," Craig asserts that (4) "if the universe has a cause, then an uncaused, personal Creator of the universe exists, who *sans* the universe is beginningless, changeless, immaterial, timeless, spaceless, and enormously powerful." Given (3) Craig concludes that (5) such a Creator exists.[29] This version of the argument is dependent on his assertion of the impossibility of the existence

27. *Theodicy*, 127.

28. Kant does allow that we can "postulate" the existence of God, but this is the operation of practical reason rather than pure theoretical reason.

29. "The *Kalam* Cosmological Argument," in *Philosophy of Religion: A Reader and Guide*, ed. Craig (New Brunswick, N.J.: Rutgers University Press, 2002), 92-113. For a more detailed argument see Craig, *The Kalam Cosmological Argument* (New York: Rowman & Littlefield, 1979).

of an "actual infinity," contradicting the general consensus of neo-Cantorian meta-mathematics.[30] We should not be surprised that Craig rejects the idea of an actual infinite; he begins (like Al-Ghazali) with Aristotelian assumptions about actuality and possibility and ends with an Aristotelian conclusion. Perhaps this underlying mathematical or "extensive" view of infinity explains his curious description of God as "enormously powerful."

This approach is open to several other philosophical and theological objections. The attempt to "prove" the existence of God by appeal to a generic experience of cause and effect is overly reliant on a foundationalist epistemology, which has lost its plausibility in late modern discourse (cf. §2.4). The argument also presupposes that the principle of sufficient reason applies to the universe as a whole; this may be intuitively plausible to many, especially those who already believe in a Creator, but it cannot be "proven." This logical move has often been cited as an example of the compositional fallacy — inappropriately transferring categories that apply to the parts of a whole to the whole itself. Craig's depiction of the uncaused cause as an immaterial person timelessly related to a world that "began" to exist also illustrates the unfortunate abstraction of the cosmological argument from the Christian experience of God's trinitarian and eschatological agency. Reconstructing the argument in light of the recovery of these late modern categories can open up space for a fresh articulation of God's relation to the cosmos.

The Origin, Condition, and Goal of Moral Desire

We can begin by describing the agency of the biblical God as the origin, condition, and goal of the *moral* desire of human creatures. Once again our interest here is not in specific questions about which particular goods we ought to desire, but in the underlying longing that structures our orientation toward the good life. The agency of human persons is characterized by ethical anxiety, by our existential struggle to use our power to secure objects that we love. This agency emerges from within a field of interpersonal relations in which we find ourselves already oriented by the

---

30. Cf. § 2.4 above. Cf. also Craig, *The Cosmological Argument from Plato to Leibniz* (London: Macmillan, 1980), 290.

customs of our social context, which conditions our understanding of which actions are right and good.

How can we make sense of this moral desire theologically? Early in the Greek tradition, the good life was understood as a life of virtue *(aretē)*. The Platonists, Aristotelians, and Stoics argued about the shape of the just life, and the way in which it could be achieved, but they all agreed on an intrinsic link between the divine and the human desire to become good.[31] In an attempt to escape a rigid fideism, the Enlightenment challenged this connection; reason was elevated above revelation and became the arbiter of what is "just." Deconstructive forms of postmodernity have emphasized the relativity of every such attempted arbitration, calling for the end to all universalizing ethical meta-narratives. Not only do such relativist claims have self-referential difficulties,[32] they are also unable to make sense of the irrepressible human longing for the good life.

Although the theistic "proof" of a necessary being[33] with a causal will does not seem like good news in contemporary culture, we find a growing openness to the reforming power of altruistic spirituality and the message of Jesus' call to love. This opens up space for theological articulation of human virtue not as a static external norm but as a dynamic intensification of relational agency that takes shape as we share in the infinite goodness of God. We can refigure the intuitions of the cosmological argument within an overall presentation of the omnipotent love of God. After all, John described the relation between God and the cosmos not in terms of causal necessity but in terms of love: "For God so loved the world [*cosmos*] that he gave his only Son" (3:16). We experience this love as the power that calls us into the truly good life of Eternity. The whole cosmos groans in labor pain (Rom. 8:22) as it is "subjected" by the trinitarian God who orients it

31. For a historical survey, see Alasdair MacIntyre, *After Virtue*, 2nd ed. (Notre Dame: University of Notre Dame Press, 1984); cf. idem, *Whose Justice? Which Rationality?* (Notre Dame: University of Notre Dame Press, 1988).

32. Cf. Roger Trigg, *Morality Matters* (Oxford: Blackwell, 2004).

33. Is the thesis that an intelligent substance, with a will that is causally efficacious over against the contingency of the world, is metaphysically necessary really what we want to prove? The categories of necessity and contingency are defined in contrast to one another. Defining God as a "necessary" being over against "contingent" beings fails the criterion of true Infinity. If God *is* necessary being, then God is dependent on the distinction between necessity and contingency. God is related to the distinction but precisely as the intensively infinite presence of trinitarian life — the origin, condition, and goal of this and all other creaturely distinctions.

toward liberation through the Logos and in the Spirit. This groaning takes shape in human life as moral desire, a longing to love and be loved in just community.

The conceptual space in which we make sense of the origin of the world is inextricably woven into the practical and liturgical space in which our moral desire is conditioned and oriented toward goodness. The intuition that the omnipotent love of God is the origin of the experience of necessity and contingency in the universe (as creation) may be conserved by articulating this "originating" as the provision of a conditioning goal. Divine agency presents itself to us in a way that evokes moral desire, which we try to satisfy with our own ethical striving to secure objects we think will bring the good life. We experience the omnipotent love of God as advent, an evocative presence that calls us to love. This "calling," this destiny that is ours and makes us what we are, constitutes moral desire by opening us up to our selves and others in love. The absolute Futurity of the infinite trinitarian God is the all-powerful love that originates temporality in all its modes, upholding creatures through an evocative constitution of the conditions for sharing in divine righteousness. This originating power of love is the intensively infinite presence of the trinitarian God, a faithful and promising agency that opens up space and time for finite agency.

Arguing that the first cause of the cosmos is *also* a person of a certain sort is an attempt to link this power to the human experience of moral desire, but it pushes the uniquely Christian emphasis on the trinitarian dynamics of divine love into the background.[34] However, the trinitarian understanding of God, woven together with the insights of Infinity and Futurity, provides its own solution to philosophical conundrums. Is an act morally good because it is willed by God or is there a moral standard to which divine decrees must conform? Accepting the former seems to make the criteria for moral (or loving) behavior arbitrary and capricious, but admitting the latter means separating the divine will from the Good. If we think of the dynamic loving and being loved of the trinitarian life *as* truly infinite Goodness, we can avoid being impaled by either horn of this dilemma (famously posed to Euthyphro by Socrates). God is not a single

---

34. For a discussion of the importance of the doctrine of the Trinity for theological dialogue with science, cf. my "The Role of Trinitarian Reflection in the Science-Religion Dialogue," in *Preparing for the Future: The Role of Theology in the Science-Religion Dialogue*, ed. Niels Henrik Gregersen and Marie Vejrup Nielsen (Aarhus: University of Aarhus Press, 2004), 27-40.

subject who "wills" objects of desire (goods) that are over against God. The eternally shared omnipotent love of the Father, Son, and the Spirit *is* the absolute Good, manifested in creation as an invitation to fellowship in this truly infinite life. Divine agency is not open to the future or oriented toward external "goods" — it is the opening of Eternity, which creatures experience as the modes of time. This constitutive opening is the condition for the dynamics of moral desire. Human agency "becomes" the righteousness (or justice) of God as it shares in the suffering of Christ through intensification in the Spirit of justice.

§9.5. The Gospel of Divine Acting

Divine acting is good news in Scripture. The ancient Israelites longed to experience the mighty acts of God, whose powerful liberating activity was the basis of their hope: "Who is like you . . . working wonders?" (Exod. 15:11). The Psalmist praised YHWH for the divine agency that brings salvation: "My mouth will tell of your righteous acts, of your deeds of salvation all day long" (Ps. 71:15). Edom has oppressed Israel, but Isaiah prophesies: "It is I, announcing vindication, *mighty to save*" (Isa. 63:1b). Divine judgment is not good news for the oppressor, but even here the ultimate intention is to evoke repentance and bring redemption, as Jonah learns in his encounter with the Ninevites. God's acting may also be experienced as an agony — all of creation groans in response to the "subjectivity" of divine agency (Rom. 8:20-23), but this too is oriented toward the ecstasy of hope through life in the Spirit of Christ.

Saving Work

The gospel *is* the *power* of God for *salvation* (Rom. 1:16). The power of divine acting is displayed in the atoning work of Christ. "God was in Christ reconciling the world to himself" not as a force that pushes us along, but as a personal dynamic love that calls us to share in the ministry of reconciliation (2 Cor. 5:19). The divine reign evokes trembling delight in the power of divine salvation, which is why the "good news of the kingdom of God" was basic to the message of Jesus (Luke 8:1), his disciples (Luke 10:9) and the apostles (Acts 8:12). Our struggle to secure finite goods cannot fulfill our longing for unity in loving community. The rich young ruler (Matt. 19:16-17; Mark 10:17-18; Luke 18:18-19) was unable to respond to the gospel because of the problem of good — the "goods" of this world had seduced him into relying on his own moral agency. We cannot ultimately protect ourselves from the causal forces of the cosmos, from the evil and suffering that threaten to crush our finite agency. The gospel is that the atoning work of Jesus Christ graciously frees us from our sinful bondage to the decaying goods and evils of the world through life in the Spirit. This does not mean that we get all the goods we want, nor that we never suffer evil, but that our finite agency is no longer dependent on our own power but on the gracious presence of omnipotent love.

Can we articulate the relation between God's saving work and human agency in a way that moves beyond the early modern structuring of the debate as monergism vs. synergism? These categories make it difficult to make sense of the Scriptural insistence that both God and humans "work" in the process of salvation (e.g., Phil. 2:13) without collapsing into salvation by "works" rather than by faith and grace (Gal. 2:16; Rom. 3:24). Weaving together the late modern trajectories can help. If the *ergos* ("work") of God is only quantitatively more powerful than — but qualitatively the same as — creaturely *ergos,* then divine and human "working" are potentially in competition. Either God does all the work in salvation (mon-ergism), or God works to only some "extent" and creatures do the rest of the work (synergism). Notice that this presupposes an extensive view of divine infinity. The issue is further complicated when the discussion is abstracted from the saving work of the trinitarian God and focused only on the "will" of a single subject. Relying on the categories of faculty psychology leads us to frame the debate in terms of the potential compatibility between human and divine "free will." The category of God as first cause also lurks in the background, for the divine work of salvation is often conceived as settled in the (timeless) past, worked out mechanically in the line of time.

However, if we imagine God's saving work as intensively infinite, then human works can be done "in" God; "those who do what is true come to the light . . . their deeds have been done *in* God" (John 3:21). Our "becoming" the righteousness of God is wholly dependent on the gracious justifying agency of God, but this agency is not threatened by our working as though both were operative within a closed energy system. God's "working" is not the effect of one finite power among many powers, for then it would limit (and be limited by) human working; divine agency would determine creaturely agency the way a bully determines the actions of another child. The *ergos* of the trinitarian God is the originating condition of human agency. As the goal of the "working" of moral desire, divine acting does not compete with us for "control" over earthly affairs. We are called to be "in" the will of God but this means entering into the very life of God, the "willing" of the triune persons in their mutual love. In the process of redemption we experience divine acting as a power that awakens us into an intensification of life, a personal presence that calls us toward just agency. Christian explication of the "cause" of the universe should therefore be embedded within our participatory manifestation of God's saving work in and to the world through concrete acts that "demonstrate" omnipotent love.

God's work is not a finite dynamic that excludes our working, but an infinite agency in which we are invited to share. The crowds ask Jesus, "what must we do to perform the works of God?" He answers, "this is the work of God, that you believe in him whom he has sent" (John 6:28-29). The infinite *ergos* of the trinitarian God invites creatures into a faithful binding of their own agency to the divine love revealed in Christ. Jesus explains that he must "work the works" (John 9:4) of the Father, and he calls the disciples to "do" the works of the One who sent him (14:10-14). This sharing in the infinite working of the trinitarian God can occur only because God's agential presence opens up a "place" for us to do "good works," which becomes our "way of life" (Eph. 2:10). God's gracious agency is "before" us precisely as the absolute goal that conditions and orients our moral desire. Divine working does not *exclude* our good working by determining good works to occur; it opens us up to a new way of life in which our agency is *included* in God's atoning work.

The Creative Providence of God

The late modern trajectories also open up space for articulating the doctrine of divine *providence* in a way that shows its intrinsic connection to the gospel of the infinitely good *creative* agency of the trinitarian God. The biblical experience of God as a providing presence that makes all things new challenges the notion that "creation" refers primarily to a past event, separated from ongoing special acts of divine "providence."[35] In the He-

---

35. It was not mere coincidence that the rise of anti-providential thought occurred in the early modern period, during the rise of modern theism (and a-theism) and alongside

brew Bible, the creativity of God is not limited to the foundation of the world — it also is connected to the active, redeeming presence of YHWH in the lives of the people of Israel. For example, Isaiah 41:20 uses the verb "create" to refer to God's redemptive provision for the poor and needy: "the hand of the LORD has done this, the Holy One of Israel has created it" (cf. Isa. 48:6-7; 65:17-18). The psalmist understands that nature itself is dependent on the ongoing creative presence of the Spirit: "When you send forth your spirit, they are created; and you renew the face of the ground" (Ps. 104:30; cf. 51:10).

The creative provision of space and time allows creatures to emerge and grope after (Acts 17:27) the truly infinite God, whose life is the love of the trinitarian persons. Is being Provider an essential attribute of the eternal God, or does God become Provider only in relation to creation? If the former, God needs an eternal world as the object of provision; if the latter, that which we experience as Provider is not really the eternal God. We can overcome this early modern way of framing the discussion by emphasizing the perichoretic relations of the Father, Son, and the Spirit, who eternally provide and are provided love to, in, and for one another. Because God's trinitarian life *is* truly infinite eternal love, this mutual provision is not characterized by a temporal distinction from the Good, as it is for creatures. These eternal loving relations are manifested in our temporal experience as the arrival of the reign of divine peace that makes us a new creation. Divine providence is mediated to creatures as an experience of absolute Futurity; we cannot grasp the infinite love of God. However, our very coming-to-be is provided to us as a being-grasped by, for, and in divine love. This absolute Gift that creates us anew is the gracious presence of God's providential agency.

Since all of creation is formed by and for the Word, and enlivened and renewed in and through the Spirit, the Christian experience of redemptive sharing in the relations of the trinitarian persons may be described as a gracious intensification of the creaturely experience of the provision of space and time. We experience the gracious arrival of our destiny as an intensification of the experience of being-provided-for, which is also an experience of being-created anew. The intensive Infinity of this providing

---

the diminishing of the significance of the role of suffering in the Christian life. Cf. Ann Thompson, *The Art of Suffering and the Impact of Seventeenth-Century Anti-Providential Thought* (Aldershot: Ashgate, 2003).

creative agency is closer to us than we are to ourselves, constituting us by opening us up into a longing to love and be loved. Divine agency invites us into the good life of trinitarian love, empowering us to participate in a righteousness that is not our own (Phil. 3:9). We are called to share in this providential agency as the reign of divine peace takes form in a community of just persons who learn to provide graciously for one another and to tend lovingly to the rest of creation.

The truly good news is that the saving power of God revealed in Jesus' dependence on the life-giving Spirit is a gracious agency that calls us into an eternal goodness that liberates our moral desire from the painful tension between finite evils and goods. The empowering goal of the emergence of moral desire within the cosmos is the constitutive presence of an all-powerful incursive agency that conditions our longing for goodness by inviting us into eternal life. Facing this divine power that creatively provides the conditions for the becoming of the whole cosmos can be terrifying, but as we learn to interpret this presence as the saving work of infinite divine love, we come to consider "trials of any kind" as "nothing but joy" (Jas. 1:2). This radical understanding of the infinitely excellent power of God does not lead us to a passive acceptance of the crushing oppression of our neighbor's agency, but to an active self-giving that bears her burdens so that she too may be drawn even now into the arriving glory of an eternal life that is "beyond measure" (2 Cor. 4:17). The saving work of God is good news because it *is* the gracious provision of an invitation to creatures to share in the infinite joy of trinitarian life. As a coming that makes us well and good, the welcoming omnipotent love of the biblical God provides the way for creaturely well-being. This understanding of divine acting is pure gospel.

· 10 ·

OMNIPRESENT HOPE

Our experiences of divine knowing and acting imply the presence of
God, and so the theme of divine *being* has been with us throughout
our analysis and reconstruction. In this chapter we turn our full attention
to this theme, exploring a pattern of issues that include omnipresence,
timelessness, freedom, and the ontological argument. This brings us to another deep intuition within the biblical tradition: *God's being embraces all
things.* In other words, nothing escapes the divine presence. Moreover, the
divine "nature" is not susceptible to the corruptibility that threatens
creaturely existence. This understanding of divine being, which has been
expressed in a variety of ways in the Christian tradition, derives from the
religious experience of being confronted by an absolutely inescapable and
unmanipulable presence that bears down upon human existence. Our critique of substance metaphysics in general, and the late modern retrieval of
the patristic insistence that God is "beyond being" in particular, raise questions about the appropriateness of the phrase "divine being." However,
even the statement that God is beyond being uses the copulative "is,"
which reintroduces the question of "being." Rather than exclude the term
from theological discourse, I will qualify it in light of the biblical ideas of
face, presence, and *parousia,* attempting to accommodate the apophatic
tradition and the insights of the linguistic turn.

The first step is to connect the doctrine of omni-*presence* to the biblical understanding of the "God of hope" (Rom. 15:13). Linking the concept
of *hope* to God initially appears more difficult than speaking of divine

faithfulness and love. This may be due in part to the popular use of the term "hope" to indicate a kind of wishful but tentative optimism, which would be wholly inappropriate to God. However, if we look carefully at the metaphysically weighty meaning of hope in Scripture and at the ontological significance of the human experience of hope, we can make more sense out of the biblical idea that hope, like faith and love, remains or "abides" (1 Cor. 13:13). In the Hebrew Bible, hope is connected to life and to the presence of God; the godless have no hope and are perishing (Job 8:13; 27:8). To be alive is to have hope (Eccl. 9:4). Those who find their hope in God (Ps. 33:22) and from God (Ps. 62:5) are receiving salvation and life. God is the "hope" of all the ends of the earth (Ps. 65:5), and this all-embracing presence provides a future in which the hope of the wise will not be cut off (Prov. 23:18; 24:14). In a theological interpretation of the human experience of becoming, *hope* and *being* are inseparable.

The New Testament authors also link hope to the experience of the presence of God (e.g., Eph. 2:12). The "hope of Israel" (Jer. 14:8) was one of the titles for God in the Hebrew Bible, and this is taken over by Paul in Acts 28:20. In Christian experience the hopeful relation to God is not a passive wishing but a "living hope" (1 Pet. 1:3), a hope that "enters" into the intimacy of the divine presence (Heb. 6:19). The biblical writers speak of hope in much the same way that they do of faith and love. Like faith, we are saved in, by, and through hope (e.g., Rom. 8:24; Heb. 7:19). Like love, hope is also described as a reality into which and for which we are saved (e.g., Eph. 1:18). If our redemptive relation to God has to do not only with faith and love but also with hope — and these three *remain* — then hope, too, must really have something to do with the eternal being of God.

We can get an intimation of the way in which hope, like faith and love, "abides" in our relation to God by reflecting on these dynamics in human relationships. My trusting orientation to my betrothed does not end when the object of my faithfulness is bound to me in marriage. This fiduciary binding intensifies my faithfulness, and opens me up for new ways of manifesting fidelity. If faithfulness ended, the relationship would become static and begin to decay. In the same way, love for my beloved takes the form of desire, a longing to be loved in love. But this desire is not quenched when the beloved returns love; it intensifies and empowers the relationship. Hope, too, may be understood in a similar way. I anticipate belonging in a harmonious personal relationship, but this hopefulness does not end when I am immersed in interpersonal harmony. The enjoyment of the relation with the one who evokes hope in me is intensified, and I desire an open future in which her beauty appears to me in ever new ways. Faith, love, *and* hope remain because they structure our desire to know, to act, and to be in relation eternally.

Moving beyond human relations, we may speak of the *presence* of the God of *hope* as embracing all *(omnia)* things; the intensive Infinity of the trinitarian life, which human persons experience as absolute Futurity, opens creaturely life up in(to) a hopeful relation to being. The theological category of hope refers not to wishful dreaming about a future point on a time-line, but to an intensive experience of the ongoing renewal of personal life, which is called (in)to being by the incursive divine *parousia* that graciously welcomes creatures into the fellowship of infinite trinitarian peace. While inquiry into the "nature" of God includes a search for conceptual clarity, we should not ignore the intensely existential dimension of this quest. Our interest in the existence and attributes of God is ultimately driven by our hope that God will *be there* for us. What we most deeply long for is not a definition of the divine essence, but finding our own being harmoniously surrounded by and immersed in eternal peace. The omnipresent hope of the biblical God promises us a life that is truly eternal and presents us a share in Eternity that is truly life. But how can we make sense of this if God is "timeless"?

§10.1. Beyond the Antinomy of Divine Timelessness

Is the being of God essentially outside of time or inside of time? When the debate is framed in terms of these options, theologians are forced to choose between (or reinterpret) those passages in Scripture that indicate that God is unchanging (e.g., Mal. 3:6-7; Ps. 102:25-28; cf. Heb. 13:8; Jas. 1:17) and those that describe God as changing (e.g., Gen. 18:25; Hos. 11:8-9; Exod. 32:14). The intuition of divine impassibility is that the being of God is not passively dependent on creaturely change. As we saw in Part I, this intuition was sometimes buttressed with the help of the Platonic concept of immutability and the Aristotelian concept of simplicity. For both of these philosophers, the dualism between passible and impassible substance is correlated to the dualism between the temporal and the eternal. If creaturely (temporal) and divine (eternal) substance are defined over against each other, then the dilemma arises: is God "outside" (or apart from) time or "inside" (a part of) time? The former makes it difficult to make sense of God's real presence to creatures in time, but the latter threatens God's transcendent freedom over or beyond creaturely temporality.

Understanding the Impasse

The first step is to recognize the underlying philosophical categories that uphold the horns of the dilemma. This can be illustrated by pointing to another *Four Views* book on *God and Time.* The contributors are asked to answer this kind of question about God: "is he standing outside time? . . . is he in time the way we are?"[1] The four answers may be plotted on a continuum created by these options. Imagine the view that defends God's "timeless eternity" as representing the right side of the spectrum, and the position described as "unqualified divine temporality" as representing the left side. The former argues that God must be outside of time because God is immaterial (pure spirit), and time only affects material (mutable) substances. The latter insists that God must be in time because God is a person, and we cannot think of a person (a single subject with knowledge and will) who does not have temporal experience.

The other two proposals fall in the middle of the continuum. Both the description of divine eternity as "relative timelessness" and the claim that God is "timeless without the universe, temporal with the universe" are attempts to maintain both God's timelessness and God's temporality (in some sense). However, these views struggle (in different ways) with the implication that God's timelessness is somehow "before" God's relation to time, which seems to contradict the very idea of timelessness. In the "Response" sections each author points out the existential difficulties with and philosophical inconsistency of those positions to the right or left of his part of the continuum. My task here is not to engage in critical debate with these proposals, but to suggest that the horns of the dilemma concerning the rela-

---

1. Gregory E. Gannsle, ed., *God and Time: Four Views* (Downers Grove, Ill.: InterVarsity, 2001), introduction, 10. In his contribution to this book, Alan Padgett hints that his view (Eternity as relative timelessness) allows us to speak of "our time" as taking place "*within. . .* God's own time" (p. 107; emphasis added), but he does not spell out the implications in this context. Cf. his *God, Eternity and the Nature of Time* (Eugene, Ore.: Wipf & Stock Publishers, 2000).

tion of the divine essence to time are based on the same categories that have contributed to the antinomies of foreknowledge and predestination.

Although the patristic theologians were nearly unanimous in their insistence on the impassibility of God, they varied widely on how this was expressed. For most theologians during this period the doctrine of impassibility was not driven primarily by abstract philosophical concerns but by their desire to maintain the biblical intuition that God cannot be grasped with creaturely categories.[2] It was part of the apophatic insistence that the Creator cannot be comprehended by creaturely predicates. So while Irenaeus, Clement of Alexandria, Tertullian, and Athanasius believed that God was (in some sense) passionate and related to the world, God's passion was not dependent upon or modified by events in the world.[3] Although the Greek "timelessness" models of the divine — which were connected to a "negative" view of infinity (cf. §5.1 above) — remained influential, many in the tradition resisted the temptation to imagine divine Eternity as merely negatively related to time. For example, Clement of Alexandria incorporated a "positive" view of Eternity into his doctrine of God,[4] and even Boethius's definition of Eternity is characterized by an emphasis on *life:* "Eternity is a possession of life, a possession simultaneously entire and perfect, which has no end."[5]

Both Platonic and Aristotelian categories were appropriated by Augustine and Thomas Aquinas in their attempts to explain how God could be impassible and yet truly related to a changing creation.[6] For the most part, these theologians insisted that God's relation to the world is manifested in terms of the divine will (which is intrinsically related to the divine intellect) but the divine *essence* is unchangeable and unaffected by tempo-

2. See Thomas Weinandy, *Does God Suffer?* (Notre Dame: University of Notre Dame Press, 2000), 83-112; Brian Davies, O.P., "Classical Theism and the Doctrine of Divine Simplicity," in idem, ed., *Language, Meaning and God* (London: Geoffrey Chapman, 1987), 67.

3. E.g. Irenaeus, *Adversus Haereses*, 2.12.1; Clement of Alexandria, *Stromata*, 5.11; Tertullian, *Adversus Marcionem*, I.8.

4. Clement, *Stromata*, 5.11.71; 6.16.138. Cf. Paul Plass, "The Concept of Eternity in Patristic Theology," *Studia Theologica* 36 (1982): 11-25 at 17.

5. *Consolation of Philosophy*, 144.

6. Cf. Wilma Gundersdorf von Jess, "Divine Eternity in the Doctrine of St. Augustine," *Augustinian Studies* 6 (1975): 75-96; Harm J. M. J. Goris, *Free Creatures of an Eternal God* (Nijmegen: Stichting Thomasfonds, 1996); Narve Strand, "Augustine on Predestination and Divine Simplicity: The Problem of Compatibility," *Studia Patristica* 38 (Louvain: Peeters, 2001), 290-305.

rality. However, both were tempted by what we might call the *essentialist* ideal, construing God's relation to the world in terms of the essence of God, rather than through knowledge or acts of will.

The danger with the "essentialist" ideal, and the most likely reason for its relative unpopularity, is that it can easily lead to emanationism: the view that the being of the world emanates from the divine being.[7] This makes it difficult to uphold the infinite qualitative distinction between Creator and creation. Nevertheless, Thomas's understanding of the doctrine of simplicity, which entails the identity of the intellect, will, and essence of God, sometimes led him to speak also of the "emanation" of creaturely *esse* from divine *esse* as the basis for finite existence (e.g., *SumTh*, I.45.1, 4). This creates a tension because Thomas also wants to insist that God does not create by "natural" necessity but by the free choice of the divine will (e.g., *SCG*, II.23.1). Augustine's voluntarism similarly came into conflict with his desire to maintain that God's understanding and activity are strictly identical to the divine Essence or Self (*De Trin.* XV.5, 7-8; *Conf.* VII.4, 6; XII), leaving him susceptible to the charge of emanationism.

The most obvious and worrisome example of the "essentialist" ideal is undoubtedly Spinoza, who followed out the logic of substance metaphysics and equated God and the world *(Deus sive Natura)*. The hardening of the categories of immaterial substance, single subject, and first cause in early modernity contributed to the rise of deism (a timeless God seems irrelevant) and ultimately to atheism (since a timeless omni-causality seems to leave no room for the freedom of creaturely temporality). The timeless essence of the divine nature in "theistic" apologetics was divorced from the religious experience of eschatological hope in the trinitarian God of the New Testament. Moreover, the nagging question of how a timeless God could "cause" in any meaningful sense increasingly came to the fore.

As they reacted to this outworking of the implications of the concepts of divine timelessness and impassibility, many theologians increasingly became convinced that these ideas were simply incompatible with other basic Christian intuitions about God's active presence in the world. By the nineteenth century, the doctrines of God's *essential* impassibility, simplicity, and immutability had become dispensable in the work of

---

7. Of course, the others have their own dangers; intellectualism leans toward idealism and voluntarism easily collapses into fatalism.

many Christian theologians. For example, I. A. Dorner argued that God is not immutable in God's essential being *(Sein)*, nor in God's relation to space and time, nor in God's "*knowing* and *willing* of the world." He insisted that God really enters into a "relation of mutual and reciprocal influence"; if we are to speak of divine immutability, it will be in reference to God's "ethical being [*Wesen*]."[8]

God and Temporality

The late modern trajectories, however, offer us resources for recovering emphases in the Christian tradition that open up space for reconstructing the doctrine of divine being in relation to time. The retrieval of divine Infinity reminds us that temporality and the tensed language that we use to carve up our temporal experience are creaturely categories that ultimately cannot be applied to God. Language itself emerges within temporality, and we cannot escape this embeddedness in order to compare Eternity with time. The need to integrate eschatological reflection into our presentation of the relation of the trinitarian God to time has been increasingly recognized among theologians in a variety of contexts.[9] Incorporating these themes immediately into the doctrine of God does not have to take the shape of an appeal *to* mystery — it may instead be an articulation *of* the appealing mysterious all-embracing presence that constitutes human temporal experience. Our becoming as creatures, which is our very being, is constituted by the evocative incursion of the eternal trinitarian God. Although human language cannot escape its dependence on this gracious presence, we may search for theological ways of interpreting our experience of temporality that make sense of this inescapable dependence.

Rather than placing God's being "outside" of time or "inside" of time, I suggest we begin with the claim of Romans 11:36 — all things are from, through, and to God. "All things" includes temporality itself, so we should say that in some sense "time" is from, through, and to God. Divine being as

8. I. A. Dorner, *Divine Immutability: A Critical Reconstruction,* trans. Robert R. Williams and Claude Welch (Minneapolis: Fortress, 1994), 148, 165; emphasis added. Original German 1856.

9. Cf. Antje Jackelén, *Zeit und Ewigkeit: Die Frage der Zeit in Kirche, Naturwissenschaft und Theologie* (Neukirchen-Vluyn: Neukirchener, 2002); Jean-Louis Leuba, ed., *Temps et Eschatologie: Données bibliques et problématiques contemporaines* (Paris: Cerf, 1994).

"true Eternity" is the life of the trinitarian God, which originates, encompasses, and orients "all things." The biblical God constitutes the spatio-temporal conditions in which creatures come to be. If we accept Paul's insistence that God is the one "in" whom we "live and move and have our being" (Acts 17:28), then we can also say that temporal experience itself is a movement "in" God. The danger of "panentheism" looms only if we continue to think about God and time in the categories of substance metaphysics. If divine Eternity is a "thing" and creaturely time is a "thing," then we would have to ask whether God is essentially outside of and separate from time or inside of and participating within time. The latter denies the very idea of God as a truly infinite all-encompassing creative presence, and the former makes God and creatures parts of a larger whole ("Eternity and time").

Weaving together the late modern trajectories can help us avoid these spurious models of Eternity. If God is "that than which nothing greater (or better) can be conceived" (Anselm), then the concept of absolute Futurity more adequately expresses the relation of divine Eternity to time than do concepts that emphasize the past (first cause), the present (eternal now), or sheer timelessness. We can always conceive of a temporal reality that is greater (or better) than the past or the present; in fact, hope for such a reality keeps us moving. We can also conceive of various "futures," some of which are better and greater than others. But we cannot conceive of anything greater or better than an infinitely shared life of joy and peace that provides the conditions for an ever-intensifying share in that life. The all-encompassing real presence of absolute Futurity is closer to us than we are to ourselves, but precisely as an intensively infinite presence that opens us up to being in hope. The absolute Futurity of God is not simply the temporal mode of "relative" futurity that is out ahead of us, "over there" at a "further" point on a timeline. God's intensively infinite Eternity embraces the whole of creation, opening up the distinctions that we call past, present, and future.

The incursive "coming" of God is not from one place to another ("from" the future to the present), for this would require us to imagine some larger space-time "in" which God comes "to" the world. What we call "temporality" is the mediated experience of self-conscious creatures in relation to the constitutive, incursive, and evocative *parousia* of the trinitarian God. This upholds both intuitions: God is not susceptible to dissolution as temporal creatures are, and God is really related to temporal events.

What was God doing "before" creation? We must reject the question not because it is impious, but because it commits a category mistake. The concept "before" emerges only for us as a result of our longing for what is "ahead." It is only from within our experience of the constitutive inbreaking of Eternity into time that the categories "before and after" make sense. The incursive being-there of the trinitarian God is the evocative presence of absolute Futurity, which constitutes all creaturely becoming and is experienced by human persons as hope. These categories can help us conserve the intuition that divine being embraces all things while also making sense of the religious experience of the biblical God.

§10.2. A Trembling Delight in the Face of God

The biblical emphasis on the divine presence as the "face of God"[10] provides us with an inherently reformative concept of divine being. Both of the basic biblical terms for "presence," *panim* in Hebrew and *prosōpon* in Greek, may also be (and often are) translated as "face." The biblical experience of divine being is interpreted as a being-faced by the mysterious divine countenance. Scripture witnesses to what is most real in this manifestation of the divine — the delightful terror of being promised into intimacy by an infinite presence that is absolutely beyond our control. A "face" is present to us in a way that is different from other presences. This is evident already in the way an infant's sense of well-being (grace) and secure belonging (peace) is mediated through the face of the primary caregiver. The absence of this face is devastating, and its presence is soothing. Human development is characterized by the struggle to find well-being in relation to a face that absolutely secures a pleasurable future of belonging to and being longed for in harmonious community. Of course, no human face can do this, and so the religious search for an eternal loving presence haunts all of our futile attempts to face others in a way that fulfills this deep desire.

---

10. Some of the material in the following sections is derived from chap. 4 of F. LeRon Shults and Steven J. Sandage, *The Faces of Forgiveness: Searching for Wholeness and Salvation* (Grand Rapids: Baker Academic, 2003), where I outline the biblical experience of the "face of God" in more detail.

The Hebrew Bible

The ontological significance of the face of God is a theme that may be traced through every genre of the Hebrew Bible. The Aaronic blessing (Num. 6:24-26) is one of the most important early references to the *panim* of YHWH: "The LORD bless you and keep you; the LORD make his *face* to shine upon you, and be gracious to you; the LORD lift up his *countenance* upon you, and give you peace."[11] The first point to observe is that the blessing and keeping of the LORD take concrete form in the manifestation of *grace* and the provision of *peace*. The community's experience of wholeness and salvation depends wholly on the face of God. The people of Israel are called into existence and held together by YHWH, whose facing of them brings the promise of gracious and peaceful life. The deepest existential longing of the righteous Israelite would be satisfied with nothing less than the joy of being in the presence of God. "My soul thirsts for God, for the living God. When shall I come and behold the face of God?" (Ps. 42:2; cf. Ps. 27:8-9a). On the other hand, nothing is more to be feared than being hidden from the shining glory of the divine countenance. The Israelites expressed this sense of divine absence, or we might say this presence of the divine absence, with the idiomatic phrase: the "hiding" of the face of God.[12] If the divine face is "hidden," sickness or death is at hand. "Do not hide your *face* from me, or I shall be like those who go down to the Pit" (Ps. 143:7b; cf. 132:10; 30:7b).

The Hellenistic categories of transcendence and immanence are not equivalent to the Hebrew categories of the hiding and shining of the face of God. The divine countenance is not a "presence" like finite presences, which are either close or far. On the one hand, it cannot be escaped — it searches out and gazes upon the Psalmist, addressing him and obliging him to respond. "Where can I flee from your presence [face]?" (Ps. 139:7). On the other hand, the face of God cannot be manipulated, not even by the religious cultic sacrifice. The divine blessing is not mechanistic; it can-

---

11. Notice that the name and reign of God (cf. §8.2 and §9.2) are connected to the theme of the divine facing (Num. 6:27).

12. "When you hide your *face*, they [living creatures] are dismayed; when you take away their breath, they die and return to their dust" (Ps. 104:29). Cf. Samuel Balentine, *The Hidden God: The Hiding of the Face of God in the Old Testament* (Oxford: Oxford University Press, 1993); Richard Elliott Friedman, *The Hidden Face of God* (San Francisco: Harper-Collins, 1995).

not be reduced to simple cause and effect. This is a major point of the Book of Job. In the climactic last chapter, the Lord announces (42:8) that he will "accept Job's prayer" ("lift up Job's face"); the Lord showed favor (42:9) to Job ("lifted up Job's face"). The divine face (like the divine name and glory) are "present" differently from the way finite objects are present to (or absent from) other finite objects. The Israelites cannot make God's face appear through ritual magic or incantations. This experience led to the idea of divine sovereignty; this mysterious countenance elicits both fascination and terror because it is wholly beyond human control, and yet humans cannot escape its constitutive presence.

The experiences of the face of God and the face of the neighbor are mutually implicated. This is illustrated in the stories of both Jacob and Moses, whose experiences of the divine face were particularly intense. Even in these intimate encounters with the face of God, its "presence" remains essentially mysterious: the presence of the Lord is not simply "given" to them in a way that can be manipulated or objectified. At the same time, encountering the divine countenance reorients the way in which they face and are faced by others. Jacob is anxious about facing his brother Esau, and he spends the night near Jabbok wrestling a stranger. After receiving the blessing from this "man," the next day Jacob (whose name is changed to Israel) goes to confront his brother with great fear. When Esau is gracious and offers peace, Jacob exclaims, "truly to see your face is like seeing the face of God" (Gen. 33:10).

The terror and delight of being faced by God are also evident in the redemption of Israel from slavery and the giving of the law at Mt. Sinai. After the people worship the golden calf, Moses prays for God to be present to him and the people; he does not want to lead them unless the *face* of God goes with them. YHWH promises "My presence [face, *panim*] will go with you, and I will give you rest" (Exod. 33:14). Moses asks to see God's *glory,* but is told that he cannot see God's *face.* Yet he does hear the Lord pronounce the *name.* "I will make all my *goodness* pass before you, and will proclaim before you the *name,* 'The Lord'; . . . But . . . you cannot see my face; for no one shall see me and live" (33:18-20). Once again, the divine presence is an ambiguous reality that evokes desire but cannot be manipulated. Here too we see that Moses' facing and being faced by God is related to his communal facing; his experience with the divine presence was so intimate and transforming that his fellow Israelites spoke of his face as "shining" — which both fascinated and frightened them (Exod. 34:29-35).

In Moses' final "song" these words are attributed to the LORD: "I will *hide my face* from them, I will see what their end will be" (Deut. 32:20a). By the end of the narrative in 2 Kings, this judgment had been realized: of both Israel (17:23) and Judah (23:27), it is said that the LORD removed them "out of his sight" ("turned out from before his *face*"). The classical prophets also speak of the terrible judgment of God's "hidden" face. Isaiah says (45:15), "Truly, you are a God who hides himself, O God of Israel, the Savior." God is portrayed as actively hiding his face, but it is precisely this hidden presence that the righteous person in Israel finds alluring. From the human side, it can be said that "your sins have hidden his face from you" (Isa. 59:2).[13] Yet the hope and promise of restoration remains a theme both in the classical prophets (e.g., Ezek. 39:29) and in the historical books. "For the LORD your God is gracious and merciful, and will not turn away his face from you, if you return to him" (2 Chron. 30:9b).

The New Testament

If the face of God was as important to the Israelites as this brief survey suggests, it is not unreasonable to think that they would have been able to understand the "first commandment" (Exod. 20:3) in a way that was a more intimate calling into fellowship: "You shall not have other gods before my face," or "Let no other gods get in the way of my facing you."[14] In other words, *Just look at my face!* Attending to the divine countenance frees a person to attend to his or her neighbors with grace and peace. Resting under the gaze of the smiling face of God is an experience of absolute loving attentiveness in which one's being is secured in relation to the living God. This is what the Israelites longed for in their relation to YHWH. In Jesus Christ, they were confronted by a person who fulfilled this commandment, manifesting throughout his life a focus on his heavenly Father, relying on the life-giving presence of the Spirit, even to death on a cross.

In 2 Corinthians Paul compares the glory of Jesus' face with the glory

---

13. "Then they will cry to the LORD, and he will not answer them; he will hide his face from them at that time, because they have acted wickedly" (Mic. 3:4). In reference to the siege of Jerusalem by Babylon, the LORD tells Jeremiah (32:31) that he will "remove it from my sight" ("from before my face"). "I have hidden my face from this city because of all their wickedness" (33:5b).

14. This passage reads literally, "Other gods shall not be to-you before the face-of-me."

of Moses' face, which had to be veiled. Because the Israelites rely on the law of Moses, some are still veiled and unable to see "the light of the gospel of the glory of Christ, who is the image of God" (4:4). However, God "has shone in our hearts to give the light of the knowledge of the glory of God in the face [*prosōpon*] of Jesus Christ" (2 Cor. 4:6). This is the context in which Paul claims that "all of us, with unveiled faces, seeing the glory of the Lord as though reflected in a mirror, are being transformed into the same image from one degree of glory to another; for this comes from the Lord, the Spirit" (3:18).

How did Jesus' way of being present to the disciples and in his broader community transform their understanding of divine being? Jesus' facing of the Father as he depended on the life-giving presence of the Spirit in his confrontations with his neighbors was not a mere formality. The relational dynamics of his life manifested the nature of God, revealing the faithful, promising love that is the trinitarian life. In his sermons and parables, in his practice of table fellowship with sinners, in his healing of the sick, and ultimately in laying down his life, Jesus showed us what love is (1 John 3:16). He taught and manifested the fulfillment of the greatest commandments: face God in love with all of your being, and face your neighbor in love as you face yourself (cf. Matt. 22:37-39). Jesus looked only to his Father for sustenance, and his ministry was immersed in the Spirit. The history of this man who called others to share in his relation to God disclosed the trinitarian shape of the eternal divine life.

The connection between the Spirit and divine facing is explicit in the Psalmist's cry: "Do not cast me away from your *presence* [face], and do not take your holy spirit from me" (Ps. 51:11). This link is also evident in Ezekiel's prophecy, "I will never again hide my *face* from them, when I pour out my *spirit* upon the house of Israel" (39:29). In the New Testament experience of this outpouring, a new interpretation of the divine presence is opened up. The Holy Spirit is the manifestation of the divine countenance, bringing grace and peace to the community of God. The "face" (presence) of the Spirit unifies the community and opens up the future, granting space and time for loving fellowship. As we saw in §4.5 (above), the longing for the presence of God was intensified and fulfilled for early Christian believers as they attended to the *parousia* of the risen Christ, which they already experienced proleptically through the indwelling Holy Spirit (Eph. 1:14) while still expecting an eschatological consummation in which "they will see his *face*, and his name will be on their foreheads" (Rev. 22:4).

The New Testament witnesses to an experience of the "being" of God as an evocative presence that calls persons to participate in the peaceful communion of the Son's facing of the Father in the Spirit (cf. Acts 2:38; 3:19-20; 1:5, 8; 2:18, 33; 10:43). The eternal fellowship of delightful facing that is the divine life is experienced by human persons as a call, an infinitely gracious and peaceful *prosōpon* that invites creaturely participation. Our *koinōnia* within this facing and being-faced is wholly dependent upon the intensely gracious presence of the Creator. The promising "face" of God welcomes temporality into being, constituting human hope by its incursive evocation. Our doctrine of divine being should not be abstracted from the redemptive experience of sharing in Jesus Christ's way of facing the Father in hopeful reliance on the life-giving Spirit. The main goal of the doctrine of "divine being" is not defining the negative attributes of timelessness and impassibility, but testifying to the illuminative and transformative power of the truly eternal and intensively infinite trinitarian passion that calls creaturely freedom to being in hope.

§10.3. Jesus Christ and the Spirit of Freedom

In the New Testament, God's presence in Christ through the Spirit is not a timeless substance detached from the temporal experience of freedom nor a causal force that threatens to overpower and crush human freedom; it is a promising presence that makes *true freedom* possible. Paul tells the Galatians that he has freedom "in Christ Jesus" (2:4) and that they have been "called to freedom" (5:13). It is "for freedom that Christ has set us free" (5:1). The one whom the Son sets free is free indeed (John 8:36). The beautiful life of *hopeful* being emerges in relation to the presence of the Spirit, for "where the Spirit of the Lord is, there is *freedom*" (2 Cor. 3:17).

If we believe that the reality of God is most clearly manifested in the person of Jesus Christ, who is "the exact imprint of God's very being" (Heb. 1:3) and in whom "all the fullness of God was pleased to dwell" (Col. 1:19), and that the presence of God is mediated through our experience of the Spirit, through whom we are being transformed from glory to glory (2 Cor. 3:18), then these themes ought to be integrated into the heart of our doctrine of God. Although a fuller treatment of the issue of human freedom in the Spirit of Christ would require a more detailed programmatic outline for reforming Pneumatology and Christology, it is important to indicate its relevance for our understanding of divine being.

Paul links the temporal experience of longing for freedom to the idea of glory: "creation itself will be set free from its bondage to decay and will obtain the freedom of the glory of the children of God" (Rom. 8:21). The theme of divine glory is explicitly linked both to hope and to the presence of eternal life: The "*hope* of sharing the *glory* of God" (Rom. 5:2) secures our being "through the Holy Spirit who has been given to us" (5:5) and is leading us "to eternal life through Jesus Christ our Lord" (5:21). The gospel "of the glory of Christ, who is the image of God" (2 Cor. 4:4), is good news because God "has shone in our hearts to give the light of the knowledge of the glory of God in the face of Jesus Christ" (4:6). In the Hebrew Bible as well, the reality or presence of God is often described in terms of the divine "glory," which "fills the tabernacle" (Exod. 40:34) and "appears" to the congregation (Num. 16:19). In the New Testament, readers are encouraged to *seek* the glory that comes from God (John 5:44; 12:41-43).

The author of 1 Peter writes that the "Spirit of glory" rests upon believers, so that they are able to rejoice as they share in Christ's sufferings and shout for joy when "his glory" is revealed. In this way they "glorify God" (1 Pet. 4:13-16). He speaks of himself as "one who *shares* in the glory [*doxēs koinōnos*] to be revealed" (5:1). In 2 Peter, the phrase "sharers of the divine nature" (1:4) is preceded by the announcement that God has "called us to his own *glory* and excellence" (1:3). Resistance to the Eastern emphasis on *theosis* is usually most intense at this point. Participating in the knowing or acting of the trinitarian God seems less worrisome than participating in divine *being*. The early modern categories of rational causative substance made it difficult to articulate the relation between timelessly glorious divine being and a temporally dynamic creaturely being. Weaving together the late modern trajectories can help us make sense of the biblical emphasis on seeking divine glory as well as the human experience of freedom.

The first step toward reforming this aspect of the doctrine of God is to remember that divine glory and human glory are not on the same scale of being; God's glory is a truly infinite glory that does not lose some of its being when shared. The Hebrew word for glory *(kabod)* has the root meaning of "heaviness," and it indicates the metaphysical weightiness of a presence. In our confrontation with other finite presences, we fear that they will crush us or we worry that we will not be able to hold them close to us.

Our *gravitas* is insufficient to secure our being in the world in relation to other beings; we become anxious as our ontological status is threatened by what seems to us to be the ultimate heavyweight — death. In Scripture, divine glory can dwell in creation and community, and they can dwell in this glory without being crushed. In fact, this intensively infinite presence promises that which no metaphysically finite being can offer: a mutual indwelling of glorious life beyond the threat of death itself. The Pauline insistence that we are being prepared "for an eternal weight of glory *beyond all measure*" (2 Cor. 4:17) indicates that we are here confronted with an intensively infinite glory that escapes the quantitative more-or-less that characterizes finite being.

We should also recognize that divine glory is outlined in the New Testament in explicitly trinitarian terms. John testifies that "we have beheld his glory, glory as of the only Son from the Father" (1:14). Jesus' glory is manifested through signs (2:11), but he does not seek his own glory — it is "my Father who glorifies me" (8:54). Jesus tells the disciples, "Now is the Son of man glorified, and in him God is glorified; if God is glorified in him, God will also glorify him in himself, and glorify him at once" (13:31-32). Further, it is the coming "Spirit of truth" who "will glorify" Christ "*because* he will take what is mine and declare it to you" (16:14). What does the Spirit take and declare in this act of glorifying? "All that the Father has" (16:15), which he has given to the Son.

God's glory is not the possession of a single subject who tries to keep it all to himself, but a mutual glorification among the trinitarian persons. "Glorify your Son so that the Son may glorify you," Jesus prays to the Father, for "I glorified you on earth by finishing the work that you gave me to do" (John 17:4). The disciples are called to do the same works that Jesus did so "that the Father may be glorified in the Son" (14:12-13). Jesus is glorified "in" the disciples (17:10), who are drawn by the Spirit into this mutual glorifying of the Father and the Son. This sharing in the trinitarian glory of God is made possible by the unifying work of the Spirit (14:16), who mediates the promise of Jesus: "The glory you have given me *I have given them,* so that they may be one, as we are one" (17:22).

The gloriously liberating presence of God is intensively infinite and robustly trinitarian, but we also need to emphasize that divine reality confronts creatures as the evocative presence of absolute Futurity — calling creaturely *freedom* into *being.* When all of our focus is on trying to make sense of the (in)compatibility between competing human and divine "voluntaristic" powers, or the relation between an immaterial timeless substance and the dynamic creaturely experience of time, we are led into a theological cul-de-sac. I believe that the refigured conceptual map provided by the late modern trajectories can help us find a more compelling way to articulate the relation of God to human freedom. The focus on the potency of an individual's faculty of "free will" is misplaced. "Freedom" is an *ontological* category. Our very "being" as human persons is an experience of be-coming, of coming-to-be as time is opened up before us. This experience of being-created is constituted by the incursive glory of absolute divine Futurity.

The omnipresence of the God of hope does not compete with human freedom, but calls it (in)to being. Human freedom is the real and actual *being* of personal existence, which is a becoming in hope that finds its origin and condition in the call of the triune Creator to an ever-intensifying fellowship with the Father through the Son in the Spirit. The absolute Futurity of divine being confronts us as a redemptive presence that evokes hope in an ever-intensifying share in the truly infinite weightiness of trinitarian glory, which *is* eternal life. Our "sharing" is not becoming part of the divine substance, but a substantive intensification of our coming-to-freedom in the relational life of God. The ontological intensity of creaturely becoming that human persons experience as freedom is constituted by the incursive and evocative trinitarian presence, which graciously opens up time in(to) the life of Eternity.

The importance of the concept of "life" for the doctrine of God has often been emphasized by Christian theologians, even when it has not been the main point of the doctrine.[15] Both the Hebrew Bible and the New Testament testify to an experience of divine being as a *living* presence that constitutes the conditions of creaturely life. The God of Israel is the "living God" (1 Sam. 17:26; Pss. 42:2; 84:2; Jer. 10:10; Heb. 12:22). Paul argues that God is the one who "gives to all mortals life and breath and all things," for "in him we *live* and move and have our *being*" (Acts 17:25, 28).

In the New Testament the trinitarian life of God — and human participation within it — is manifested in Jesus' way of freely orienting his

---

15. Cf. Irenaeus, *Adversus haereses*, III.6; ANF 1:418-20; Gregory of Nyssa, *Contra Eunomium*, 8.5; Cyril of Jerusalem, *Catechetical Lectures*, 18.29; NPNF2, 7:141; Thomas Aquinas, *SumTh*, I.18.1; NPNF2, 5:210.

whole being toward the Father in hopeful dependence on the Spirit of life. Jesus deconstructs our image of a beautiful human life and its relation to glory and being. His own way of appearing is not what one would expect of a glorious king. After the resurrection, the apostles interpreted his life in terms of Isaiah's suffering servant, who "had no form or majesty that we should look at him, nothing in his appearance that we should desire him. He was despised and rejected by others, a man of suffering and acquainted with infirmity; and as one from whom others hid their faces" (53:2-3).

Jesus did not secure his being in the world by throwing around his metaphysical weight like the political and religious leaders of his day. His peaceful well-being was infinitely secured by the presence of the Father through his hope in the life-giving Spirit, so that he found delight in all of nature and was able to exhaust his own being for the sake of his neighbors. Jesus also challenged the way we respond to the appearance of others. He was not seduced by the aesthetic pleasures of his culture nor did he turn his face away from those with physical or social deformities. Many of those whom we have been raised to admire appear beautiful on the outside but are decaying on the inside (Matt. 23:27), for their way of being in relation to others is oppressive.

Those who try to secure their own glory at the expense of others are unable to participate in the reign of divine peace. Jesus' life was beautiful because it was not his own; he was able to give himself wholly for others because the freedom of his being was secured by his dependence on being-glorified by the Father through the Spirit. Sharing in the glory of Jesus Christ is less about the "communication of attributes" than actually following his way of facing God and neighbor. As we enter with Christ into the beautiful fellowship of divine life, we learn to face our neighbors (and our selves) with grace and peace. We re-present God as we invite others into the presence of eternal life.

§10.4. Reconstructing the Ontological Argument

The (re)turn to relationality in the late modern theological trajectories also provides us with an opportunity to reform the "ontological" argument. It is important to recognize that Anselm's intention in the *Proslogion* (the *locus classicus* of the argument) was not to isolate this proof from a material presentation of the doctrine of God. The whole book is a "single argument" that aims to "prove whatever we believe about the Divine Being." The first chapter calls the mind to contemplation, and what is usually called the "ontological argument" appears in chapters two to four; the remaining twenty-two chapters spell out many of the traditional attributes of God. We should imitate Anselm's incorporation of the intuition of the ontological argument into a presentation of the doctrine of God. However, rather than an objective "proof" of a rational causative substance, our goal is to outline the illuminative and reformative power of the Christian understanding and experience of the living God.

Classical and Contemporary Formulations

As we saw in §5.1, the underlying intuition that drove Anselm's argument was the Christian insistence on (what later came to be called) the "true Infinity" of the Creator. Our reconstructive efforts have attempted to conserve this intuition. In this section, however, we turn to some of the problematic aspects of and challenges to traditional formulations of the ontological argument. Anselm assumed that existence in reality is a quality that is *greater* than existence in the mind. Even the fool admits that he has in his mind the idea "something than which nothing greater can be thought."[16] If this "something" existed only in the mind, then something else could be thought of as greater; namely, a something than which nothing greater can be thought that existed both in the mind and in reality. So this "something" must exist in reality, otherwise we would be thinking a contradiction. That is to say, since "something can be thought to exist that cannot be thought not to exist, and this is greater than that which can be thought not to exist," the something "than which nothing greater can be thought" exists truly and cannot be thought not to exist (*Proslogion*, II-III). "And you, Lord our God, are this being."

This argument, as a "proof," did not remain popular during the rest of the Middle Ages. Thomas Aquinas preferred the cosmological and teleological arguments, although he did discuss the *a posteriori* self-evident nature of the idea of divine existence (*SumTh*, I.2.1; cf. *SCG*, I.43.11; *De Veritate*, X.12). Duns Scotus adds the idea of non-contradiction to the for-

16. *Aliquid quo nihil maius cogitari possit.*

mula: "God is that than which, having been thought without contradiction, a greater cannot be thought without contradiction." However, for Scotus it does not function as a "proof," but more as a persuasion to probability.[17] These versions of the argument focused on God as the source of an idea in the human "mind."

Augustine had formulated a similar kind of argument in Book II of *On Free Choice of the Will*, where he aimed to convince Evodius that, given his own existence, it is manifest that God exists. Evodius experiences his intellect as fallible and susceptible to deceit; Augustine points out that "if you did not exist, it would be impossible for you to be deceived."[18] Therefore, Evodius exists. However, this existence is characterized by a longing for truth (and goodness), the source of which cannot be his own fallible consciousness. Therefore, there must exist something superior that is the basis of the good and the true. Augustine argues that the existence of God is therefore an "indubitable fact," maintained not only by faith but through reasoning.[19] In the context of his treatment of the image of God in *The City of God*, Augustine also linked his certainty about his own existence to his desire for God. There he notes: "For if I am deceived, I am. For he who is not, cannot be deceived; and if I am deceived, by this same token I am."[20]

As we saw in §2.1, these Augustinian insights were taken up and refigured by René Descartes in the seventeenth century. His *Meditations* serve as a valuable resource for clarifying the idea of the Infinity of God. However, the Cartesian version of the argument as a "proof" did not fare well in the centuries that followed, and those who hear it today rarely find it compelling. Several factors led to its demise. First, the collapse of the foundationalist model of rationality has led to the realization that Descartes's form of the argument was circular. The foundation of our clear and distinct ideas is the existence of God, but the foundation of our knowledge of the existence of God is the existence of our own clear and distinct ideas.[21]

Second, the argument presupposed the idea of causative substance,

17. Scotus, *Opus Oxoniense* I.2.2.; translated and quoted in F. Copleston, S.J., *A History of Philosophy*, 9 vols. in 3 (New York: Doubleday, 1985), 2:525-26.

18. Augustine, *On Free Choice of the Will*, II.3; trans. A. S. Benjamin and L. H. Hackstaff (Indianapolis: Bobbs-Merrill, 1964), 40.

19. Ibid., 71.

20. *City of God*, XI.26; NPNF1, 2:220.

21. Cf. "Introduction" by George Heffernan in René Descartes, *Meditationes de prima philosophia*, trans. and ed. G. Heffernan (Notre Dame: University of Notre Dame Press, 1990).

which had been mediated to Descartes through Suarez: "It is perspicuous that there must be at a minimum just as much [reality] in the cause as there is in the effect."[22] From this premise Descartes could argue that a finite thinking self could not be the cause of the idea of a perfect being, and so a perfect being (with greater substance) must exist as the cause of this idea. These notions of causation and substance also shaped Spinoza's attempt to prove that God necessarily exists (*Ethics*, I.11). As this early modern understanding of force was slowly undermined by developments in the natural sciences (cf. §4.4 above), the validity of this "proof" was also challenged.

A third reason for the increasing implausibility of the argument was the rise of British empiricism. Descartes spoke of the idea of a perfect being as an "innate" idea, and he tried to build his knowledge from this rationalist foundation. Locke rejected the notion of innate ideas and insisted that knowledge is derived from empirical experience. Therefore, arguments for the existence of God cannot be *a priori* (based on innate ideas) but must proceed *a posteriori* — beginning with empirical experience (e.g., the observation of order in the cosmos).

Fourth, the emergence and eventual dominance of nominalism also impacted the viability of the ontological argument. If general (or "universal") ideas are merely names and have no "real" being outside the mind, then the basis for the argument's movement from an idea "in the mind" to an "idea in reality" is severely undercut. It is not surprising, therefore, that Ockham did not believe God's existence can be proved through the use of "natural reason" (*Quodlibet*, I).

Finally, Descartes assumed (with the medieval scholastics) the convertibility of "good" and "being." On this metaphysical model, the attributes of perfection and existence are mutually entailed. Since "existence" is "valuable," a being with all perfections would also have existence because existence is a perfection.[23] Kant was particularly critical of this idea in his rejection of the ontological argument; he argued that "existence" is not a real predicate but merely the positing of a thing with all its predicates.[24]

In contemporary philosophical theology several proponents of "Perfect Being Theology" have attempted to revive Anselm's version of the proof, without paying sufficient attention to the underlying categories of

---

22. Descartes, *Meditationes*, trans. Heffernan, 145.
23. Ibid., 175.
24. *Critique of Pure Reason*, 504.

substance metaphysics that shape its formulation. For example, Stephen T. Davis interprets Anselm's famous phrase — "than which no greater can be conceived" — as indicating the existence of a "greatest conceivable being." He defends this interpretation of Anselm by arguing that "conceiving one's self" is a great-making property. This property must be predicated of God *qua* "perfect being," and so God must conceive God's self. Therefore, God is a conceivable being and *ex hypothesi* the "greatest" conceivable being.[25]

This form of the argument presupposes both the projection of faculty psychology onto the divine being (a single intellect) and the substance-property structure of Aristotelian predication theory. It also misinterprets the *Proslogion*. Anselm makes it quite clear that God is *not* a conceivable being. This apophatic insistence is explicit in chapter XV: "thou art a being greater than can be conceived."[26] Like the patristic theologians before him, Anselm recognized that describing God as among all conceivable beings "the greatest" would place God under the constraints of an "extensive" understanding of infinity. In light of these challenges, how might we reconstruct the intuition of the ontological argument in a way that liberates it for dialogue in late modern culture?

The Origin, Condition, and Goal of Aesthetic Desire

We can begin by articulating an understanding of the God of the Bible as the origin, condition, and goal of *aesthetic* desire. Here I am not referring to particular experiences of specific objects of beauty or pleasure that lure us, but to the underlying desire to hold and be held in a harmonious matrix of being. For most of the great Western philosophers, beauty has to do with relationality, symmetry, and proportionality.[27] The beauty of a great story, piece of music, sunset, painting, sculpture, or human face draws us

---

25. *God, Reason and Theistic Proofs* (Edinburgh: Edinburgh University Press, 1997), 17. Thomas V. Morris relies on similar categories in *Our Idea of God* (Downers Grove, Ill.: InterVarsity, 1991), 39-40. For a critique of the concept of "perfection" as utilized by "Perfect Being Theology," cf. Philip Clayton, *The Problem of God in Modern Thought* (Grand Rapids: Eerdmans, 2000).

26. *Proslogion*, 137.

27. Wladyslaw Tatarkiewicz, "The Great Theory of Beauty and Its Decline," *The Journal of Aesthetics and Art Criticism* 31 (1972): 165-80. Cf. Monroe C. Beardsley, *Aesthetics from Classical Greece to the Present* (University: University of Alabama Press, 1966).

toward it, embraces us, wraps us up in a longing to belong in pleasurable relation (with)in it. However, these are only mediated intimations of a deeper existential longing for a future in which our particularity belongs with(in) an absolutely peaceful harmony of being.

Human hope is drawn into existence through the gracious gift of the Aesthetic. Beauty, hope, and the human fascination with the future are intimately related. "The aesthetic perception of *beauty* has long evoked in man [*sic*] the feeling of being drawn from the present moment toward a *future*, however imperceptible the actual consciousness of temporal sequence may be, which offers the promise of higher value."[28] We can hope for and in others, but as finite creatures they (like us) do not have the ontological weight to secure a beautiful future. The ultimate origin, condition, and goal of this hopeful longing that constitutes personal becoming is the presence of the truly infinite Beauty of divine life.

The origin and condition of creaturely aesthetic desire *is* the presence of its goal — the absolute Futurity of the infinite trinitarian God. The human experience of temporality is the gift of God (cf. Eccl. 3:11), but we must express this theologically in a way that is consistent with the intuition that God's presence embraces all things. Divine Eternity is the fullness of life and so the fullness of hope. However, the "hope" of the trinitarian persons does not look forward to a future time, but is a truly eternal perichoretic giving and receiving of being. The harmonious life of the Trinity is infinitely joyful. This fullness of joy is the intensively infinite *telos* that conditions the creaturely desire for peaceful being-in-relation.

Our experience of being-embraced by divine Eternity takes the form of an orientation toward the future; thus hope "abides" in the eschatological consummation of creation. This way of understanding aesthetic desire in relation to God leads me to commend the eschatological dynamism of Nyssa and Edwards rather than the eschatological "final states" of Thomas and Turretin. We may think of the absolute Beauty of God as "that perfect joy in the other by which God is God," which draws us on "into an endless *epektasis*, a stretching out toward an ever greater embrace of divine glory."[29] We long to be truly free — to find ourselves existing harmoni-

28. Yandell Woodfin, "The Futurity of Beauty: Aesthetic Intimation and Eschatological Design," *Theologische Zeitschrift* 29 (July-August 1973): 256-79 at 256; emphasis in original.

29. David Bentley Hart, *The Beauty of the Infinite: The Aesthetics of Christian Truth* (Grand Rapids: Eerdmans, 2003), 167, 20.

ously within a pattern of being in which we are liberated from the pain of self-determination and free for the joy of relating to others without fear that they will smother or abandon us. This is the life of God.

One aspect of the ontological argument that has often been overlooked in contemporary theology is the fact that its classical formulations are bathed in the language of *joy*. For Anselm, the experience of the divine presence evokes an intensification of aesthetic desire that breaks out in joyful delight in the face of God. His *Proslogion* begins with a cry of desire to be in the divine presence, a longing to be taken into the "light inaccessible" of God: "When will You enlighten our eyes and show 'Your *countenance*' to us?" The final chapter is his exultation that this is the "fullness of *joy*" in the divine promise. Anselm's desire not only to know and to love God, but also to *rejoice* eternally in God, pervades the last chapters of the *Proslogion*. He concludes: "Let my soul hunger for it, let my flesh thirst for it, my whole *being* desire it, until I enter into the '*joy* of the Lord' [Matt. 25:21], who is God, Three in One, blessed forever. Amen."[30] We find the same doxological outbreak at the end of Descartes's Third Meditation, where he pauses to "gaze with wonder and adoration on the *beauty* of this immense light, so far as the eye of my darkened intellect can bear it. For just as we believe through faith that the supreme happiness of the next life consists solely in the contemplation of the divine majesty, so experience tells us that this same contemplation, albeit much less perfect, enables us to know the greatest *joy* of which we are capable in this life."[31]

The life of the trinitarian persons is the eternal joy of the fullness of being-in-relation. This intensively infinite freedom-in-being is manifested in relation to creation as omnipresent hope, as the origin and goal of the spatio-temporal conditions in which self-conscious creatures emerge and come to long for eternally hopeful and joyful being. C. S. Lewis describes the experience of joy not simply as "aesthetic experience" but as a desire for something "other," something beyond ourselves. No finite object of pleasure can satisfy us because our desire for joy is a longing for a unity with the Absolute that surpasses all finite "appearances" in the world.[32] No natural happiness can fulfill this longing for an experience of the "Weight of Glory," because it is a thirst for "acceptance by God, response, acknowl-

---

30. *Proslogion*, 143-55; emphasis added.
31. *PWD*, II:36; emphasis added.
32. C. S. Lewis, *Surprised by Joy* (New York: Harcourt & Brace, 1955), 213-14.

edgement, and welcome into the heart of things." Seeing this or that beautiful object is not enough; "we want something else which can hardly be put into words — to be united with the beauty we see, to pass into it, to receive it into ourselves, to bathe in it, to become part of it."[33] Our absolute ontological dependence on the life of God is good news indeed, for it is the gift of being-oriented toward eternal joy.

§10.5. The Gospel of Divine Being

In Scripture the being of God is good news. Neither the Hebrew Bible nor the New Testament uses the contrastive categories "immanence" and "transcendence" to describe the relation of the Creator to creation, nor are they overly concerned about the "existence" or "essence" of God. As we have seen, however, an intense longing for the divine *presence* pervades the text. The shining face (or presence, *panim*) of God is the best news possible, for it brings the Israelites the blessing of YHWH, who keeps them in grace and peace (Num. 6:24-26). The (omni)presence of God may also evoke terror, for it is a convicting presence: "Where can I go from your spirit? Or where can I flee from your presence [or face, *panim*]" (Ps. 139:7). However, this being-convicted is also gracious, for it calls us toward an ever-intensifying joyful way of coming-to-be.

Saving Face

The good news of the divine presence is expressed beautifully throughout the Psalms. The idiom of the "shining divine countenance" is often used to express the author's desire to be in relation with the source of salvation. "Let your *face shine* upon your servant; *save* me in your steadfast love" (Ps. 31:16). "Let your *face shine*, that we may be *saved*" (Ps. 80:3; cf. 67:1-2). The link between the ideas of presence and face in the Hebrew Bible could lead us to translate Ps. 16:11 as "your face fills me with joy." We could even take the liberty of paraphrasing the prayer in Ps. 43:5 as a calling out to "my *saving face* and my God." The presence of God mediates salvation in the New Testament as well. The glory of God is manifested in the face *(prosōpon)* of

---

33. C. S. Lewis, *The Weight of Glory* (San Francisco: Harper Collins, 1949), 41-42.

Jesus Christ (2 Cor. 4:6), and the community of believers is held in being by the indwelling presence of the Holy Spirit (1 Cor. 12:4-13). For Paul it is the *eschatos Adam,* who became a life-giving Spirit (1 Cor. 15:45), that reorients his understanding of the living God. It is through the *parousia* — or coming presence — of the resurrected one that God already gives us life in the Spirit (cf. Rom. 8:11).

We try to secure our own lives by using our metaphysical weight to hold ourselves in patterns of harmony that bring us pleasure. These efforts emerge within and are shaped by our communities; we want to find our "place" within a social group without losing our own particularity. We fear being crushed by the existential heaviness of the "faces" of others, but we also worry about losing our gravitational connection to them. Our "facing" of others is not ultimately powerful enough to secure reality — ours or theirs. This ontic weightlessness terrifies us. We desire to hold and be held, but we do not have the ontological *gravitas* to ground this desirable future. Facing the lightness of our being is intensely painful because here we are confronted by the ultimate existential threat to our hope for an eternally peaceful life of beauty. The gospel is the liberating announcement that we will not be crushed under the weighty threat of nonbeing, for the "law of the Spirit of life in Christ Jesus has set you free from the law of sin and death" (Rom. 8:2). This existential liberation grants us being beyond the threat of death.

In the face of God we find our being eternally secured in hope. Anxiety about life "after" death, which has often driven the insistence on a dualism between the substances of body and soul — despite the holism of biblical anthropology and contemporary science — is misplaced. Our hope is not simply for a life "after" death but for newness of life "beyond" death. The good news to the Colossians is that they "*have been* raised with Christ" and their lives are hid "with Christ in God" (Col. 3:1, 3). The Christian already shares in the glory of divine life, and not even death can separate us from this eternally beautiful facing and being-faced. We still anticipate an intensification of our "being-with" Christ, when we will be "further clothed" and our mortality is "swallowed up by life" (2 Cor. 5:4). The eternal life that is present and promised to Christians is a participation in the Son's liberation by the Spirit into and for fellowship with the Father. The glorious beauty of the divine life confronts us as an omnipresent hope that welcomes us into face-to-face intimacy. This being-gifted-as-called, this gift of living as called-to-be with others, *is* the freedom of human persons. Salvation is the transformation of this experience into true freedom — a being made new that originates with the call of God to participate in the infinitely beautiful divine life.

In the ever-new intensification of salvation in relation to divine facing, creatures do not become God; the temporal cannot catch up to Eternity. However, as personal creatures we can joyfully accept the gracious gift of our finitude in freedom, which is a real relation to the reality of the trinitarian God. If God was confronted by a real future that is ahead of God in time then God would not be the truly infinite Creator of all things; God would be partially conditioned by this future that is outside of God. If the omnipresence of God was simply the presence of one "other" being (even the "greatest" conceivable being) in the world, then we would still be threatened by the possibility of being crushed or abandoned by this "face." However, the divine presence is the intensively infinite eternal facing and being faced of the trinitarian God — the absolute reality from, through, and to whom *all things* are (Rom. 11:36). The "saving face" of the Creator is present as divine Futurity — the origin, condition, and goal of the creaturely experience of temporality. The dynamic experience of temporal openness *is* personal human freedom, which is redemptively called into being by the creative presence of God.

The Creative Presence of God

The all-encompassing presence of the eternal trinitarian God constitutes the temporal creation by calling it into being. In the Hebrew Bible, the term "creation" refers not merely to a past event, but to the ongoing renewal of life, which is dependent on the divine presence: "when you send forth your spirit, they are created; and you renew the face of the ground" (Ps. 104:30). God is not "present" to the world as temporal things are present to each other. The reality of God, which is the eternal coming from, with, and to one another of the trinitarian persons, is present to creatures in a way that calls them into a share in that life. Paul writes that those who live by faith live "in the *presence*" of God, who "gives life to the dead and *calls into existence* the things that do not exist" (Rom. 4:17).

The presence of the Creator calls into being that which has no being of its own. As the gracious incursion of the life of the triune God, the evocative presence of Eternity creates temporal becoming. This evocation is the constitutive presence of truly infinite trinitarian life, which grants to creatures a longing for fellowship with the divine. This incursion of the promising presence of God faithfully addresses creatures as it calls them into being. It is through God's "precious and very great *promises*" that believers are called to God's "own glory and excellence" and invited to share in the divine nature (2 Pet. 1:3-4).

Maintaining the true Infinity of the Creator in relation to creation can help us avoid either a deistic separation or a pantheistic fusion of God's presence and God's creativity. A recurrent temptation for Christian theology has been to define divine creativity analogously to finite creativity. When we create something, we have an effect on another "thing." But the Creator does not "cause" an "effect" in the same way. Divine creation is not dependent upon other "things" nor does it result in "more" things. As Vladimir Lossky explains, the "newness" of creation adds nothing to the being of God: "our concepts proceed by juxtaposition, according to a 'thingist' imagery, but one cannot add up God and the world."[34] Diogenes Allen expresses the intuition in this way: "God is not more with a world than without a world. . . . The world plus God is not more than God alone. God less the world is not less than God alone."[35] The creation of the world does not "limit" God because God is truly infinite, and so not susceptible to limitation like finite creatures. This is why we cannot measure or quantify God in relation to the world. The creative presence of God cannot be reduced to a *relatum* in comparison to the world (or any part of it) because God cannot be confined onto one "side" of any relation. God is the all-embracing origin, condition, and goal of any and all relationality whatsoever. This truly infinite "surplus" of trinitarian being is good news for creatures, who are graciously called into being by the eschatological arrival of the absolute fullness of divine relationality.

The New Testament interest in divine "creation" is primarily oriented toward the "new creation" that is manifested by God's saving presence in Christ through the Spirit. As we saw in §4.5, this experience of being created anew is made possible by the *parousia* of the trinitarian God. Paul reinterprets reality in light of this new creation: "So if anyone is in Christ, there is a new creation: everything old has passed away; see, everything has become new!" (2 Cor. 5:17). The world no longer bears down on Paul in the

---

34. Lossky, *Orthodox Theology: An Introduction,* trans. Ian and Ihita Kesarcodi-Watson (Crestwood, N.Y.: St. Vladimir's Press, 1989), 54.

35. Allen, *Philosophy for Understanding Theology* (Atlanta: John Knox Press, 1985), 10.

same way; he has "died" to the world and its way of measuring and judging appearances: "For neither circumcision nor uncircumcision is anything; but a new creation is everything!" (Gal. 6:14-15). This new being-in-relation frees us to face one another with grace and peace because we no longer have to rely on our own "presence" to overcome ontological anxiety. The authors of the Hebrew Bible emphasized that the creative presence of God liberates persons into new forms of communal praxis, oriented toward setting free those who have borne the weight of political oppression (e.g., Exod. 6:6; Pss. 69:18; 144:7; Isa. 58:6; Jer. 34). As a joyful and thanksgiving (eucharistic) community, the church gathers together to celebrate its hopeful being and mediates the real presence of God in the world as it calls others to share in the reign of divine peace.

For those feeling crushed by the ontological weight of the world, the all-embracing presence of God is good news, evoking hope that grants new being even now, as we attend to the infinite divine countenance that brings grace and peace. The absolute beauty of omnipresent hope calls human freedom into being as a hopeful becoming. Hebrews 11:1 describes faith as the "hypostasis" of "hoped-for things." Christian life is subsisting in the infinite hope-fullness of the trinitarian God. The divine presence holds believers in an ever new experience of ecstatic becoming. The being of the biblical God is gospel, because being confronted by this welcoming presence is an invitation to be transformed by and in a living hope. God's gracious creative presence orients us in hope toward the future of our own well-being, which is already being made new. We long to belong eternally within the infinitely joyful harmony that is the life of God. This is the chief end of human becoming — to glorify and enjoy God forever.

Epilogue

Our goal has been to conserve the intuitions of the biblical tradition by liberating them for illuminative and transformative dialogue in contemporary culture. Part I outlined the challenges facing formulations of the doctrine of God that rely on early modern construals of the concepts of immaterial substance, single subject, and first cause. Our analysis of the proposals of significant Western theologians — especially Augustine, Thomas Aquinas, and several of the Protestant Scholastics — was an appreciative interrogation of ways in which they engaged the philosophical categories of Neoplatonism, Aristotelianism, and Materialism. Today we honor them by following their example, critically refiguring the categories that shape our own context. In Part II, we traced three late modern trajectories that have recovered traditional resources for the reconstructive task: the retrieval of divine Infinity, the revival of trinitarian doctrine, and the renewal of eschatological ontology. Part III was an attempt to weave together the insights of these developments into a presentation of the gospel of the knowing, acting, and being of the biblical God.

This programmatic proposal has emerged out of the particularities of my own context, and is guided by my concerns as an evangelical Reformed theologian interested in ecumenical and interdisciplinary dialogue. Some of my evangelical colleagues will find it strange that I have taken these other voices so seriously, while some of my colleagues from other traditions will find it odd that I have devoted so much space to issues framed by seventeenth-century debates. I believe we need each other:

the ability of evangelical theology to engage contemporary society can be strengthened by the depth of resources in the broader tradition, and the vitality of ecumenical and interdisciplinary dialogue can be enhanced by the evangelical passion for the gospel.

The reconstructive efforts of Part III are embedded within a broader matrix of theological inquiry, which organizes the presentation of the themes of Christian doctrine in a way that explicitly links them to the religious longing for truth, goodness, and beauty. Outlining the intuitions of the biblical tradition in relation to desire (and fear) facilitates an emphasis on the *reformative* task of theology, as well as an engagement with general philosophical concerns about epistemology, ethics, and metaphysics. Through faith, love, and hope we are welcomed into a redemptive relation with the biblical God — the absolute origin, condition, and goal of our longing to know, act, and be in peaceful and joyful communion. In *Reforming Theological Anthropology* and *The Faces of Forgiveness*, I treated the traditional loci of anthropology, soteriology, and ecclesiology within a thematic organization that was guided by this matrix of theological inquiry (Table 1).

TABLE 1

Longing for Truth	Longing for Goodness	Longing for Beauty
Epistemic Anxiety	Ethical Anxiety	Ontological Anxiety
Faith	Love	Hope
Finding Identity with Jesus Christ	Dying to Sin with Jesus Christ	Conforming to the Image of Jesus Christ
Knowing in Sacramental Community	Acting in Baptized Community	Being in Eucharistic Community

The traditional themes of the doctrine of God were organized and presented within this matrix in Part III of the current book (Table 2).

TABLE 2

Omniscient Faithfulness	Omnipotent Love	Omnipresent Hope
Antinomy of Foreknowledge	Antinomy of Predestination	Antinomy of Timelessness
The Name of God	The Reign of God	The Face of God
The Teleological Argument and Noetic Desire	The Cosmological Argument and Moral Desire	The Ontological Argument and Aesthetic Desire
The Gospel of Divine Knowing	The Gospel of Divine Acting	The Gospel of Divine Being

Each chapter (represented by the columns) attempted to weave together the insights of Part II in response to the challenges outlined in Part I. This formal organization of the themes allowed us to bring the material concerns of Christology and Pneumatology immediately into our presentation of the doctrine of God.

However, we are still faced with the task of reforming these traditional loci in more detail. In forthcoming books I explore ways in which we can conserve the intuitions of Christology and Pneumatology in our late modern context (Table 3).

TABLE 3

Knowing in the Spirit (Becoming Wise)	Acting in the Spirit (Becoming Just)	Being in the Spirit (Becoming Free)
Incarnation: The Identity of Jesus Christ	Atonement: The Agency of Jesus Christ	Parousia: The Presence of Jesus Christ

The proposal for reforming the doctrine of the Holy Spirit is integrated with the practical concerns of spiritual transformation. I outline the process of "intensification" in the Spirit in more detail, describing the transformational dynamics of becoming wise, becoming good, and becoming free.[1] The presentation of Christology involves bringing the themes of incarnation, atonement, and parousia into concrete dialogue with some of the significant philosophical categories and scientific theories that shape the plausibility structures of contemporary Western society.[2] All of these proposals aim to contribute to the ongoing task of *reforming* Christian theology.

1. F. LeRon Shults and Steven J. Sandage, *Transforming Spirituality: Integrating Theology and Psychology* (Grand Rapids: Baker Academic, forthcoming 2006).

2. F. LeRon Shults, *Christology and Contemporary Science* (Aldershot: Ashgate, forthcoming).

Bibliography

Achtner, Wolfgang, Stefan Kunz, and Thomas Walter. *Dimensions of Time: The Structures of the Time of Humans, of the World, and of God.* Grand Rapids: Eerdmans, 2002.

Adams, Marilyn McCord. *Horrendous Evils and the Goodness of God.* Ithaca, N.Y.: Cornell University Press, 1999.

———. "Philosophy and the Bible: The Areopagus Speech." *Faith and Philosophy* 9, no. 2 (April 1992): 135-50.

Adams, Robert M. *Finite and Infinite Goods.* Oxford: Oxford University Press, 2002.

Albert, David Z. *Quantum Mechanics and Experience.* Cambridge, Mass.: Harvard University Press, 1992.

Alison, James. *Raising Abel: The Recovery of the Eschatological Imagination.* New York: Crossroad, 1996.

Allen, Diogenes. *Philosophy for Understanding Theology.* Atlanta: John Knox Press, 1985.

Althaus, Paul. *The Theology of Martin Luther.* Translated by Robert C. Schultz. Philadelphia: Fortress Press, 1966.

Alvarez, Daniel. "On the Possibility of an Evangelical Theology." *Theology Today* 55, no. 2 (July 1998): 175-94.

Anastos, Thomas L. "Gregory Palamas' Radicalization of the Essence, Energies, and Hypostasis Model of God." *Greek Orthodox Theological Review* 38, no. 4 (1993): 335-49.

Arfeuil, Jean-Pierre, O.P. "Le dessein sauveur de Dieu: La doctrine de la prédestination selon saint Thomas d'Aquin." *Revue Thomiste* 74 (October-December 1974): 591-641.

298

Aristotle. *The Complete Works of Aristotle.* Edited by Jonathan Barnes. 2 volumes. Princeton: Princeton University Press, 1984.

Asendorf, Ulrich. *Eschatologie bei Luther.* Göttingen: Vandenhoeck & Ruprecht, 1967.

Ashworth, William B., Jr. "Christianity and the Mechanistic Universe." In *When Science and Christianity Meet,* 61-84. Edited by D. Lindberg and R. Numbers. Chicago: University of Chicago Press, 2003.

Arminius, James. *The Works of James Arminius.* Translated by J. Nichols and W. Nichols. 3 volumes. Grand Rapids: Baker, 1983.

Augustine. *Confessions.* Translated by F. J. Sheed. Indianapolis: Hackett Publishing Co., 1993.

――――. *On Free Choice of the Will.* Translated by Anna S. Benjamin and L. H. Hackstaff. Indianapolis: Bobbs-Merrill, 1964.

――――. *The City of God: Against the Pagans.* Translated and edited by R. W. Dyson. Cambridge: Cambridge University Press, 1998.

Bak, Per. *How Nature Works: The Science of Self-Organized Criticality.* New York: Copernicus, 1996.

Balentine, Samuel. *The Hidden God: The Hiding of the Face of God in the Old Testament.* Oxford: Oxford University Press, 1993.

Barbour, Julian. *The End of Time: The Next Revolution in Physics.* Oxford: Oxford University Press, 1999.

Barnes, Michel René. "Augustine in Contemporary Trinitarian Theology." *Theological Studies* 56 (1995): 237-50.

Barrett, C. K. *The Acts of the Apostles.* Edinburgh: T&T Clark, 1994.

Barth, Karl. *Church Dogmatics.* 4 vols. Translated by G. W. Bromiley and T. F. Torrance. Edinburgh: T&T Clark, 1936-1969.

――――. *The Epistle to the Romans.* Translated by Edwyn C. Hoskyns. London: Oxford, 1933.

――――. *Evangelical Theology: An Introduction.* Translated by Grover Foley. Grand Rapids: Eerdmans, 1963.

――――. *Ethics.* Translated by G. W. Bromiley. New York: Seabury Press, 1981.

――――. *The Humanity of God.* Translated by J. N. Thomas. Richmond, Va.: John Knox, 1960.

Bauckham, Richard, ed. *God Will Be All in All: The Eschatology of Jürgen Moltmann.* Edinburgh: T&T Clark, 1999.

Bauckham, Richard, and Trevor Hart. "The Shape of Time." In *The Future as God's Gift,* 41-72. Edited by D. Fergusson and M. Sarot. Edinburgh: T&T Clark, 2000.

Beale, Greg K. "The Eschatological Conception of New Testament Theology." In *Eschatology in Bible and Theology,* 11-52. Edited by Kent E. Brower and Mark W. Elliot. Downers Grove, Ill.: InterVarsity Press, 1997.

Beardslee, John W., III. *Reformed Dogmatics*. New York: Oxford University Press, 1965.

Beardsley, Monroe C. *Aesthetics from Classical Greece to the Present*. University: University of Alabama Press, 1966.

Behe, Michael. *Darwin's Black Box*. New York: Simon and Schuster, 1998.

Beilby, James, and Paul Eddy, editors. *Divine Foreknowledge: Four Views*. Downers Grove, Ill.: InterVarsity Press, 2001.

Belenky, Mary Field, et al. *Women's Ways of Knowing: The Development of Self, Voice and Mind*. New York: Basic Books, 1986.

Bloch, Ernst. *The Principle of Hope*. Translated by Neville Plaice et al. 3 volumes. Cambridge, Mass.: MIT Press, 1986.

Bobrinskoy, Boris. *The Mystery of the Trinity: Trinitarian Experience and Vision in the Biblical and Patristic Tradition*. Crestwood, N.Y.: St. Vladimir's Seminary Press, 1999.

Boethius. *Consolation of Philosophy*. Translated by Joel C. Relihan. Indianapolis: Hackett, 2001.

Boff, Leonardo. *Holy Trinity, Perfect Community*. Translated by Phillip Berryman. Maryknoll, N.Y.: Orbis, 2000.

Bohm, David. *Wholeness and the Implicate Order*. London: Routledge, 1980.

Braaten, Carl E. *The Futurist Option*. New York: Newman Press, 1970.

———. "God and the Idea of the Future." *Dialog* 7 (Autumn 1968): 252-58.

———. "The Reunited Church of the Future." *Journal of Ecumenical Studies* 4, no. 4 (Fall 1967): 611-28.

———. "Toward a Theology of Hope." *Theology Today* 24, no. 2 (July 1967): 208-26.

———. "The Recovery of Apocalyptic Imagination." In *The Last Things: Biblical and Theological Perspectives on Eschatology*. Edited by Carl E. Braaten and Robert W. Jenson. Grand Rapids: Eerdmans, 2002.

Braaten, Carl E., and Robert W. Jenson. *The Future of God*. New York: Harper & Row, 1969.

Braaten Carl E., and Robert W. Jenson, eds. *Christian Dogmatics*. 2 volumes. Philadelphia: Fortress, 1984.

Breck, John. *Spirit of Truth: The Origins of Johannine Pneumatology*. Crestwood, N.Y.: St. Vladimir's Press, 1991.

Bright, John. *The Kingdom of God*. New York: Abingdon, 1953.

Brightman, Robert S. "Apophatic Theology and Divine Infinity in Gregory of Nyssa." *The Greek Orthodox Theological Review* 18, no. 2 (1973): 97-114.

Brueggemann, Walter. *The Land*. Philadelphia: Fortress, 1977.

———. "Theodicy in a Social Dimension." *Journal for the Study of the Old Testament* 33 (1985): 3-25.

Brunner, Emil. *The Christian Doctrine of God*. Translated by Olive Wyon. Philadelphia: Westminster, 1949.

—————. *Eternal Hope.* Translated by H. Knight. Philadelphia: Westminster, 1954.

Brunschwig, Jacques, and David Sedley. "Hellenistic Philosophy." In *Greek and Roman Philosophy.* Edited by David Sedley. Cambridge: Cambridge University Press, 2003.

Buber, Martin. *I and Thou.* Translated by Ronald Gregor Smith. Second edition. New York: Charles Scribner's Sons, 1958.

—————. *The Knowledge of Man.* Edited and translated by Maurice Friedman. New York: Harper & Row, 1965.

Buckley, Michael J., S.J. *At the Origins of Modern Atheism.* New Haven: Yale University Press, 1987.

Buckley, James J., and David Yeago. *Knowing the Triune God: The Work of the Spirit in the Practices of the Church.* Grand Rapids: Eerdmans, 2001.

Bultmann, Rudolph. *The Presence of Eternity: History and Eschatology.* New York: Harper & Row, 1955.

—————. *Theology of the New Testament.* New York: SCM Press, 1952.

Burrell, David. "Distinguishing God from the World." In *Language, Meaning and God.* Edited by B. Davies. London: Geoffrey Chapman, 1987.

—————. *Freedom and Creation in Three Traditions.* Notre Dame: University of Notre Dame Press, 1993.

—————. *Knowing the Unknowable God.* Notre Dame: University of Notre Dame Press, 1986.

—————. "Reflections on 'Negative Theology' in the Light of a Recent Venture to Speak of 'God Without Being.'" In *Postmodernism and Christian Philosophy.* Edited by Roman T. Ciapalo. Washington, D.C.: The Catholic University of America Press, 1997.

Caird, G. B. "Predestination — Romans 9–11." *The Expository Times* 68 (October 1956–September 1957): 324-27.

Calvin, John. *Concerning the Eternal Predestination of God.* Translated by J. K. S. Reid. Louisville: Westminster/John Knox, 1997.

—————. *Institutes of the Christian Religion.* Edited by John T. McNeill. Translated by Ford Lewis Battles. Philadelphia: Westminster Press, 1960.

Čapek, Milič. "Determinism in Western Theology and Philosophy." In *Religious Pluralism.* Edited by Leroy Rouner. Notre Dame: University of Notre Dame Press, 1984.

—————. *The Philosophical Impact of Contemporary Physics.* New York: Van Nostrand Reinhold Co., 1961.

—————. "Time in Relativity Theory: Arguments for a Philosophy of Becoming." In *The Voices of Time,* 343-54. Edited by J. T. Fraser. Second edition. Amherst: University of Massachusetts Press, 1981.

Carr, Anne. "The God Who is Involved." *Theology Today* 38, no. 3 (October 1981): 314-28.

—————. *Transforming Grace.* New York: HarperCollins, 1990.

Carstairs-McCarthy, Andrew. *The Origins of Complex Language: An Inquiry into the Evolutionary Beginnings of Sentences, Syllables and Truth.* Oxford: Oxford University Press, 1999.

Chaitin, Gregory J. *The Limits of Mathematics.* London: Springer-Verlag, 2002.

————. *The Unknowable.* London: Springer-Verlag, 1999.

Charry, Ellen. "Spiritual Formation by the Doctrine of the Trinity." *Theology Today* 54, no. 3 (October 1997): 367-80.

Chopp, Rebecca S., and Mark Lewis Taylor, editors. "Introduction: Crisis, Hope and Contemporary Theology." In *Reconstructing Christian Theology.* Minneapolis: Fortress, 1994.

Clarke, Samuel. *A Demonstration of the Being and Attributes of God.* Edited by Ezio Vailati. Cambridge: Cambridge University Press, 1998.

Clarke, F. Stuart. "Christocentric Developments in the Reformed Doctrine of Predestination." *Churchman* 98, no. 3 (1984): 229-45.

Clayton, Philip. *The Problem of God in Modern Thought.* Grand Rapids: Eerdmans, 2000.

Clayton, Philip, and Arthur Peacocke, editors. *In Whom We Live and Move and Have Our Being: Panentheistic Reflections on God's Presence in a Scientific World.* Grand Rapids: Eerdmans, 2004.

Coakley, Sarah. "Gender and Knowledge in Western Philosophy: The 'Man of Reason' and the 'Feminine' 'Other' in Enlightenment and Romantic Thought." In *The Special Nature of Women?* Edited by Anne Carr and Elisabeth Schüssler Fiorenza. London: SCM Press, 1991.

Coakley, Sarah, editor. *Re-thinking Gregory of Nyssa.* Oxford: Blackwell, 2003.

Coffey, David. *Deus Trinitas: The Doctrine of the Triune God.* New York: Oxford University Press, 1999.

Copleston, Frederick. *A History of Philosophy.* 9 volumes. Garden City, N.Y.: Image Books, 1985.

Cosgrove, Charles S. "The Divine *dei* in Luke-Acts." *Novum Testamentum* 26, no. 2 (1984): 168-90.

Craig, William Lane. *The Cosmological Argument from Plato to Leibniz.* London: Macmillan, 1980.

————. *The Kalam Cosmological Argument.* New York: Rowman & Littlefield, 1979.

————. "The Kalam Cosmological Argument." In *Philosophy of Religion: A Reader and Guide.* Edited by William Lane Craig. New Brunswick, N.J.: Rutgers University Press, 2002.

————. "Middle Knowledge: A Calvinist-Arminian Rapprochement?" In *The Grace of God, the Will of Man,* 141-64. Edited by Clark Pinnock. Grand Rapids: Zondervan, 1989.

Cranz, F. Edward. "A Common Pattern in Petrarch, Nicholas of Cusa and Martin

Luther." In *Humanity and Divinity in Renaissance and Reformation*. Leiden: Brill, 1993.

Cullmann, F. Edward. *Christ and Time: The Primitive Christian Conception of Time and History*. Translated by Floyd V. Filson. London: SCM, 1962.

Cunningham, David S. *These Three Are One: The Practice of Trinitarian Theology*. Oxford: Blackwell, 1998.

Damasio, Antonio. *Descartes' Error: Emotion, Reason, and the Human Brain*. New York: Avon, 1994.

―――. *The Feeling of What Happens: Body and Emotion in the Making of Consciousness*. New York: Harcourt and Brace, 1999.

―――. *Looking for Spinoza: Joy, Sorrow and the Feeling Brain*. New York: Harcourt, 2003.

Davis, Stephen T. God, *Reason and Theistic Proofs*. Edinburgh: Edinburgh University Press, 1997.

Dirk L. Couprie, Robert Hahn, and Gerard Naddaf. *Anaximander in Context: New Studies in the Origins of Greek Philosophy*. Albany: State University of New York Press, 2003.

Dunn, James D. G. *Romans 1–8*. Word Biblical Commentary, v. 38A. Dallas: Word Books, 1988.

Dalferth, Ingolf. *Existenz Gottes und christlicher Glaube: Skizzen zu einer eschatologischen Ontologie*. Munich: Kaiser Verlag, 1984.

―――. "Karl Barth's Eschatological Realism." In *Karl Barth: Centenary Essays*, 14-45. Edited by S. W. Sykes. Cambridge: Cambridge University Press, 1989.

Dauben, Joseph W. "Georg Cantor and Pope Leo XIII: Mathematics, Theology and the Infinite." *Journal of the History of Ideas* 38, no. 1 (1977): 85-108.

Davenport, Anne Ashley. *Measure of a Different Greatness: The Intensive Infinite 1250-1650*. Leiden: Brill, 1999.

Davies, Brian, O.P. "Classical Theism and the Doctrine of Divine Simplicity." In *Language, Meaning and God*. Edited by Brian Davies, O.P. London: Geoffrey Chapman, 1987.

Davies, Oliver. *A Theology of Compassion: Metaphysics of Difference and the Renewal of Tradition*. Grand Rapids: Eerdmans, 2003.

Deacon, Terrence W. *The Symbolic Species: The Co-evolution of Language and the Brain*. New York: W. W. Norton, 1997.

Deats, Paul, and Carol Robb, editors. *The Boston Personalist Tradition in Philosophy, Social Ethics and Theology*. Macon, Ga.: Mercer University Press, 1986.

D'Costa, Gavin. *The Meeting of Religions and the Trinity*. Maryknoll, N.Y.: Orbis, 2000.

del Colle, Ralph. *Christ and the Spirit: Spirit-Christology in Trinitarian Perspective*. New York: Oxford University Press, 1994.

Dembski, William. *Intelligent Design: The Bridge Between Science and Theology*. Downers Grove, Ill.: InterVarsity, 1999.

————. *Mere Creation: Science, Faith and Intelligent Design.* Downers Grove, Ill.: InterVarsity, 1998.

De Régnon, Louis. *Etudes de théologie positive sur la Sainte Trinité.* 3 volumes. Paris: Retaux, 1892-1898.

Derrida, Jacques. *Of Grammatology.* Translated by G. C. Spivak. London: Johns Hopkins University Press, 1998.

————. *Writing and Difference.* Translated by Alan Bass. Chicago: University of Chicago, 1978.

Descartes, René. *The Philosophical Writings of Descartes.* 3 volumes. Translated by John Cottingham et al. Cambridge: Cambridge University Press, 1985-1991.

————. *Meditationes de prima philosophia.* Translated, edited, and with an introduction by George Heffernan. Notre Dame: University of Notre Dame Press, 1990.

Dixon, Philip. *Nice and Hot Disputes: The Doctrine of the Trinity in the Seventeenth Century.* London: Continuum, 2003.

Dorner, I. A. *Divine Immutability: A Critical Reconstruction.* Translated by Robert R. Williams and Claude Welch. Minneapolis: Fortress, 1994.

Downey, Michael. *Altogether Gift: A Christian Spirituality.* Maryknoll, N.Y.: Orbis, 2000.

Drozdek, Adam. "Beyond Infinity: Augustine and Cantor." *Laval théologique et philosophique* 51, no. 1 (1995): 127-40.

Duns Scotus, John. *Philosophical Writings.* Translated by Allan Wolter. Indianapolis: Hackett, 1987.

Durkheim, E. *The Elementary Forms of Religious Life.* Translated by J. W. Swain. New York: Free Press, 1915.

Einstein, Albert. *Ideas and Opinions.* New York: Bonanza, 1954.

————. *Relativity: The Special and the General Theory.* New York: Crown, 1961.

Einstein, Albert, and Leopold Infeld. *The Evolution of Physics.* New York: Simon and Schuster, 1938.

Engberg-Pedersen, Troels. *Paul and the Stoics.* Louisville: Westminster/John Knox, 2000.

Epictetus. *The Discourses as Reported by Arrian.* Translated by W. A. Goldfather. 2 volumes. Cambridge, Mass.: Harvard University Press, 1925.

Erickson, Millard. *Christian Theology.* Second edition. Grand Rapids: Baker, 1998.

Farrow, Douglas. *Ascension and Ecclesia: On the Significance of the Doctrine of the Ascension for Ecclesiology and Christian Cosmology.* Grand Rapids: Eerdmans, 1999.

Farthing, John L. "Christ and the Eschaton: The Reformed Eschatology of Jerome Zanchi." In *Later Calvinism: International Perspectives.* Edited by W. Fred Graham. Kirksville, Mo.: Sixteenth Century Journal Publishers, 1994.

Fatio, Oliver. "Remarques sur le temp et l'éternité chez Calvin." In *Temps et*

Eschatologie: Données bibliques et problématiques contemporaines, 161-72. Edited by Jean-Louis Leuba. Paris: Cerf, 1994.

Feferman, Solomon. "Does Mathematics Need New Axioms?" *American Mathematical Quarterly* 106, no. 2 (February 1999): 99-11.

Ferguson, Everett. "God's Infinity and Man's Mutability: Perpetual Progress according to Gregory of Nyssa." *The Greek Orthodox Theological Review* 18, no. 2 (1973): 59-78.

Feuerbach, Ludwig. *The Essence of Christianity.* Translated by George Eliot. New York: Harper & Row, 1957.

Fiddes, Paul S. *Participating in God: A Pastoral Doctrine of the Trinity.* Louisville: Westminster/John Knox Press, 2000.

Force, James E. "Newton's God of Dominion: The Unity of Newton's Theological, Scientific, and Political Thought." In James E. Force and Richard H. Popkin, *Essays on the Context, Nature, and Influence of Isaac Newton's Theology.* Dordrecht: Kluwer, 1990.

Ford, Lewis S. "Creativity in a Future Key." In *New Essays in Metaphysics,* 179-97. Edited by Robert Neville. Albany: SUNY, 1987.

Ford, Lewis S. "God as the Subjectivity of the Future." *Encounter* 41, no. 3 (1980): 287-92.

———. *The Lure of God.* Philadelphia: Fortress, 1978.

———. "Nancy Frankenberry's Conception of the Power of the Past." *American Journal of Theology and Philosophy* 14, no. 3 (1993). 287-300.

———. "The Nature of the Power of the Future." In *The Theology of Wolfhart Pannenberg,* 75-94. Edited by P. Clayton and C. Braaten. Minneapolis: Augsburg, 1988.

———. *Transforming Process Theism.* Albany: SUNY, 2000.

Forde, Gerhard. "The Formula of Concord Article V: End or New Beginning?" *dialog* 15, no. 3 (Summer 1976): 184-91.

Forrest, Barbara C., and Paul R. Gross. *Creationism's Trojan Horse: The Wedge of Intelligent Design.* Oxford: Oxford University Press, 2003.

Fox, Patricia A. *God as Communion: John Zizioulas, Elizabeth Johnson, and the Retrieval of the Symbol of the Triune God.* Collegeville, Minn.: Liturgical Press, 2001.

Freud, Sigmund. *The Future of an Illusion.* Translated by James Strachey. London: Hogarth Press, 1968.

Friedman, Richard Elliott. *The Hidden Face of God.* San Francisco: HarperCollins, 1995.

Gannsle, Gregory E., editor. *God and Time: Four Views.* Downers Grove, Ill.: InterVarsity Press, 2001.

Gardner, H. *Frames of Mind: The Theory of Multiple Intelligences.* New York: Basic Books, 1985.

Garman, Michael. *Psycholinguistics.* Cambridge: Cambridge University Press, 1990.

Gibbs, Raymond W., Jr. "Intentions as Emergent Products of Social Interactions." In *Intentions and Intentionality: Foundations of Social Cognition,* 105-22. Edited by Bertram F. Malle, Louis J. Moses, and Dare A. Baldwin. Cambridge, Mass.: MIT Press, 2001.

Gilson, Étienne. *History of Christian Philosophy in the Middle Ages.* London: Sheed and Ward, 1955.

Gleick, James. *Chaos: Making a New Science.* New York: Viking, 1987.

Goris, Harm J. M. J. *Free Creatures of an Eternal God.* Nijmegen: Stichting Thomasfonds, 1996.

Grant, Edward. *The Foundations of Modern Science in the Middle Ages: Their Religious, Institutional, and Intellectual Contexts.* Cambridge: Cambridge University Press, 1996.

Gregersen, Niels Henrik. "Beyond the Balance: Theology in a Self-Organizing World." In *Design and Disorder: Perspectives from Science and Theology,* 53-91. Edited by Niels Henrik Gregersen and Ulf Görman. London: T&T Clark, 2002.

—————. "From Anthropic Design to Self-Organized Complexity." In *From Complexity to Life,* 206-34. Edited by Niels Henrik Gregersen. Oxford: Oxford University Press, 2003.

—————. "The Idea of Creation and the Theory of Autopoietic Process." *Zygon* 33, no. 3 (September 1998): 336-67.

Gregersen, Niels Henrik, et al., editors. *The Human Person in Science and Theology.* Edinburgh: T&T Clark, 2000.

Gregory of Nyssa. *Life of Moses.* Translated by E. Ferguson and A. J. Malherbe. New York: Paulist Press, 1978.

Grenz, Stanley J. *Rediscovering the Triune God: The Trinity in Contemporary Theology.* Minneapolis: Augsburg Fortress, 2004.

Griffin, David Ray, editor. *Physics and the Ultimate Significance of Time: Bohm, Prigogine, and Process Philosophy.* Albany: SUNY, 1986.

Gundersdorf, Wilma von Jess. "Divine Eternity in the Doctrine of St. Augustine." *Augustinian Studies* 6 (1975): 75-96.

Gunton, Colin. *Act and Being: Towards a Theology of the Divine Attributes.* Grand Rapids: Eerdmans, 2002.

—————. *The Actuality of Atonement.* Edinburgh: T&T Clark, 1998.

—————. *Becoming and Being: The Doctrine of God in Charles Hartshorne and Karl Barth.* Oxford: Oxford University Press, 1978.

—————. "Between Allegory and Myth: The Legacy of the Spiritualising of Genesis." In *The Doctrine of Creation.* Edited by Colin Gunton. Edinburgh: T&T Clark, 1997.

—————. *A Brief Theology of Revelation.* Edinburgh: T&T Clark, 1995.

—————. *The Christian Faith.* Oxford: Blackwell, 2002.

————. "Dogmatic Theses on Eschatology." In *The Future as God's Gift*, 139-43. Edited by D. Fergusson and M. Sarot. Edinburgh: T&T Clark, 2000.

————. "The End of Causality." In *The Doctrine of Creation*. Edited by Colin Gunton. Edinburgh: T&T Clark, 1997.

————. "God, Grace and Freedom." In *God and Freedom*. Edited by Colin Gunton. Edinburgh: T&T Clark, 1995.

————. *Intellect and Action*. Edinburgh: T&T Clark, 2000.

————. *The One, the Three, and the Many*. Cambridge: Cambridge University Press, 1993.

————. *The Promise of Trinitarian Theology*. Edinburgh: T&T Clark, 1991.

————. "Relation and Relativity: The Trinity and the Created World." In *Trinitarian Theology Today*. Edited by Christoph Schwöbel. Edinburgh: T&T Clark, 1995.

————. "Trinity, Ontology and Anthropology: Towards a Renewal of the Doctrine of the *Imago Dei*." In *Persons, Divine and Human*. Edited by C. Schwöbel. Edinburgh: T&T Clark, 1991.

————. *The Triune Creator: A Historical and Systematic Study*. Grand Rapids: Eerdmans, 1998.

————. *Yesterday and Today: A Study of Continuities in Christology*. Grand Rapids: Eerdmans, 1983.

Gunton, Colin, editor. *Trinity, Time, and Church: A Response to the Theology of Robert W. Jenson*. Grand Rapids: Eerdmans, 2000.

Guth, Alan. *The Inflationary Universe: The Quest for a New Theory of Cosmic Origins*. Cambridge: Perseus, 1997.

Guthrie, Shirley. *Christian Doctrine*. Revised edition. Louisville: Westminster/John Knox, 1994.

————. "Romans 11:25-32." *Interpretation* 38, no. 2 (April 1984): 286-91.

Gutiérrez, Gustavo. *A Theology of Liberation*. Translated by Sister Caridad Inda and John Eagleson. Maryknoll, N.Y.: Orbis, 1988.

————. *The Truth Shall Make You Free*. Translated by Matthew J. O'Connell. Maryknoll, N.Y.: Orbis, 1990.

Hankinson, R. J. "Stoic Epistemology." In *The Stoics*. Edited by Brad Inwood. Cambridge: Cambridge University Press, 2003.

Harries, Karsten. *Infinity and Perspective*. Cambridge, Mass.: MIT Press, 2001.

Harris, Errol E. *The Reality of Time*. Albany: SUNY, 1988.

Hart, David Bentley. *The Beauty of the Infinite: The Aesthetics of Christian Truth*. Grand Rapids: Eerdmans, 2003.

Hasker, William. "The Openness of God." *Christian Scholar's Review* 28, no. 1 (Fall 1998): 111-23.

————. "A Philosophical Perspective." In Clark Pinnock et al., *The Openness of God*, 126-54. Downers Grove, Ill.: InterVarsity Press, 1994.

Haught, John F. *God after Darwin: A Theology of Evolution.* Boulder, Colo.: Westview, 2000.

Hayes, Zachary, O.F.M. *Visions of a Future: A Study of Christian Eschatology.* Wilmington, Del.: Michael Glazier, 1992.

Hegel, G. W. F. *Lectures on the Philosophy of Religion.* Translated by P. C. Hodgson et al. 3 volumes. Berkeley: University of California Press, 1998.

————. *Phenomenology of Spirit.* Translated by A. V. Miller. Oxford. Oxford University Press, 1977.

————. *Science of Logic.* Translated by A. V. Miller. Amherst, N.Y.: Humanity Books, 1999.

Heidegger, Martin. *Being and Time.* Translated by John Macquarrie and Edward Robinson. San Francisco: HarperCollins, 1962.

————. *Identity and Difference.* Translated by Joan Stambaugh. Chicago: University of Chicago Press, 2002.

Heim, Mark. *The Depths of Riches: A Trinitarian Theology of Religious Ends.* Grand Rapids: Eerdmans, 2001.

Henry, John. "'Pray do not ascribe that notion to me': God and Newton's Gravity." In *The Books of Nature and Scripture: Recent Essays on Natural Philosophy, Theology, and Biblical Criticism in the Netherlands of Spinoza's Time and the British Isles of Newton's Time,* 123-48. Edited by James E. Force and Richard H. Popkin. Dordrecht: Kluwer, 1994.

Heppe, Heinrich. *Reformed Dogmatics: Set Out and Illustrated from the Sources.* Revised and edited by E. Bizer. Translated by G. T. Thomson. London: George Allen & Unwin, 1950.

Heron, Alasdair I. C. *The Holy Spirit.* Philadelphia: Westminster, 1983.

Hill, Craig. *In God's Time: The Bible and the Future.* Grand Rapids: Eerdmans, 2002.

Hobbes, Thomas. *Leviathan.* Oxford: Oxford University Press, 1996.

Hodge, Charles. *Systematic Theology.* 3 volumes. Grand Rapids: Eerdmans, 1981.

Holwerda, R. "Eschatology and History: A Look at Calvin's Eschatological Vision." In *Exploring the Heritage of John Calvin.* Edited by R. Holwerda. Grand Rapids: Baker, 1976.

Hülser, Karlheinz, editor. *Die Fragmente zur Dialektik der Stoiker.* 4 volumes. Stuttgart: Frommann-Holzboog, 1987-1988.

Hunt, David. "On Augustine's Way Out." *Faith and Philosophy* 16, no. 1 (January 1999): 3-26.

Hutton, Sarah. "More, Newton and the Language of Biblical Prophecy." In *The Books of Nature and Scripture: Recent Essays on Natural Philosophy, Theology, and Biblical Criticism in the Netherlands of Spinoza's Time and the British Isles of Newton's Time,* 25-38. Edited by James E. Force and Richard H. Popkin. Dordrecht: Kluwer, 1994.

Inwood, Brian, and L. P. Gerson, editors. *The Epicurus Reader*. Indianapolis: Hackett, 1994.

Jackelén, Antje. *Zeit und Ewigkeit: Die Frage der Zeit in Kirche, Naturwissenschaft und Theologie*. Neukirchen-Vluyn: Neukirchener, 2002.

James, William. "The Dilemma of Determinism." In *The Will to Believe and Other Essays in Popular Philosophy*. New York: Dover, 1956.

Jammer, Max. *Concepts of Force*. New York: Dover, 1999.

Jané, Ignacio. "The Role of the Absolute Infinite in Cantor's Conception of Set." *Erkenntnis* 42 (1995): 375-402.

Jenson, Robert W. *Alpha and Omega: A Study in the Theology of Karl Barth*. New York: Nelson, 1963.

————. *America's Theologian: A Recommendation of Jonathan Edwards*. Oxford: Oxford University Press, 1988.

————. "Aspects of a Doctrine of Creation." In *The Doctrine of Creation*, 17-28. Edited by Colin Gunton. Edinburgh: T&T Clark, 1997.

————. *Essays in Theology of Culture*. Grand Rapids: Eerdmans, 1995.

————. *God after God: The God of the Past and the God of the Future, Seen in the Work of Karl Barth*. Indianapolis: Bobbs-Merrill, 1969.

————. *On Thinking the Human: Resolutions of Difficult Notions*. Grand Rapids: Eerdmans, 2003.

————. *Story and Promise: A Brief Theology of the Gospel about Jesus*. Philadelphia: Fortress Press, 1973.

————. *Systematic Theology*. 2 volumes. Oxford: Oxford University Press, 1997, 1999.

————. *The Triune Identity: God According to the Gospel*. Philadelphia: Fortress, 1982.

————. "What Is the Point of Trinitarian Theology?" In *Trinitarian Theology Today*, 31-43. Edited by C. Schwöbel. Edinburgh: T&T Clark, 1995.

Johnson, Elizabeth. *She Who Is: The Mystery of God in Feminist Theological Discourse*. New York: Crossroad, 1997.

————. "Trinity: To Let the Symbol Sing Again." *Theology Today* 54, no. 3 (October 1997): 298-311.

Johnson, William Stacey. *The Mystery of God: Karl Barth and the Postmodern Foundations of Theology*. Louisville: Westminster/John Knox, 1997.

Jorgenson, James. "Predestination according to Divine Foreknowledge in Patristic Tradition." In *Salvation in Christ: A Lutheran-Orthodox Dialogue*, 159-83. Edited by John Meyendorff and Robert Tobias. Minneapolis: Augsburg, 1992.

Jüngel, Eberhard. *Death: The Riddle and the Mystery*. Translated by Iain and Ute Nicol. Philadelphia: Westminster, 1974.

————. *The Freedom of a Christian*. Translated by Roy A. Harrisville. Minneapolis: Augsburg, 1988.

————. *God's Being Is in Becoming: The Trinitarian Being of God in the Theology of Karl Barth.* Translated by John Webster. Grand Rapids: Eerdmans, 2001.

————. *God as the Mystery of the World: On the Foundation of the Theology of the Crucified One in the Dispute between Theism and Atheism.* Translated by Darrell L. Guder. Grand Rapids: Eerdmans, 1983.

————. *Justification: The Heart of the Christian Faith.* Translated by Jeffrey F. Cayzer. Edinburgh: T&T Clark, 2001.

————. "Quae supra nos, nihil ad nos." *Evangelische Theologie* 3 (June 1972).

————. *Theological Essays.* Translated by J. B. Webster. Edinburgh: T&T Clark, 1989.

————. *Theological Essays II.* Edited and translated by J. B. Webster and A. Neufeld-Fast. Edinburgh: T&T Clark, 1995.

————. "Thesen zur Ewigkeit des ewigen Lebens." *Zeitschrift für Theologie und Kirche* 97 (2000).

————. "Thesen zum Verhältnis von Existenz, Wesen und Eigenschaften Gottes." *Zeitschrift für Theologie und Kirche* 96, no. 3 (September 1999).

————. "Das Verhältnis von 'ökonomischer' und 'immanenter' Trinität." *Zeitschrift für Theologie und Kirche* 72, no. 3 (September 1975): 353-64.

————. "Zukunft und Hoffnung." In *Müssen Christen Sozialisten sein?* Edited by W. Teichert. Hamburg: Lutherisches Verlaghaus, 1975.

Kahn, Charles H. "Discovering the Will: From Aristotle to Augustine." In *The Question of "Eclecticism": Studies in Later Greek Philosophy.* Edited by J. M. Dillon and A. A. Long. Berkeley: University of California Press, 1988.

Kant, Immanuel. *Critique of Pure Reason.* Translated by Norman Kemp Smith. New York: St. Martin's Press, 1965.

Karkkainen, Veli-Matti. *Toward a Pneumatological Theology: Pentecostal and Ecumenical Perspectives on Ecclesiology, Soteriology and Theology of Mission.* Edited by Amos Yong. Lantham, N.Y.: University Press of America, 2002.

Kearney, Richard. *The God Who May Be: A Hermeneutics of Religion.* Bloomington: Indiana University Press, 2001.

Kegan, Robert. *The Evolving Self: Problem and Process in Human Development.* Cambridge, Mass.: Harvard University Press, 1982.

————. *In over Our Heads: The Mental Demands of Modern Life.* Cambridge, Mass.: Harvard University Press, 1994.

Kelly, J. N. D. *Early Christian Doctrines.* San Francisco: HarperSanFrancisco, 1978.

Kierkegaard, Søren. *The Concept of Anxiety.* Edited and translated by Reidar Thomte. Princeton: Princeton University Press, 1980.

————. *Concluding Unscientific Postscript.* Edited and translated by Howard V. and Edna H. Hong. 2 volumes. Princeton: Princeton University Press, 1992.

————. *Eighteen Upbuilding Discourses.* Edited and translated by Howard V. and Edna H. Hong. Princeton: Princeton University Press, 1990.

————. *Philosophical Fragments.* Translated by Howard V. and Edna H. Hong. Princeton: Princeton University Press, 1985.

————. *Purity of Heart Is to Will One Thing.* Translated by Douglas V. Steere. New York: Harper & Row, 1948.

————. *The Sickness Unto Death.* Translated by Howard V. and Edna H. Hong. Princeton: Princeton University Press, 1980.

————. *Works of Love.* Edited and translated by Howard V. and Edna H. Hong. Princeton: Princeton University Press, 1995.

Kirk, G. S., J. E. Raven, and M. Schofield. *The Presocratic Philosophers.* Second edition. Cambridge: Cambridge University Press, 1987.

Koyré, Alexandre. *Newtonian Studies.* Chicago: University of Chicago Press, 1965.

Kubrin, David. "Newton and the Cyclical Cosmos." In *Science and Religious Belief.* Edited by C. A. Russell. London: University of London Press, 1973.

Kunz, E. *Protestantische Eschatologie: Von der Reformation bis zur Aufklärung.* Freiburg: Herder, 1980.

LaCugna, Catherine Mowry. *God for Us: The Trinity and Christian Life.* San Francisco: HarperCollins, 1991.

————. "God in Communion with Us." In *Freeing Theology: The Essentials of Theology in Feminist Perspective,* 83-114. Edited by Catherine Mowry LaCugna. San Francisco: HarperCollins, 1993.

Ladd, George Eldon. *The Gospel of the Kingdom.* Grand Rapids: Eerdmans, 1959.

————. *The Presence of the Future: The Eschatology of Biblical Realism.* Grand Rapids: Eerdmans, 1974.

Laertius, Diogenes. *Lives of the Philosophers.* Translated by R. D. Hicks. 2 volumes. Cambridge, Mass.: Harvard University Press, 1925.

Lakatos, Irme. *The Methodology of Scientific Research Programmes.* Cambridge: Cambridge University Press, 1978.

Lan, Kwok Pui. "Discovering the Bible in the Non-biblical World." *Semeia* 47 (1989): 25-42.

Laudan, Larry. *Progress and Its Problems: Towards a Theory of Scientific Growth.* Berkeley: University of California Press, 1977.

LeBlanc, Jill. "Infinity in Theology and Mathematic." *Religious Studies* 29 (1993): 51-62.

Lee, Jung Young. *The Trinity in Asian Perspective.* Nashville: Abingdon, 1996.

Leff, Gordon A. *Medieval Thought.* Atlantic Highlands, N.J.: Humanities Press, 1980.

Leibniz, G. W. *Theodicy: Essays on the Goodness of God, the Freedom of Man and the Origin of Evil.* Translated by E. M. Huggard. LaSalle, Ill.: Open Court, 1985.

Leuba, Jean-Louis, editor. *Temps et Eschatologie: Données bibliques et problématiques contemporaines.* Paris: CERF, 1994.

Levinas, Emmanuel. "God and Philosophy." In *Basic Philosophical Writings.* Edited by Adriaan T. Peperz et al. Bloomington: Indiana University Press, 1996.

————. *God, Death and Time.* Translated by Bettina Bergo. Stanford: Stanford University Press, 2000.

————. *Otherwise than Being or Beyond Essence.* Translated by A. Lingis. Pittsburgh: Duquesne University Press, 1998.

————. *Totality and Infinity.* Translated by A. Lingis. Pittsburgh: Duquesne University Press, 1961.

————. *Time and the Other.* Translated by Richard A. Cohen. Pittsburgh: Duquesne University Press, 1987.

Lewis, C. S. *Surprised by Joy.* New York: Harcourt & Brace, 1955.

————. *The Weight of Glory.* San Francisco: Harper Collins, 1949.

Locke, John. *An Essay concerning Human Understanding.* Edited and with an introduction by Peter H. Nidditch. Oxford: Clarendon Press, 1975.

Lossky, Vladimir. *In the Image and Likeness of God.* Crestwood, N.Y.: St. Vladimir's Press, 1985.

————. *The Mystical Theology of the Eastern Church.* Crestwood, N.Y.: St. Vladimir's Press, 1998.

————. *Orthodox Theology: An Introduction.* Translated by Ian and Ihita Kesarcodi-Watson. Crestwood, N.Y.: St. Vladimir's Press, 1989.

Lucas, J. R. *The Future: An Essay on God, Temporality and Truth.* Oxford: Blackwell, 1990.

Luther, Martin. *The Bondage of the Will.* Translated by J. I. Packer and O. R. Johnston. Grand Rapids: Baker, 1957.

MacIntyre, Alasdair. *After Virtue.* Second edition. Notre Dame: University of Notre Dame Press, 1984.

————. *Whose Justice? Which Rationality?* Notre Dame: University of Notre Dame Press, 1988.

Malherbe, Abraham J. "Determinism and Free Will in Paul: The Argument of 1 Corinthians 8 and 9." In *Paul in His Hellenistic Context.* Edited by Troels Engberg-Pedersen. Minneapolis: Fortress, 1995.

Manuel, Frank. *The Religion of Isaac Newton.* Oxford: Clarendon, 1974.

Masao, Abe. "The Japanese View of Truth." *Japanese Religions* 14, no. 3 (December 1986): 1-6.

Maor, Eli. *To Infinity and Beyond: A Cultural History of the Infinite.* Princeton: Princeton University Press, 1987.

Marcel, Gabriel. *Homo Viator: Introduction to a Metaphysic of Hope.* Translated by Emma Craufurd. New York: Harper & Row, 1962.

Martin, James. *The Last Judgment in Protestant Theology from Orthodoxy to Ritschl.* Grand Rapids: Eerdmans, 1963.

Martin, Luther H. "Fate, Futurity and Historical Consciousness in Western Antiquity." *Historical Reflections/Réflexions Historiques* 17, no. 2 (1991): 151-69.

Martyn, J. Louis. *Theological Issues in the Letters of Paul.* Nashville: Abingdon, 1997.

Maurer, Arnold. *The Philosophy of William of Ockham.* Toronto: PIMS, 1999.

Bibliography

May, Gerhard. *Creatio ex nihilo: The Doctrine of 'Creation out of Nothing' in Early Christian Thought.* Translated by A. S. Worrall. Edinburgh: T&T Clark, 1994.

Malebranche, Nicolas. *Dialogues on Metaphysics and on Religion.* Translated by M. Ginsburg. London: Allen and Unwin, 1923.

Manson, Neil A. *God and Design: The Teleological Argument and Modern Science.* London: Routledge, 2003.

McCormack, Bruce. *Karl Barth's Critically Realistic Dialectical Theology: Its Genesis and Development 1909-1936.* Oxford: Clarendon, 1995.

McFague, Sallie. *The Body of God.* Minneapolis: Fortress, 1993.

McIntosh, Mark A. *Mystical Theology: The Integrity of Spirituality and Theology.* Oxford: Blackwell, 1998.

Menke-Peitzmeyer, Michael. *Subjektivität und Selbstinterpretation des dreifaltigen Gottes: Eine Studie zur Genese und Explikation des Paradigmas "Selbstoffenbarung Gottes" in der Theologie Karl Barths.* Münsterische Beiträge zur Theologie, 60. Münster: Aschendorff, 2002.

Mensch, James Richard. *Postfoundational Phenomenology: Husserlian Reflections on Presence and Embodiment.* University Park, Pa.: The Pennsylvania State University Press, 2001.

Mettinger, Tryggve. *In Search of God: The Meaning and Message of the Everlasting Names.* Minneapolis: Fortress, 1998.

Metz, J. B. "The Church and the World." In *The Word in History.* Edited by T. Patrick Burke. New York: Sheed and Ward, 1966.

———. *Theology of the World.* Translated by William Glen-Doepel. London: Burns & Oates, 1969.

———. "The Future in the Memory of Suffering." In J. B. Metz and J. Moltmann, *Faith and the Future.* Maryknoll, N.Y.: Orbis, 1995.

Meyendorff, John. *A Study of Gregory Palamas.* London, 1974.

Milroy, Leslie, and Matthew Gordon. *Sociolinguistics: Method and Interpretation.* Second edition. Oxford: Blackwell, 2003.

Mithen, Steven. *The Prehistory of the Mind: The Cognitive Origins of Art, Religion and Science.* London: Thames and Hudson, 1996.

Molina, Luis. *On Divine Foreknowledge (Part IV of the Concordia).* Translated by Alfred J. Freddoso. Ithaca, N.Y.: Cornell University Press, 1988.

Moltmann, Jürgen. "'Behold, I make all things new': The Category of the New in Christian Theology." In *The Future as the Presence of Shared Hope.* Edited by Maryellen Muckenhirn. New York: Sheed and Ward, 1968.

———. *The Church in the Power of the Spirit.* Translated by Margaret Kohl. New York: Harper & Row, 1977.

———. *The Coming of God.* Translated by Margaret Kohl. Minneapolis: Fortress, 1996.

———. *The Crucified God: The Cross of Christ as the Foundation and Criticism of*

Christian Theology. Translated by R. A. Wilson and John Bowden. New York: Harper & Row, 1974.

—————. *Experiences in Theology.* Minneapolis: Fortress, 2000.

—————. *The Future of Creation.* Philadelphia: Fortress, 1979.

—————. *God for a Secular Society: The Public Relevance of Theology.* Translated by Margaret Kohl. Minneapolis: Fortress, 1999.

. *God in Creation.* Translated by Margaret Kohl. San Francisco: Harper & Row, 1985.

—————. "God's Kenosis in the Creation and Consummation of the World." In *The Work of Love: Creation as Kenosis.* Edited by John Polkinghorne. Grand Rapids: Eerdmans, 2001.

—————. *Gottes Zukunft: Zukunft der Welt.* Edited by H. Deuser et al. Munich: Chr. Kaiser Verlag, 1986.

—————. "Hope and the Biomedical Future of Man." In *Hope and the Future of Man.* Edited by Ewert H. Cousins. Philadelphia: Fortress, 1972.

—————. *History and the Triune God.* New York: Crossroad, 1992.

—————. "Religion, Revolution and the Future." In *The Future of Hope.* Edited by Walter Capps. Philadelphia: Westminster, 1971.

—————. *The Source of Life.* Translated by Margaret Kohl. Minneapolis: Fortress, 1997.

—————. *The Spirit of Life.* Translated by Margaret Kohl. Minneapolis: Fortress, 2001.

—————. *The Trinity and Kingdom.* Translated by Margaret Kohl. Minneapolis: Fortress, 1993.

—————. *The Triune Creator.* Grand Rapids: Eerdmans, 1998.

—————. *Theology of Hope.* Translated by James Leitch. Minneapolis: Fortress, 1993.

Montague, George T., S.M. *The Holy Spirit: Growth of a Biblical Tradition.* New York: Paulist Press, 1976.

Moore, A. W. *The Infinite.* Second edition. London: Routledge, 2001.

Morgan, Robert. "From Reimarus to Sanders: The Kingdom of God, Jesus and the Judaisms of His Day." In *The Kingdom of God and Human Society.* Edited by Robin Barbour. Edinburgh: T&T Clark, 1993.

Morris, Thomas V. *Our Idea of God.* Downers Grove, Ill.: InterVarsity Press, 1991.

Mostert, Christian. *God and the Future: Wolfhart Pannenberg's Eschatological Doctrine of God.* London: T&T Clark, 2002.

Muller, Richard. *Christ and the Decree: Christology and Predestination in Reformed Theology from Calvin to Perkins.* Durham, N.C.: The Labyrinth Press, 1986.

—————. *God, Creation and Providence in the Thought of Jacob Arminius.* Grand Rapids: Baker, 1991.

—————. "God, Predestination and the Integrity of the Created Order: A Note on Patterns in Arminius' Theology." In *Later Calvinism,* 431-46. Kirksville, Mo.: Sixteenth Century Journal Publishers, 1994.

Bibliography

————. *Post-Reformation Reformed Dogmatics.* 4 volumes. Grand Rapids: Baker Academic, 2003.

Murphy, Nancey. *Anglo-American Postmodernity.* Boulder, Colo.: Westview, 1997.

Murphy, Nancey, and George Ellis. *On the Moral Nature of the Universe: Theology, Cosmology and Ethics.* Minneapolis: Fortress, 1996.

Murray, John Courtney, S.J. *The Problem of God.* New Haven: Yale University Press, 1964.

Nellas, Panayiotis. *Deification in Christ: The Nature of the Human Person.* Translated by Norman Russell. Crestwood, N.Y.: St. Vladimir's, 1997.

Nesteruk, Alexei V. *Light from the East: Theology, Science and the Eastern Orthodox Tradition.* Minneapolis: Fortress, 2003.

Neville, Robert. *Creativity and God: A Challenge to Process Theology.* New edition. Albany: SUNY Press, 1995.

————. *A Theology Primer.* Albany: SUNY, 1991.

Newton, Isaac. *Opticks.* New York: Dover, 1952.

————. *The Principia: Mathematical Principles of Natural Philosophy.* Translated by I. Berard Cohen and Anne Whitman. Berkeley: University of California Press, 1999.

Nicholas of Cusa. *God as Not-Other.* Translated by Jasper Hopkins. Minneapolis: University of Minnesota Press, 1979.

Noble, William, and Iain Davidson. *Human Evolution, Language and Mind: A Psychological and Archaeological Inquiry.* Cambridge: Cambridge University Press, 1996.

Oberman, Heiko. "Teufelsdreck: Eschatology and Scatology in the 'Old' Luther." *The Sixteenth Century Journal* 19, no. 3 (Fall 1988): 435-50.

Ockham, William. *Predestination, God's Foreknowledge and Future Contingents.* Translated by Marilyn McCord Adams and Norman Kretzmann. Indianapolis: Hackett, 1983.

————. *Quodlibetal Questions.* Translated by Alfred J. Freddoso and Francis E. Kelley. New Haven: Yale University Press, 1991.

O'Collins, Gerald, S.J. *The Tripersonal God: Understanding and Interpreting the Trinity.* New York: Paulist, 1999.

Okechukwu, Ogbonnaya. *On Communitarian Divinity: An African Interpretation of the Trinity.* New York: Paragon House, 1994.

Olson, Roger, and Christopher Hall. *The Trinity.* Grand Rapids: Eerdmans, 2002.

Ouspensky, Leonid, and Vladimir Lossky. *The Meaning of Icons.* Crestwood, N.Y.: St. Vladimir's Press, 1999.

Pannenberg, Wolfhart. *Anthropology in Theological Perspective.* Translated by Matthew J. O'Connell. Philadelphia: Westminster, 1985.

————. *Basic Questions in Theology II.* Translated by George H. Kehm. Philadelphia: Fortress, 1971.

———. "The Christian Vision of God: The New Discussion on the Trinitarian Doctrine," *The Asbury Theological Journal* 46, no. 2 (Fall 1991).

———. "Eternity, Time and the Trinitarian God." In *Trinity, Time and Church*, 62-70. Edited by C. Gunton. Grand Rapids: Eerdmans, 2000.

———. "God's Presence in History." *The Christian Century*, March 11, 1981, 260-63.

———. *Grundfragen systematischer Theologie II*. Gottingen: Vandenhoeck & Ruprecht, 1980.

———. *The Idea of God and Human Freedom*. Translated by R. A. Wilson. Philadelphia: Westminster, 1973.

———. *Jesus — God and Man*. Second edition. Translated by Lewis L. Wilkins and Duane A. Priebe. Philadelphia: Westminster, 1977.

———. *Metaphysics and the Idea of God*. Translated by P. Clayton. Edinburgh: T&T Clark, 1988.

———. "Problems of a Trinitarian Doctrine of God." *Dialog* 26, no. 4 (1987): 250-57.

———. *Theology and the Kingdom of God*. Philadelphia: Westminster, 1969.

———. *Toward a Theology of Nature: Essays on Science and Faith*. Edited by Ted Peters. Louisville: Westminster/John Knox, 1993.

———. *Systematic Theology*. Translated by G. W. Bromiley. 3 volumes. Grand Rapids: Eerdmans, 1991, 1994, 1998.

———. *What Is Man?* Translated by D. A. Priebe. Philadelphia: Fortress, 1970.

Pannikar, Raimundo. *The Trinity and the Religious Experience of Man*. Maryknoll, N.Y.: Orbis, 1973.

Pao, David W. *Acts and the Isaianic New Exodus*. Grand Rapids: Baker Academic, 2000.

Patrick, Dale. "The Kingdom of God in the OT." In *The Kingdom of God in Twentieth-Century Interpretation*, 67-79. Edited by Wendell Willis. Peabody, Mass.: Hendrickson, 1987.

Peacocke, Arthur. *Theology for a Scientific Age*. Minneapolis: Fortress, 1993.

Peirce, C. S. *The Essential Peirce*. Edited by Nathan Houser and Christian Kloesel. 2 volumes. Bloomington: Indiana University Press, 1992, 1998.

Pennock, R. *Intelligent Design and Its Critics*. Cambridge, Mass.: MIT Press, 2001.

Peters, Ted. "Eschatology — Eternal Now or Cosmic Future?" *Zygon* 36, no. 2 (June 2001): 349-56.

———. *Fear, Faith and the Future*. Minneapolis: Augsburg, 1980.

———. "Future Consciousness and the Need for Theology." *Dialog* 13 (Autumn 1974): 251-57.

———. *Futures — Divine and Human*. Atlanta: John Knox Press, 1978.

———. *God — The World's Future*. Second edition. Minneapolis: Fortress, 2000.

———. "God as Spirit — and Natural Science." *Zygon* 36, no. 4 (2001): 783-93.

———. *God as Trinity: Relationality and Temporality in Divine Life*. Louisville: Westminster/John Knox, 1993.

————. "Resurrection: The Conceptual Challenge." In *Resurrection: Theological and Scientific Assessments.* Edited by T. Peters, R. J. Russell, and M. Welker. Grand Rapids: Eerdmans, 2002.

Phan, Peter C. *Eternity and Time: A Study of Karl Rahner's Eschatology.* London: Associated University Presses, 1988.

Phillips, D. Z. *Faith after Foundationalism.* Boulder, Colo.: Westview, 1995.

Philo, *De Opificio Mundi.* Translated by F. H. Colson and G. H. Whittaker. Loeb Classical Library. London: Heinemann, 1929.

Picht, Georg. "Die Zeit und die Modalitäten." In *Hier und Jetzt.* Stuttgart: Klett-Cotta, 1980.

Plantinga, Alvin. *God and Other Minds.* Ithaca, N.Y.: Cornell University Press, 1967.

————. "On Ockham's Way Out." In *The Concept of God.* Edited by Thomas V. Morris. Oxford: Oxford University Press, 1987.

————. "Reason and Belief in God." In *Faith and Rationality.* Edited by A. Plantinga and N. Wolterstorff. Notre Dame: University of Notre Dame Press, 1983.

Plass, Paul. "The Concept of Eternity in Patristic Theology." *Studia Theologica* 36 (1982).

Plato. *Complete Works.* Edited by John M. Cooper. Cambridge: Hackett Publishing Co., 1997.

Plotinus. *Enneads.* Translated by A. H. Armstrong. Loeb Classical Library. Cambridge, Mass.: Harvard University Press, 1988.

Polkinghorne, John. "Eschatology: Some Questions and Some Insights from Science." In *The End of the World and the Ends of God.* Edited by J. Polkinghorne and M. Welker. Harrisburg, Pa.: Trinity Press International, 2000.

————. "Chaos Theory and Divine Action." In *Religion and Science.* Edited by W. Mark Richardson and Wesley Wildman. London: Routledge, 1996.

Prenter, Regin. *Spiritus Creator: Luther's Concept of the Holy Spirit.* Translated by John M. Jensen. Philadelphia: Muhlenberg, 1953.

Prestige, G. L. *God in Patristic Thought.* London: Heinemann, 1936.

Preus, Robert D. *The Theology of Post-Reformation Lutheranism.* 2 volumes. London: Concordia, 1972.

Prigogine, Ilya, and Isabelle Stengers. *Order out of Chaos.* New York: Bantam, 1984.

Prior, A. N. *Past, Present and Future.* Oxford: Clarendon Press, 1967.

Pseudo-Dionysus, *The Complete Works.* Translated by Colm Luibheid. New York: Paulist Press, 1987.

Quistorp, Heinrich. *Calvin's Doctrine of Last Things.* Translated by H. Knight. London: Lutterworth Press, 1955.

Rahner, Karl. *Foundations of Christian Faith.* Translated by William Dych. New York: Crossroad, 2000.

————. *Theological Investigations.* 20 volumes. Translated by C. Ernst et al. London: Darton, Longman and Todd, 1961-1979.

————. *The Trinity.* Translated by J. Donceel, with an introduction by C. M. LaCugna. New York: Crossroad, 1997.

————. *Spirit in the World.* Translated by W. Dych, S.J. New York: Herder and Herder, 1968.

Reid, Duncan. *Energies of the Spirit: Trinitarian Models in Eastern Orthodox and Western Theology.* Atlanta: Scholars Press, 1997.

Rescher, Nicholas. *A Useful Inheritance: Evolutionary Aspects of the Theory of Knowledge.* Savage: Rowman and Littlefield, 1990.

Ripley, Jason J. "Covenantal Concepts of Justice and Righteousness, and Catholic-Protestant Reconciliation: Theological Implications and Explorations." *Journal of Ecumenical Studies* 38, no. 1 (Winter 2001).

Rist, J. M. *Epicurus: An Introduction.* Cambridge: Cambridge University Press, 1972.

Rolston, Holmes, III. *Genes, Genesis and God.* Cambridge: Cambridge University Press, 1999.

Rorty, Richard. *Philosophy and the Mirror of Nature.* Princeton: Princeton University Press, 1979.

Rowland, Christopher. *The Open Heaven: A Study of Apocalyptic in Judaism and Early Christianity.* New York: Crossroad, 1982.

Ruether, Rosemary Radford. *Sexism and God-Talk: Toward a Feminist Theology.* Boston: Beacon, 1983.

Russell, Robert J. "Eschatology and Physical Cosmology." In *The Far-Future Universe: Eschatology from a Cosmic Perspective.* Edited by George F. R. Ellis. Philadelphia: Templeton Press, 2002.

————. "Finite Creation without a Beginning: The Doctrine of Creation in Relation to Big Bang Quantum Cosmologies." In *Quantum Cosmology and the Laws of Nature.* Edited by Robert J. Russell et al. Berkeley: CTNS, 1996.

————. "The God Who Infinitely Transcends Infinity." In *How Large Is God? The Voices of Scientists and Theologians.* Edited by J. M. Templeton. Philadelphia: Templeton Press, 1997.

Sailor, Danton B. "Moses and Atomism." In *Science and Religious Belief.* Edited by C. A. Russell. London: Open University Press, 1973.

Sauter, Gerhard. *What Dare We Hope? Reconsidering Eschatology.* Harrisburg, Pa.: Trinity Press International, 1999.

Schillebeeckx, Edward. *God the Future of Man.* Translated by N. D. Smith. New York: Sheed and Ward, 1968.

————. *God Is New Each Moment.* Translated by David Smith. Edinburgh: T&T Clark, 1983.

Schleiermacher, Friedrich. *The Christian Faith.* Translated by H. R. MacKintosh and J. S. Stewart. Edinburgh: T&T Clark, 1989.

————. *On Religion: Speeches to Its Cultured Despisers.* Translated and edited by Richard Crouter. Cambridge: Cambridge University Press, 1996.

Schmemann, Alexander. *The Eucharist.* Translated by P. Kachur. Crestwood, N.Y.: St. Vladimir's Press, 2000.

Schmid, Heinrich. *The Doctrinal Theology of the Evangelical Lutheran Church.* Third edition. Edited and translated by C. A. Hay and H. E. Jacobs. Minneapolis: Augsburg, 1961.

Schrag, Calvin. *God as Otherwise than Being: Toward a Semantics of the Gift.* Evanston, Ill.: Northwestern University Press, 2002.

Schwarz, Hans. *Eschatology.* Grand Rapids: Eerdmans, 2000.

Schweitzer, Albert, *The Quest of the Historical Jesus.* Translated by W. Montgomery. New York: Macmillan, 1961.

Seils, Martin. "Luther's Significance for Contemporary Theological Anthropology." In *Luther's Ecumenical Significance,* 183-202. Edited by P. Manns et al. Philadelphia: Fortress, 1984.

Seppänen, Jouku. "Infinity — An Outline of Conceptions in Mythology, Cosmology and Natural Philosophy." In *Finite Versus Infinite: Contributions to an Eternal Dilemma,* 257-83. Edited by C. S. Calude and G. Paun. London: Springer-Verlag, 2000.

Shaull, Richard, and Waldo Cesar. *Pentecostalism and the Future of the Christian Churches.* Grand Rapids: Eerdmans, 2000.

Sheldrake, Philip. *Spirituality and Theology: Christian Living and the Doctrine of God.* Maryknoll, N.Y.: Orbis, 1998.

Shimizu, Teturo. "Time and Eternity. Ockham's Logical Point of View." *Franciscan Studies* 50 (1990): 283-307.

Shults, F. LeRon. *Christology and Contemporary Science.* Aldershot: Ashgate, forthcoming.

———. *The Postfoundationalist Task of Theology: Wolfhart Pannenberg and the New Theological Rationality.* Grand Rapids: Eerdmans, 1999.

———. *Reforming Theological Anthropology: After the Philosophical Turn to Relationality.* Grand Rapids: Eerdmans, 2003.

———. "The Role of Trinitarian Reflection in the Science-Religion Dialogue." In *Preparing for the Future: The Role of Theology in the Science-Religion Dialogue.* Edited by Niels Henrik Gregersen and Marie Vejrup Nielsen. Aarhus: University of Aarhus Press, 2004.

———. "Sharing in the Divine Nature: Transformation, *Koinonia* and the Doctrine of God." In *On Being Christian . . . and Human.* Edited by T. Speidell. Eugene, Ore.: Wipf & Stock, 2002.

———. "A Theology of Chaos." *Scottish Journal of Theology* 45 (1992): 223-35.

Shults. F. LeRon, and Steven J. Sandage. *Transforming Spirituality.: Integrating Theology and Psychology.* Grand Rapids: Baker Academic, forthcoming 2006.

Shults, F. LeRon, and Steven J. Sandage. *The Faces of Forgiveness: Searching for Wholeness and Salvation.* Grand Rapids: Baker Academic, 2003.

Smith, Roger. *The Human Sciences.* New York: Norton, 1997.

Smullyan, Raymond M. *Gödel's Incompleteness Theorems*. Oxford: Oxford University Press, 1992.

Sokolowski, Robert. *The God of Faith and Reason*. Washington, D.C.: Catholic University Press, 1995.

Spinoza, Baruch. *Ethics*. Translated by Samuel Shirley. Cambridge: Hackett, 1992.

Starr, James M. *Sharers in Divine Nature: 2 Peter 1:4 in Its Hellenistic Context*. Coniectanea Biblica New Testament Series 33. Stockholm: Almqvist & Wiksell, 2000.

Stead, Christopher. *Divine Substance*. Oxford: Clarendon, 1977.

Strand, Narve. "Augustine on Predestination and Divine Simplicity: The Problem of Compatibility." In *Studia Patristica* 38, 290-305. Louvain: Peeters Publishers, 2001.

St. Victor, Richard. *The Twelve Patriarchs: The Mystical Ark, Book Three of the Trinity*. Translated by Grover A. Zinn. New York: Paulist Press, 1979.

Sweeney, Leo, S.J. *Divine Infinity in Greek and Medieval Thought*. New York: Peter Lang, 1992.

———. "Presidential Address: Surprises in the History of Infinity." In *Infinity*, 3-23. Edited by D. O. Dahlstrom et al. Washington, D.C.: The American Catholic Philosophical Association, 1981.

Swinburne, Richard. *The Coherence of Theism*. Second edition. Oxford: Clarendon, 1993.

———. *The Existence of God*. Revised edition. Oxford: Clarendon Press, 1991.

Tatarkiewicz, Wladyslaw. "The Great Theory of Beauty and Its Decline." *The Journal of Aesthetics and Art Criticism* 31 (1972): 165-80.

Tavard, George H. *The Starting Point of Calvin's Theology*. Grand Rapids: Eerdmans, 2000.

Teilhard de Chardin. *The Phenomena of Man*. Translated by Bernard Wall. New York: Harper & Row, 1959.

Thiselton, Anthony. *The First Epistle to the Corinthians*. Grand Rapids: Eerdmans, 2000.

———. "Human Being, Relationality and Time in Hebrews, 1 Corinthians and Western Traditions." *Ex Auditu* 13 (1997): 76-95.

Thomas Aquinas. *Summa Contra Gentiles*. Translated by Anton C. Pegis. Notre Dame: University of Notre Dame Press, 1975.

———. *Summa Theologiae*. Blackfriars edition. New York: McGraw-Hill, 1964.

Thompson, Ann. *The Art of Suffering and the Impact of Seventeenth-Century Anti-Providential Thought*. Aldershot: Ashgate, 2003.

Tillich, Paul. *The Courage to Be*. New Haven: Yale University Press, 1952.

———. *Systematic Theology*. 3 volumes. Chicago: University of Chicago Press, 1951-1963.

Tipler, Frank. *The Physics of Immortality: Modern Cosmology, God and the Resurrection of the Dead*. New York: Anchor, 1994.

Templeton, John Marks, editor. *Evidence of Purpose: Scientists Discover the Creator.* New York: Continuum, 1994.

Torrance, Alan. *Persons in Communion: An Essay on Trinitarian Description and Human Participation.* Edinburgh: T&T Clark, 1996.

Torrance, T. F. *The Christian Doctrine of God: One Being, Three Persons.* Edinburgh: T&T Clark, 1996.

———. *Kingdom and Church: A Study in the Theology of the Reformation.* London: Oliver and Boyd, 1956.

———. "The Modern Eschatological Debate." *The Evangelical Quarterly* 25, no. 1-4 (1953): 45-54, 94-106, 167-78, 224-32.

———. *The Trinitarian Faith.* Edinburgh: T&T Clark, 1998.

———. *Trinitarian Perspectives: Toward Doctrinal Agreement.* Edinburgh: T&T Clark, 1994.

Trigg, Roger. *Morality Matters.* Oxford: Basil Blackwell, 2004.

Trueman, Carl R., and R. Scott Clark, editors. *Protestant Scholasticism: Essays in Reassessment.* Carlisle: Paternoster Press, 1999.

Tsirpanlis, Constantine N. "What Is Truth: An Orthodox Response." *The Patristic and Byzantine Review* 5, no. 2 (1986): 85-90.

Turner, Denys. *The Darkness of God: Negativity in Christian Mysticism.* Cambridge: Cambridge University Press, 1995.

Turretin, Francis. *Institutes of Elenctic Theology.* Translated by George Musgrave Giger. 3 volumes. Philipsburg, N.J.: P&R Publishing, 1992.

Tymoczko, Thomas. *New Direction in the Philosophy of Mathematics: An Anthology.* Revised edition. Princeton: Princeton University Press, 1998.

Vagaggini, Cyprian, O.S.B. *Theological Dimensions of the Liturgy.* Translated by L. J. Doyle and W. A. Jurgens. Collegeville, Minn.: Liturgical Press, 1976.

van Asselt, Willem J., and Eef Dekker. *Reformation and Scholasticism: An Ecumenical Enterprise.* Grand Rapids: Baker Academic, 2001.

van den Brom, Luco J. "Eschatology and Time: Reversal of the Time Direction?" In *The Future as God's Gift: Explorations in Christian Eschatology,* 159-67. Edited by D. Fergusson and M. Sarot. Edinburgh: T&T Clark, 2000.

van Huyssteen, J. Wentzel. *The Shaping of Rationality.* Grand Rapids: Eerdmans, 1999.

van Leeuwen, Mary Stewart. *The Person in Psychology: A Contemporary Christian Appraisal.* Grand Rapids: Eerdmans, 1985.

Vanhoozer, Kevin J., editor. *The Trinity in a Pluralistic Age: Theological Essays on Culture and Religion.* Grand Rapids: Eerdmans, 1997.

Vogel, Winfried. "The Eschatological Theology of Martin Luther — Part I: Luther's Basic Concepts." *Andrews University Seminary Studies* 24, no. 3 (Autumn 1986): 249-64.

von Arnim, H. *Stoicorum Veterum Fragmenta.* 3 volumes. Leipzig: Teubner, 1903-1905.

von Balthasar, Hans Urs. *Theo-Drama*, vol. 5: *The Last Act*. Translated by G. Harrison. San Francisco: Ignatius Press, 1998.

von Rad, Gerhard. *Old Testament Theology*. Translated by D. M. G. Stalker. 2 volumes. Louisville: Westminster/John Knox, 2001.

von Schelling, F. W. J. *Die Weltalter*. Ausgewählte Schriften, Band 4. Frankfurt: Suhrkamp, 1985.

Voth, Steven M. "Justice and/or Righteousness: A Contextualized Analysis of *scdcq* in the KJV (English) and RVR (Spanish)." In *The Challenge of Bible Translation*, 321-45. Edited by Glen G. Scorgie, Mark L. Strauss, Steven M. Voth. Grand Rapids: Zondervan, 2003.

Vyshelslavtsev, B. P. *The Eternal in Russian Philosophy*. Translated by Penelope V. Burt. Grand Rapids: Eerdmans, 2002.

Ward, Graham. *Barth, Derrida and the Language of Theology*. Cambridge: Cambridge University Press, 1995.

Ware, Kallistos. *In the Image of the Trinity*. Crestwood, N.Y.: St. Vladimir's Press, 2004.

Watts, Fraser. *Theology and Psychology*. Aldershot: Ashgate, 2002.

Watts, Rikki E. *Isaiah's New Exodus and Mark*. Tübingen: Mohr Siebeck, 1997.

Webster, John. *Eberhard Jüngel: An Introduction to His Theology*. Cambridge: Cambridge University Press, 1986.

Weil, Simone. *Gravity and Grace*. Translated by Arthur Wills. Lincoln: University of Nebraska Press, 1997.

Weinandy, Thomas. *Does God Suffer?* Notre Dame: University of Notre Dame Press, 2000.

Weiss, Johannes. *Jesus' Proclamation of the Kingdom of God*. Translated by Richard Hyde Hiers and David Larrimore Holland. Philadelphia: Fortress, 1971.

Welker, Michael. *God the Spirit*. Translated by John F. Hoffmeyer. Minneapolis: Fortress, 1994.

Westfall, Richard S. "The Rise of Science and the Decline of Orthodox Christianity: A Study of Kepler, Descartes and Newton." In *God and Nature*, 218-33. Edited by David C. Lindberg and Ronald L. Numbers. Berkeley: University of California Press, 1986.

Westphal, Merold. *Overcoming Onto-theology*. New York: Fordham University Press, 2001.

Whitehead, Alfred. *Process and Reality*. Corrected edition. Edited by David Ray Griffin and Donald W. Sherburne. New York: Free Press, 1978.

Wildiers, N. Max. *The Theologian and His Universe: Theology and Cosmology from the Middle Ages to the Present*. New York: Seabury, 1982.

Wildman, Wesley, and Robert John Russell, "Chaos: A Mathematical Introduction with Philosophical Reflections." In *Chaos and Complexity: Scientific Perspectives on Divine Action*, 49-90. Second edition. Edited by Robert John Russell et al. Berkeley: CTNS, 1997.

Wilson, A. M. *The Infinite in the Finite*. Oxford: Oxford University Press, 1995.

Wingren, Gustaf. *Man and the Incarnation: A Study in the Biblical Theology of Irenaeus*. Translated by R. MacKenzie. Philadelphia: Muhlenberg, 1959.

Woodfin, Yandall. "The Futurity of Beauty: Aesthetic Intimation and Eschatological Design." *Theologische Zeitschrift* 29 (July-August 1973): 265-79.

Worthing, Mark. *God, Creation and Contemporary Physics*. Minneapolis: Fortress, 1996.

Wright, N. T. *Jesus and the Victory of God*. Minneapolis: Fortress, 1996.

———. *The New Testament and the People of God*. Minneapolis: Fortress, 1992.

———. *The Resurrection of the Son of God*. Minneapolis: Fortress, 2003.

Wright, Robert. *Nonzero: The Logic of Human Destiny*. New York: Pantheon, 2000.

Zimmerli, Walther. *Man and His Hope in the Old Testament*. Naperville, Ill.: Allenson, 1971.

Zizioulas, John. *Being as Communion*. Crestwood, N.Y.: St. Vladimir's Press, 1997.

———. "Déplacement de la perspective eschatologique." In *La chrétienté en débat*, 89-100 at 93. Edited by G. Alberigo et al. Paris: Les Éditions du Cerf, 1984.

———. "The Doctrine of the Holy Trinity: The Significance of the Cappadocian Contribution." In *Trinitarian Theology Today*. Edited by C. Schwöbel. Edinburgh: T&T Clark, 1995.

———. "Human Capacity and Human Incapacity: A Theological Exploration of Personhood." *Scottish Journal of Theology* 28 (1975): 401-48.

——— "On Being a Person: Toward an Ontology of Personhood." In *Persons, Divine and Human*, 33-46. Edited by C. Schwöbel and C. Gunton. Edinburgh: T&T Clark, 1991.

———. "La vision Eucharitique du Monde et L'homme Contemporain." *Contacts: Revue française de l'orthodoxie* 19 (1967): 83-92.

Zwingli, Ulrich. *On Providence, and Other Essays*. Edited by William John Hinke. Durham, N.C.: Labyrinth Press, 1983.

Index